JAPAN IN ASIA

Post-Cold-War Diplomacy

JAPAN LIBRARY

JAPAN IN ASIA

Post-Cold-War Diplomacy

Tanaka Akihiko

Translated by
Jean Connell Hoff

Japan Publishing Industry Foundation for Culture

Translation Note

The local custom of placing the family name first has been followed for the names of Japanese, Chinese and Korean persons.

Japan in Asia: Post-Cold-War Diplomacy
Tanaka Akihiko. Translated by Jean Connell Hoff.

Published by
Japan Publishing Industry Foundation for Culture (JPIC),
3-12-3 Kanda-Jinbocho, Chiyoda-ku, Tokyo 101-0051, Japan

First edition: 2007
Second edition: 2017

This book is a translation of *Ajia no naka no Nihon*, first published in Japanese by NTT Publishing Co., Ltd. in 2007 and especially updated and revised by the author for the English edition.

English language rights arranged with NTT Publishing Co., Ltd.

Jacket and cover design by Niizuma Hisanori
Jacket and cover photo ©Jakkree Thampitakkull
Jacket and cover image ©GelatoPlus
Author photo by Kawamoto Seiya

As this book is published primarily to be donated to overseas universities, research institutions, public libraries and other organizations, commercial publication rights are available. For all enquiries regarding those rights, please contact the publisher at the following address:
japanlibrary@jpic.or.jp

Printed in Japan
ISBN 978-4-916055-63-7
http://www.jpic.or.jp/japanlibrary/

Contents

Chapter 4

"Asia-Pacific" Experiments

Chapter 5

The Rise of China and the Crisis on the Korean Peninsula

Chapter 6

The "History" Flare-up and Strains in Japan-China Relations

Preface to the English Edition

Nearly ten years have passed since the publication of the Japanese edition of this book. Since then, Asia has undergone further transformations. China has surpassed Japan in terms of GNP to become the world's second largest economic power. The standard of living in Singapore, Hong Kong, South Korea and Taiwan is now equal to that of any Western country in the developed world. In 2015, the Southeast Asian countries established three ASEAN communities. The Southeast Asian and East Asian countries' relations with India have also deepened. Even in Myanmar, where a military regime held sway for so long, the democracy movement is firmly under way. Only North Korea remains isolated, repeatedly conducting tests of its nuclear weapons and missiles, but with that sole exception, Asia is increasingly becoming the most economically, socially and culturally vibrant region in the world.

During this period, Japan too has greatly changed. After the Koizumi administration exited the scene, it was followed by three short-lived Liberal Democratic governments, but the LDP suffered a major defeat in the 2009 general election and ceded power to the Democratic Party of Japan. Once in office, the DPJ failed to provide a stable government, however, and in 2012 the LDP again returned to power. In the meantime, relations between Japan and Asia were also strained at times. The relationship with China and South Korea in particular has given rise to a state of affairs that might well be called the worst since Japan normalized relations with those two countries.

For those reasons, I have combined the sections on the Koizumi administration in Chapters 9 and 10 of the Japanese edition to form a new Chapter 9 in the English edition, and in two chapters, Chapters 10 and 11, I have analyzed the period from the first Abe administration on. In addition to paying close attention to structural changes, crises and the formation of institutions in Asia, as I had in the preceding chapters, the perspective I decided to emphasize was the connection to internal affairs. That is because the changes in government in

Japan, as well as the domestic political situation in each of the other countries, had a huge impact on international relations. Also, during this period, the symbolic subject of the "understanding of history" especially became a major issue between Japan and its nearest neighbors, South Korea and China. Because the details of the "history" flare-up in the 1980s and 1990s are essential for an adequate understanding of how the history problem has unfolded during the past ten years, I have made substantial revisions and additions in Chapter 6 to the account in the Japanese version. In the other chapters as well, I have reviewed everything I originally wrote and made the necessary additions and corrections. In that sense, the English edition is not a mere translation of the Japanese publication of 2007; I hope it will be viewed as an enlarged and updated version in English.

Consequently, I have had to do quite a bit of new research for the analysis in the English edition. That research has in part made use of the results from the following two projects sponsored by the Ministry of Education, Culture, Sports, Science and Technology (MEXT), Grants-in-Aid for Scientific Research Program (KAKENHI), Grant-in-Aid for Scientific Research (A)—"Political Process of Developing Regional Cooperation Frameworks in East Asia" (FY2009–2011) and "China's Role in East Asian Regional Cooperation" (FY2012–2014)—as well as a MEXT Grant-in-Aid for Publication of Scientific Research Results for the "Database of Japanese Politics and International Relations (DJPIR)" (2016), part of "The World and Japan" Database Project of the Institute for Advanced Studies on Asia, University of Tokyo.

In addition, between April 2012 and September 2015, I served as president of the Japan International Cooperation Agency (JICA) and was engaged in the practical side of Japanese development cooperation. During that time, I had the opportunity to visit almost all the countries in East Asia and South Asia. Although my primary objective was to confer with the governments of these countries about Japanese development cooperation and to supervise and direct local staff, the ability to visit all these places was beneficial in helping me experience "Japan in Asia" firsthand. Let me take this opportunity to express my thanks to the staff at JICA and to all the experts, affiliated companies and JICA volunteers that work on the frontlines of Japanese development cooperation.

The translating and editing of this book by Jean Connell Hoff was carried out with support from the Japan Library project. Ms Hoff also translated my book *The New Middle Ages: The World System in the 21st Century*, which came out in 2002. Not only did she provide a translation with the same level of accuracy as the last time, she also checked the historical sources and where possible tracked down English translations of the documents cited. Endō Chiho of NTT Publishing Co. gave timely instructions to the author, who has a tendency to procrastinate, and oversaw the process of revising the book. As was the case in the Japanese edition, "The World and Japan" Database (as of April 1, accessed at http://worldjpn.grips.ac.jp/front-ENG.shtml), which crops up frequently in the notes and for which I serve as representative, makes political and diplomatic documents available online. At the time the Japanese version was published, the number of documents it contained was around 3,500; now approximately 8,000 documents can be accessed online. In addition to managing and maintaining the database, Ikeda Kyōko also manages my schedule. That this English edition has somehow been able to materialize is thanks to their efforts. I am very grateful.

Naturally enough, if, despite all their contributions, there are any apologies to be made in regard to facts or interpretation, these are solely the author's responsibility.

Tanaka Akihiko
May 2017

Preface to the Japanese Edition

Asia is becoming one.

Of course, Asia still isn't there yet. Nor is it likely that the vast Asian continent, which stretches from Japan in the east to Turkey in the west, will ever become a single entity. And yet, isn't Asia slowly but surely achieving some sort of interconnectedness? Isn't at least part of it—"East Asia" ranging from Japan to Southeast Asia, for example—becoming one? Southeast Asia took the lead; now "East Asia," which includes Southeast Asia, is following suit; and in the future "Asia," which includes "East Asia," is headed toward integration. Isn't that the trend?

That is the visceral sensation I have come to have whenever I board an airplane and fly to different parts of Asia. If I look back and try to remember when I came to feel this way, I realize it wasn't all that long ago. As I rather hazily recall, it was around the year 2000, I think. Once I had that feeling, I next began to wonder whether it was true or not. Wasn't it nothing more than sheer romanticism? Wasn't it, in fact, more accurate to say that Asia was becoming more divided than ever? Wasn't international politics in Asia really one crisis after another? Would the international political agenda ever move in a direction that would give Asia some cohesion? Then again, assuming my feeling was correct, I wanted to know when the process had begun and what were the causes for it.

Considering the matter from a different angle, what had Japan been doing in an Asia like this? That was also a theme I was curious about. I had previously written books on topics such as the modern history of Sino-Japanese relations and changes in Japan's security policy.[1] And at the request of the media, I have made numerous assessments of Japan's foreign policy and world politics. So it isn't as if I didn't have some sort of impression of Japanese diplomacy vis-à-vis Asia. But because up until that point I had never undertaken a full-scale overview and analysis of Japan's diplomatic efforts in the various places there, I was unable to explain what Japan had achieved, or failed to achieve, in

Asia. I slowly came to realize I needed to investigate Japan's Asian diplomacy as a whole.

Just as I was becoming conscious of these issues, I received an invitation to write a book for the "Japan 'Now'" series. If, under the title "Japan in Asia," I wrote a contemporary history of Asian international relations and Japan's foreign policy, I thought I might be able to clarify to some extent whether Asia is becoming one and what the special features of Japan's Asian diplomacy are. It must, however, be added that this is not a work on "regionalization" or "regional integration" per se. The material on international relations and international politics that this book deals with are not data that show the various interactions and degrees of integration which are often discussed in studies of regionalism or regional integration. Rather, it treats such topics as the political events that the leaders and the people who live in the region had to seriously contend with; the methods they used to deal with them; and the mechanisms they created to do so. It is a standard history of international politics, the themes of which are crises, responses to crises and cooperative institution-building to prevent crises before they happen. It was written with the aim of giving, to the best of my ability, a readily understandable overview of political trends in Asia from the second half of the 20th century into the 21st, and Japan's diplomatic response to them.

That does not mean, however, that there is no theoretical perspective behind the account in this book. As is true of any history, underlying a narrative that seems to be a mere enumeration of facts are the author's biases and beliefs about international politics. For those beliefs themselves, all the reader needs to do is to take a look at other books of mine,[2] but to make my opinions and biases clear in advance, allow me to sum up my general views in this book as being the following three.

The first proposition is that "regionalization in Asia in the second half of the 20th century occurred in the course of three structural changes: the end of the Cold War, globalization and democratization." There are, of course, many factors behind regionalization. The end of the Cold War, it would be fair to say, was a factor in breaking down barriers, so to speak. Removing the political and military obstacles created by the worldwide Cold War is likely to have had the effect of increasing contacts between one place and another. Moreover, places where the Cold War developed into a hot war never experienced regional integration in the first place, just ongoing fragmentation as battlegrounds. Consequently, if the end of the Cold War also brought about an end to hot wars, the possibility was high that regionalization would proceed. If peace resulted from the end of the Cold War, interaction would improve, and regionalization, too, would be accelerated.

Globalization isn't a regional movement. But the globalization of economies and finance increases general interaction and inter-dependence among people and businesses where these barriers have been removed. As a result of globalization, geographic proximity has the potential to strengthen relationships with places nearby rather than with places elsewhere. Thus, the trend toward globalization is thought to be related to an intensification of regional cohesiveness. Or to put it another way, at each of the stages of globalization, we can probably say that a region undergoes reorganization in the hopes of creating an optimum "region."

Democratization, too, I believe, leads to regionalization. People living under political systems that are not democratic cannot make free judgments about those who live somewhere else. Even as the diffusion of information advances, the potential exists under authoritarian and totalitarian regimes to powerfully distort the flow of information. As a result, the major aim of regionalization—empathy with those who live elsewhere—is beset with difficulties under undemocratic regimes.

Other factors that may promote regionalization and integration are theoretically conceivable—the existence of a strong "enemy" or an iron-fisted dominant power, for example. If a common enemy exists, it is possible that people in places that are geographically close will unite and form a region. And it is perhaps also possible that a strong dominant power will bring neighboring countries together into a single region by force. But judging from the present-day situation in Asia, it doesn't seem that either a common enemy or an iron-fisted power exists. Of course, we can't exclude the possibility that these factors may one day occur. But I don't believe that, up to now at least, either of them has been operating in the current regionalization process.

This book's second proposition is that "although regionalization has been progressing thanks to the end of the Cold War, globalization and democratization, these three structural factors, on the other hand, also hold the potential to cause all sorts of crises." In the case of all three, crises may occur if any one of them brings about an international and/or domestic state of affairs that is different from what previously existed and that is incompatible with the prevailing political, economic or cultural framework. It is not the case that with the end of the Cold War all countries saw their perceived threats take a turn for the better. Globalization gives rise to economic and financial crises, which in turn give rise to crises in political systems. And pro-democracy movements also have the potential to produce a backlash, while, on the other hand, changes in the structure of popular consciousness brought about by democratization may also have an affect on international relations. Thus, the structural factors behind regionalization can also create crises.

The third proposition in this book is that "advances in regionalization and a series of crises have been the motivating factors behind the formation of regional systems." The need arose for frameworks to further advance the regionalization that was already proceeding as a result of the three structural factors and to coordinate the interests involved in doing so. The occurrence of a number of crises also led to the creation of frameworks to deal with them. These sorts of system-building, needless to say, do not happen automatically and in the process become a diplomatic game in which all kinds of diplomatic haggling takes place.

The reason the account in this book begins roughly in the second half of the 1970s is simply a reflection of my view of international politics already stated here. The latter half of the 1970s was the first period in which the end of the Cold War, the impact of globalization and pro-democracy movements began to extend to Asia. Thereafter the account becomes the story of an intricate chain composed of three links: the structural factors discussed above, crises, and the system-building to deal with those crises and with regionalization.

Although the feeling that Asia is becoming one is the basis for this book, Asia is an exceedingly vast place, and it is impossible to know about all of it. I have visited various parts of Asia, held discussions with local experts and learned much from books and studies on the different countries. Nevertheless, however, my experience and knowledge of Asia, besides being inadequate, is slanted toward "East Asia." The reason the account in this book is virtually limited to East Asia is the result of my own limitations. Yet it may itself also be proof that this is the place, in an Asia which is becoming one, which is doing so particularly rapidly.

I am indebted to many people for the completion of this book. My special thanks must be given to everyone on the staff of "The World and Japan" Database Project that my Institute operates (http://www.ioc.u-tokyo.ac.jp/~worldjpn/front-ENG.shtml). This database, which comprises more than 3,500 documents dealing with Japanese politics and international relations as well as detailed chronological tables containing more than 200,000 items from the 20th to the 21st centuries, is updated daily. Almost every page of this book makes use of the material and chronologies found there. I am particularly grateful to Ikeda Kyōko, Komuro Sanae, Sasa Waki, Hori Yūko, Matsumoto Ritsuko and Yanagita Yōko.

Thanks to the skillful handling of the author by Makino Akihisa and Miya Kazuho, this book finally took shape. With the scary Mr Miya backing up the genial Mr Makino, their teamwork created an atmosphere that made it utterly impossible for me to slack off.

Needless to say, any factual errors or misinterpretations are entirely the author's responsibility.

Tanaka Akihiko
September 2007

Chapter 1

Asia before the End of the Cold War

The Cold War in Asia

The end of the Cold War was an important event that marked the end of an era in 20th-century Asia as well as in the rest of the world. And yet it is quite difficult to speak about the Cold War in Asia— not to mention its ending and aftermath—because these events took on a very different guise there than they did in Europe, the Cold War's main battleground. Generally speaking, the Cold War can be thought of as an international political phenomenon that, after the development of nuclear weapons, arose from and was compounded by the confrontation between two ideologies, Marxism-Leninism and liberalism, and two military superpowers, the United States and the Soviet Union.[1] The basic features of this Cold War were visible most prominently in Europe. Most countries there clearly sided with either the US or the USSR, and in terms of actual troop deployment, the East and the West faced each other head on. Thus, broadly speaking, the countries in the US camp supported a capitalist economy under a liberal democratic government, and those in the USSR camp adopted a centrally planned Marxist-Leninist economy. It was within this sort of Cold-War-produced confrontational schema that economic interdependence, economic integration and the formation of a community rarely found in history would evolve in Western Europe.

By contrast, the situation in Asia was more complex. First of all, the Cold War in Asia, militarily, had sides to it that cannot be compressed into a simple bipolar confrontation between the United States and the Soviet Union. The main cause for this was the looming presence of China. China had announced its policy of "leaning to one side" (*yibiandao*), or allegiance to the Soviet cause, and maintained a strong alliance with the USSR in the 1950s; as long as this Sino-Soviet monolith continued, the Cold War in Asia was as clear-cut as it was in Europe. But Chinese-Soviet tensions deepened in the 1960s, and when Mao Zedong made the strategic decision to make peace with the United States in 1971, the Cold War in Asia changed from a face-off between East and West to a complex strategic game played by three countries, the US, China and the USSR. In the 1970s, China fanned fears that the USSR was a more dangerous hegemonist of "social imperialism" than the US was.[2]

Secondly, the Cold War in Asia had ideological features that cannot simply be reduced to a conflict between liberalism and Marxism-Leninism. Most Asian countries had been colonies, had gained their independence and were now engaged in nation-building. For them, nationalism—trying to create a new political entity of their own independent choosing—took precedence over the doctrines of liberalism and Marxism-Leninism. With the exception of Japan, most countries that belonged to the American camp were not all that liberal or democratic, nor were the countries in the Soviet camp that professed to be socialist all that faithful of Soviet-style socialism.

Thirdly, the Cold War in Asia was a race among developing countries to industrialize rather than a competition among advanced economies to become even more industrially advanced. Here, too, with the exception of Japan, there were no advanced industrial countries in Asia. Trends like those in Western Europe, which, over the course of the Cold War, saw the advanced industrialized countries further strengthen their economic integration, achieve even greater economic development and head toward the formation of a community, were not found in Asia. Regional cooperation in Asia was either economic cooperation with a strong military component or development cooperation carried out by Japan and the US in the developing countries. The Cold War in Asia was a race to see which countries would succeed in escaping third-world status and become economically developed, those that sided with the US or those that sided with the USSR.

As a result, in order to think about "post-Cold-War" Asia, we must consider what sort of changes this complex state of affairs in Asia brought about as the process of ending the Cold War unfolded. If the appearance of the Cold War was different in Asia than it was in Europe, the impact that the end of the Cold War had on Asia was also different. Briefly put, if, from a military perspective, the Cold

War in Asia had previously been a "complicated confrontation," the end of the Cold War brought with it a "normalization of international relations." If, from the political ideology perspective, the Cold War in Asia had been about national unity without being particular about what form that might take, the end of the Cold War was a process of "liberalization" and "democratization." And if, from an economic perspective, the Cold War in Asia had been a "race to escape from developing-nation status," the post-Cold War was a search for regional cooperation that would lead to "economic interdependence and economic integration."

Within this Cold-War Asia, the situation for Japan was extremely different. On the one hand, the position it was in was quite similar to that of the countries of Western Europe. Unlike other Asian countries, it did not seem all that unnatural to Japan that an East-West military confrontation and a conflict between two ideologies would determine where a country stood. On the other hand, for an Asian country, this put Japan in an anomalous position. In particular, from the perspectives of Asian nationalism and the race to develop among the developing countries, Japan's position was more like that of Europe and North America. In the past, Japan had invaded many of the countries in Asia, and yet from the perspective of economic development, it was now a source of aid. It is often said that Japanese identity in Asia is complicated; if we think about the state of affairs in Asia during the Cold War using the above schema, the nature of this complexity becomes clear. When most people in Asia looked back on the past from the perspective of nationalism, Japan was an imperialist country that had to be overthrown. But when they considered the present and future from the perspective of economic development, Japan was an advanced industrialized nation from whom they ought to ask for aid and cooperation.

From the end of World War II to the 1970s, however, Japan was focused on the postwar cleanup and its own economic revival. For most Japanese, these complex Cold-War trends in Asia were just stories about faraway lands. Most Japanese were not even fully aware of the complexity of their own identity in Asia. From the Japanese standpoint, the period from the end of the Cold War into the post-Cold-War era was a process of rediscovering Asia and Japan's place in it.[3]

The Cambodian Civil War

What came to symbolize the complexity of the late Cold-War period was the Cambodian Civil War. That war was not one that could be reduced to a simple confrontation between East and West. And the process of ending it was the very thing that brought about the normalization of international relations throughout Asia. Usually, the Cold War in the world system is regarded as having ended as the result of a process that began with the fall of the Berlin Wall in 1989 and concluded with the breakup of the Soviet Union at the end of 1991. The Cambodian Civil War, too, officially ended with the Paris Peace Agreement in October 1991. It might be said that the Cold War in Asia also ended at roughly the same time as it did in the rest of the world.

The reason why Cambodia, the country of Angkor Wat, became the stage on which the end of the Cold War in Asia was played out is very complicated. But the immediate cause was the seizure of power in Cambodia by Khmer Rouge forces at about the same time the Vietnam War ended in 1975. As the Khmer Rouge regime carried out its horrifyingly inhumane revolutionary policies, relations with Vietnam soured, giving rise to a conflict that dragged in China and then the US and the USSR.

Pol Pot, the leader of the Khmer Rouge, was obsessed with the idea of an agricultural communism that was anti-urban, anti-industrial and anti-intellectual and that pushed the ideas behind Mao Zedong's Cultural Revolution to an even further extreme. He forcibly sent city residents into the countryside and is said to have had between 1.5 and 1.7 million of his fellow countrymen tortured and killed.[4] His economic policies, land policies and agricultural policies were all reckless in the extreme and drove his people to the brink of starvation. Ieng Sary, the Khmer Rouge's second in command, told the Japanese diplomat, Miyake Wasuke, who visited Cambodia in September 1978, "All inequality derives from the existence of money, Mr Miyake. Because money exists, it makes wealth accumulation possible and gives rise to inequality." When Miyake asked the cost of a batik which was hanging in the display room of a government building, "one calf" was the answer.[5]

Beginning around August 1977, the Khmer Rouge repeatedly initiated military clashes along the border in an effort to reclaim territory taken by Vietnam. When it encountered large-scale resistance from

Vietnam at the end of 1977, the Khmer Rouge accused Vietnam of "aggression" and on December 31 of that year broke off diplomatic relations.[6] By early 1978, military clashes were constantly occurring along the Vietnamese-Cambodian border.

The relationship between Vietnam and the Khmer Rouge thus deteriorated into full-scale hostilities. For Vietnam, which felt betrayed by China after the Chinese-US rapprochement in 1971, the fact that China supported the Khmer Rouge was intolerable. China, too, allowed its hostile sentiments toward Vietnam to fester because of the increasingly anti-Chinese attitude Vietnam showed after its victory in the Vietnam War. Beginning in the spring of 1978, large numbers of Vietnam residents of Chinese descent fled the country and became refugees. Many of them attracted worldwide attention as "boat people." Both the Chinese and Vietnamese sides repeatedly hurled accusations at each other, and in July 1978, China completely halted aid to Vietnam. Vietnam showed its defiance of China by joining the Soviet-led COMECON (Council for Mutual Economic Assistance) in June 1978 and by concluding a treaty of friendship and cooperation with the Soviet Union that November. With Soviet backing, it invaded Cambodia in large numbers on December 25, 1978, quickly forcing Phnom Penh to surrender and launching the pro-Vietnamese Heng Samrin regime. As Chinese-Vietnamese relations grew more strained, China sent troops across the Chinese-Vietnamese border to "punish" Vietnam in February 1979, right after Deng Xiaoping's historic visit to the United States. But Vietnam proved a formidable opponent to the Chinese, who withdrew in March; in short order, the Chinese-Vietnamese war was over.[7]

Normally it would have been natural for the US to roundly criticize the inhuman behavior of the Khmer Rouge and perhaps even support Vietnam's military involvement as a "humanitarian intervention," to use the later terminology of international society. But having lost the Vietnam War, it was, in fact, impossible for the United States to establish friendly relations with Vietnam. In any event, Vietnam strengthened its ties with the USSR, America's Cold-War enemy; Cam Ranh Bay, which had already been turned into a naval port for the Soviet fleet, became the base for the Soviets in the South. Given the logic of the Cold War, it was inevitable that the US would take a hard line against Vietnam.

Vietnam's intervention in the Cambodian Civil War came at a time when the West's sense of being under global threat from Soviet aggression was intensifying. The USSR was strengthening its strategic influence in Africa, increasing its deployment of SS20 intermediate-range ballistic missiles and promoting the buildup of the Far Eastern Soviet Army in East Asia. This was also the time that the Soviets redeployed their land army in Japan's Northern Territories. As America's sense of the danger of these Soviet moves deepened, on December 15, 1978, it agreed to normalize relations with China as of January 1979. Vietnam's full-scale invasion of Cambodia took place ten days later. About a year after that, the Soviet Union invaded Afghanistan. As the course of this so-called "new" Cold War became more ominous, the East-West conflict in a form that included China on the West's side was becoming an insoluble dilemma.

Thus, the Cambodian Civil War became the military setting for a "new" Cold War in Asia. Within Cambodia, the Khmer Rouge and the Heng Samrin regime opposed each other; China supported the Khmer Rouge; Vietnam, which was sending its army into Cambodia, supported the Heng Samrin regime. America backed China, and the Soviets backed Vietnam. ASEAN and most of the Western countries accused Vietnam of invading Cambodia, supported Democratic Kampuchea, the Khmer-Rouge-controlled government, and blocked a bid by Vietnam and the Soviet Union to deprive Democratic Kampuchea of the right to represent Cambodia in the United Nations. As the confrontation took a classic Cold-War pattern, it was impossible for the permanent members to reach an agreement, and so the Cambodian problem remained unresolved in the UN Security Council. The US, Japan and the other Western countries found themselves in the utterly incomprehensible position of continuing to support the Khmer Rouge, who had committed mass atrocities, but given the logic of the Cold War, the situation could not help but become complicated. (It must, however, be said that neither the US nor the countries of Europe recognized the Democratic Kampuchea government.) Both the opposing regimes within Cambodia were ostensibly socialist; socialist China and socialist Vietnam took opposing sides in this conflict between socialist regimes, while the US and the West supported one side and the USSR supported the other. This fact, as well as the fact that the regime that the West supported committed genocide, are emblematic of how complicated the Cold War in Asia was.

The Fukuda Doctrine Frustrated

The period during which the Cambodian Civil War was being fought in earnest was also a period of major adjustment in Japan's postwar foreign policy.[8] For most Japanese, who understood international relations in schematic terms as a bipolar US-USSR conflict, the rapprochement between America and China that Richard Nixon and Mao Zedong reached in July 1971 was truly a "Nixon shock." Coupled with the subsequent dramatic change in the international economic order and the 1973 oil shock, it made the task of reconsidering the course of Japan's foreign policy a pressing problem. Of course, voices in Japan had been calling for normalization of relations with the People's Republic of China even before then, and in response, the Cabinet of Tanaka Kakuei had normalized relations in September 1972. Looking in the direction of Southeast Asia, however, there were two tasks for Japan. First, as the US withdrawal from Vietnam became clear, there was the question of what to do about relations with post-Vietnam-War Indochina. The second was how to build a comprehensive relationship of mutual trust with the countries of Southeast Asia. The anti-Japanese demonstrations in Jakarta and Bangkok that Prime Minister Tanaka Kakuei encountered on his visit to Southeast Asia in January 1974 had been a shock to the Japanese. Although it is true that domestic factors were also involved in both these demonstrations, nevertheless, the very fact that Japan was targeted was a major problem. By thinking only of economic expansion Japan had failed to take into consideration the countries of Southeast Asia where many held the view that Japan had once invaded them militarily and was now about to invade them economically.[9]

The situation in Japan during this period was one of confusion: the international economic environment was in a state of upheaval as the result of the oil shocks and other factors; Japan's domestic economy was suffering from unprecedented inflation; scandals were rocking the government; and the administration changed every two years in dizzying succession from Tanaka Kakuei (1972–74) to Miki

Takeo (1974–76) and Fukuda Takeo (1976–78). Although that made it impossible to work out a firm foreign policy strategy or an Asian strategy, each government tried to come up with its own policies. The Fukuda administration, in particular, began to advocate an "omni-directional peace policy" and set forth a course of action that attached importance to Southeast Asia.[10]

These trends were revealed in a clear form in a policy speech that Prime Minister Fukuda made during a visit to Southeast Asia in August 1977. Because of the importance of this speech, which later came to be called the Fukuda Doctrine, I will quote from it here in some detail. Prime Minister Fukuda made three main points. The first was that Japan would not become a military superpower.

> Throughout the world's history, great economic powers have always been great military powers as well. Japan, however, has set for herself a new ideal, unprecedented in history, of relying for [her] safety and survival on the justice and good faith of nations. We have chosen not to take the path to great military power. Although we possess the economic and technological capability needed to produce nuclear arms, we have firmly rejected the acquisition of such weapons.
>
> This is a challenging experiment, without parallel in history. I am, however, persuaded there can be no other proper course for Japan. My country, densely populated and with few natural resources, depends for its survival on free intercourse and cooperation with all countries. Moreover, I believe the path Japan has chosen also serves the best interests of Asia and, in the final analysis, of the world as a whole. A Japan which does not pose any threat to its neighbor countries, either in a military way or in any other way whatever, can only be viewed as a stabilizing force in the world, devoting its energies exclusively to peaceful and constructive purposes, at home and abroad. Thus can Japan best contribute to world peace, stability and development.

The second point was the need for "heart-to-heart understanding" among the peoples of Japan and the Southeast Asian countries.

It is not enough for our relationship to be based solely on mutual material and economic benefit. Our material and economic relations should be animated by heartfelt commitments to assisting and complementing each other as fellow Asians.

This is the message I have carried everywhere on this tour, speaking repeatedly of the need to communicate with each other with our hearts as well as our heads, the need in other words for what I call "heart-to-heart" understanding among the peoples of Japan and Southeast Asia.

You, fellow Asians, will understand what I mean. For it is in our Asian tradition, and it is in our Asian hearts, always to seek beyond mere physical satisfaction for the richness of spiritual fulfillment.

The third point was the need to take advantage of the opportunity that the end of the Vietnam War afforded to build a stable and peaceful Southeast Asia.

Finally, we all recognize that the future stability and prosperity of the ASEAN area can only be assured within a framework of peaceful progress throughout Southeast Asia as a whole. Now that decades of war and destruction have finally come to an end, we have a chance to work for enduring peace and stability in the whole region. Let me pay tribute here to the ASEAN countries for having expressed, in the joint communique of the ASEAN summit, their desire to develop peaceful and mutually beneficial relations with the nations of Indochina, enunciating their policy that "further efforts should be made to enlarge the areas of understanding and cooperation with those countries on the basis of mutuality of interests." I believe that these patient efforts will eventually expand the scope of mutual understanding and trust throughout the breadth of Southeast Asia. Towards this same objective, Japan will also seek to place its relations with the nations of Indochina on a solid foundation of mutual understanding.[11]

Prime Minister Fukuda himself is said to have placed special importance on the first and second of these three points.[12] Even before he became prime minister, he had repeatedly stated the message that Japan would not become a military power. In addition, as was already mentioned, Prime Minister Tanaka Kakuei, who visited Southeast Asia in January 1974, had been greatly shocked by the anti-Japanese demonstrations he met with in Jakarta and Bangkok. Japan regretfully recognized that its dealings with Southeast Asia up to that point had been economy-centered, and its efforts to win popular understanding in Asia had been totally ineffectual. Fukuda may have hoped that, along with the clear statement that Japan would not become a military power, the emphasis on "heart-to-heart understanding" would improve the view of Japan among the people of Southeast Asia.

Although the prime minister may have placed the emphasis on these areas, among the professionals in the Ministry of Foreign Affairs and elsewhere, the third point, developing relations with the countries of ASEAN and Indochina, was especially important.[13] Already by the late stages of the Vietnam War, the Japanese foreign ministry had been working to improve relations with North Vietnam, and Japan established diplomatic relations with the North in 1973. After the fall of Saigon in 1975, Japan immediately began to provide official development assistance to a unified Vietnam, an 8.5 billion yen grant in 1975, a 5 billion yen grant in 1976, a 4 billion yen grant as well as a 10 billion yen concessional loan in 1978.[14] Furthermore, in December 1978, just as Vietnam was launching a full-scale invasion of Cambodia, Japan made the decision to provide 14 billion yen in aid for FY1979.

Japan also carried out negotiations to normalize diplomatic relations with Cambodia, signed a joint communiqué on normalization in Beijing at the end of July 1976 and established diplomatic relations on August 2. Because the situation in Phnom Penh was not conducive to setting up an embassy there, the Japanese ambassador to China also held the post of ambassador to Cambodia. In September 1978, however, Satō Shōji, the ambassador to China and Cambodia, visited Phnom Penh, and the following October the deputy prime minister of the Khmer Rouge visited Japan. Right up until the time that relations between Vietnam and Cambodia broke down, Japan was engaged in diplomatic efforts aimed at improving relations with both countries.

From today's perspective when the atrocities committed by the Khmer Rouge after the Vietnam War and the complicated actions involving Vietnam and Cambodia examined earlier are well known, it is hard to understand why the Japanese Ministry of Foreign Affairs, which up until then had been eager to improve relations with Vietnam, was also in such a hurry to establish relations with the Khmer Rouge regime, which was likely to become Vietnam's enemy. Interpreted in a favorable light, the expectation may have been very strong that, now that the difficult problem of the Vietnam War was over, international relations in Asia were bound to head toward something "normal." Be that as it may, faced with the realities of international politics, the third point in the Fukuda Doctrine, which had been worked out by the pros in the Ministry of Foreign Affairs, became utterly impossible to put into practice.

Thus, no progress was made in diplomatic relations with Indochina. Anti-Japanese sentiments lingered on in Southeast Asia well into the 1980s. What took the central role in Japan's foreign policy vis-à-vis Southeast Asia was official development assistance (ODA). Originally, relations between Japan and the countries of Southeast Asia had started out in the form of the payment of reparations or quasi-reparations as part of the postwar cleanup after World War II.[15] Because these payments had mostly ended by the late 1970s, the policy came to be adopted to provide official development assistance to succeed them. As a result, aid to Southeast Asia has occupied an extremely large portion of Japanese ODA from the very outset. A look at the records for 1980 shows that it was the most important region, with ASEAN countries accounting for 35.9 percent. Because aid to China began in 1980, the proportion that the Southeast Asian countries received decreased. But since the total amount of Japanese ODA vastly increased at this time, the absolute amount these countries received did not decline but steadily increased. East Asia as a whole, including China, accounted for 46 percent in 1990. Likewise, the importance of aid from Japan among Asian countries continued to increase throughout the 1980s. In 1987, for example, the number of countries for whom Japan was the largest provider of aid rose to 17: Bangladesh, Bhutan, Burma, India, Maldives, Nepal, Pakistan, Sri Lanka, Brunei, China, Indonesia, Laos, Malaysia, Mongolia, Philippines, Singapore and Thailand. For most of the Asian countries, foreign aid meant aid from Japan.[16]

One aspect that Japan explored in its ODA projects was human resource development. In order to facilitate "heart-to-heart understanding" and help achieve economic development in Southeast Asia, Japanese aid workers began to realize that a human-centered approach was useful and necessary. When Prime Minister Suzuki Zenkō visited ASEAN countries in January 1981, he promised to extend about USD 100 million to establish human resource development centers in each of the five ASEAN member countries, where Japanese experts would engage in various technical cooperation projects for a period of nearly ten years.[17] In 1983, in his speech at Kuala Lumpur, Prime Minister Nakasone Yasuhiro promised to start a "Friendship Program for the 21st Century," in which Japan would invite 3,750 young administrators and teachers from ASEAN countries to Japan to participate in training and exchange programs in the coming five years. This program has continued into the 21st century, expanding the number of participating countries and celebrating its 30th anniversary in 2015; as of the end of FY2013, roughly 22,000 people had attended this program.[18]

In addition to human resource development, what Japan's ODA emphasized was infrastructure development. This emphasis on infrastructure can be explained by Japan's own experiences of industrial development since the Meiji Restoration. Networks of roads and railroads, port facilities and power production constituted the foundation upon which Japan modernized in the late 19th to early 20th centuries. The effectiveness of the World Bank loans extended to Japan in the 1950s and 1960s, financing the Shinkansen, Tōmei and Meishin Highways, Kurobe No. 4 hydropower station and so on, reinforced Japanese belief in the significance of infrastructure.[19] In Japan's ODA to Southeast Asia, therefore, infrastructure was another important sector.

One typical mega-project built with Japanese assistance was the Eastern Seaboard Development program in Thailand, an ambitious national program to transform the coastal region east of Bangkok from barren fields into an industrial region for export-oriented production.[20] Japan provided technical cooperation to make a series of master plans on water, port facilities and industrial development and extended ODA loans to 16 projects amounting to about 180 billion yen from 1982 to 1993. The region, now home to some 1,400 companies, has become one of the largest production centers of Southeast Asia.

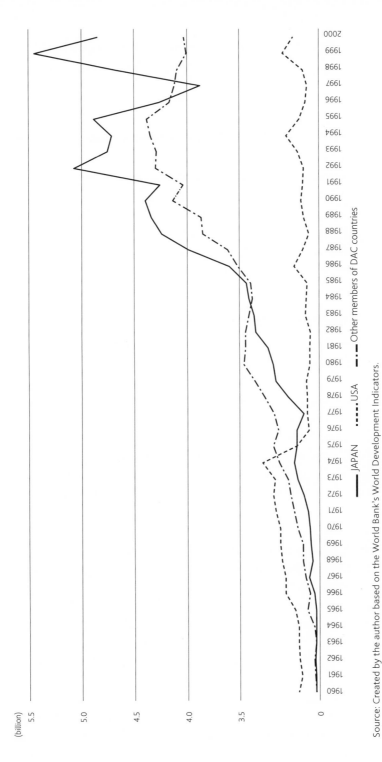

Source: Created by the author based on the World Bank's World Development Indicators.

Figure 1.1 ODA to the Developing Countries of East Asia and the Pacific

Prime Minister Fukuda's appeal for "heart-to-heart under-standing" might be called naive, but seen from these results, it was backed up by the continuation and steady expansion of official development assistance emphasizing human resources and infra-structure. The subsequent miraculous economic development of Southeast Asia was made possible by many factors—the appropriate economic policies of the national governments, the state of the world economy that attracted foreign direct investment into Southeast Asia and the sheer effort of the people in the region. But Japan's ODA also contributed to the improvement of the basic requirements needed to support economic development: human resources and infrastructure (See Figure 1.1). Anti-Japanese sentiment had ceased to be a concern in Southeast Asia by the early 1990s.

Movements toward Peace in Cambodia

The Cambodian Civil War continued unabated throughout the 1980s. There were various attempts at peace-making, but none was successful. Not surprisingly, it was hard to adopt policies that showed utter disregard for humanity by supporting only the Khmer Rouge (Pol Pot) faction, and so, in 1982, there was a movement among the ASEAN countries and the West to add other groups to it and estab-lish a Coalition Government of Democratic Kampuchea consisting of three parties, the Khmer Rouge's Democratic Kampuchea, the Sihanouk faction led by Prince Norodom Sihanouk and the Son Sann faction led by conservative politician Son Sann. In June of that year, the three groups finally agreed to form a coalition government. This government, however, was actually extremely weak. Militarily, only the Pol Pot faction was capable of resisting the Heng Samrin regime; both the Sihanouk faction and the Son Sann faction were only able to maintain a presence in a small area along the Thai border.

By the latter half of the 1980s, the parties involved began to make serious efforts to find a way out of the impasse. The first of these was Sihanouk's attempt to hold direct talks with the Heng Samrin regime. In May 1987, he announced that he was taking a leave of absence as president of the three-party coalition government. The aim, it is said, was to distance himself somewhat from the Pol Pot and Son Sann factions and to open a dialogue with Vietnam and the

Heng Samrin regime.[21] In response to this move, the Heng Samrin regime approached Sihanouk. At the beginning of June 1987, through a representative of the Palestine Liberation Organization in Pyongyang, North Korea, it requested a meeting with Sihanouk, who was in Pyongyang at the time. Sihanouk accepted, but because the Heng Samrin regime later criticized him, Sihanouk got angry, and the talks went back to square one. In August 1987, however, Sihanouk met with Thai Foreign Minister Siddhi Savetsila in Pyongyang and told him that he was confident that direct and frank discussions with Prime Minister Hun Sen of the Heng Samrin regime would be beneficial for the country and the Cambodian people and that he had already conveyed to the other side his willingness to meet them.[22] In October of that year, Sihanouk related at length to the Japanese ambassador to France, Motono Moriyuki, his pet theory about what an unmanageable and destructive bunch the Khmer Rouge were and expressed his strong desire to achieve a breakthrough in the deadlock and move toward peace in Cambodia by holding direct talks with Hun Sen.[23] A meeting between Sihanouk and Hun Sen actually took place as Sihanouk said it would in December 1987 in the Paris suburb of Fère-en-Tardenois. The two met again in January 1988 and pushed the discussion forward even further. Difficult issues were involved, such as a time frame for the withdrawal of Vietnamese troops; whether or not to dissolve the Heng Samrin regime before general elections once peace was made; and the disarmament of the Pol Pot forces. When the Son Sann side and the Pol Pot side resisted these moves, Sihanouk responded by saying that he would resign as president of the coalition. Since both sides would be placed in an awkward position were Sihanouk to give up the presidency, they pressed him to reconsider. Sihanouk agreed and remained president.

By this time, the countries of Southeast Asia were putting forth a number of ideas in an attempt to mediate a settlement. In the summer of 1987, Foreign Minister Mochtar Kusumaatmadja of Indonesia met with Foreign Minister Nguyen Co Thach of Vietnam in Ho Chi Minh City, and they agreed to hold informal discussions in Indonesia among the countries concerned, including Vietnam and the other parties involved in the Cambodian conflict. This proposal did not win the approval of the other ASEAN countries, and as a result nothing came of it. However, while no progress was being made in the talks between Sihanouk and Hun Sen, in what once again seemed to be a valuable attempt, the conflict's participants and the countries concerned held informal discussions over cocktails in Bogor, a suburb of Jakarta, between July 25 and July 28, 1988. But, in fact, ASEAN's candid "cocktail party" atmosphere did not go as planned. On the contrary, the outlines of the conflict only became even clearer, and no agreement was reached.

Democratization and the Cold War

The Cold War in Asia cannot be reduced to an ideological confrontation between liberalism and Marxism-Leninism. As the Sino-Soviet split shows, in the 1960s, the rift within the socialist camp was already growing wider. What is more, in Asia, most of the countries in the American camp were neither liberal nor democratic. In South Korea, authoritarian regimes had tightened their grip on power since the days of its first president, Rhee Syng-man, and the administration of Chang Myon, which had grown out of the student-led revolution of 1960, was short-lived. The Park Chung-hee administration that succeeded it established an authoritarian regime that lasted a long time. It invoked martial law in 1972 and ruled with an iron fist, even kidnapping the opposition leader Kim Dae-jung in Japan. After President Park had been assassinated by Kim Jae-gyu, the head of the Korean Central Intelligence Agency (KCIA) in 1979, the Chun Doo-hwan administration was also military-led.

Having being defeated in the Chinese Civil War and fleeing to Taiwan in 1949, the Republic of China was also a classic authoritarian regime. The Kuomintang (the Chinese Nationalist Party) itself had originally been organized under the leadership of the Soviet Communist Party during the period of the First United Front in the 1920s and was a political party deeply tinged with Leninist features. Those who had lived in Taiwan since the time of Japanese colonial rule (the "islanders") and who openly called for Taiwanese independence were thrown in jail or forced into virtual exile in Japan or the United States.

In the Philippines, an American-style democracy had been introduced after independence, and politically the country maintained a democratic system despite abuses such as preserving the rights of a large land-owning class (the oligarchy). In 1972, however, on the pretext of abolishing oligarchic control, Ferdinand Marcos, who had been elected president in 1965, declared martial law, revised the constitution to extend the term of the presidency (only two terms, or a total of eight years, had been previously allowed) and set up a dictatorship. In Indonesia, as well, President Suharto, who seized power after the fall of the Sukarno regime, formed an authoritarian system, which, it was thought, would last forever. Malaysia and Singapore under their strong-willed leaders Mahathir Mohamad and Lee Kuan Yew created unique political systems that might be called soft authoritarian regimes. Although an authoritarian system under a single strong leader was never established in Thailand, the pattern was set that once every few years, a military coup d'état would occur, and there would be a change of government. Burma, which had become independent from Britain, took an internationally independent course after the coup d'état of 1962 under General Ne Win and advocated "Burmese-style Socialism." As a result, around 1980, the only countries in Asia that were regarded as having stable democratic governments were Japan and India.

Democratization in the Philippines

Once into the 1980s, however, the pro-democracy movement grew stronger even in Asia.[24] Leading the way was the Philippines.[25] The turning point was the August 21, 1983 assassination at Manila International Airport of Benigno Aquino, a former senator and anti-Establishment leader who had just returned home from exile in the United States. Criticism of the "Marcos dynasty"—the friends and relatives especially of Imelda Marcos that had solidified around the center of power—spiked.[26] In addition to the local bosses whom Marcos had deprived of their vested interests, the urban middle class, who had borne the brunt of the impact of economic recession on the Philippines, also turned their backs on the Marcos regime.

In 1972, when Marcos imposed martial law, the gross national product per capita of the Philippines had been USD 207; in 1983, it had risen to USD 642. But this was in nominal prices; in terms of real prices estimated in American dollars for the year 2000, the increase was only from USD 765 to USD 997. Moreover, because of the rise in the price of crude oil after the second oil shock and the subsequent slump in commodity prices, the Philippine economy continued to be depressed; the economic growth rate for both 1984 and 1985 was minus 7 percent. On the other hand, consumer prices soared; there was double-digit inflation: 12.5 percent in 1983, 44 percent in 1984, and 23 percent in 1985.[27]

The assassination of Benigno Aquino occurred in the midst of the ongoing economic slump, and the anti-Marcos movement gained speed. A month after the assassination, memorial services were held in ten cities throughout the country including Manila. Near the presidential palace several thousand demonstrators clashed with security forces, and 15 people were killed. On November 27, Benigno Aquino's birthday, 100,000 people gathered for an anti-Marcos protest. On August 21, 1984, 500,000 anti-government protesters held a demonstration in Manila. Despite this, Marcos showed no signs of accepting their demands for his resignation and even indicated his intention to run again in the next presidential election scheduled for 1987. On November 3, 1985, he appeared on an American news program on ABC television and said he was moving the election forward a year.[28] If there were an election, he claimed, it would be clear that the people supported him.

Meanwhile, the trial to establish the facts behind the assassination of Benigno Aquino continued, and on December 2, 1985, a verdict of not guilty was handed down on all 26 defendants, including General Fabian Ver, chief of staff of the Philippine armed forces. This not-guilty verdict deepened suspicions not only about the fairness of the trial but also about the very nature of the Marcos regime. There have always been many questions about the investigation into the facts of this incident. In October 1983, a fact-finding committee composed of five civilians had been set up, but it failed to reach a conclusion that all the members could agree upon. In October 1984, Corazon Agrava, the head of the committee, presented her report to President Marcos that seven military officers had been involved. But the remaining four members were dissatisfied with her report and submitted a separate report stating that all 26 members of the armed forces including General Ver had taken part. In any case, however, the involvement of the military was thought to be clear. Thus, there were doubts about the court's fairness when all of them were found not guilty.

On December 2, the day this verdict was handed down, a law was passed moving presidential elections forward to February 7, 1986. When the anti-Marcos side heard this, they united behind the candidacy of Corazon Aquino, the assassinated Benigno Aquino's widow. Because of strong international doubts about whether fair elections could be held, a total of 20 countries including the US sent observers. The American observation team was led by Senator Richard Lugar, chairman of the Foreign Relations Committee. Tensions heightened as the election drew near. There were even reports through US information channels that Mrs Aquino might be assassinated. And, in fact, right before the election, she appealed to US Ambassador Stephen Bosworth to find a safe place for her.[29]

No election in a developing country had ever been given as much worldwide coverage as this one. CNN broadcast live the opening of the polls throughout the Philippines. CNN is a network founded in 1980 to handle world news programs, and while its images were being carried throughout the world, domestic media in the Philippines were also rebroadcasting them. It was these images that determined the impression not only among the Philippine people but among people throughout the world that Mrs Aquino had won the election.[30] Despite the fact that the international observers reported unanimously that there had been numerous irregularities in the election, on February 15, the Philippine Assembly announced that President Marcos had been elected for a fourth term. In response, the US government, which had not taken a very clear position up until then, issued a statement saying, "It has already become evident, sadly, that the elections were marred by widespread fraud and violence perpetrated largely by the ruling party." The international tide of support for Mrs Aquino was decisive.

On February 16, Mrs Aquino declared victory at a large gathering in Manila. On February 20, the US Senate passed a resolution condemning the corruption in the Philippine presidential elections. On the 22nd, Secretary of National Defense Juan Ponce Enrile and Chief of Staff of the Philippine Constabulary Fidel Ramos, important pillars of the Marcos regime, handed in their resignations, signifying that they no longer recognized Marcos as the supreme commander in chief, and took refuge in Camp Aguinaldo. Here the People Power Revolution faced its moment of truth. The government army under

General Ver lined up its tanks and encircled the opposition forces. As images of the face-off in Manila were broadcast throughout the world, civilians gathered around Camp Aguinaldo to support the opposition troops. With fears mounting that the situation would end in bloodshed, on the 23rd, the White House decided it would no longer support the Marcos regime.[31] President Reagan's message to President Marcos warning that the US would suspend military aid immediately if any attack were made on the anti-Marcos camp was made public. On the 24th, Enrile announced that a provisional government would be set up under President Corazon Aquino. General Ver asked President Marcos for permission to attack, but the president refused.[32] The American government issued a statement that the only way out of this dangerous situation was a "peaceful transition to a new government" and, in fact, put pressure on Marcos to resign.[33] On the 25th, an extraordinary state of affairs occurred when Mrs Aquino announced that she would take office at 10:40 that morning, and Marcos announced that he would take office an hour later at 11:50. Ultimately, Marcos was forced to decide to resign, and at 9 o'clock that evening he left Malacañan Palace on an American military helicopter for Clark Air Force Base; the Marcos dictatorship had come to an end.

Democratization in South Korea

The People Power Revolution in the Philippines had an enormous impact on other authoritarian countries where the first stirrings of a pro-democracy movement were being felt. The first to be affected was South Korea.[34] Pro-democracy sentiments heightened right after the assassination on October 26, 1979 of President Park Chung-hee. Choi Kyu-hah, who assumed the office of acting president immediately afterward and later became president, lifted the presidential Emergency Measure No. 9, which had continued throughout the Park administration, and freed political prisoners including Kim Dae-jung, who had been placed under house arrest. In December, however, General Chun Doo-hwan, head of the Defense Security Command, and others in the military staged a coup d'état and arrested Martial Law Commander and Army Chief of Staff Jeong Seung-hwa on suspicion of involvement in the shooting of President Park. Those who carried out the coup d'état,

Chun Doo-hwan, Roh Tae-woo and other members of the eleventh graduating class of the Korean Military Academy, seized control of the army. At the beginning of 1980, when Kim Dae-jung, Kim Young-sam and other leaders of the opposition began to act, there was support for them everywhere; students and others began to hold massive rallies demanding democratization and an end to martial law. The military, through which Chun Doo-hwan and others had seized control of martial law, tightened its guard against the pro-democracy movement and began to consider taking direct control itself. At the American embassy, its staff had become convinced that Chun intended to become president.[35] On May 18, an emergency martial law went into effect, and the Martial Law Command arrested Kim Dae-jung and other opposition leaders. When news of Kim's arrest reached his hometown of Gwangju in South Jeolla Province, a massive anti-government demonstration erupted. Special forces sent to suppress it engaged in indiscriminate attacks on civilians over three days, which only intensified the violent civilian resistance. Gwangju was finally brought under control by the 20th Division of the army and by special forces on May 27. According to the Martial Law Command, 170 people died (later revised by a 1995 inquiry to 240). In August, President Choi took responsibility for the Gwangju incident and resigned. Chun Doo-hwan succeeded him as president.

From the time of the Park assassination through the Gwangju incident to Chun's seizure of power, the US administration under President Jimmy Carter was unable to exert much influence, being preoccupied by the Soviet invasion of Afghanistan and by the occupation of the American embassy in Iran after the Iranian Revolution. At the beginning of September, the Chun regime announced that Kim Dae-jung had been sentenced to death as the mastermind behind the anti-government insurrection. President Ronald Reagan, who had defeated Carter in the November election, made a deal with Chun that he would welcome Chun to Washington in return for Kim's life;[36] as a result, international recognition of the Chun regime was secured. On February 2, 1981, Reagan welcomed Chun and his entourage to the White House. The following September, Seoul succeeded in securing the 1988 Olympics, defeating Nagoya. This, too, strengthened international recognition of the Chun regime.

In addition, the Chun regime maintained a confrontational attitude toward North Korea, and on the grounds that South Korea was a fortress protecting Japan, it demanded that, for security reasons, Japan should provide it with economic assistance. The Suzuki Zenkō administration rejected this demand, saying that it was inconceivable to give economic aid to a military regime, and Japanese-South Korean relations deteriorated badly. To resolve the situation, Prime Minister Nakasone Yasuhiro, who took over in November 1982, asked Sejima Ryūzō, part of his brain trust, to enter into secret negotiations with the South Korean government. The agreement was reached that Japan would give economic aid amounting to a total of USD 4 billion and that Nakasone's first official overseas visit would be to South Korea. It would be the first official visit to South Korea by a Japanese prime minister.[37] In this way, Japan also assumed the role of internationally backing the Chun regime.

As the regime garnered international support, it managed the economy with a steady hand in much the same way that the Park regime had, in what could be called a typical developmental dictatorship, causing economic conditions to improve. In 1972, when the Park regime strengthened its authoritarian rule, the GDP per capita of South Korea was only USD 323, not much different from the Philippines. When Park was assassinated in 1979, however, it had risen to USD 1,747. When Chun took over in 1980, the economy had a negative growth rate of minus 1 percent as a result of the second oil shock, but it subsequently recovered and grew at the high rates of 6 percent in 1981, 7 percent in 1982, 11 percent in 1983, 8 percent in 1984, 7 percent in 1985, and 11 percent in 1986. In 1986, the GDP per capita was USD 3,368.[38]

Economic growth, however, did not translate into stronger popular support for the authoritarian regime. Memories of the Gwangju incident forced strong anti-government sentiments in Jeolla to go underground. Students and the urban middle class in Seoul and other big cities came to demand greater freedom as well as a higher standard of living. If the overthrow of the authoritarian regime in the Philippines had come about because of economic mismanagement and corruption—its failures as a regime, so to speak—the pro-democracy movement in South Korea had its origins in the very success of its developmental dictatorship.

From a historical perspective, President Chun himself made an important decision. In June 1980, he told Richard Walker, who later became the American ambassador to South Korea, "If I were to become president, I would like the history books to say that I was the first one in Korea to turn over power in a legitimate and constitutional manner."[39] The constitutional revision he decided upon on becoming president was to limit the presidential term of office to seven years and prohibit a second term, and he announced right from the moment he took power that he would abide by the constitution. Consequently, he kept his promise and did indeed become the first president "to turn over power in a legitimate and constitutional manner."

The way the Chun regime conducted itself, however, was authoritarian enough to raise doubts as to whether or not he would keep his promise. His handling of the student-led anti-government demonstrations had been extremely harsh, and he did not hesitate to place Kim Dae-jung and other anti-government leaders under house arrest. Also intensifying these doubts was the fact that, in response to demands to revise the South Korean constitution, which had grown stronger around the time of the People Power Revolution in the Philippines, Chun had mentioned changing to a parliamentary cabinet system. There were suspicions that under a parliamentary system he might become prime minister himself or try to manipulate power from behind the scenes.[40]

Thus, from the latter half of 1986 into 1987, a movement demanding direct presidential elections spread throughout the country. At the center of these activities were the students. The death of Seoul University student Park Jong-chul on January 14, 1987 after being tortured by the police poured oil on the fire of anti-government sentiment. A large-scale memorial service for him planned for February 7 was blocked by the police. Although the Cabinet of Prime Minister Roh Shin-yeong took responsibility for the incident and resigned, this failed to stop the student movement. On June 10, while the governing party, the Democratic Justice Party, was holding its convention and officially nominating Roh Tae-woo as its candidate for president, opposition forces trying to hold a rally to protest the torture death of the Seoul University student clashed with police. The next day demonstrations consisting not just of students but for the most part ordinary citizens spread throughout the country; as many as 700,000 people in 33 cities took part in the demonstrations, and 12,686 of them were taken into custody. The participation of middle-class citizens in political demonstrations had never been seen in South Korea before.

As in the case of the revolution in the Philippines a year earlier, CNN and other television networks transmitted the local situation to the rest of the world, broadcasting the uprising in South Korea in real time. With the Seoul Olympics a year away, the world's interest focused on South Korea. On the morning of June 19, President Chun decided that if the unrest continued any longer he would have no choice but to call in the army and directed army leaders to send in troops the next morning to every city and university. The young army officers, however, protested vehemently against this decision. And Roh Tae-woo himself, who had been nominated as the presidential candidate, told Chun he was opposed to mobilization. The American ambassador to South Korea, James Lilley, with the tacit agreement of General William Livesey, commander of the ROK-US combined forces, gave the president strong warnings against sending in the troops. American opposition, the opposition of his successor and opposition within the army ultimately made the president to decide to call the mobilization off.[41] Bloodshed was avoided.

On June 29, Roh Tae-woo announced an eight-point plan to bring the situation under control and advised President Chun to accept it. The plan included a revision of the constitution to allow direct presidential elections, which the opposition had been demanding, as well as the pardoning of Kim Dae-jung, freedom of the press and autonomy for the universities. Chun did so, and the government of South Korea dramatically changed course and headed toward democratization. The proposal to revise the constitution to a direct presidential election system was subsequently passed by the National Assembly and approved with the overwhelming support of the popular vote, 93.1 percent. The opposition was unable to unite behind a single candidate, and, as a result, in the election on December 16, Roh Tae-woo won by a simple majority with 36 percent of the vote; Kim Young-sam received 28 percent, and Kim Dae-jung 27 percent. Roh's image as somebody who had forced an unwilling Chun Doo-hwan to accept bold plans for democratization was perhaps useful in wiping away his image as a military officer succeeding the unpopular dictator. It must be added, however, that those involved have made it clear that the eight-point plan of June 29 was the decision of Chun Doo-hwan himself.[42] If so, the role that Chun played in South Korean democratization will need to be reevaluated.

Democratization in Taiwan

Even Taiwan, another "bastion of anticommunism" in the Asian Cold War, saw the beginnings of a pro-democracy movement in the 1980s.[43] Democratization in Taiwan, however, did not follow the dramatic trajectory of street clashes and the overthrow of a dictator as it did in the Philippines and South Korea. The Chinese Nationalist Party—the Kuomintang—that had backed the authoritarian government of Chiang Kai-shek is still a powerful political party in Taiwan well into the 21st century.

Taiwanese society is a complicated society in many senses. In terms of demographics, it can roughly be divided into three groups. The first are the "aborigines," people with strong affinities with Polynesian peoples who have inhabited Taiwan since before the 17th century; the second are the "islanders" (*benshengren*), people of Han Chinese descent who moved there from the mainland after the 17th century; and the third are the "mainlanders" (*waishengren*) who moved there from all parts of China with the Kuomintang after 1945 in the aftermath of the defeat of Japan and the Chinese Civil War. The second group, the islanders, can be further broken down into the "Hakka," who have their own unique identity, and the Hoklos, whose ancestors came from the southern part of Fujian (Hokkien) Province and who are also known as the Min Nan, or the Southern Min people, because Fujian was also called Min. As of 1989, the aborigines made up 1.7 percent of the population, the Hoklos 73.3 percent, the Hakka 12 percent and the mainlanders 13 percent.[44] The situation is complex even with respect to the languages people speak. Under Japanese rule, Japanese was taught as the national language, but under the control of the Kuomintang, the official language has been Mandarin, which for the most part the mainlanders speak. Thus, the islanders and the aborigines are forced to speak several languages in addition to the language that they speak at home.[45]

Moreover, the mainlanders to a certain extent had the attitude of "conquerors." The government of Taiwan under the Kuomintang right after 1945 was regarded not only as authoritarian because of its exclusion of the islanders but also as incompetent and corrupt. Discontent exploded on February 28, 1947 when riots by the islanders occurred everywhere in Taiwan and were totally suppressed by the Kuomintang (the 228 Incident).[46] Since then, the center of political power in Taiwan has mostly been in the grip of the mainlanders. Furthermore, because of the ongoing Civil War with the Communist Party, the government of the Republic of China, which lost the mainland in 1949, suspended the democratic portions of the constitution under martial law, drew up the Temporary Provisions Effective During the Period of Communist Rebellion and gave dictatorial authority to the president. Since its official stance was that it was the government of national unity that ruled all of China, members of the National Assembly and the Legislative Yuan, who had been elected in all parts of China between 1947 and 1948, remained in office without being reelected even when their term came to an end.[47]

The authoritarian government of Chiang Kai-shek that had been imposed on this complicated Taiwanese society could not help but encounter rough sailing in international society as well. In July 1971, the US government indicated its intention to improve relations with China, which it had previously regarded as an enemy, and announced that President Nixon would visit China the following year (the "Nixon shock"). That autumn the UN General Assembly adopted a resolution granting the government of the People's Republic of China in Beijing the right to represent China and deciding to expel the Republic of China from the UN, in protest against which the ROC announced its withdrawal from the United Nations. Nixon visited China in February 1972, and in September, Japan normalized diplomatic relations with China and broke off relations with Taiwan. PRC-US negotiations advanced further in 1978, and on January 1, 1979, the US established diplomatic relations with Beijing and severed its ties with Taiwan.

The period of these continuing international difficulties was also a time of transition in terms of political power in Taiwan. Chiang Kai-shek's eldest son, Chiang Ching-kuo, succeeded to power after his father. He had been vice president of the Executive Yuan in 1969 and took office as its president in 1972; when Chiang Kai-shek died in 1975, he became leader of the Kuomintang, was named president of the Republic of China in 1978 and seized complete control of Taiwan both in name and in reality.

For Chiang Ching-kuo, in international isolation, it was no easy matter to manage a political system that was supposed to control "one China." First of all, no matter how autocratic his regime might be, it was impossible to govern Taiwan with only mainlanders. The emergence of talented islander technocrats such as Lee Teng-hui was unavoidable. In addition, the members of the National Assembly and the Legislative Yuan brought over from the mainland, even though not reelected, could not live forever. If a seat for a representative of Taiwan Province became vacant, a provincial election could be held to fill it; there was no excuse, then, for reelections not to be held on the grounds that elections were impossible. As a result, in 1969, elections were held to fill vacancies in the "free areas" (as opposed to the mainland, i.e., Taiwan, Penghu, Kinmen, Matsu, etc.). In addition, in 1972, although the existing members and representatives of the National Assembly and the Legislative Yuan would not be up for reelection, a reform was put into effect to increase the quota and hold regular elections in the "free areas." In order for the Kuomintang to continue to maintain legitimacy in international isolation, this sort of partial election may have been judged to be useful. In fact, as elections were carried out under martial law and with freedom of speech virtually nonexistent, the Kuomintang won an overwhelming majority. No matter how limited they may have been, however, the very fact that elections had been held led to the emergence of an anti-Kuomintang movement demanding greater democracy among people with no party affiliation.

While Chiang Ching-kuo's Taiwan may have been isolated from the international community politically, economically it had achieved economic growth that can only be called exemplary. The per capita GNP in Taiwan in 1970 was USD 384, not much higher than in the Philippines. But in 1980 it had risen to USD 2,293 and to USD 3,125 in 1985. Looking at the GNP growth rate as a whole, the GNP continued to grow on an average of more than 7 percent during the 1980s.

Amid international isolation, economic development and the stirrings of a domestic pro-democracy movement, the Kuomintang government under Chiang Ching-kuo at first responded to demands for democratic reform with even greater repression. But doing so increasingly tarnished the international image of Taiwan, which was internationally isolated as it was. Despite authoritarian measures and terror at home, the pro-democracy movement was getting stronger, and criticism from the US and elsewhere was intensifying. Right after the People Power Revolution in the Philippines in February 1986, Chiang Ching-kuo finally decided on "government reform." When the Tangwai (literally, "outside the party," i.e., outside the Kuomingtang) forces demanding democratization formed the Democratic Progressive Party that September, he recognized it conditionally and lifted martial law the following July. Chiang Ching-kuo died in January 1988 right after he made the decision to allow Taiwan to move toward democracy. Although the demand had come from below, democratization in Taiwan got its start as the result of a decision by the leader of an authoritarian regime.

Democratization in Taiwan, however, did not transform the political system or the leadership in a single stroke through constitutional reform and presidential elections. Under the Kuomintang administration, whose official stance was that it was the government of all of China, lifting martial law and restoring freedom of speech meant liberalization, but democratization in the sense that the government was being run by the will of the people had not immediately been achieved. To be sure, Lee Teng-hui, who succeeded Chiang Ching-kuo as president, represented a huge change. Born to a Hakka family and educated in Japan during Japanese colonial rule—he was a graduate of Kyoto Imperial University—he was regarded as a technocrat, a specialist in agronomics who had never been to the Chinese mainland. Nevertheless, the fact that he became president was because Chiang Ching-kuo had appointed him vice president under an authoritarian system; he had not been elected by the Taiwanese people. Both the National Assembly, which elected the president, and the Legislative Yuan, which made the laws, had members serving lifelong terms who represented all the mainland provinces despite the fact that the Nationalists had lost the mainland. The democratic elections held after Chiang Ching-kuo's succession to power were only local elections and "elections to increase the membership" over and above the seats of the "permanent legislators." Democratization in Taiwan in the sense that leaders were chosen by election would have to wait until the 1990s.

The Failure of Democratization in Burma

Discontent with a rigid political system was also growing stronger in Burma in the late 1980s. Burma, which had become independent of Britain as a federal state in 1948 just after the leader of the independence movement Aung San had been stabbed to death, is a country with an area 1.8 times the size of Japan and an extremely complex demography. From the time of independence on, uprisings by the Karen and other ethnic minorities were constantly occurring, making governance extremely difficult. Ne Win, the leader of the Burmese Army, who had staged a coup d'état in 1962 to prevent the federation from collapsing, upheld the ideal of a "Burmese Way to Socialism." He carried through policies of self-sufficiency and non-alliance and pursued a course of international isolation, as a result of which the economy stagnated. The Constitution of the Socialist Republic of the Union of Burma was promulgated in 1974, and a transition was made to civilian rule under the Burmese Socialist Programme Party; in fact, however, it was a "system of indirect military rule" with a strong army influence.[48] With aid from Japan and elsewhere, for a while the economy seemed to take a turn for the better, but the economic infrastructure had not been laid, and ultimately the only thing that grew was the debt. As the economy grew steadily worse in the 1980s, the government's lack of a consistent economic policy fanned social unrest.

In March 1988, popular discontent flared up over a minor incident. As the result of a fight in a teashop between students at Rangoon Institute of Technology and the son of a powerful local leader, a student demonstration led to bloodshed when the security forces quelled it. As demonstrations spread into the countryside, the atmosphere became tense. On July 3, a state of emergency was declared in Rangoon. At a special congress of the Burma Socialist Programme Party on July 23, Ne Win announced the resignations of the party leaders, himself included, and proposed to put to a popular vote whether or not there should be a transition to a multi-party system. This proposal for popular elections was rejected by the party congress, however, and on July 26, it elected hardliner Sein Lwin to succeed Ne Win as party chairman. He took office as president the following day. On August 3, he declared martial law and adopted hardline policies, but the anti-government movement's resistance just grew stronger, and riots broke out throughout the country. Ultimately, Sein Lwin was forced to resign a mere 17 days after he had been elected.

The person who succeeded him was Maung Maung, the chairman of the Council of People's Inspectors, who seemed to be a moderate civilian. When he repealed martial law, however, even larger numbers of students took part in mass meetings. Through Burmese-language short-wave-radio broadcasts over the BBC, the students who participated in the general strike knew about the collapse of the Marcos regime in the Philippines in 1986 and Roh Tae-woo's announcement of democratic reforms in South Korea in 1987 and realized that the democratization of their own country was in line with these world trends.[49] As these students expected, former prime minister U Nu, retired Brigadier General Aung Gyi, and Aung San Suu Kyi, the daughter of the hero of Burmese independence, became the leaders of the anti-government movement. Between two and three million people, including civil servants and members of the armed forces, are said to have participated in the countrywide demonstrations that took place on September 1.[50] However, the leaders of the anti-government movement at this point did not seem to have a firm strategy. Although they were able to hold huge rallies on a national scale, they could not come to a clear agreement on how to oppose the regime.[51]

The Maung Maung government held a special party congress on September 12 and decided to introduce a multi-party system and hold general elections. But the anti-government leaders rejected these proposals, which could be described as moderate, and demanded the immediate resignation of the current regime. As a result, the masses, fired up with anti-government fervor, broke out into rioting all over the country. On September 18, the army led by General Saw Maung, commander-in-chief of the armed forces, staged a coup d'état to end the chaos; he formed the State Law and Order Restoration Council (SLORC), seized complete control, and in 1989 the military regime renamed the country "Myanmar." The SLORC announced that its position was only temporary and, with a view to carrying out elections, introduced a law on the registration of political parties and a law of association.

Hearing this news, on September 24, the leaders of the opposition formed the National United Front for Democracy, later the National League for Democracy (NLD). But because they were not unified, the military government forced Aung San Suu Kyi and other opposition leaders into house arrest. The military regime may have thought that if elections were held while the opposition leaders were under arrest, the opposition would not win. But when general elections were held on May 27, 1990, the NLD won an overwhelming 392 of the 491 seats in the National Assembly with a 59.87 percent turnout.[52] Taken by surprise, the military government froze the election results, claiming to delay a transition to a new government until the new constitution could be drawn up. The "provisional government," set up by the military, became a long-term repressive military dictatorship. The pro-democracy movement had, for the moment, failed.

Chapter 2

Northeast Asia and the End of the Cold War

The Tiananmen Square Incident

While pro-democracy movements were making strides in the Philippines, South Korea and Taiwan, in the spring of 1989 the focus of the world's attention was on Tiananmen Square in China. Sparked by the death of the Chinese Communist Party's former general secretary, Hu Yaobang, on April 15, 1989, students and intellectuals poured into Tiananmen Square, demanding greater freedom and mourning Hu Yaobang, who had fallen from power because he sought reform. At first, the Chinese government under General Secretary Zhao Ziyang did nothing to stop the student movement, and the Western media were even allowed to report on it actively. While the Western media were broadcasting these events in real time, however, Deng Xiaoping and others in the Communist Party leadership increasingly felt that the Party's political power was in danger of being undermined if the liberalization movement were allowed to continue; after labeling it "turmoil" (*dongluan*), finally on June 4 they forcibly suppressed it.

In the background to this movement in China were the pro-democracy movements in Asia already discussed, but also playing a major role was the fact that China itself in the latter half of the 1970s had abandoned the policy of "self-reliance" (*zili gengsheng*) that Mao Zedong advocated and steered a course to what Deng Xiaoping called "reform and opening up" (*gaige kaifang*) that de facto embraced a market economy.[1] If Mao had changed the nature of the Cold War in Asia by seeking rapprochement with the United States for strategic reasons, Deng's "reform and opening up" policy, too, decisively changed the nature of the Cold War as a development race among late-developing countries. As South Korea, Taiwan, Hong Kong and Singapore, the so-called "newly industrializing economies," were achieving growth one after another on the basis of a market economy, even China was moving away from its centrally planned economy. Which side would win the Cold War as an economic competition among late-blooming economies was becoming obvious.

That does not mean, however, that the course of openness and reform itself was unreservedly accepted in China. Despite its hostile relations with the USSR, the Chinese Communist Party had been founded on Marxist-Leninist principles. Accepting a market economy was not all that simple. As the standard bearer for reform and opening up in the early 1980s, Hu Yaobang had been expected to succeed Deng Xiaoping. An open-minded person, he attached importance to relations with Japan and built a staunch friendship with Prime Minister Nakasone Yasuhiro; in 1984, he invited 3,000 young Japanese to China. When Nakasone's visit to the Yasukuni Shrine became an issue in 1985, he came under criticism in China for being too pro-Japanese. Conservatives also criticized the understanding he showed toward the students' proclivity for greater freedom of speech. When a student demonstration calling for liberalization occurred in December 1986, he was criticized a month later in January 1987 for being too soft in his response, fell from power and resigned as general secretary. The movement for greater freedom did not stop there, however. Zhao Ziyang, the acting general secretary after Hu Yaobang who subsequently assumed that post, also cautiously supported the direction of reform. During the winter of 1988–89, Fang Lizhi and other pro-democracy leaders gave new life to the movement. In the media as well, there was a considerable amount of free speech; a televised documentary entitled *Heshang* (River Elegy), for example, contained the message that China would never develop without greater reform and opening up. The conservatives must have regarded these activities warily.

Under the Zhao Ziyang administration, students and the intelligentsia took advantage of the funeral of Hu Yaobang to press for even greater freedom. They thronged to Tiananmen Square for the funeral and once again began demonstrating for freedom of speech and democratization. The end of the Cold War had not yet become evident at this point, but a student movement demanding some sort of liberalization was itself typical of the atmosphere in the months leading up to the Cold War's end. The fact that Western television

Student demonstration in Tiananmen Square, Beijing (May 4, 1989).
Photo: Kyodo News

was able to cover the student movement in China and continued to broadcast it in real time also portended a change in the times.

As the groups of students that gathered in Tiananmen Square demanding freedom swelled to enormous proportions, however, the conservatives in the Chinese Communist Party became more and more wary. On April 26, while Zhao Ziyang was on a visit to North Korea, the *People's Daily* made clear its opposition to the demonstration, calling it "turmoil." When Zhao Ziyang returned, he disagreed with the conservatives, took issue with the label "turmoil" and showed his understanding of the students' actions, calling them "patriotic calls for democracy." The demonstrators, who rejected the label "turmoil," reached their high-water mark in mid-May when 1.2 million people gathered in central Beijing. Seeing this sea of humanity, Deng Xiaoping, the dominant political figure, must have been terrified. The situation could not be allowed to go on like this. Perhaps he was afraid that if nothing was done, China would once again descend into chaos as it had during the time of the Cultural Revolution. Deng removed Zhao Ziyang from office and made the decision to invoke martial law. On the morning of May 19, Zhao Ziyang appeared in front of the students. "We came too late," he said. He was never seen in public again.[2]

At the beginning of June, Deng finally ordered the People's Liberation Army to use armed force to remove the demonstrators occupying
Tiananmen Square. In the early hours of June 4, the sight of the People's Liberation Army heading for Tiananmen Square and the acts of
suppression taking place in other parts of Beijing were televised live
to the world, causing shock all over the globe. An official statement
by the Chinese government later reported 319 dead and 900 injured.
Reports at the time gave the number of dead as around 2,000.

The Western Reaction

Criticism from around the world was fierce. The most trenchant
of all came from the West. On the morning of June 4, French
Foreign Minister Roland Dumas said that the French government
was "dismayed by the bloody repression" of a popular movement
trying to bring about democracy. He criticized the Chinese authorities for taking military action and stated his hope that they would
unconditionally abandon the use of force and open the way to dialogue with its own citizens. President François Mitterrand also
denounced the Chinese government for having "degraded itself to
shoot at youth who had stood up in the name of freedom," saying
there was "no future" for such a government. On June 6, Prime Minister Michel Rocard announced that France was freezing relations
with China at all levels.[3]

Immediately after the incident occurred, President George H.W.
Bush of the United States said that he deeply deplored "the decision
to use force against peaceful demonstrators and the consequent loss
of life," and on June 5 he announced that he was putting into effect
measures to suspend arms exports to China and US-Chinese military exchanges. These measures included (1) an immediate embargo
on the export of weapons to China by the American government
and the private sector; (2) the suspension of exchanges among
military-related personnel of the two countries; (3) assistance to
Chinese students currently in the United States, such as extending
their stay; (4) care for the wounded through the Red Cross; (5) a
review of other aspects of US-Chinese relations. The Bush administration itself had a rather restrained attitude toward China. But it
could not help but harden when China demanded that Fang Lizhi,

a leader of the pro-democracy movement who had taken refuge in the US embassy in Beijing, be handed over and put under arrest. In the US Congress, in particular, a hard line against China gained momentum. On June 6, the Senate and the House of Representatives each unanimously passed resolutions condemning China. Speaker of the House Thomas Foley warned that if the Chinese used violence against the American embassy to arrest Fang Lizhi, the US should immediately break off diplomatic relations. On June 29 by a vote of 418 to 0. On July 14, the Senate also passed a sanctions bill with almost identical contents.[4]

The Tiananmen Incident and Japan

What was the response in Japan right after the Tiananmen incident?[5] Japan's internal political situation at the time was such that foreign relations were the last thing on its mind. The Takeshita Cabinet had fallen as a result of the Recruit scandal,[6] and the Cabinet of Prime Minister Uno Sōsuke had just been formed on June 2. All that even a pivotal figure in the new Uno administration could remember was, "I knew there was some sort of fuss going on in Tiananmen, but it was only sometime later that I realized how big an event it was. It was right after the start of the Uno Cabinet, so I don't have much recollection of the discussions about how the Cabinet should respond."[7]

Though this might have been the state of affairs in the Prime Minister's Official Residence, that does not mean that the Ministry of Foreign Affairs did nothing. On June 4, Director-General for Press and Public Relations Watanabe Taizō stated, "It is unfortunate that this situation had led to bloodshed. The Japanese government strongly hopes that it will not deteriorate any further."[8] Foreign Minister Mitsuzuka Hiroshi said, "It is very regrettable that such bloodshed occurred in the midst of China's steady economic development based on its liberalization policy. We would like to see China return to a peaceful state as soon as possible."[9]

As voices demanding sanctions against China grew stronger in the West, a certain vacillation can be detected in Prime Minister Uno's statements. On the morning of the 6th, he said, "We are not thinking of sanctions or anything like that," but ten minutes later he added, "The statement I just made does not rule out sanctions. Please take it to mean we are not yet at the stage to do so or not."[10]

At this time Japan seemed reluctant to make statements about China's domestic affairs much less comments on sanctions. In a speech to the plenary session of the House of Representatives on June 7, Prime Minister Uno said,

> We need to be aware that the Japan-China relationship is totally different from the US-China relationship. We have a past in which we were once at war with China. At a time when China is in disarray, I think we should avoid statements that try to paint the situation in black-and-white terms. However, I cannot help but say that turning guns on one's own citizens is extraordinary. I hope that peace will be restored as soon as possible.[11]

At a speech to the plenary session of the House of Councillors the following day, he went on to say,

> I have great concern about our neighbor's painful situation. A situation in which guns are turned on one's own citizens is extraordinary. The Japanese government has also conveyed to the Chinese embassy here the view that this is "not acceptable from a humanitarian standpoint." Some have said that the Japanese government should make a bolder statement, but China is an important neighbor, and if we think about the safety of the lives of Japanese citizens living in China, I believe we should refrain from incautious statements and not make our feelings public. . . . The imposition of sanctions would be discourteous to our neighbor. Because I hope that the situation will return to normal as soon as possible, I will not make any protest.[12]

The idea that sanctions in this situation "would be discourteous to our neighbor" is an odd sentiment but may have reflected his sense of guilt about Japan's wartime aggression; in any case, there must have been a lot of hesitation. And yet it would have been awkward if Japan were to be thought to have different values from the Western countries that had taken a stern view of China. Accordingly, on June 16, Foreign Minister Mitsuzuka stated, "The recent intensification of the crackdown on students and ordinary citizens by the Chinese government is a Chinese internal issue, but, even so, it is incompatible with the basic values of our country as a democratic nation. . . . Considering the position China occupies in the international community, we expect that in future the Chinese government will take international public opinion fully into account and make efforts toward normalization."[13]

The sanctions that Japan actually imposed on China, however, were not particularly milder than those taken by the West (or, to put it the other way, the sanctions against China taken by the West, including the US, were not particularly harsher than Japan's). Basically, the measures consisted of advising Japanese travelers to voluntarily refrain from going to China; freezing its third yen loans;[14] and suspending high-level contacts. Nevertheless, much of Japan's subsequent diplomatic efforts were spent trying to convince the other Western countries that isolating China would not be desirable. In fact, despite the American Congress's strong anti-Chinese stand, the Bush administration itself also made the strategic decision to oppose any plan to isolate China. Thus, at a meeting with President Bush and Secretary of State James Baker on June 26, Foreign Minister Mitsuzuka was able to reach the agreement that, from a broader perspective, Japan and the US "should not push China into a position of isolation."[15] Although it was done in secret at the time, at the beginning of July, the Bush administration sent its National Security Advisor Brent Snowcroft and Deputy Secretary of State Lawrence Eagleburger to China.

At the Arche Summit in France on July 15, the Western countries were demanding that China be stiffly censured; Japan, however, insisted that they should guard against isolating China. Ultimately, the Summit settled for a statement that said, "We look to the Chinese authorities to create conditions which will avoid their isolation and provide for a return to cooperation based upon the resumption of movements towards political and economic reform, and openness."[16] Thereafter, Japan would make even more active efforts to lift the sanctions against China.

The Fear of "Peaceful Evolution" and a Pragmatic Approach

The period immediately after the Tiananmen incident was truly a time of upheaval for the world that culminated in the end of the Cold War. From the perspective of people critical of China as a result of

Tiananmen, the world was moving in quite the opposite direction from that of China. Symbolic of this was the fact that on June 4, the very day of the military suppression in Tiananmen Square, a partially free election for the upper and lower houses of the legislature was held in Poland, the first time an opposition party in a socialist bloc country had been allowed to participate. That party, the Independent Self-governing Labor Union "Solidarity," won overwhelmingly. On a day when there was repression in China, one of the Communist countries of Eastern Europe took a step towards liberalization.

Thereafter, an administration that listened to the views of Solidarity was formed in Poland, and in August, Tadeusz Mazowiecki, a Solidarity adviser, became prime minister. On August 19, at Sopron, Hungary, near the Austrian border, a gathering took place for what was called a "picnic." A thousand East Germans who had gathered there crossed the border all at once and escaped to Austria. The Hungarian border guards did nothing to stop them, and on September 11, the Hungarian government officially decided to open its borders with Austria. East German citizens streamed out to the West via Hungary. Others converged on Czechoslovakia and Poland as well, seeking to escape to the West from there. Under this pressure, on November 9, the East German government finally decided to liberalize travel to the West for its citizens, and on the 10th, work began to physically tear down the Berlin Wall.

That December, on the Mediterranean island of Malta, President Bush and General Secretary Mikhail Gorbachev held a US-Soviet summit, which is regarded as symbolizing the end of the Cold War. Immediately after that, the Communist regimes in Eastern Europe collapsed one after another. The most dramatic episode in this regime-change drama was the execution of Romanian dictator Nicolae Ceauşescu. Movement toward the unification of East and West Germany, something unimaginable at the beginning of 1989, progressed at a rapid rate in 1990, and on October 3, the two Germanys were unified. With the break-up of the Soviet Union in December of the following year, the Cold War finally came to an end.

The changes that beset these Communist countries were nothing less than terrifying for the leaders of China who had just gone through the Tiananmen incident. It no doubt justified the use of force there because if they had not put down the demonstration at that time, it might have been China where regime change had been the first to occur.

The West's attempt to topple Communist regimes by peaceful means was termed a plot to effect "peaceful evolution" (*heping yanbian*). In September 1989, Deng Xiaoping stated, "The West really wants unrest in China. It wants turmoil not only in China but also in the Soviet Union and Eastern Europe. The United States and some other Western countries are trying to bring about a peaceful evolution towards capitalism in socialist countries."[17] But if China merely tightened its internal system, Deng thought, it would end up like the Soviet Union and Eastern Europe. In a speech given immediately after the Tiananmen incident, he was already saying, "What about the other basic point, keeping to the policies of reform and opening to the outside world? Is that wrong or not? It is not wrong. How could we have achieved the success we have today without the reform and the open policy?"[18] Likewise, during China's international isolation immediately after Tiananmen, he formulated a strategy that China should slowly implement for the future. Later called the "28-character strategy," the plan was to be able to "watch and analyse [developments] calmly; secure [our own] positions; deal [with changes] with confidence; conceal [our] capacities; be good at keeping a low profile; never become the leader; and do what we can."[19] In other words, it was to maintain a strategically defensive posture while pursuing economic development.

Repairing Japanese-Chinese Relations

From mid-1989 on, the search continued for ways to improve Japanese-Chinese relations. On August 18, the Japanese government lifted its travel advisory for all of China except Beijing, and on September 25, it lifted that as well. On November 9, a Japanese-Chinese economic cooperation delegation composed of leaders of Japanese industry (led by Kawai Ryōichi, chairman of the Japan-China Economy Association) visited China and met with Premier Li Peng and General Secretary Jiang Zemin as well as Deng Xiaoping. On December 6, the fifth Japan-China consultative conference on cultural exchange convened in Beijing, the first government level talks since the Tiananmen incident.

Immediately after that, it was revealed that US National Security Advisor Brent Snowcroft and Deputy Secretary of State Lawrence Eagleburger had secretly visited Beijing; when signs appeared that the US was somewhat softening its policies on China, it became clear that Japan needed to speed up the normalization process as well.

Early in 1990, on January 16, state councillor and chairman of the State Planning Commission Zou Jiahua was invited to Japan by the Japanese government. This was the first Chinese cabinet-level visit to Japan since the Tiananmen incident. While Zou Jiahua was in Japan, Matsuura Kōichirō, director-general of the Ministry of Foreign Affair's Economic Cooperation Bureau, was in China from the 18th to the 19th to discuss economic cooperation. At the non-governmental level, the launching of the Japan-China Investment Promotion Organization, which had been scheduled for June 1989 but put off indefinitely after Tiananmen Square, took place at the end of March. Diplomatic contacts also continued. The tenth Japan-China vice-ministerial consultation was held in Beijing on April 11. In attendance were Deputy Foreign Minister Owada Hisashi on the Japanese side and Vice-Minister of Foreign Affairs Qi Huaiyuan on the Chinese side.

In the Diet in March 1990, Foreign Minister Nakayama Tarō said,

> It is truly important for the peace and stability of the Asia-Pacific region, and indeed for the whole world, that China does not take the path of isolation but develops and maintains cooperative relations with other countries. The role that Japanese-Chinese relations have to play in this is a large one, and so it is important to develop and maintain good and stable relations between Japan and China. When State Councillor Zou Jiahua was in Japan recently, we made it clear once again to the Chinese side that efforts are needed on both sides to improve relations with the West and that we especially hope for greater efforts on China's part. We believe it is important from now on for both sides to make repeated efforts to restore Japanese-Chinese relations to what they had been before as soon as possible.[20]

He hinted at the possibility that Japan would work out a proactive plan to improve relations depending on China's response.

Meanwhile, at the beginning of April, with the interim report of the Structural Impediments Initiative with the US complete and trade frictions between Japan and the US settled for the time being, there was activity within the Japanese government to resume yen loans and advance Japanese-Chinese relations. In the period between 1989 and 1990, American attitudes toward Japan were extremely strained, and the Japanese government must have regarded the danger of an overly hasty rapprochement with China as being too great. It was the Ministry of Finance that made the first move. On April 10, Minister of Finance Hashimoto Ryūtarō said, "The time has come to resume untied loans which do not restrict the providers of goods and services to Japanese firms. Such loans would not arouse international mistrust that Japan is trying to get a head start on doing business [with China] and would be vital for the stability of [the Chinese] people's livelihoods."[21] On the 13th, he added, "We ought to discuss this regardless of the July summit. Japan is [China's] neighbor; we must make efforts both to prevent China from being isolated from international society and to say clearly what we think to China."[22] The proactive argument was also gaining strength within the Liberal Democratic Party. LDP Secretary-General Ozawa Ichirō on April 16 told Foreign Minister Nakayama, "We ought to persuade the US [which was asking for a stiffer stance against China] and lift the freeze. Japan's position vis-à-vis China is different from that of the United States."[23]

On June 25, 1990, Fang Lizhi and his wife, who had taken refuge in the US embassy in Beijing since the Tiananmen incident, were allowed to leave the country. Although this was mainly a concession on the Chinese side to get the US to soften its Chinese policies, especially the continuation of most-favored-nation status, it was also judged by Japan to be a positive step toward improving Japanese-Chinese relations. When the final report of the Structural Impediments Initiative was concluded at the end of June, a major stumbling block to Japanese-US relations leading up to the Houston Summit had disappeared. As a result, the Ministry of Foreign Affairs, which has been described as passive up until then, also began to move toward resuming aid to China.

In the meantime, Japan had also gradually begun to invite powerful Chinese to Japan. On June 30, Li Tieying, a state councillor and minister of the National Board of Education, visited Japan to attend China Day at the International Garden and Greenery Exposition in Osaka and met with Prime Minister Kaifu Toshiki and others. On

July 2, Zhu Liang, head of the International Department of the Central Committee of the Communist Party of China, came to Japan at the invitation of the LDP.

Based on the progress of these exchanges between Japan and China, Prime Minister Kaifu announced at the Houston Summit in July that Japan would be gradually rescinding its freeze on economic cooperation with China. Although some summit participants were critical of Japan for lifting the sanctions on China, the Japanese government went ahead and implemented its decision.

On September 20, former Prime Minister Takeshita went to China at the invitation of Premier Li Peng to attend the opening ceremonies of the Asian Games. Minister of Education Hori Kōsuke also attended the opening ceremonies. It was the first visit to China by a sitting Japanese cabinet member since Tiananmen Square.

Thus, the resumption of Japan's third yen loans headed toward negotiations at the administrative level. On October 18, Nishigaki Akira, president of the Overseas Economic Cooperation Fund, visited China at the invitation of the Ministry of Foreign Economic Relations and Trade for an exchange of views on the third yen loans. On November 2, an exchange of notes to the effect that the first installment for FY1990 would be 36.5 billion yen was signed by Vice-Minister of Foreign Affairs Qi Huaiyuan and Hashimoto Hiroshi, the Japanese ambassador to China. The exchange of notes for the second installment for FY1990 of 42.633 billion yen was signed on December 21 and for the third for 43.38 billion yen on March 15, 1991.

By 1991, a year and a half after the Tiananmen incident, it would be fair to say that relations between Japan and China had been more or less restored to normal. But, during that time, something had decisively changed: the feelings of most Japanese toward China. After diplomatic normalization, especially in the early 1980s, the Japanese view of China was extremely warm. In government-conducted public opinion polls, China was always at the top of countries the Japanese people felt close to (see Figure 2.1). As a result of the Tiananmen incident, however, Japanese views of China hardened. Even though it was desirable from an international relations perspective that China be stable, the images of Tiananmen Square and the Chinese Communist

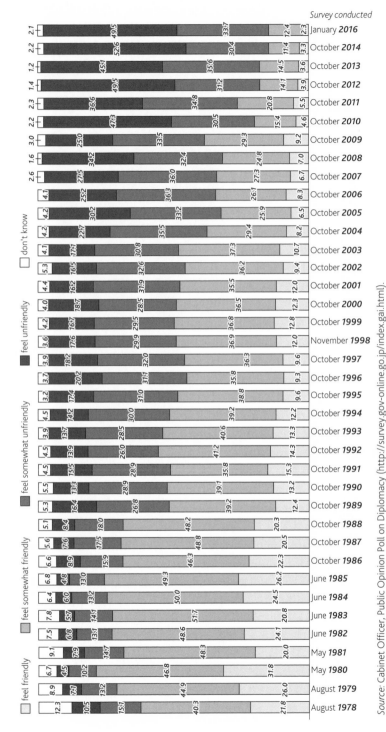

Source: Cabinet Officer, Public Opinion Poll on Diplomacy (http://survey.gov-online.go.jp/index.gai.html).

Figure 2.1 Japanese Feelings toward China

regime's suppression of its own citizens would influence the Japanese assessment of China for a long, long time.

Nordpolitik

Trends in the Soviet Union after the appearance of Gorbachev had a tremendous effect not only on Southeast Asia but on Northeast Asia as well, especially the Korean peninsula. Roh Tae-woo, who had assumed office as president of South Korea, seeing the rapid advance of *perestroika* in the USSR and the "new thinking" there on foreign diplomacy, concluded that now was the time for South Korea to pursue a *Nordpolitik*, a policy modeled after the *Ostpolitik* that West German Chancellor Willy Brandt had once adopted vis-à-vis East Germany. In his inauguration address in February 1988, Roh Tae-woo had said, "We will broaden the channel of international co-operation with the continental countries with which we have hitherto had no exchanges, with the aim of pursuing a vigorous northern diplomacy."[24] In its first incarnation articulated on July 7, 1988 (the July 7th Declaration), Roh said that it was desirable for South Korea to move toward better relations with the Soviet Union and China and for North Korea to pursue better relations with the US and Japan, what was called "cross-recognition."[25] In a speech that he gave to the UN General Assembly, President Roh put forward the idea that ultimately it would be desirable to form a six-party Consultative Conference for Peace in Northeast Asia, consisting of North and South Korea, the US, USSR, China and Japan. The aim of "cross-recognition" and the six-party conference framework was to serve as common ground during the end-of-the-Cold-War process.[26]

What developed rapidly as the Cold War drew to a close was the establishment of South Korean relations with the countries of Eastern Europe. When diplomatic relations were implemented with Hungary in September 1988, the end of the Cold War was not yet clear, and relations with Poland were established just before the fall of the Berlin Wall in November 1989. Thereafter, the Communist regimes in Eastern Europe collapsed like dominoes one after the other; South Korea entered into diplomatic relations with Yugoslavia in December 1989, Czechoslovakia, Bulgaria and Romania in March 1990, and Albania in August 1991. With the restoration of relations

between a democratized South Korea and the similarly democratized Eastern European countries, ideology and Cold-War antagonism altogether ceased to be a problem. Moreover, South Korean aid
and investment were extremely attractive to the Eastern European
countries, which had economic problems.

The biggest targets of President Roh's *Nordpolitik*, of course, were
China and the Soviet Union. In Gorbachev's speeches in Vladivostok
in 1986 and in Krasnoyarsk in September 1988 just before the Seoul
Olympics, he had alluded to developing economic relations with
South Korea. The aim of Gorbachev's *perestroika*, it hardly needs
saying, was to rebuild the Soviet economy, not to break up the Soviet
Union. Never dreaming that by the end of 1991 the USSR would
cease to exist, Gorbachev was trying to establish friendly relations
with countries that had the potential to cooperate in rebuilding the
economy. At a meeting of the Soviet Communist Party's Politburo on
November 10, 1988, Gorbachev made a speech in which he said, "We
will firmly proceed on the way to rapprochement and establishing
relations with South Korea."[27] South Korea, which had approached
the Soviet Union and was showing a positive attitude toward economic aid, was attractive to Gorbachev. At the end of 1988, however,
he probably did not imagine that this would lead to the normalization
of diplomatic relations with South Korea. When Foreign Minister
Eduard Shevardnadze visited Pyongyang that December, he told the
North Korean side, "I am a communist, and I give you my word as a
party member: the USSR leadership does not have any intention and
will not establish diplomatic relations with South Korea."[28] Despite
this statement, North Korea had misgivings about where the Soviet
Union was heading. In May 1989, Gorbachev visited Beijing in order
to normalize Soviet relations with China; at this time, North Korea
invited him to visit Pyongyang, but Gorbachev refused.[29] North
Korea's doubts intensified even further.

The decisive event occurred in June 1990. President Roh Tae-woo
headed for San Francisco expressly to meet Gorbachev, who was on a
visit to the United States. It was the first talks ever held by the leaders
of the Soviet Union and South Korea. In Gorbachev's memoirs he
writes, "It was clear that we could not, for obsolete ideological reasons
(i.e. because of our ties with North Korea), continue opposing the
establishment of normal relations with his country, which showed

an exceptional dynamism and had become a force to be reckoned with, both in the Asia-Pacific region and in the wider world."[30] On the heels of the San Francisco talks, he said, he made the decision to normalize diplomatic relations between the USSR and South Korea as of January 1, 1991.

The task of conveying this decision to North Korea fell to Foreign Minister Shevardnadze, who less than two years earlier had told the North that diplomatic relations with South Korea were out of the question. Shevardnadze visited Pyongyang at the beginning of September 1990. He argued that the normalization of relations with South Korea did not mean there would be any change in the Soviet Union's relation with the North, but Foreign Minister Kim Yong Nam representing the North Korean side reacted furiously.[31] "If . . . the . . . Alliance Treaty will automatically be reduced to a dead letter . . . it will leave North Korea no other choice but to seek independent measures to procure weapons by itself."[32] This was clearly a threat that North Korea would move to develop nuclear weapons. Immediately afterwards at the United Nations General Assembly, Shevardnadze was making arrangements with the South Korean Foreign Minister Choi Ho-joong on the agreement to normalize diplomatic relations. When the latter proposed moving up the date of normalization, Shevardnadze with his own pen drew a line through the date on the agreement, January 1, 1991, and wrote September 30, 1990 instead. It is the view of Don Oberdorfer, an American journalist who has written the definitive account of international politics on the Korean peninsula, that Shevardnadze's anger at North Korea during his stay in Pyongyang had not yet cooled down.[33] With a stroke of Shevardnadze's angry pen, the global Cold War vanished from the Korean peninsula. The South Korean government promised to lend the Soviet government USD 3 billion dollars on January 1, 1991.

Kanemaru's Visit to North Korea

The Soviet Union's move to normalize relations with South Korea meant that part of the international political structure surrounding North Korea had collapsed. During the Cold War, North Korea had tried to ensure its own security against threats from the US and

South Korea by drawing on support from both the USSR and China. Economically as well, North Korea was "so fragile that if aid from China and the Soviet Union, especially the latter, were delayed, its economy would quickly face serious problems."[34] Though dependent on China and the USSR from both an economic and security stand-point, when it came to domestic matters, however, North Korea did not do what it was told to do. Quite the contrary; Kim Il Sung in the late 1950s purged the leaders of the Russian and Chinese factions and built a system based on "the *juche* idea," which was centered solely around himself. The political system based on *juche*, which is usually translated "self-reliance," is similar in appearance to a socialist system in the modern sense but quite different in nature. Suzuki Masa-yuki, an expert on Korean politics, argues that the system is based on a "*Suryōng* (Great Leader) System," a theory of society as a social organism guided by a Great Leader.[35] Formed presumably under the influence of Confucianism and the prewar Japanese Emperor system, it conceived of North Korea as a socio-political organism with the Great Leader as its brain.

Indeed, precisely because the political system was such, it was possible to officially admire hereditary succession in the traditional sense. Thus, as preparations got under way for Kim Il Sung to hand the reins of power over to his son Kim Jong Il, North Korea in the 1970s and the 1980s engaged repeatedly in aberrant behavior against other countries. In the late 1970s, as it later became clear, the North kidnapped Japanese nationals and others, and in 1983, it carried out a terrorist bombing in Rangoon whose intended victim was South Korean President Chun Doo-Hwan then on a visit to Burma. In 1987, it committed an act of terrorism by blowing up a Korean Air Lines plane over the Indian Ocean. Maintaining its idiosyncratic system at home, while engaging in terrorist activities abroad—that was North Korea at the end of the 1980s. Then, before North Korea's very eyes, the Cold War was suddenly coming to an end, and the Soviet Union, which was supposed to be its protector, had begun making contact with South Korea. That did not mean, however, that North Korea was content to do nothing while South Korea was fast-tracking rela-tions with the Soviet Union.

An important episode that occurred in this period was the development of Japanese-North Korean relations.[36] It goes without saying that Japan had entered into diplomatic relations with South Korea through the Treaty on Basic Relations between Japan and the Republic of Korea in 1965. Finally, 20 years after Japan's colonial rule had ended, relations were established with the country that controlled the southern half of the Korean peninsula. There were various problems that had to be resolved before an agreement was reached with South Korea. On the issue of the right of claims that South Korea demanded from Japan, the two sides agreed to settle all these matters en bloc by carrying out "economic cooperation"; they also agreed that all treaties related to Japanese colonial rule "are already null and void" and that no mention would be made to the territorial dispute over the islands known respectively as Takeshima and Dokdo. The Japanese government took the interpretation that the scope of the treaty applied to the southern half of the Korean peninsula.[37] Because it was the position of the Republic of Korea that it was the sole lawful government of the entire Korean peninsula, Japan's interpretation habitually aroused criticism in the South.

As for Japan's stance vis-à-vis North Korea, given that criticism in the South was so strong, the policies Japan actually took toward the North were extremely limited. It might have negotiated immediately with the northern half of the peninsula on the grounds that the Treaty on Basic Relations was only with the southern half, but it did not do so. Japanese contacts with North Korea were limited to small trading companies, the General Association of Korean Residents in Japan (*Sōren*) and, on the political side, the Japanese Socialist Party. "The Japanese government was afraid of arousing criticism from South Korea; in fact, it was stuck when it came to the Korean peninsula issue," was how Tanabe Makoto of the Socialist Party assessed the situation.[38]

The situation changed, however, with President Roh Tae-woo's July 7th Declaration in 1988. That declaration made it clear that South Korea was "willing to co-operate with North Korea in its efforts to improve relations with countries friendly to us, including the United States and Japan." The Japanese government immediately responded to this, and on the same day Chief Cabinet Secretary Obuchi Keizō stated that "if the North Korean side shows a constructive attitude, in close cooperation with the countries concerned, we will move vigorously to improve Japanese relations with North Korea, while taking into consideration a balance in our relations with South Korea, China and the Soviet Union": he made it plain that, "We are prepared to talk with the North Korean side on all aspects of all Japanese-North Korean issues" provided that the No. 18 Fujisan Maru affair was resolved.[39] (Since November 1983, North Korea had detained on suspicion of espionage the captain and chief engineer of the freighter No. 18 Fujisan Maru, which had been engaged in trade between North Korea and Japan). And in September 1988, right before the Seoul Olympics, Japan lifted measures that had been taken against North Korea after the bombing of the Korean Air Lines flight. In January 1989, a delegation of the Workers' Party of North Korea was allowed to enter Japan to attend the general meeting of the Japan Socialist Party. Furthermore, when, on January 11, 1989, a spokesman for the North Korean Ministry of Foreign Affairs rejected any contact between the two governments, citing the "insincere attitude of the Japanese government," on January 20 the Japanese government announced "our country's policy on the Korean peninsula." "The Japanese government does not regard North Korea as an enemy and has no desire to see the North and South permanently divided. . . . We are ready to discuss all aspects between Japan and North Korea without any preconditions."[40]

Around this time, the Takeshita government, although under concerted attack from the opposition and the mass media over the Recruit scandal and in the end stages of its administration, strengthened its ties with the Socialist Party on North Korean policy. On March 30, at the House of Representatives' Budget Committee meeting Prime Minister Takeshita responded as follows to a question from Diet member Murayama Tomiichi:

As we have previously made clear on repeated occasions, the Japanese government and the Japanese people are deeply aware that the actions of our country in the past caused great suffering and loss to the citizens of neighboring nations. Out of our regret and resolve never to repeat such actions again, we have been pursuing a course as a peace-loving nation ever since. This awareness and regret, I believe, must especially be kept in mind in the relationship between our country and the Korean peninsula, which is closest to us both geographically and historically.

On this occasion, as the situation in the Korean peninsula is about to enter a new phase, we want to express once again our deep regret and remorse for this past relationship to all the people of that region.

On the subject of Japanese-North Korean relations, it is a fact that there has been an estrangement since this unfortunate period in the past right up to the present day. As a government, we have come to believe we should take the basic position that issues pertaining to the Korean peninsula ought to be settled through discussions by the parties concerned in the North and the South and that we should pursue diplomatic relations with the Korean peninsula based on this new resolve. As for relations with the Democratic People's Republic of Korea, taking into consideration the new situation in the Korean peninsula, we hope to improve our relationship based on the understanding stated earlier.

From this perspective, ever since last year, the government has expressed its desire to discuss unconditionally all aspects of the unresolved issues between Japan and North Korea; if we receive a positive response from the other side, we hope to be able to initiate a dialogue at the earliest date possible and to carry on talks in good faith on both sides.[41]

The expression of "deep regret and remorse" toward all the people on the Korean peninsula and the use of North Korea's official name, the Democratic People's Republic of Korea, attracted attention. Immediately after Takeshita made the statement, Tanabe Makoto, the former secretary-general of the Socialist Party, visited Pyongyang and met with Chairman Kim Il Sung on April 4. Tanabe carried a letter addressed to Kim Il Sung from former Deputy Prime Minister Kanemaru Shin.[42] When Kim Il Sung met Tanabe, he said, "Some Japanese authorities are making good remarks."[43] The North Korean side indicated it would welcome a visit by Kanemaru to Pyongyang. Since Tanabe's visit to North Korea as secretary-general of the Japan Socialist Party in May 1985, he had developed a friendship with Ho Dam, secretary of the Workers' Party of North Korea, and had wrestled with relations with North Korea. He had also had experience as chairman of the Diet Affairs Committee and had deepened his friendship with Kanemaru Shin, who had been chairman of the LDP's Diet Affairs Committee at the same time. Before visiting Pyongyang this time, Tanabe had asked Abe Shintarō, secretary-general of the LDP, and

Prime Minister Takeshita respectively for messages for North Korea. He had made arrangements with Takeshita beforehand, he said, telling him, "I am going to North Korea . . . , please mention an apology in your answer to a question from my man, Murayama Tomiichi, at the House of Representatives' Budget Committee meeting."[44]

In the spring of 1989, however, both Japan and the world were entering a period of violent change, and progress on Japanese-North Korean relations came to a standstill. During this time of upheaval from the Tiananmen incident to the end of the Cold War, North Korea was anxious that the sparks at some point might land there. In Japan, the Takeshita Cabinet collapsed as a result of the Recruit scandal right after Tanabe's visit. Then the Pachinko scandal involving the Socialist Party and the General Association of Korean Residents in Japan (*Sōren*) became an issue. The Pachinko scandal had to do with whether or not to introduce prepaid cards into the pinball business; *Sōren*, which opposed their introduction, was suspected of having made contributions to the Socialist Party. North Korea with its close ties with *Sōren* was deeply offended by this.

It was the spring of 1990, while relations between South Korea and the Soviet Union were progressing rapidly, that the situation began to develop. At the end of March, unofficial contacts between Japan and North Korea were held in Paris through the intermediation of a private individual involved in trade between the two countries. Later, in May, the North told Fukada Hajime, the head of the Socialist Party's National Movement Bureau who was visiting North Korea, "We would welcome a delegation of LDP representatives led by Mr Kanemaru and will cooperate actively in resolving the Fujisan Maru issue."[45] In mid-July, Socialist Party Deputy Chairman Kubo Wataru visited North Korea and agreed to the formulation that "there would be three-party talks among the LDP, the Socialist Party and the Workers' Party of North Korea, and then negotiations would be transferred to the government level." On September 4, an advance group headed by the LDP's Ishii Hajime and the Socialist Party's Kubo Wataru was sent ahead to North Korea, and the decision was made that the Kanemaru-Tanabe delegation would come to North Korea on September 24. The advance group's negotiations were said to have reached broad agreements, including the resolution of the No. 18 Fujisan Maru affair.[46] Kanemaru seems to have wanted to move relations ahead with the North one way or another. He publicly stated that, "When I go to North Korea, I will be bringing a suitable gift"; was annoyed with the Ministry of Foreign Affairs for saying that "without diplomatic relations financial aid was out of the question"; and had called Asian Affairs Bureau chief Tanino Sakutarō "that blockhead."[47]

According to the understanding in Japan at the time, it was thought that North Korea would be unlikely to agree to establishing diplomatic relations with Japan. It should be added, however, that both South Korea and North Korea since the 1970s had permitted foreign countries to have diplomatic relations with both governments. On this point, they were unlike China, which would sever diplomatic relations if a country maintained ties with Taiwan and would establish relations only on the condition that existing ties be cut. For North Korea, however, Japan and the United States were regarded as special. Since the 1970s, Professor Kamiya Fuji of Keio University and former US Secretary of State Henry Kissinger had advocated the idea of "cross-recognition": that in order to solve the Korean problem, China and the Soviet Union should recognize South Korea, and Japan and the US should recognize North Korea. The understanding up to that point was that North Korea would not accept this idea. If North Korea did not accept cross-recognition, it was unlikely that talks would proceed as far as normalizing diplomatic relations. And if talks didn't get as far as normalization, it was impossible for Japan to give North Korea anything in return. That was the position of the Ministry of Foreign Affairs.

What awaited the Kanemaru-Tanabe delegation in Pyongyang, however, was a proposal from North Korea "to establish diplomatic relations right away." On September 25, soon after their arrival, the LDP-Socialist delegation held talks with the Workers' Party of North Korea and viewed the mass gymnastics of which the North Koreans were particularly proud. On the 26th, the site of the discussions moved to Kim Il Sung's presidential guesthouse in the Myohyang Mountains, 170 kilometers north of Pyongyang.

Kanemaru handed over a personal letter to Kim Il Sung from Kaifu Toshiki in his capacity as LDP President, in which the prime minister said, "Regrettably, an unfortunate past existed between our country and the Korean peninsula for a period of time in the present century. Former Prime Minister Takeshita expressed deep regret and remorse over this unfortunate past in the Diet in March of last year. I, as Prime Minister, have repeatedly made it clear that I completely share his views." He also alluded to the fact that, "the issue of the right of claims still remains unresolved."[48]

During the banquet at the guesthouse, Kim Il Sung is said to have walked around and offered drinks to all the Japanese delegation members. That evening, just before the delegation was to return to Pyongyang, Kim Il Sung proposed that he and Kanemaru hold two-man talks; Kanemaru alone remained in the Myohyang Mountains and met with Kim Il Sung. Probably based on the outcome of these talks, at the second round of negotiations on the 27th, secretary of the Party Central Committee Kim Yong Sun formally proposed that, "diplomatic relations be established as soon as possible." Up to that point, the Japanese government had assumed that there was no way that North Korea would agree to negotiations to normalize Japanese-North Korean relations. Kawashima Yutaka, deputy director-general of the Ministry of Foreign Affairs Asian Affairs Bureau who was part of the delegation, said he couldn't believe his ears. Kanemaru himself showed no visible signs of surprise. At the two-man talks with Kim Il Sung, this topic had probably already come up.

As a result, in the three-party joint declaration of the LDP, the Socialist Party and the Workers' Party of North Korea on the 28th, it was agreed that, "the abnormal state between the DPRK and Japan must be eliminated and diplomatic relations be established as soon as possible." In addition, "The three parties agreed to strongly recommend the start of inter-governmental negotiations for the realization of the establishment of diplomatic relations and the solution of all the outstanding problems within November 1990." But what later came under strong attack in Japan was the following: "The three parties consider that Japan should fully and officially apology [sic] and compensate to the Democratic People's Republic of Korea for the enormous misfortunes and miseries imposed upon the Korean people for 36 years and the losses inflicted upon the Korean people in the ensuing 45 years after the war," because it could be read as an agreement that Japan must pay reparations not only for the period of colonial rule but also for the "45 years after the war."[49] In October the captain and chief engineer of the No. 18 Fujisan Maru were handed over to the Japanese side.

In any event, having received the news from Shevardnadze in September that the Soviet Union and South Korea were normalizing their relationship, North Korea changed its policy toward Japan. Presumably it decided to move in the direction of cross-recognition with an eye to future diplomatic relations with the US as well. The impact on North Korea of the Soviet defection followed by the end of the Cold War was enormous. It is not known how much Japan was aware of these geopolitical influences. Of course, the Japanese side, too, had information at a general level that the Soviet Union and South Korea were moving closer to one another. If they had taken note of the talks between Gorbachev and Roh Tae-woo in June, these trends would have been apparent. But there is virtually no indication that the Japanese side attached any importance to these factors. What was most important to those involved in the Kanemaru visit to North Korea was the settlement of the No. 18 Fujisan Maru affair and the matter of Japanese "compensation" in the event diplomatic relations were normalized.

Progress in North-South Relations and Nuclear Suspicions

One more approach that North Korea attempted when faced with the Soviet Union's overtures to South Korea was to make overtures of its own to the South. There is a hypothesis that when North Korea judges itself to have been abandoned by a great power, it has a tendency to turn to North-South dialogue,[50] and this time was a classic example of that. On July 12, after Gorbachev's meeting with Roh Tae-woo, North Korea agreed to hold North-South prime ministerial level meetings with South Korea. And on September 5–6, 1990, right after Shevardnadze's visit to North Korea to announce that the USSR was normalizing relations with the South, the first such meeting was held in Seoul. It was the first time since the establishment of two governments on the peninsula that the two prime ministers had sat down with one another. Premier Yon Hyong Muk on the North Korean side paid a courtesy call on President Roh Tae-woo at the Blue House, the South Korean President's official residence. The second prime ministerial meeting was held on October 17–18 in Pyongyang, and this time Prime Minister Kang Young-hoon paid a courtesy call on Chairman Kim Il Sung. Addressing the South Korean delegation at this time, Kim Il Sung called for unification through "a federal system based on one people, one nation, two systems and two governments." It was the first time that North Korea had indicated that "two governments" could coexist on the Korean peninsula.[51] The third meeting was held in December in Seoul.

Thus, to counter the USSR's rapprochement with South Korea, North Korea made approaches to Japan and South Korea and also tried to get close to the United States. Beginning in December 1988, councillor level diplomats from the US and the North held meetings in Beijing; these meetings were held 12 times prior to USSR-South Korean diplomatic normalization.[52] But the Japanese-North Korean negotiations agreed upon at the Kanemaru visit, the North-South prime ministerial level talks that began after the beginning of USSR-South Korean talks and US-North Korean contacts all came to a standstill because of suspicions that North Korea was developing nuclear weapons.

When North Korea seriously began planning its own nuclear development program is still uncertain, but in April 1982, an American reconnaissance satellite confirmed for the first time that what appeared to be a nuclear reactor facility was being built at Yongbyon, 100 kilometers north of Pyongyang. According to North Korea, this first domestically produced nuclear reactor was capable of generating 5 megawatts of electricity. But in 1988, it acknowledged that it had begun to build a bigger reactor aimed at producing 50 megawatts of electricity.[53] Both reactors were of a type known as graphite moderated. In addition to these reactors of their own making, North Korea tried to acquire civil nuclear reactors from the Soviet Union. Eventually, the Soviet Union agreed to provide one on the condition that North Korea join the Nuclear Non-Proliferation Treaty (NPT); North Korea became a treaty member on December 12, 1985.

Treaty members are obligated to accept inspections by the International Atomic Energy Association (IAEA) in order to prove that all their nuclear facilities are for peaceful purposes. Under the treaty, member countries must sign the security measures agreement (inspection agreement) with the IAEA within 18 months of joining. Strictly speaking that would have been the middle of 1987, but there was a slipup on the IAEA's side, and the deadline was extended to

December 1988. But even by that time, North Korea showed no signs of signing the inspections agreement.

As a result, in 1989, the US conveyed its suspicions about the nuclear development program at Yongbyon to China, the USSR, South Korea, Japan and other interested parties, and this news was reported in the media.[54] A Japanese "foreign ministry official" acknowledged in November 1989, for example, that there were suspicions that North Korea was developing nuclear weapons. "If it is thinking of building a nuclear bomb," he said, "it will have a grave impact on the situation on the Korean peninsula, and Japan will not be able to sit by and do nothing."[55]

But although the international situation was against them, the North Koreans seem to have regarded nuclear development as the most important means of ensuring their own safety. As has already been noted, in September 1990, in response to Foreign Minister Shevardnadze's announcement that the USSR was normalizing relations with South Korea, it hinted that if the Soviet Union joined hands with the South, the North would have no choice but to rely on nuclear weapons.

After the Kanemaru visit, Japan and North Korea held preliminary discussions three times between November and December 1990 and agreed to hold formal talks beginning in January 1991. These talks began in January and were held five times during that year but without any progress being made. There were a number of controversial issues, but the biggest of all was Japan's insistent demand that North Korea accept IAEA inspections. North Korea retorted that the nuclear question was not a topic for discussion with Japan. As for the other issues, there was the matter of compensation for the "45 years after the war" in the three-party agreement and the news that the Japanese language teacher of Kim Hyon Hui, who had carried out the 1987 bombing of the Korean Air Lines flight, had been a Japanese woman called "Lee Un Hae." These were all tough problems, but the situation in the 1991 negotiations was such that if no progress was made to resolve the suspicions about nuclear development, no progress could be made on anything else.

Chapter 3

Southeast Asia and the End of the Cold War

What eventually led to the settlement of the stalemate that was the Cambodian Civil War were developments in the process that ended the Cold War. Just as movements toward democratization, openness and reform could be found in the American camp in the 1980s, the Soviet camp, too, along with steps to end the Cold War in the late 1980s, was beginning to take decisive steps in those directions. Mikhail Gorbachev, who had become General Secretary of the Soviet Communist Party in 1985, was pushing ahead with *perestroika* (reform) in domestic affairs and *novoe myshlenie* (new thinking) in foreign relations. These moves on Gorbachev's part were both a model for Vietnam as it headed toward reform and a message that it could not expect aid from the Soviet Union forever. What was driving these efforts to end the Cold War were the prospects for economic development in Southeast Asia, which were becoming obvious at that time. As the major powers ended the Cold War and recalibrated their diplomatic relations, each of the countries concerned in the region was beginning to feel the need to somehow stop the fighting for the sake of their own economic development. Both the USSR and the US were slowly trying to extricate themselves from the rigid state of affairs imposed on each of them by the force of circumstances of the Cold War. China was trying to escape from isolation after the Tiananmen incident. And Japan, troubled by economic frictions with the US, was seeking some sort of role for itself in international society.

Doi Moi

In December 1986, the Sixth Vietnamese Communist Party Congress chose the reformer, Nguyen Van Linh, a member of the

Politburo, to be General Secretary and officially set forth the policy of *Doi Moi* (innovation) aimed at economic reform.[1] There were many factors behind Vietnam's adoption of *Doi Moi*, but the biggest objective was to overcome its economic difficulties. In the background, however, was pressure from the Soviet Union under Gorbachev. For Gorbachev, who wanted a way out of the USSR's own economic difficulties, economic and military aid to Vietnam, which continued to intervene in Cambodia, was becoming the "number-two money drain" after Cuba.[2] Among the powerful people promoting reform inside Vietnam, Soviet views seem to have been extremely important. Nguyen Van Linh, who visited the Soviet Union in May 1987, told Gorbachev that receiving his support would be very significant on his return home to Vietnam. According to Gorbachev, Nguyen Van Linh came to Moscow several times after that to receive the "live ammunition" for reform, returning home with the promise that Gorbachev and the Soviet leadership supported his policies.[3]

Sino-Soviet relations, which had been very hostile in the late 1970s, were beginning to get better in 1982, and after Gorbachev's arrival on the scene, they improved rapidly. In July 1986, Gorbachev made an important speech in Vladivostok in which he said that the normalization of Chinese-Vietnamese relations was essential for resolving the Cambodian problem and indicated his desire to improve relations especially with China. Deng Xiaoping later said to Gorbachev that this speech was welcomed with satisfaction in Beijing and became the impetus behind steps to respond.[4] Qian Qichen in his memoirs writes that this was "a ray of hope for a political settlement of the Cambodian issue."[5] In Vietnam as well, it was becoming impossible to continue to assume that China and the USSR would always be in a state of conflict. Vietnam was gradually being forced to rethink the Cambodian problem as well as its relationship with China.

Reminiscing about those days, Nyugen Co Thach, who had been foreign minister at the time, said the following to Professor Tomoda Seki in 1994:

The general current in the world then was aiming at peace in Cambodia, and we thought it was in Vietnam's interest to facilitate the peace process by withdrawing troops from Cambodia.

The economic difficulties we experienced in those days were very serious, and inflation was approaching a three-digit peak in 1987.

For that reason, as Tomoda notes, "the need to end international isolation, which had accelerated economic difficulties, was all the more pressing."[6] Although Vietnam had previously "withdrawn" its troops stationed in Cambodia, in fact, it was said to have sent other units to replace the troops it was withdrawing. The "sixth withdrawal" in November 1987, however, was a real troop withdrawal.[7]

As for relations with China, in 1988 the provision in the Vietnamese constitution labeling China a "hegemonist" was removed.[8] According to Qian Qichen, Foreign Minister Nguyen Co Thach twice indicated his desire to visit China.[9] China refused because it felt that Vietnam's position had not really changed. But when Nguyen Co Thach repeated his request at the end of 1988, finally in January 1989, China agreed to a visit by Vietnam's First Deputy Foreign Minister Dinh Nho Liem. Dinh told China that Vietnam planned to completely withdraw its troops from Cambodia. And on April 5, 1989, Vietnam and the Heng Samrin regime announced Vietnam's unconditional withdrawal.

From a Battlefield into a Marketplace

The economic development that was rapidly proceeding in the ASEAN countries also put pressure on ending the Cambodian Civil War. Vietnam itself, in a government announcement at the Sixth Party Congress in December 1986, said, "In the coming years, the tasks of our party and state in the field of external affairs are to strive to combine the strength of the nation with that of the epoch." According to Tomoda, "the more limited political as well as economic implications of the 'strength of the epoch' might have been the structural changes in the international environment, namely, the improvement in relations between Moscow and Washington as well as the end of the antagonism between Moscow and Beijing, on the one hand, and the startling economic dynamism becoming visible in the Southeast Asian nations, on the other."[10]

The person who most clearly articulated this change in policies from the perspective of globalization was Thai Prime Minister

Chatichai Choonhavan, who appeared on the scene in August 1988. Up until then the attitude of Thailand toward the Cambodian problem was to wholeheartedly oppose Vietnam. As soon as he took office, however, Prime Minister Chatichai said he wanted to put an end to the long disputes with three of the other Indochinese countries and begin a new era that would "turn a battlefield into a marketplace."[11] To begin with, he planned to improve relations with Laos, with whom Thailand had a longstanding territorial dispute, and in November 1988, he visited Laos and normalized relations between the two countries. In tandem with this, the Chatichai government made contact with the Heng Samrin regime in Cambodia. In October 1988, Chavalit Yongchaiyudh, Supreme Commander of the Royal Thai Armed Forces, held secret talks with the Heng Samrin's Prime Minister Hun Sen in the Laotian capital of Vientiane.[12] At the end of the year, Prime Minister Chatichai said he would welcome a visit to Thailand from Prime Minister Hun Sen; Hun Sen's visit to Bangkok took place in January 1989.

Under pressure from globalization and the winding down of the Cold War, the second round of informal talks was held in Jakarta in February 1989, but the talks ultimately collapsed. The Heng Samrin side still maintained that Vietnamese troop withdrawal was conditional. Despite this, however, on April 5, Vietnam and the Heng Samrin regime announced that Vietnam forces were unconditionally withdrawing from Cambodia.

In the fall of 1988, Prince Sihanouk, who was attending the UN General Assembly, proposed to President Mitterrand of France that an international conference consisting primarily of the permanent members of the UN Security Council be held to settle the Cambodian problem. Thus, after ongoing talks among France, the UK, the US, and especially China and the USSR, on July 30, 1989, the Paris International Conference on Cambodia convened in Paris. In addition to the UN Secretary General, the participating countries were the four Cambodian factions, the six ASEAN countries, Vietnam, Laos, the permanent members of the Security Council, Japan, Australia, India and, representing the nonaligned countries, Zimbabwe. It was assumed that after the meeting of the foreign ministers, the deliberations of the working group would take about a month. But it did not work out that way. No one could agree on the formula for power sharing in the provisional government that was to be set up after peace was made. Technically speaking, there were four political factions involved—the Heng Samrin regime, Pol Pot's group (the Khmer Rouge), Sihanouk's group and Son Sann's group. The three groups that opposed the Heng Samrin regime attached importance to this format; they demanded that all four factions set up a provisional government and that power be divided equally among them at 25 percent each. The Heng Samrin regime, on the other hand, demanded that the Pol Pot group be excluded. By the end of August, no agreement had been reached, and the Paris Conference was suspended indefinitely.[13]

As was mentioned in the preceding chapter, the time of this Paris Conference saw the beginning of dramatic changes that would result in the end of the Cold War. As *perestroika* and *glasnost* proceeded in the Soviet Union, the stream of people leaving Hungary and entering Austria became an unstoppable flood; then, people entered West Germany from East Germany; finally, in November 1989, the Berlin Wall, which could rightfully be called the symbol of the Cold War, was torn down. In December of that year, a US-USSR summit was held in Malta, and the Communist regimes in Eastern Europe collapsed one after another.

In Cambodia, when the Vietnamese troop withdrawal began in September 1989, the Civil War heated up again as the three anti-Heng Samrin factions joined forces. But because the Heng Samrin regime had strengthened its military capability, it was clear that there was no possibility the regime would immediately collapse after the pullout of Vietnamese troops. In any event, it was becoming obvious that the withdrawal of Vietnamese forces alone would not solve the Cambodian problem. The four factions in Cambodia had to come to an agreement on what sort of political framework to form. But the "Informal Meeting on Cambodia" held in Jakarta in 1990 broke down because no written statement of principles was acceptable.

That does not mean, however, that there were no positive developments during this time. Australia presented a plan that would involve the UN after a peace treaty had been signed and would give the UN Secretary General transitional authority until general elections could be held. Australia prepared a 154-page working paper and presented the plan at Jakarta. To get around the basic conflict over power sharing in the provisional government, it was based on the idea that each faction would first entrust all government powers to a "Supreme National Council," and this Council would transfer these powers to the UN Secretary General. The Pol Pot faction adamantly rejected this plan, however, and ultimately no agreement was reached.[14]

Japan and the Cambodian Peace

Up until the latter half of the 1980s, Japan's position on the Cambodian problem was not particularly noteworthy; basically, Japan agreed with ASEAN and supported the three anti-Vietnamese factions. It did not grant recognition to the Heng Samrin regime that had been set up as a result of Vietnam's invasion of Cambodia and instead recognized Democratic Kampuchea and subsequently the three-party coalition government. In any case, postwar Japan was not actively involved in international disputes that were not directly related to it; in that sense, there was nothing especially unprecedented about Japan's muted response to the Cambodian problem.

For most Japanese citizens, Cambodia was a country far away. Mention Cambodia, and Angkor Wat was about all anyone knew. Very few if any Japanese were even aware that genocide had taken place there. That was about the extent of most people's knowledge of Cambodia. In short, it was inconceivable to most Japanese that Japan would become actively involved in the Cambodian problem.

At the end of the 1980s, however, in the midst of Japan-US economic frictions, Japan was a country who, it was feared, might overtake the United States. Having consolidated its position as an economic superpower, despite the sharp rise in the value of the yen after the 1985 Plaza Accord, Japan was regarded as having no equal anywhere in terms of economic strength. There were even voices in the US saying that Japan must be "contained." Sony purchased Columbia Pictures; Mitsubishi Estate Co., Ltd. bought up Rockefeller Center in Manhattan. The land value of the Imperial Palace alone, it was said, was enough to be able to buy the entire state of California. If a major civil war in Asia were to come to an end, naturally, Japan as an economic superpower was expected to make a significant financial contribution to postwar aid.

In addition, there was growing discontent even in Japan that Japan was regarded as a "free rider," a country that made no international contribution but was only interested in making money, as many American critics of Japan often said. The reason that Takeshita Noboru, who became prime minister in November 1987, formulated an International Cooperation Initiative as "Japan's contribution to the world" and made it a guiding principle of his foreign policy was in order to respond to this international perception and to the mood at home. Takeshita made public his International Cooperation Initiative while on a visit to Great Britain in May 1988. He made clear that his plan consisted of three main pillars: "the strengthening of cooperation to achieve peace," "the strengthening of international cultural exchange" and "the expansion of Japan's official development assistance." In particular, as regards strengthening cooperation for peace, he said,

> As you may know, Japan is firmly committed to the furtherance of world peace, and its Constitution does not permit it to extend any military cooperation. This does not mean, however, that Japan should stand idly by with regard to international peace. I believe that Japan, from a political and moral viewpoint, should extend cooperation to the utmost of its ability. I will pursue "Cooperation for Peace" as a new approach toward enhancing Japan's contributions to the maintenance and reinforcement of international peace. This will include positive participation in diplomatic efforts, the dispatch of necessary personnel and the provision of financial cooperation, aiming at the resolution of regional conflicts.[15]

This speech made clear his policy to be actively involved henceforth in international dispute resolution. Likewise, concerning the third pillar, the strengthening and expansion of official development assistance, he subsequently decided specifically that, as the new interim target for ODA in June 1988, the amount to be extended during the five-year period from 1988 to 1992 would be USD 50 billion. This was double the amount of ODA given in the previous five-year period.

A member of the foreign ministry task force assigned to draw up draft plans for the International Cooperation Initiative who subsequently became continuously involved in the Cambodian problem was Ikeda Tadashi. In his memoirs, he writes, "At the time the International Cooperation Initiative was announced, it was felt that there were three areas of international conflict in the Asian region that it would apply to: the Korean peninsula, Cambodia and the Northern Territories." But "of these three, there was a growing awareness within the foreign ministry while the International Cooperation Initiative was being drafted that we should take some kind of action with respect to Japan's contribution to solving the Cambodian conflict, and that, first of all, we had to become directly involved in the peace negotiating process."[16]

Japan at the time was in the midst of the Recruit scandal, and the Emperor Showa had just died; during this period of floundering as the Takeshita government was replaced by the Uno government, which in turn was replaced by the Kaifu government, there was little public interest in foreign affairs. Even for those who took an interest in such matters, the biggest focus of attention in Asia was on China and the Tiananmen incident, and in the rest of the world on the fall of the Berlin Wall. It would probably be accurate to say that getting involved in Cambodia existed as a problem that only the pros, so to speak, were aware of. "Few Diet members voiced their personal opinions about the Cambodia problem. Since that was the case, the government gave us quite a significant free hand to come up with a policy plan," Kōno Masaharu, director of the First Southeast Asian Division, recalled.[17]

What is more, the international community asked for Japan to become involved in the Cambodian problem. Japan was invited to participate in the Paris Initiative on Cambodia Conference, which was held in July 1989. This was the first time since the Versailles Peace Conference, which ended World War I, that Japan had taken part in an international conference on peace in other countries. Not only did it participate, Japan also served as chair of a subcommittee to discuss postwar reconstruction. At this stage, however, Japan was not involved in discussions of the most difficult issues such as power sharing. As usual, Japan was confined to participate only as a source of funding for postwar reconstruction.

Seeing this state of affairs, the idea arose within the Japanese government that Japan ought to play more of a role than just as a source of funds. The Ministry of Foreign Affairs attempted to make contact with the Heng Samrin regime. Thai Prime Minister Chatichai's plan to turn Indochina "from a battlefield into a marketplace" was appealing to Japan. If ASEAN was solidly anti-Vietnamese, that left Japan little room to maneuver. But if Thailand, which up to then had been the most unbending of all toward the Vietnamese, was exploring relations with Vietnam and with the Heng Samrin regime, Japan, too, had room to act. Even on the issue of power sharing, which had been the cause of the breakdown of the Paris Conference, the thinking within the Japanese government was that an even 25 percent for each of the four factions was unrealistic, that the "correct" answer was 50–50.[18] In any case, they were coming to believe that the reality of the Heng Samrin regime had to be accepted.

Thus it was that, in February 1990, Director Kōno went to Phnom Penh. As a gesture to signify that the trip did not mean that the Japanese government had officially recognized the Heng Samrin regime, Kōno traveled on a regular passport instead of a diplomatic passport. This step was not one that the US necessarily approved of. Just before his trip to Cambodia, Kōno visited the United States, where the parties concerned in the State Department and the White House (Assistant Secretaries of State Richard Solomon and John Bolton and presidential aide Karl Jackson) told him, "If you go to Phnom Penh at this time, it will send the wrong signal to Vietnam." Kōno replied, "Japan is not at all thinking about becoming the playmaker in this offensive (the peace process) as the quarterback on the team. But it has no intention of watching this important game as a spectator and then just being made to clean up the stadium (providing reconstruction assistance) once the game is over."[19] At this point, the United States still had a confrontational attitude toward Vietnam. Against US opposition, Kōno argued that it was only natural that Japan should have some say in the peace process since it was being asked to play a role in assisting in the rebuilding of Cambodia after peace had been made. What Kōno and the Ministry of Foreign Affairs were trying to say to the US was, in effect, "no taxation without representation." Those in charge on the US side in the end grudgingly conceded. The Bush administration was probably opposed, but since it did not stop a determined Kōno, the visit could be said to forecast America's subsequent response.

Though it created a pipeline to the Heng Samrin regime, Kōno's Phnom Penh visit was far from being the route that would enable Japan to play an active part in solving the Cambodian problem. According to Tomiyama Yasushi, a journalist who actively followed this issue, at the Informal Meeting on Cambodia in Jakarta, which was held immediately after the Kōno trip, "Foreign Minister [Gareth] Evans of Australia, who had proposed UN participation in a political solution and had made possible the course of events that led to the reopening of talks, was especially invited to, and played an important role in, formulating peace plans. By contrast, ministers and other personnel from the Japanese Embassy in Thailand ran around the lobby of the hotel where the meetings were held, mixing with the scrum of reporters to pick up information. Even from the sidelines, it was a pathetic sight."[20]

The opportunity that presented itself to Japan at this time was the visit of Thai Prime Minister Chatichai to Japan in April 1990. On the evening before the top-level talks were to begin, Chatichai's son, Kraisak Choonhavan, and other foreign policy advisers to the prime minister were invited to Director Kōno's home to hold discussions. When Kraisak broached the subject that Japan ought to play more of a role in the Cambodian peace process, Kōno said, "How about Sihanouk and Hun Sen holding a two-party meeting in Tokyo?" Kraisak approved, and it was agreed that at the Japanese-Thai summit, Prime Minister Chatichai would bring up a proposal for two-party talks in Tokyo with Prime Minister Kaifu. And, in fact, when Prime Minister Chatichai proposed such a meeting, Prime Minister Kaifu responded that he would study the idea positively.[21] It was a carefully choreographed passivity, an elaborate Kabuki dance sometimes seen in Japanese foreign policy in which Japan would have ASEAN propose something that Japan wanted and then agree to go along with it.

What took place was not the two-party talks between Sihanouk and Hun Sen that had initially been planned but the Tokyo Conference between the Heng Samrin government and the three-party coalition government. Sihanouk had been reluctant to meet without the Pol Pot group on the grounds that the latter would veto any agreement and nothing would come of it. As a result, Khieu Samphan from the Pol Pot faction agreed to attend the Tokyo meetings. Although he came to Tokyo, in the end, however, he boycotted the Conference. Because the format of the Conference was between two governments, the position of the Pol Pot faction was that as a member of a three-party coalition, they were a third of a half, in short, a sixth; that was said to be the reason for Khieu Samphan's discontent. Since in the discussions up to then, the four sides had always been equal, with each having a quarter say in the proceedings, in that sense, his reaction was only natural. By the time of the Tokyo Conference, however, Sihanouk had come to accept the view of equality between two governments (the Heng Samrin and the three-party coalition) instead of four equal groups. As a result, he accepted the idea of equal representation for both governments in the participation formula for the Supreme National Council, as Australia and others had proposed. The result of the Tokyo Conference was a joint communiqué, agreed upon by Sihanouk and Hun Sen, which for the first time in an international document made it clear that both governments would be equally represented in the SNC.[22]

The Way to the Paris Peace Agreement

The United States, which had been cool to Kōno's visit to Cambodia and watched the Tokyo Conference with a critical eye, changed its policies on the Cambodian problem a month after the Tokyo Conference. On July 18, 1990, Secretary of State James Baker declared that now that Vietnamese troops had pulled out of Cambodia, it was important to prevent the Khmer Rouge (the Pol Pot faction) from ever returning to power. "In keeping with that objective," he said, "we will open a dialogue with Vietnam about Cambodia, we will be prepared to enhance our humanitarian assistance to Cambodia, and we will be prepared to and will in fact change what has been our policy regarding the seat at the United Nations which has been held by a coalition that includes the Khmer Rouge."[23] The US was now putting an end to a situation in which it had no choice, based on Cold-War logic, but to support the Pol Pot faction. In the US Congress, there had been increasing criticism of aid to the three-party coalition government, which might end up indirectly aiding the Pol Pot faction. Tomiyama explains the circumstances this way:

> Behind the reasons that made the American policy shift possible was a fundamental change in the international situation brought about by the end of the US-USSR Cold War. From the end of the 1970s on, the US had opposed Vietnamese control of Cambodia and adopted policies to isolate Vietnam and the Heng Samrin regime that Vietnam had established. The understanding that underlay this policy was that Vietnam was the "advance guard" of Soviet expansionism in Asia. However, when the end of the Cold War became virtually certain at the US-USSR summit meeting on the Mediterranean island of Malta in December 1989, America's strategic interests in maintaining policies that regarded Vietnam as an enemy disappeared.[24]

At this point, the United States and the Soviet Union had come to see that it was in their own interest to settle the Cambodian problem. As a result, the only great power that still supported the Pol Pot faction and took a hostile view of Vietnam was China. With Gorbachev's visit in May 1989, China, too, had completely normalized its diplomatic relations with the Soviet Union. And the fact that China had incurred international isolation after Tiananmen Square, which happened right in the middle of Gorbachev's visit, also put pressure on China to change the course of its Cambodian policy. China no longer felt the need to demand the dissolution of the Heng Samrin regime and the establishment of a four-party transitional government.

In tandem with this, China began to make active efforts to ease tensions with Vietnam. In September 1990, the leaders of China and Vietnam held secret talks in Chengdu. Jiang Zemin and Li Peng attended on the Chinese side, and Nguyen Van Linh, Do Muoi and Pham Van Dong on the Vietnamese side.[25] General Vo Nguyen Giap's attendance at the Asian Games in Beijing later created a stir. China would resume diplomatic relations with Vietnam in November 1991.

Thus, in November 1990, the five permanent members of the UN Security Council reached a basic agreement about Cambodian peace. While the great powers were in accord about the direction peace in Cambodia should take, both the Heng Samrin government and the anti-Vietnamese three-party coalition government, after much twisting and turning, began to move toward talks that would lead to a final agreement. Although it was difficult to work out agreements on disarmament conditions and the composition of the SNC, when the neighboring great powers reached a basic agreement, finally all those involved had no choice but to move in the direction that Sihanouk had indicated. As a result, on October 23, 1991, the Paris Peace Agreement was finalized.

The Gulf War and the UN PKO Cooperation Law

While the foreign ministry's experts on Asian affairs were making the final adjustments to the Cambodian peace and the Kanemaru delegation was heading to North Korea, Japan faced a situation that has to be called its first crisis since the end of the Cold War: the Gulf crisis and the Gulf War.[26]

On August 2, 1990, the Iraq army invaded neighboring Kuwait en masse and in no time occupied the country. The Gulf crisis graphically revealed that the Cold War had come to an end. Against this blatant act of aggression, a consensus was immediately formed that could never have happened during the Cold War. That same day a UN Security Council meeting passed a resolution (Resolution 660) demanding the immediate and unconditional withdrawal of the Iraq army from Kuwait. US Secretary of State Baker flew to Moscow from Mongolia, where he was visiting, and issued a joint statement with Soviet Foreign Minister Shevardnadze condemning Iraq.

Japan, too, took measures in response to Iraq's invasion of Kuwait: it immediately froze Kuwaiti assets in Japan, banned the import of oil from Iraq and Kuwait and placed embargoes on trade and all capital transactions with both countries. Its subsequent response, however, could not help but be deeply troubled. Naturally the prevailing mood was that it was inconceivable that Japan, which had become a global economic superpower, would do nothing against such a blatant violation of international law. One of the pillars of the International Cooperation Initiative at the time of the Takeshita Cabinet had been "strengthening cooperation for peace." But although there was public agreement that Japan "had to do something," ultimately there was no agreement as to what that "something" should be. Ozawa Ichirō, who was then secretary-general of the LDP, advanced the view that even military cooperation, if based on a UN resolution, would not be a violation of the Japanese constitution. But Prime Minister Kaifu, the upper echelons of the Ministry of Foreign Affairs and especially the Cabinet Legislation Bureau took a much more conservative view. A UN Peace Cooperation Bill was hastily drawn up within government circles and presented to the Diet but ultimately had to be withdrawn.

As a result, Japan's "contribution" was financial aid totaling USD 13 billion to the multinational force and some civilian activity. Right after the multinational force launched an offensive against Iraq on January 17, 1991, Japan decided to send Self-Defense Force airplanes to Jordan to transport refugees, but while preparations to do so were being made, the Gulf War had already ended in a coalition victory (February 28). Because the USD 13 billion in financial assistance was covered by an increase in the gas tax, etc., it worked out to 10,000 yen for every man, woman and child in Japan. But when the Kuwait government after the Gulf War took out a full-page ad in an American newspaper thanking the countries of the world, Japan's name was not included in the list.

The Japanese government sent Self-Defense Force minesweepers to clear mines in the Persian Gulf after the Gulf War and tried somehow to impress upon the world the efforts Japan was making. Although these activities were extremely useful, according to the memoirs of Ochiai Taosa, who commanded the Maritime Self-Defense Force minesweeping unit, he heard a lot of criticism of Japan at strategy planning sessions with military personnel from other countries. About the tankers heading for Japan that were constantly leaving from the Middle East, they would say, "Why do we have to protect them when we hardly import any oil from the Middle East?" When Ochiai explained that every single Japanese had contributed 10,000 yen to the war effort, he would be told, "Less than a $100 per person? If I could just pay $100 and not have to come to the Persian Gulf, I'd pay right now."[27] Unless the "contribution" involved human activities on the ground, it didn't count: this was the lesson that most Japanese learned from the Gulf crisis and the Gulf War.

As for what such a "contribution" might constitute, needless to say, under the postwar Japanese constitutional system, it was unclear what was, or was not, possible. There were many discussions about just how far Japan could go without violating the government's traditional interpretation of the constitution. For the moment, the objective was UN peacekeeping operations that, at least in some form, Japan could participate in without violating the constitution. By the time the LDP, Komeito and the Democratic Socialist Party agreed upon a bill on Cooperation with UN Peacekeeping Operations and Other Operations (the PKO Cooperation Bill) in September 1991, more than half a year had passed since the end of the Gulf War. In order to avoid any possible violation of the constitution, this bill attached a large number of restrictions on Japan's participation in international peacekeeping. Those restrictions were summarized in what was called the five PKO principles:

- Agreement on a cease-fire shall have been reached among the parties to armed conflicts.
- Consent for the undertaking of UN peacekeeping operations as well as Japan's participation in such operations shall have been obtained from the host countries as well as the parties to armed conflicts.
- The operations shall strictly maintain impartiality, not favoring any of the parties to armed conflicts.
- Should any of the requirements in the above-mentioned principles cease to be satisfied, the Government of Japan may withdraw Self-Defense Force (SDF) units.
- The use of weapons shall be limited to the minimum necessary to protect the lives of personnel, etc.[28]

Among these, the notable restriction on the use of weapons was a particularly great impediment to international activities. According to this principle, Self-Defense Forces could not protect participants in peacekeeping operations from other countries, nor could they even protect their own fellow countrymen. In addition, the consent of the parties to the conflict to Japan's participation and the agreement of all the parties to a cease-fire were provisions that would make Japan's participation very difficult on many occasions. But a considerable amount of caution had been required in order to make the sending of Self-Defense Forces overseas possible.

Despite these restrictions, there was strong opposition within Japan, most notably from the Japan Socialist Party, and vocal criticism abroad. Right after the bill was introduced, the South Korean foreign ministry stated, "It could not help but regret" that Japan was submitting the PKO Cooperation Bill to the Diet. Later, President Roh Tae-woo, too, expressed his personal concerns. China also told LDP Secretary-General Obuchi Keizō in August 1991 that General Secretary Jiang Zemin had urged caution. Even in Southeast Asia, there was uneasiness in Singapore, which had once been occupied by Japan and had suffered many losses especially among its residents of Chinese descent. In May 1991, former Prime Minister Lee Kuan Yew said of Japan's PKO participation, "As someone put it, you may be giving liqueur chocolates to an alcoholic. Whatever they do, they do to its limits."[29]

The Deployment of Peacekeeping Operations

The PKO Cooperation Bill was beginning to be discussed in the Diet just before the finishing touches were being put on the Cambodian Peace Agreement. "During the time that peacekeeping operations were first being considered as one possibility for Japan's international contribution, the topic of PKO deployment in Cambodia came up," Owada Hisashi, an architect of the Tokyo Conference on Cambodia, remembered.[30] After the Paris Peace Agreement was concluded on October 23, 1991, the link began to be made between the Cambodian peace, in which Japan continued to be actively involved on the post-Cold-War diplomatic scene, and peacekeeping operations as a way out of Japan's humiliating experiences in the Gulf War.

For the Japanese people, there was yet another development that had turned their attention to peacekeeping operations in Cambodia. Akashi Yasushi, a UN Under Secretary General at the time, had been appointed to head the United Nations Transitional Authority in Cambodia (UNTAC), the framework that would be key to Cambodian peace. As to why he had been chosen, Akashi said he had not asked Secretary General Boutros Boutros-Ghali, but probably one of his qualifications was that he was a "person from Asia." Furthermore, Prince Sihanouk and others "seem to have told the members of the Supreme National Council (SNC) that it would no doubt be advantageous as far as economic aid to Cambodia was concerned if a Japanese were to become the special representative of the Secretary General."[31]

PKO troops boarding a chartered plane (October 13, 1992). Photo: Kyodo News

Akashi's appointment as the UN Secretary General's special representative was also useful in the deliberations on the PKO Cooperation Bill in Japan. He was called as a witness by the House of Councillors' Special Committee on Peace Cooperation on May 12, 1992 and explained in minute detail the actual conditions of UN peacekeeping operations. There was also a request from Cambodia. When Cambodia's Prime Minister Hun Sen came to Japan in March, he, too, had asked Japan to send Self-Defense Forces and other military personnel necessary for UNTAC activities. At a press conference on April 13, Prime Minister Miyazawa Kiichi said, "Now that Cambodian peace is about to be implemented by UNTAC peacekeeping forces, it would be strange if Japan, which is geographically close by, were to do nothing. We have also received a request for cooperation from Cambodia. I would very much like to see the PKO Cooperation Bill passed by the present session of the Diet. If it is not passed, they [the rest of the world] will wonder what gives with Japan."[32] The Japan Socialist Party, which was resolutely opposed to this bill, tried to resist using tactics to slow the proceedings down, but in the end, it was enacted in June 1992 with the approval of the LDP, the Democratic Socialist Party and Komeito. Abroad, the media in China and South Korea were universally critical of Japanese involvement in these activities.

In Southeast Asia, on the other hand, Malaysian Foreign Minister Abdullah Ahmad Badawi, for example, welcomed the bill's passage. Expectations about Japan's role in Cambodia were beginning to grow.

Finally, on September 2, 1992, the Japanese government made a cabinet-level decision on an "International Peace Cooperation Operations" plan for Cambodia, which involved sending a 600-man Self-Defense Force engineering battalion, eight cease-fire observers, 75 civilian police and 50 election observers. By mid October, all 600 members of the Self-Defense Force engineering battalion had arrived in Cambodia. And on October 23, a ceremony was conducted in front of the PKO headquarters to commemorate the first anniversary of the signing of the Paris Peace Agreement. According to Special Representative Akashi,

> The Hinomaru was there among the flags of 44 nations. It had been the subject of so much debate in Japan, and I, too, had been the target of criticism, so I was deeply moved that Japanese participation in UN peacekeeping operations had finally become a reality. Under the Peace Constitution it would not be a good thing if the Hinomaru were to fly alone in a foreign land. But when it appears along with the flags of 44 countries as well as the flag of the United Nations, it reflects Japan's new attitude of active participation in international security. It announces that an era of unrealistic international isolationism has finally ended and that Japan has joined the world. I tried hard not to let Prince Sihanouk, next to me, see my tears.[33]

It is doubtful, however, how prepared Japan itself was for UN peacekeeping. The region UNTAC assigned the Self-Defense Force engineering battalion to operate in was Takeo Province, which was regarded as relatively peaceful and safe. According to the memoirs of Ishihara Nobuo, who was deputy chief cabinet secretary at the time, "since it was the first time, if something went wrong, popular sentiment would completely change. If possible, we hoped to be assigned a safe place where there would not be much trouble."[34] Nevertheless, though a peace agreement may have been signed, Cambodia, the Self-Defense Forces' first overseas assignment, was very far from being a safe place.

Trials and Tribulations in Cambodia

While the Diet was deliberating about the UN PKO Cooperation Bill, the UN's transitional government in Cambodia had gotten under way following the Paris Peace Agreement, and Japanese foreign diplomacy, too, was engaged in diplomatic efforts to rebuild the country after the peace. That did not mean, however, that the future prospects for postwar Cambodia were necessarily bright. In June 1992, the UN Transitional Authority in Cambodia (UNTAC), which had been launched that March under Special Representative Akashi, entered the second phase of the cease-fire: disarmament within four weeks of all 200,000 armed combatants. The Pol Pot faction, however, refused to comply, and the president of the UN Security Council was forced to issue a presidential statement censuring them. As a result, when the Japanese Self-Defense Forces arrived in Cambodia in September 1992, the Pol Pot faction's resistance to UNTAC was already strengthening, and tensions were mounting militarily as well.

While this was going on, in addition to the sending of Self-Defense Forces, on the diplomatic side, Japan was also concentrating its efforts on reconstruction assistance. In June 1992, it invited the countries involved to Tokyo and held the International Conference on the Reconstruction of Cambodia. It also tried to use diplomatic persuasion on the Pol Pot faction. According to Akashi's memoirs, "In August, joint mediation efforts were begun by Japan and Thailand. The position of Thailand, which was close to the Pol Pot faction, was respected. The team of Ikeda [Tadashi] of the Ministry of Foreign Affairs Asian Affairs Bureau and Yamamoto [Tadamichi], director of the First Southeast Asia Division, in Tokyo and Ambassador Imagawa [Yukio] in Cambodia skillfully conducted negotiations."[35] Meanwhile, Special Representative Akashi himself took the firm position that if the Pol Pot faction did not cooperate, the Cambodian general elections scheduled for May 1993 would go ahead without them. That was the division of labor: while Japan and Thailand tried persuasion, UNTAC took an unbending stand. In October, the UN Security Council adopted Resolution 783, criticizing the Pol Pot faction by name for its refusal to join Phase II of the cease-fire and requesting Japan and Thailand to continue to act as intermediaries. Although the

Japanese and Thai efforts in August had ended in failure, the significance of these discussions was that they offered one last chance to the
Pol Pot faction. In the end, despite the efforts of Japan and Thailand,
the Pol Pot did not respond to persuasion, and there were repeated
sporadic military attacks throughout Cambodia. In late November,
Ieng Sary, a high-ranking Pol Pot official, held a news conference
and hinted that the use of force would be unavoidable if the general
elections scheduled for May 1993 were held as currently planned. In
response, on November 30, the UN Security Council put pressure on
the Pol Pot faction to take part in the elections and adopted Resolution
792 that would trigger economic sanctions, such as a ban on the provision of petroleum products and the freezing of the faction's overseas
assets, in the event that it did not (China abstained).

Early in 1993, on January 27, formal registration for political parties in the Cambodian general elections scheduled for that May was
closed. Twenty parties registered, but not the Pol Pot faction, thus
confirming that it would not take part. At the end of that month,
Phnom Penh government forces launched a large-scale attack on the
Pol Pot faction, and UNTAC was forced to express its regret. As the
election drew closer, the situation became more and more tense. At
the end of March, an attack on a Bangladeshi battalion, which was
part of UNTAC, produced the first fatalities among UNTAC military personnel. On April 8, the car in which Nakata Atsuhito (25), a
UN Volunteer and election supervisor, was riding came under attack
in Kampong Thom Province in central Cambodia, and he and his
Cambodian interpreter were killed. Although a civilian, he was the
first Japanese casualty of the Cambodian peacekeeping operation.

According to UNTAC Special Representative Akashi, who met
with Nakata's parents and sister right afterwards,

> Nakata Takehito [Nakata's father] spoke quietly but with pride
> of his son, who had realized his heart's desire. While I listened, I
> recalled a short story I had once read by Akutagawa Ryūnosuke
> called "The Handkerchief." In it, a mother who has come to tell
> her son's mentor about the boy's sudden death speaks composedly,
> but her inner grief is betrayed by the shaking of the handkerchief
> that she clasps under the table. Takehito later decided to quit his
> job and work for the [same] NGO. It was an event that might

be called rare in postwar Japan of a parent and child pursuing a single ideal.[36]

From April to May, military activities by the Pol Pot faction became more frequent, and on May 3, they launched a fierce attack on the city of Siem Reap in northwest Cambodia. Phnom Penh government troops responded, and around 20 were killed from both sides. For the first time, UNTAC issued a "first standby alert" for the entire country. The following day vehicles containing UNTAC personnel in Banteay Meanchey Province in northwest Cambodia were ambushed and came under attack by guerrillas, who seem to have belonged to the Pol Pot faction. A Japanese civilian policeman, Inspector Takata Haruyuki (Okayama Prefectural Police), was killed, and four other policemen sustained major or minor injuries.

In Japan, there was shock at the death of Inspector Takata (posthumously promoted to superintendent) so soon after that of UN Volunteer Nakata. According to the memoirs of Ishihara Nobuo, "To tell the truth, when Superintendent Takata and the other civilian policemen were attacked, there was a serious debate about whether the cease-fire conditions in the five principles of participation that the government and the opposition parties had promised had been broken as a result of this situation."[37] At the time this incident occurred, Prime Minister Miyazawa was in Karuizawa, but immediately returned to Tokyo. As Miyazawa recalled,

> According to the detailed report phoned in from Tokyo, there were already strong sentiments that the death of a civilian policeman necessitated the withdrawal from all peacekeeping operations in Cambodia. While nothing specific was said, this seemed to be the sentiment of the official residence as well. I told them: "Wait until I can get back. At any rate, I'll arrive back soon after midnight, so wait a while longer."
>
> As I expected, when I returned to the Prime Minister's residence, the general mood somehow seemed to favor withdrawing. I told everyone: "I've also thought about this in the car, and I oppose withdrawing. We have an obligation to carry on with this mission." . . . In response to the prevailing atmosphere, I made the decision as Prime Minister.[38]

The decision was made, and Cabinet Secretary Kōno Yōhei announced, "The present incident is a local matter not an all-out war situation; the cease-fire agreement based on the Paris Peace Agreement has not been broken. . . . Overcoming our sadness and staying the course is the way to ensure that this death does not go in vain, I believe."[39]

Nevertheless, within the Japanese government and particularly among those in the police force, dissatisfaction and uneasiness persisted. Why had this happened in what had been described as a safe assignment? "Frankly speaking, there was great discontent in our country about UNTAC's response to concerns about the safety of personnel" (Deputy Chief Cabinet Secretary Ishihara Nobuo).[40] Japanese policemen in Cambodia decided among themselves to withdraw to Phnom Penh. Minister of Home Affairs Murata Keijirō, who had hastily come to Cambodia, demanded that UNTAC Special Representative Akashi assure the safety of Japan's election supervisors and reassign the civilian policemen.

But from UNTAC's perspective, the Japanese government's actions were an irrational response to the situation. It might be called a UN peacekeeping operation, but danger was always involved; military personnel from other countries had also sustained casualties. It was only natural that UNTAC could not give special treatment to Japan alone. As for the actions of the Japanese civilian policemen who had fled to Thai territory after the attack, Brigadier General Klaas Roos, who was responsible for the UNTAC civilian police force, protested to the Japanese Embassy that they had "deserted their posts in violation of orders."[41] Special Representative Akashi responded to Home Minister Murata that he could not give Japanese special treatment.

Despite these difficulties, the Cambodian general elections were held on May 23, and contrary to what had been feared, voting took place without any major disturbances.

At 8 o'clock in the morning, voting began simultaneously at polling stations in more than 1,300 places throughout the country. From early in the morning, crowds thronged to the polls. Women voters wore their very best clothes. UNTAC personnel, Cambodians and other nationalities, in their blue UN helmets, were dealing efficiently with the sea of people. All the polling stations I observed were full to overflowing. That was true even in the villages around Siem Reap, which had been attacked by the Pol Pot faction two or three days before. The villagers seemed to be in high spirits as if they were going to a festival. The voting participation rate was over 89 percent.[42]

As for the voting results, the FUNCINPEC party led by Prince Norodom Ranariddh came in first. Although the Cambodian People's Party led by Hun Sen called for a recount in some of the polling districts, in the end all the parties concerned agreed to accept the results, opening an epoch-making first chapter in Cambodian politics. The final number of confirmed seats for the leading parties were 58 for the FUNCINPEC party; 51 for the Cambodian People's Party; and 10 for the Buddhist Liberal Democratic Party. An agreement was reached to form the Provisional National Government of Cambodia with Prince Norodom Ranariddh, leader of the National Unified Front (FUNCINPEC), and Prime Minister Hun Sen of the Phnom Penh government as its joint prime ministers. The remnants of the Pol Pot faction subsequently tried to resist, but the trend did not change. UNTAC ended its mission in the autumn of 1993, a successful example of the most extensive UN peacekeeping operations of the post-Cold War, and Japan's Self-Defense Forces returned home without any casualties.

With Cambodian peace and the success of the subsequent Cambodian peacekeeping operations, Japan was present at a success story at the end of the Cold War in Southeast Asia. Armed clashes would later occur in Cambodia between the two largest coalition parties in 1997, confirming the impression that the road to democratization would be long and difficult, but in the election of 1998, a new party led by Prime Minister Hun Sen came to power, and the government has been stable, if increasingly authoritarian, ever since. In April 1999, Cambodia became a member of ASEAN; although still poor and experiencing difficulties with economic development, it is becoming a stable power in Southeast Asia.

Chapter 4

"Asia-Pacific" Experiments

Movements toward Large-scale Regionalism

The period between the "new" Cold War and the Cold War's end in Asia was one of increasing democratization in the Philippines, South Korea and Taiwan and ongoing civil war in Cambodia, but it was also a time of intensifying economic competition among the advanced Western industrial nations and a search for a new international economic framework. G7 Summit meetings in which Japan participated were launched in the middle of the 1970s,[1] but these alone were not capable of managing the global economy. The Tokyo Round of multilateral free trade talks conducted in the 1970s finally concluded in 1979, but although these talks had been able to substantially lower tariff barriers, the focus shifted to the problem of so-called non-tariff barriers. In the service area and agriculture especially, the gap among Japan, the United States and Europe was extremely large. From the Japanese perspective, the 1980s were a time of US-Japan economic friction, but the economic frictions between the US and Europe were also fierce.

Under these circumstances, one direction for the world economy to move in was to launch a new round of multilateral negotiations aimed at trade liberalization. Considering the difficulties of the Tokyo Round, however, it was impossible to reach a consensus that this was the only course of action. Consequently, while calls for a new round of multilateral talks continued, efforts at regional integration were also being explored. In September 1986, a ministerial-level meeting of the General Agreement on Tariffs and Trade (GATT) convened at Punta del Este in Uruguay and agreed to open multilateral negotiations as a continuation of the Tokyo Round. Named after this meeting, these talks came to be called the "Uruguay Round," but the outlook for them was far from optimistic. In Europe, on the other hand, a European Council meeting in Milan in June 1985 adopted a white paper on "Completing the Internal Market" and set the goal for the European Community to become a "single market" by 1992, which would make possible the free movement of goods, people, services and capital within the region. The Single European Act containing articles aimed at regional market integration went into effect in July 1987, and moves toward regional integration accelerated in Western Europe. In North America as well, talks between the US and Canada about concluding a Canada-United States free trade agreement were first held in 1985; the agreement was signed in January 1988 and went into effect the following January. In short, while multilateral talks were proceeding at the worldwide level with the opening of the Uruguay Round, in Western Europe and North America, efforts were already under way to make trade freer within both those regions.[2]

What was on the minds of the Japanese people in this period? It would be no exaggeration to say that, aside from national security policies and the Japan-China relationship, almost all Japan's diplomatic energy in the 1980s had been expended on trade frictions with the US. The focus during the first half of that decade had been trade frictions related to automobiles; these were settled in the form of "voluntary" export restraints. But as long as the US continued to adopt a "strong dollar" policy, there was no chance of eliminating its trade deficit with Japan, which had ballooned enormously despite these "voluntary" restraints. Finally, in 1985, the exchange rate was readjusted significantly (the Plaza Accord). Nevertheless, the momentum of Japan's economic challenge to the US seemed to have remained unchanged. In fact, quite the contrary, the steep rise in the yen had caused an abnormal bubble economy to develop and gave rise to the unwarranted arrogance on Japan's part—and the exaggerated fear on America's part—that nothing could stand in the Japanese economy's way.[3]

It is hard to imagine now, but in 1989, when asked what posed the greatest threat in the post-Cold-War period, most Americans thought it would be Japan. Now that the Cold War was over, what would be important was geo-economics not geopolitics; the threat would not be military but economic. As was touched on in Chapter 3, in 1989, there were fears that "Japanese money" would buy up almost all of the US. Mitsubishi Estate bought Rockefeller Center, and Sony bought Columbia Pictures. The journalist James Fallows even wrote an article around this time entitled "Containing Japan."[4]

The flip side of Japanese arrogance now that the country was at the pinnacle of success, however, was a consciousness of their own fragility. With Europe heading toward a single market and the US aiming at a North American Free Trade Agreement and increasingly seeming to try to contain the Japanese economy politically, there was a growing awareness that something had to be done. Hostile relations with the US had to be prevented. For Japan to be shut out of the European market would be troubling. And being shut out of the American market would be even worse. The idea they came up with as one solution was to form a large region that would include Japan.

The then Ministry of International Trade and Industry (MITI) created an Asia-Pacific Co-operative Development Group, which, in part of its report published in June 1989, argued as follows:

As the globalization of economic activities proceeds apace, now, two apparently contradictory trends toward the formation of a new global economic order exist. One is the trend toward the promotion of multilateral free trade as represented by the Uruguay Round; the other is the trend toward regional cooperation such as EC market integration and the Canada-US Free Trade Agreement. The former is aimed at the integration of the global economy; the latter at first glance seems to be aiming at its disintegration, and countries outside these regions tend to fear that they may lead to "bloc"-ism or protectionism.

In the formation of a new economic order, the aim must be to facilitate global economic activities. In that sense, the trend to promote multilateral free trade as represented by the GATT Uruguay Round is one that contributes to the globalization of economic activities and is a challenge that all nations must make every effort to come to grips with.

On the other hand, the global economy needs a strong EC. In that sense, EC integration is probably an inevitable direction. The Canada-US Free Trade Agreement, too, is regarded as necessary to further invigorate the economic activities of two countries that are already in a profoundly interdependent relationship with one another. It is to be hoped that cooperation in both regions will be promoted along with the trend to globalize economic activities.[5]

Would it be possible, however, to form a large region in Asia that would include Japan? That does not mean, of course, that Asia had no multilateral regional frameworks. Japan had also envisioned a number of such frameworks as far back as the 1950s.[6] But until the 1980s, Asia had been politically divided. A framework that would transcend Cold-War dividing lines had been difficult. And even within these dividing lines, the stages of economic development in Asia were much too different. "Regional cooperation" was a relationship based on the aid that Japan and other advanced industrial nations provided to many, many developing countries. That the only powerful regional economic framework established during the Cold War was the Asian Development Bank clearly demonstrates these tendencies.

There were exceptions, of course. An important one is the Association of Southeast Asian Nations (ASEAN), which was a cooperative framework for relatively equal countries. As it had been a grouping of small- and medium-sized developing countries when it started in 1967, no one would have predicted that ASEAN would become the nucleus of the Asian regional framework in the 21st century. From the second half of the 1970s on, however, ASEAN strengthened its partnerships with countries outside the region such as Japan to the point that every summer it holds an expanded foreign ministers meetings, the Post Ministerial Conference (PMC), with ASEAN at its core.[7]

It also does not mean that there had been no projects for an Asian- and/or Pacific-centered regional framework at the conceptual level. In the 1960s, Kojima Kiyoshi, a professor at Hitotsubashi University, had proposed a plan for a Pacific Free Trade Area consisting of the US, Japan, Canada, Australia and New Zealand.[8] And in 1980, Prime Minister Ōhira Masayoshi's personal study group announced the Pacific Basin Cooperation Concept.[9] That year also saw the founding of the Pacific Economic Cooperation Conference (PECC), in which individuals from business and industry, government, academia and other circles in the region would participate in their private capacity.[10]

Seeing these various informal movements and assessing the economic realities, the MITI study group realized that the time was right. According to its report:

The rapid growth of the 1980s has been accompanied by a noticeable deepening of interdependence. A glance at trade volumes shows that the degree of dependence that each country in the Asia Pacific has on this region as a whole has risen five to ten percentage points in the seven years from 1981 to 1987; although there are differences from country to country, it ranges from between 50 to 70 percent, for an average of 63 percent. How high the rate of interdependence in this region is can perhaps be understood from the fact that the rate of interdependence in the EC is 58 percent.

Although economic interdependence had been growing this much even without a regional framework, the lack of one was causing various problems. Now, at last, the report said, it was fully possible to create such a framework. But a regional framework in Asia and the Pacific must not lead conversely to an increase in European or American protectionism. At the time, there was great concern that when Europe became a single market, it would turn into "Fortress Europe" and discriminate against countries outside the region. An Asia-Pacific regional framework, it was thought, must not be used as an excuse for European protectionism. What should be done to prevent that? And so the motto became "open regionalism," though the expression was sometimes called an oxymoron.

Asia-Pacific cooperation must not be a movement aimed at creating an economic bloc. It is clear that "openness" is imperative in maintaining sound economies, and the revitalization of the economies in this region will be even greater through trade with countries around the world. In reducing trade barriers, for example, it naturally should be done on the basis of a most-favored-nation principle. As for the business opportunities for infrastructure development projects that will facilitate a better international division of labor, it is important that companies from throughout the world participate, provided they have superior technological skills. Only in this way will the economic development of this region be fully fledged.

If the Asia-Pacific region said it too was going to create a protectionist framework in order to defend itself against Europe becoming protectionist, it would cause Europe to adopt even greater protectionism. It would become, so to speak, a self-fulfilling prophecy. To prevent this from happening, the only choice was to argue vehemently for the necessity of "open regionalism." Of course, if Europe actually did become protectionist, to counteract this, the Asia-Pacific region would probably have considered real regionalism. But no one openly said this.

As a specific policy to implement open regionalism, the same report concluded:

> To promote policy cooperation, first, in the economic sectors of trade and industry, etc., that can be regarded as being of shared concern to many countries, it is necessary for the ministers responsible for these areas to engage in a frank exchange of views at the earliest possible opportunity. To this end, it would be appropriate to hold a meeting of the ministers concerned in the Asia-Pacific region.

It proposed starting from the mechanism of ministerial conferences.

APEC

As we have just seen, plans were moving ahead within MITI to create a framework for an Asia-Pacific region.[11] But Japan's MITI was not alone in promoting such plans. Australia, too, was formulating a project along similar lines. During discussions between Japan and Australia in December 1988, MITI Vice-Minister Muraoka Shigeo asked Australia to take the initiative for holding such a conference. Muraoka's thinking, and that of MITI, was that "Japan could not take the lead . . . 'due to the lingering memories of the last war.'"[12]

Thus, the political initiative came first from the Australian Prime Minister Bob Hawke.[13] In a speech to top business leaders in Seoul in January 1989, Prime Minister Hawke proposed creating a new framework for Asia-Pacific cooperation. Following up on this speech, Secretary Richard Woolcott of the Department of Foreign Trade and Affairs traveled around meeting personally with the leaders of each country and fine-tuning the plan. On the whole, the response was good. But when Woolcott visited Japan, he was unable to meet with Prime Minister Takeshita. Since MITI was promoting the plan in Japan, the Ministry of Foreign Affairs was said to be skeptical. Takeshita, who didn't meet Woolcott at that time, later told Funabashi Yōichi, "I heard later that Australia was pretty unhappy about it. Perhaps the Gaimushō [Ministry of Foreign Affairs] blocked it. Maybe it was because that affair [the Recruit scandal] was so big at the time."[14] In any event, in the spring of 1989, the leaders of the Japanese government had other things on their minds.

It was the ASEAN countries and the United States that would be key. Malaysia and other countries made no attempt to conceal their very strong wariness of any framework that involved the US. On the other hand, whether the US would go along with the idea was an unknown quantity. In 1989, the US was behaving as though it was engaged in economic warfare with Japan. In April, Section 301 of the Omnibus Trade and Competitiveness Act, "Super 301," cited Japan as a priority negotiating partner for its trading practices, and the Bush administration later proposed that the two countries begin talks on structural impediments issues. Australia's Prime Minister Hawke in his Seoul speech is said to have intentionally not included the US as a founding member of this Asia-Pacific framework. By not mentioning the US, he dispelled the wariness of the ASEAN countries, but, on the other hand, he administered a sort of shock therapy that made the US take an interest in the plan. Whether or not that was the strategy is, in fact, unclear, but that was the result. In June of that year, Secretary of State James Baker gave his approval to the Hawke plan.

Thus, in November 1989, the first Asia-Pacific Economic Cooperation (APEC) Ministerial Meeting was held in Canberra. The member countries at the time were Australia, Canada, Japan, South Korea, New Zealand, the US and the then-six ASEAN countries. It would be fair to say that the meeting was the fruit of Japan's behind-the-scenes initiative, but, in fact, it produced strange results. According to Funabashi Yōichi,

MITI and the Gaimushō's visions of Asia-Pacific regional cooperation were different in every respect. In the lead-up to the Canberra meeting, the one matter on which the two ministries agreed was that Chinese membership in APEC was premature. But, of course, given the Tiananmen Square incident in June of that year, the prospects of that happening were zero. At the Canberra meeting, the ministers of both ministries planned to give substantive speeches to set the tone for the occasion. Both ministers did give speeches, but because the time allotted to a single country had been divided in half, each ended up making short remarks without much substance. And though both clamored for a seat at the head table at the welcome banquet, only a single seat at the head table was reserved for the chief delegate from each country. The two Japanese ministers were offered seats at another, secondary, table, as a result. An Asian minister commenting on this situation said, "Neither minister from Japan was at the head table. Unbelievable!" and burst out laughing.[15]

Later, beginning with the Seoul meeting in 1991, China, Hong Kong and Taiwan joined APEC; Mexico and Papua New Guinea became members at the Seattle meeting in 1993; and Chile joined at the Jakarta meeting in 1994. Russia, Vietnam and Peru joined in 1998. Among these new members, the most distinctive was the participation of China, Hong Kong and Taiwan. Given China's tendency to do everything in its power to preclude the possibility of recognizing the independent existence of Taiwan, for these three to become members of APEC is noteworthy, and much of the reason for it can be traced to the special circumstances of the year 1991.

A major factor, first of all, was that at the second meeting in Singapore in 1990, South Korea was named to host the third meeting. As we shall discuss in greater detail in Chapter 5, South Korea would be extremely proactive in normalizing its relations with China. But in 1991, it still had relations with Taiwan. In fact, among the APEC member countries, it was the only one to do so. If the meeting had occurred a year later, South Korea would have already entered into relations with China and severed its ties with Taiwan so that Taiwanese membership would likely have been difficult.

Secondly, 1991 was a time when China was making desperate diplomatic efforts to be reinstated in the international community. The merits of belonging to an organization whose members included the US, Japan, ASEAN and Australia were probably considered to be extremely high. In addition, generally speaking, in the case of organizations in which China was a late joiner, things did not always go the way China wanted. If China had been a founding member of APEC, Taiwan would certainly not have been allowed to join. (Among important international organizations, another exception is the World Trade Organization. Here, too, China was not a founding member.)

The organizer in South Korea in charge of making the preparations for APEC was Lee See-young, and the conditions for membership of the "three Chinas" that were worked out thanks to his efforts were contained in the following Memorandum of Understanding.

1. The respective designations of the three parties shall be the People's Republic of China, Chinese Taipei and Hong Kong. These designations shall be used in all APEC meetings, activities, documents, materials and other publications as well as in all APEC administrative and conference arrangements;

2. Without prejudice to the rights of APEC participants to appoint their respective representatives to APEC meetings, Chinese Taipei shall be represented at Ministerial Meetings only by a minister or ministers in charge of APEC-related economic affairs, while its "foreign minister" or "vice foreign minister" shall not attend APEC meetings. Chinese Taipei's delegation may include officials of "foreign" and other ministries at or below the level of department director. Members of Chinese Taipei's delegation may use their official titles subject to the principles agreed upon in this Memorandum of Understanding;

3. Subject to the aforementioned terms, the three parties will participate in APEC meetings and activities on an equal basis with the current APEC participants.[16]

In short, if Taiwan accepted the designation "Chinese Taipei," it would be equal in all other respects. In the subsequent conduct of APEC affairs, however, many things emerged that were contrary to Taiwan's expectations.

EAEC

Meanwhile, at roughly the same time as the founding of APEC, another multinational framework focused on East Asia was being proposed— the East Asian Economic Group (EAEG) advocated by Malaysian Prime Minister Mahathir Mohamad.[17] Mahathir presented this plan to

Chinese Premier Li Peng while the latter was visiting Malaysia in December 1990. Since the GATT Uruguay Round talks were stalled at that point, Prime Minister Mahathir suggested the formation of a common market or trading bloc for the Asian region. The bloc would include the then-six ASEAN countries, Japan, China, South Korea, Hong Kong, Taiwan and the countries of Indochina.[18] Li Peng responded cautiously to this proposal, saying in effect that "it was an open question what form of co-operation countries in the region should adopt because the East Asian countries differed in their economic systems and in their level of economic development."[19]

The proposal itself was so sudden that not even Rafidah Aziz, the Malaysian Minister of International Trade and Industry, had been informed of it in advance. As a result, it was apparently not until January 1991 that Malaysia began fleshing out the idea with specifics.[20] Although the substance of the plan was still unclear, it touched off various speculations as well as strong reactions both for and against it. Since APEC had been launched in the fall of 1989, and its second meeting had just been held in the fall of 1990, in Japan, those in MITI put a damper on the proposal: "A tit-for-tat mentality [against possible Western protectionism] is too strong. Economic cooperation that excluded the US and Canada would spur the creation of an Asian economic bloc." "There is absolutely no reality to the present proposal." And Indonesian Foreign Minister Ali Alatas said, "If the aim is to become a protectionist bloc, it would violate the basic principles of ASEAN."[21] In March 1991, Michael Armacost, the American ambassador to Japan, criticized the proposal on the grounds that "it would hinder the activities of APEC, which had been formed at the end of 1989."[22]

Faced with this sort of criticism, instead of calling it a trading bloc as it had done at first, Malaysia changed the name to the East Asian Economic Group (EAEG). At the ASEAN Economic Ministers Meeting held in Kuala Lumpur at the beginning of October 1991, the expression "caucus" was used, and it was agreed that it would convene "as and when the need arises."[23] It subsequently came to be called the EAEC (East Asian Economic Caucus) proposal. At the meeting of ASEAN Economic Ministers, Prime Minister Mahathir watered down his original plan considerably, saying that it was not against free trade nor was it a trading bloc, but even so criticism was fierce. When US Secretary of State James Baker visited Japan in November of that year, he told Foreign Minister Watanabe Michio that the EAEC was absolutely unacceptable because it would draw a line down the Pacific and divide the US and Japan.[24] Baker later recalled it this way:

> Malaysian Prime Minister Mahathir Bin Mohamad, in particular, continued to hawk his idea of an East Asian Economic Group (EAEG) along the lines of the EC. Mahathir was not seen as particularly pro-American and was considered likely to cause mischief if crossed, so I took a moderate line on his idea in public. In private, I did my best to kill it. Some East Asian APEC members were inclined to go along with it merely to placate the insistent Mahathir. At the APEC meeting in Seoul, Korean Foreign Minister Lee Sang Ok suggested his country might support Mahathir's proposal out of Asian solidarity. I reminded Lee that it was Americans, not Malaysians, who had shed their blood for Korea forty years before. My message was simple: All countries are *not* equal. The South Koreans got it, and did not press for an EAEG.[25]

Within Japan, there were some who favored Prime Minister Mahathir's proposal. "The 'pro-Asia' bureaucrats who have obtained important posts in the Ministry of Finance and the Ministry of Foreign Affairs are more inclined to support the EAEC," Funabashi observes. At MITI, the issue caused a generational divide: "Younger MITI officials are more receptive to the EAEC, although the ministry's top ranks remain cautious."[26] In the face of the Bush administration's unbending opposition, however, both the Ministry of Foreign Affairs and MITI adopted a cautious attitude. Given all the concerns about US-Japan frictions that already existed, they thought that if Japan were to go along with this proposal, the rift with the US would deepen decisively.

While the US and Japan were taking a guarded stand, ultimately no movement arose within ASEAN to actively back the EAEC. An ASEAN Summit communiqué confined itself to acknowledging that "With respect to an EAEC, ASEAN recognises that consultations on issues of common concern among East Asian economies, as and when the need arises, could contribute to expanding cooperation among the region's economies, and the promotion of an open and free global trading system." Although ASEAN did not deny the significance of such a proposal out of regard for Prime Minister Mahathir, it showed no signs of immediately putting an EAEC into effect.[27] The ASEAN Ministerial Meeting (AMM) that summer also basically put off the proposal by asking a Joint Consultative Meeting (JCM) of ASEAN to "study an appropriate modality" for the EAEC.[28] The JCM submitted its report to the ASEAN Ministerial Meeting in the summer of 1993, but the meeting only went so far as to suggest that the EAEC ought to be a "caucus within APEC," and that "the ASEAN Economic Ministers Meeting (AEM) would be the appropriate body" to consider the idea further.[29] When the AEM met that autumn, however, it merely concluded that consultations were necessary among the countries expected to participate in the EAEC.[30] At the ASEAN Ministerial Meeting in 1994, it became clear that these consultations had made virtually no progress. The meeting's joint communiqué merely stated that it welcomed such consultations and that they would continue.[31]

It should be added, however, that at the time of the 1994 AMM, a symbolic meeting was held that was seemingly related to the EAEC. On July 25, an unofficial meeting of nine foreign ministers—from Japan, China and South Korea as well as the six ASEAN countries —was held in the form of a working lunch for what was called an EAEC preparatory meeting. Partly because of Foreign Minister Kōno Yōhei's cautious attitude, not much progress was made as to substance, but there was perhaps some symbolic significance to the fact that the foreign ministers of the prospective member countries of the EAEC had met together at an informal lunch. At the ASEAN Economic Ministers Meeting that autumn, however, it was obvious that no real progress had been made on the EAEC proposal.[32] Even in 1995, the attitude of ASEAN as a whole toward the EAEC was not all that positive. The Bangkok Declaration agreed upon at the ASEAN Summit at the end of 1995 confined itself to saying that "ASEAN shall continue with efforts to advance further the East Asian Economic Caucus (EAEC)."[33]

ARF

On the security side, the founding of the ASEAN Regional Forum (ARF) was a watershed in the history of multilateral frameworks for the Asia-Pacific region.[34] The initiative to found ARF arose out of the ideas of ASEAN diplomacy experts who wanted to create a framework that would enable them to display their countries' strengths and hold their own against the great powers of the Asia Pacific. In 1988, a network called the ASEAN Institutes of Strategic and International Studies (ASEAN ISIS) was formed as a coalition of think tanks in all the ASEAN countries to deal with international and strategic issues. In this network, ASEAN experts in these areas analyzed the global situation at the end of the Cold War and came up with proposals as an ASEAN response to them. One of these results was entitled "A Time for Initiative," which was published in June 1991. This proposal urged that after the annual meeting of ASEAN foreign ministers, an expanded ASEAN conference of foreign ministers be held to deal with security issues and conduct an Asia-Pacific political dialogue.[35] This could be called the ASEAN response to the many proposals for framework building that Canada and Australia had put forth around the end of the Cold War. These perceptions were shared by the relevant personnel in the ASEAN governments, and at the ASEAN Post Ministerial Meeting in July 1992, in addition to Japan and the US, which were already members as "dialogue partners," Russia and China were invited as guests.

Japan, too, tried to work out plans of its own for some sort of regional security framework. An example can be found in the speech of Foreign Minister Nakayama Tarō, who attended the Post Ministerial Meeting in July 1991. In it, Nakayama expressed his approval of ASEAN's use of the Post Ministerial Meetings as a security framework and proposed that "in order for such dialogue to be effective, it might be advisable to organize a senior officials' meeting which would then report its deliberations to the ASEAN Post Ministerial Conference for further discussion."[36] This proposal has often been interpreted as the starting point out of which ARF arose, but though there are aspects to it that may have been a motivating factor in a broad sense, the ASEAN Regional Forum that was consequently created differed considerably from the one that Foreign Minister Nakayama had originally proposed. Nakayama's speech envisioned a membership that would include only those who were then members of the Post Ministerial Meetings and assumed that the political dialogue would be devoted to dispelling fears about Japan and the

US-Japan Security Treaty. By contrast, discussions within ASEAN were conceptualizing a framework that would include major countries outside ASEAN such as Vietnam, China and the Soviet Union in addition to Japan and the United States.[37]

The founding of ARF was agreed upon at the ASEAN Post Ministerial Meeting in 1993, and its first meeting was held in 1994. The members at the time, in addition to the six ASEAN countries, were Vietnam, Laos, Japan, the US, Canada, Australia, New Zealand, South Korea, China, Russia, Papua New Guinea and a representative from the EU.

As in the case of APEC, ARF had no grand designs when it started out. Its stated aims were extremely vague. The first meeting was even described as nothing more than a "talk shop." It was not until the second meeting that the member states agreed on mid-term goals. These goals were that ARF would attempt to promote dialogue in the security area in three stages: confidence building, preventive diplomacy and conflict resolution, and it was agreed to tackle confidence building first. As the means to do so, members agreed to strengthen political/security dialogues; increase transparency by making public documents related to defense policies; deepen exchanges among military personnel; and promote membership in the United Nations Register of Conventional Arms.

Asia-Pacific Regionalism

In 1993, yet another innovation occurred in APEC. Before the ministerial meeting scheduled to take place in Seattle, President Bill Clinton proposed holding an unofficial summit meeting in addition to the ministerial meeting. Although Prime Minister Mahathir of Malaysia did not participate in the Seattle Summit, the heads of all the other member countries attended. It was the first time in history that leaders of the Asia-Pacific region had gathered together in one place, a sign that in Asia, too, the Cold War was over, and relations among countries were normalizing. As has already been stated, the founding of ARF had also been agreed upon in 1993, and so at this point in time international relations in the Asia Pacific, in a framework that included the US and Australia, were beginning to get on track.

Informal summit meeting in Seattle. Prime Minister Hosokawa at the end on the right (November 20, 1993). Photo: Kyodo News

Looking back from the perspective of Japanese diplomacy, the two or three years after 1989 were a period in which Japan had been buffeted by violent upheavals in the world situation with no time for an in-depth consideration of policies. MITI and the Ministry of Foreign Affairs, each in its own area of expertise, did develop policies: Cambodian peace was one; the founding of APEC was another. In the case of Tiananmen Square, the Gulf War and Kanemaru's visit to North Korea, however, Japan basically had to play catch-up as far as policy was concerned.

When Prime Minister Miyazawa Kiichi took office at the end of 1991, it is no wonder that he thought Japan should be pursuing more systematic policies. For Miyazawa, who had always been in the postwar political mainstream and who prided himself on being a pro among pros as far as Japanese diplomacy and politics were concerned, there was nothing strange about trying to work out policies of his own.

Within the Ministry of Foreign Affairs, too, there were those who were trying to make Japan's post-Cold-War security policies more systematic. Compared to earlier Bluebooks, the Heisei 3 (1991) edition of the Diplomatic Bluebook, for example, in the section that discussed the "Objectives and Priorities of Japan's Foreign Policy," looked back on the past and observed that Japanese diplomacy had now entered a new era. As regards Asian diplomacy especially, it argued that Japan must have a multilateral outlook instead of the traditional focus on bilateral foreign relations. And in the section on security, it methodically discussed "Ensuring Peace and Stability in the Asia-Pacific Region" and made a distinction between the region's security environment and that of Europe.[38]

There were also calls from the private sector for Japan to take a fresh look at its foreign policy. Kobayashi Yōtarō, the president of Fuji Xerox, for example, attracted attention in the spring of 1991 when he published an article calling for the "re-Asianization" of Japan.[39]

As views of these kinds about Asia and Japan's foreign policy emerged, there was a sense that the various opinions that existed within the country and the bureaucracy needed to be consolidated, and so in May 1992, Prime Minister Miyazawa set up the Panel on "Japan and the Asia-Pacific Region in the 21st Century." Its members included experts from academia, the industrial world and the media in Japan at that time who had knowledge and experience of Asia. In his speech at the founding of the panel, Prime Minister Miyazawa expressed his understanding of the situation as follows.

> In Indochina, Cambodian peace has been achieved, and the process of rebuilding the country has begun. On the Korean peninsula, there have been positive movements toward an easing of tensions now that both the North and the South are members of the United Nations, and some progress in the North-South dialogue is being made. The further development of China's openness and reform policies, the *doi moi* policy in Vietnam, democratization and openness policies in Mongolia, each based on the situations of their respective countries, are also regarded as forward-looking trends. Major policy changes can also be seen in Southwest Asia. In India, economic liberalization is well under way, and democratization is being achieved in Nepal and Bangladesh. ASEAN, which this year is celebrating the 25th anniversary of its founding, is increasingly strengthening trends toward regional cooperation and attempting to widen its scope to include Indochina. APEC, which last year saw the People's

Republic of China, Taiwan and Hong Kong become members, has grown into a large regional cooperative body that accounts for nearly half the world's GNP, and the further expansion of cooperation can be expected.[40]

In other words, as of June 1992, many positive factors were thought to be appearing in Asia as seen from Japan. As we now know, in the autumn of 1991, Japan's bubble economy had burst, but few people imagined that the Japanese economy would subsequently plunge into as severe a stagnation period as it turned out to be. Prime Minister Miyazawa himself was bullish. He thought he was laying the foundations for Japan's Asia policy.

After several discussions, the panel presented its report to Prime Minister Miyazawa on December 25. In addition to emphasizing the need to think flexibly about the region in regard to each objective without giving a particularly restrictive definition as to the scope of the Asia Pacific, the report mentioned relations with China, ASEAN and Indochina, and the situation on the Korean peninsula (especially the suspicions about North Korea's nuclear weapons), Russia and South Asia as major factors affecting the region's future, and cited "respect for diversity" and the "promotion of openness" to achieve "peace and prosperity" as ideals that Japan ought to maintain. "It goes without saying that freedom and democracy are goals that should also be pursued in this region," but "if we consider that many countries [in the region] have had the experience of suffering under harsh colonial regimes, when it comes to the issues of freedom, democracy and human rights, we need to stand on our own accumulated experiences and engage in quiet and repeated dialogue with these countries." Citing three points as tasks for the future— security, a regional framework and the understanding of the past—the report also singled out the importance of an American presence as the basis of security; the value of openness in a regional framework; and the importance of "a sincere and humble attitude" in respect to the problems of the past. As specific means to these ends, it cited deepening the dialogue on regional security, improving economic cooperation and promoting mutual understanding in the Asia-Pacific region. As regards the security dialogue in particular, it noted the importance of involving China and Russia in the region's security dialogue and also proposed adopting an initiative on disarmament and arms control. On Japanese economic cooperation, acknowledging that Japan's achievements thus far "have produced results that we can speak of with pride," the report recognized the effectiveness of Japanese aid and said it ought to be strengthened even further.

Considering the subsequent developments in the situation on the Korean peninsula and the Taiwan Strait, these proposals can be seen to have lacked a sense of short-term danger. Despite this, however, the report contained all the items necessary for Japan's subsequent Asian policy: an awareness of the importance of the US-Japan security system; the value of a multilateral security dialogue; the need to improve economic cooperation; the significance of an understanding of history; the importance of mutual understanding, etc. Unfortunately, right around the time this proposal was announced, Japanese domestic politics would be beset by violent change, and everyone was too preoccupied to even think about foreign policy.

Although problem areas in the Japanese political system had been pointed out for many years, beginning around the time that the Takeshita administration was dissolved as a result of the Recruit scandal, political reform was becoming a bigger theme with every passing day. The public had no great expectations for the Miyazawa Cabinet that succeeded the Uno and Kaifu administrations, and the support rate hovered in the low 30 percent range. Around this time suspicions arose about the LDP's Vice-President Kanemaru Shin, who had visited North Korea in 1990, and popular distrust reached its peak. When it became clear that Kanemaru, who was then a dominant figure in the LDP, had accepted 500 million yen in illegal contributions from Sagawa Express Co., he was subsequently forced to resign from the Diet. As a result of this affair, the Takeshita faction, the largest in the LDP, split, and the political world was thrown into chaos. Miyazawa dealt with the political situation with the intention of carrying out political reform himself, but the Ozawa Ichirō group sided with the opposition, and a vote of non-confidence in the Miyazawa Cabinet was passed and enacted. Miyazawa immediately dissolved the House of Representatives, and in the general election held in July 1993, the LDP failed to win a majority. As a result, the LDP, which had governed continuously since its founding in 1955, fell from power, and a cabinet was formed by Hosokawa Morihiro of the New Japan Party, who became prime minister.

Even after the formation of the Hosokawa Cabinet, Japan's domestic politics were by no means stable. At the beginning of 1994, a reform of the electoral system involving proportional representation and single-seat constituencies went into effect, but immediately afterward, Prime Minister Hosokawa announced he was stepping down, and Hata Tsutomu took over the administration. As a result of dissension within the ruling coalition, however, the Japan Socialist Party defected, and at the beginning of July, it joined forces with the LDP, its mortal enemy for the past 40 years, and together they formed a cabinet headed by Murayama Tomiichi, the chairman of the Socialist Party.[41]

During all these upheavals in domestic politics, needless to say, diplomacy continued. But those who recalled the proposals of the Panel on Japan and the Asia-Pacific Region in the 21st Century had all but disappeared. Thus, as we shall see in the next chapter, in 1994, not just Japan's domestic politics but all of East Asia found itself peering into the abyss.

Chapter 5

The Rise of China and the Crisis on the Korean Peninsula

The Diplomacy of Normalization

China, which had been isolated from the West after the Tiananmen Square incident, was making all-out diplomatic efforts to lessen its isolation while stubbornly rebuffing American and Western demands to respect human rights and thereby prevent "peaceful evolution" (*heping yanbian*) from having any impact on the country. Although Japan's moves to oppose isolation had been advantageous to China, these alone were not enough. Given that the Cold War had ended, international relations with the countries around China were anything but normal. Although it had normalized relations with the Soviet Union at the height of the Tiananmen incident, China did not have normal diplomatic relations at this time with the following six countries: Mongolia, South Korea, Vietnam, Indonesia, Singapore and Brunei.

With respect to Mongolia, during Gorbachev's visit to China in May 1989, the Soviet Union had promised to withdraw the troops it had stationed there, and China's relations with Mongolia subsequently began to improve. In July, a Chinese Communist Party delegation visited Ulan Bator, met with the Mongolian People's Revolutionary Party and restored party relations. In August and September, Foreign Minister Qian Qichen visited Mongolia, and in May 1990, Mongolia's Gombojavyn Ochirbat, general secretary of the People's Party, paid an official visit to China. The first visit to China by a Mongolian head of state in 28 years, it confirmed that relations between the two countries, which had deteriorated after the Chinese-Soviet split, were now fully restored.[1]

In Southeast Asia, relations between China and Indonesia had remained severed since 1967. The reason for the split was the widespread perception in Indonesia that China had provided behind-the-scenes support to the Indonesian Communist Party, which had backed an abortive coup d'état in 1965 called the September 30th Movement. Although the facts of the matter are still unclear, even so, that there had been a relationship of support between the Indonesian Communist Party and the Chinese Communist Party is not in doubt. As a result, President Suharto, who suppressed the September 30th Movement and subsequently took power, had an extremely strong mistrust of China. In addition, China adopted the view toward ethnic Chinese living in Indonesia that nationality was determined by the citizenship of one's parent/s, thus provoking the issue of dual citizenship. But as economic development in East Asia advanced, the lack of diplomatic relations became inexpedient for both countries. Because direct trade was essential, trade was recognized first in 1985. Movements toward normalizing political relations then began around 1988, and discussions officially started in February 1989, with the meeting of President Suharto and Foreign Minister Qian Qichen, who were both in Japan to attend Emperor Hirohito's funeral. When the Tiananmen Square incident occurred and the West stepped up its anti-Chinese policies, according to Qian Qichen's memoirs, Indonesia adopted a "wait and see" attitude.[2] At the Paris Conference on Cambodia in August, however, Qian met with Indonesian Foreign Minister Alatas, and they agreed to move ahead with normalization talks. China continued to adopt an active attitude. According to Qian Qichen,

> China considered Indonesia the leader of ASEAN, and believed that our resumption of diplomatic relations with Indonesia would lead the only ASEAN countries which did not have diplomatic ties with China—Singapore and Brunei—to establish relations quickly, thus improving our overall relations with ASEAN. Also, these moves would impede the "flexible diplomacy" advocated by the Taiwan authorities and weaken the sanctions against China imposed by Western countries.[3]

From Indonesia's perspective it was important to have China take a proactive stance on the Cambodian problem as well as on Indonesian domestic issues. And so, on July 1, 1990, Foreign Minister Alatas visited China and agreed to normalize diplomatic relations as of August 8. Although China did not make the apology that Indonesia had demanded for the September 30th Movement, it did promise not to support the Indonesian Communist Party, declaring that it would "not interfere in the other party's [i.e., Indonesia's] internal affairs." Nor would it insist on the principle of "dual nationality" for Indonesia's ethnic Chinese.[4]

From today's 21st-century perspective, it is difficult to imagine that no diplomatic relations existed between Singapore and China until 1990. With a territory around the area of Tokyo's 23 wards and a population of 5.5 million, Singapore is an Asian country with a per capita national income higher than Japan. Seventy-four percent of the population is of Chinese descent, and if you go to Singapore today, the same simplified Chinese characters that are found in mainland China are used on the street signs. No place in East Asia has stronger cultural ties to China than Singapore. Indeed, this very "Chineseness" was the major reason that there were no diplomatic relations between Singapore and China during the Cold War.[5] For a small country like Singapore, relations with its two neighbors, Indonesia and Malaysia, were vital for its security. Moreover, although citizens of Chinese descent were influential economically in both these neighbors, the majority of the citizenry in these two countries was of Malay descent. It was thus far from desirable for Singapore to be regarded as some sort of stalking horse for China. Another decisive factor was that, during the Cold War, China was under a Communist regime, and the governments of Malaysia and Indonesia were both anti-Communist. In the past, China had supported both the Indonesian Communist Party and the Malay Communist Party, and ever since the 1970s, there were those in both countries who strongly mistrusted the Chinese Communist Party's relationship with the Communist Parties of Southeast Asia. Under these circumstances, if Singapore were to establish diplomatic relations with China before Malaysia and Indonesia did, it could not help but be regarded as a base for a Communist revolution in Southeast Asia. Consequently, until those two countries had diplomatic relations with China, Singapore would not do so. Although Malaysia normalized relations with China in 1974, Singapore's Foreign Minister Sinnathamby Rajaratnam, who visited China right after that in 1975, told Zhou Enlai, "Because our neighbor Indonesia is extremely nervous about trends in Singapore, which has an overwhelmingly large Chinese population, we will establish relations with China after Indonesia has done so."[6]

Thus, when the normalization of relations between Indonesia and China was decided upon in the summer of 1990, Singapore immediately moved to normalize its own relations with China. When Prime Minister Li Peng, who had visited Indonesia for the normalization ceremonies, stopped over in Singapore, Prime Minister Lee Kuan Yew took advantage of the opportunity. "I told Li Peng that I wanted to solve the diplomatic relations issue with China before I stepped down as prime minister in November. Li Peng expressed his appreciation for the development of Chinese-Singapore relations during my long tenure, agreed to establish relations before I retired and invited me to visit Beijing in mid-October."[7]

In the case of Brunei, the sultanate gained its independence only in 1984. It has vast oil and natural gas reserves, and its people rank with Singapore in terms of wealth; politically, however, it is an Islamic state under the absolute authority of Sultan Bolkiah. After independence, President Li Xiannan sent a congratulatory telegram indicating China's willingness to recognize Brunei, but Brunei responded that it had no intention of having relations with a country ruled by the Communist Party.[8] Seeing that Singapore had now taken steps to normalize relations with China, however, it in turn did so. It established relations on September 30, a few days before Singapore would on October 3, 1990.

As was mentioned in the previous chapter, China also moved to improve relations with Vietnam. Talks continued after the leaders of the two countries made secret contact in Chengdu in September 1990, and in November 1991, two weeks after the Cambodian Peace Agreement was signed, the two countries agreed to normalize relations.

China and the Korean Peninsula

For China, the relationship with the Korean peninsula has always been an important strategic issue.[9] The Korean peninsula under the control of a strong hostile power has been something China would like to avoid at all costs. That was the reason Chinese leaders sent the People's Volunteer Army to fight against the Americans in the Korean War: they recognized that their vital interests were at stake. Consequently, after the Korean War, China maintained diplomatic relations only with North Korea and had hostile relations with the

South. This inflexible situation began to change with the introduction of China's openness and reform policy. Beginning first with indirect trade, economic ties deepened; China also sent a team to the Seoul Olympics in 1988.

Of the two countries, South Korea, through its efforts to promote *Nordpolitik*, was more proactive than China. The Roh Tae-woo administration devised a number of plans to improve relations through unofficial channels. The Chinese side responded cautiously because of its relationship with North Korea, but at the beginning of 1989, it went so far as to hold discussions about opening trade offices in each other's country. The movement to improve relations was subsequently stalled for a while as a result of the Tiananmen Square incident on June 4, but sometime around the end of 1989, the Chinese side once again began to explore relations with South Korea. The agreement between the two countries to establish mutual trading offices took place on October 20, 1990, following normalization of diplomatic relations between South Korea and the Soviet Union. And right afterward, China set up a trading office in the South. North Korea is not likely to have been happy about these activities. But China probably thought that it was only natural to improve relations with the South since the North had led the way to cross-recognition as a result of the Kanemaru visit, which also took place at more or less the same time as USSR-South Korean normalization. In any event, improving relations with near neighbors was all the more necessary for China, which was internationally isolated after Tiananmen Square.

The next problem to arise for China in its attempt to advance relations with South Korea was the issue of membership of the North and the South in the United Nations. Originally, the government of the Republic of Korea (South Korea) had been formed as the result of a general election carried out under a UN resolution, and from the outset South Korea had applied for membership in the UN as the sole government on the Korean peninsula. During the Cold War, however, the Soviet Union had used its veto power in the Security Council to shelve all the South's applications. In the early 1970s, the South changed its views on UN membership and proposed joint membership for both North and South Korea. But this, too, did not come to fruition. North Korea maintained that the North and South must be unified first under a federal system and then join the UN as a united country.

Now, however, the Soviet Union had brushed aside North Korea's objections and normalized relations with South Korea. Since the USSR no longer opposed joint UN membership for the North and the South, the focus shifted to how another member of the Security Council—China—would move. South Korea hoped that China would not block it from joining the UN. Although China publicly took the position that the issue of UN membership was for the North and the South to decide, when Li Peng visited North Korea in May 1991, he made it known that "if the ROK again proposed joining the UN during the Assembly that year, China would find it difficult to oppose this. Moreover, once the ROK became a member, it would be difficult for the DPRK to join the UN."[10] If the North accepted cross-recognition in principle, logically, joint admission to membership in the United Nations, too, should not be all that difficult a matter. What the North was afraid of at the time was that the South alone would join the UN, and the North would be left out in the cold. On this point, China assured them that this would not happen. Finally, on May 28, 1991, North Korea announced it would accept joint membership in the UN. As a result, at the UN General Assembly meeting in September 1991, the North and the South were jointly admitted as members of the United Nations.

Even after the North and South both had UN membership, a huge problem still remained—the North's development of nuclear weapons. As has already been discussed, both the North-South talks and the normalization negotiations between the North and Japan had reached an impasse because the North refused to accept IAEA inspections. If no progress were made in either North-South relations or Japanese-North Korean relations, the prospects for cross-recognition were not good. Though the South became more and more insistent, China found it difficult to move forward.

That does not mean, however, that the objections North Korea raised against these demands for nuclear inspections were totally without reason. That reason was the large quantities of American nuclear weapons in South Korea. During the Cold War, the United States had deployed a considerable number of tactical nuclear weapons in the South. But there had long been many doubts about the effectiveness of such weapons, and, in fact, the US had been reducing their deployment so that at the beginning of the Bush administration, the number of nuclear warheads in the South was said to be around a hundred.[11] Although the US adopted a "neither confirm nor deny" policy on nuclear deployment, North Korea's vehement arguments about the American nuclear threat were not unfounded.

What caused this situation to change was a US decision: on September 27, 1991, President Bush announced that the United States was withdrawing all its land- and sea-based tactical nuclear weapons from American bases around the world. Doing so, it was assumed, would nullify North Korea's reason for refusing nuclear inspections. In addition, the US decided to remove the tactical nuclear weapons on its aircraft carriers deployed in South Korea and even allowed North Korea to inspect American bases in the South.

These moves by the United States caused the stalled North-South relations to move ahead. During October 23–25, 1991, the fourth round of North-South summit talks were held in Pyongyang, and the fifth was held December 11–13 in Seoul. On December 13, both sides signed an "Agreement on Reconciliation, Nonaggression, and Exchanges and Cooperation between South and North Korea." This was the most important agreement between the two sides since the North-South joint communiqué of July 4, 1972. In it both sides recognized "that their relationship, not being a relationship as between states, is a special one constituted temporarily in the process of unification" and agreed to "recognize and respect the system of each other . . . not interfere in the internal affairs of each other . . . not slander or defame each other . . . refrain from any acts of sabotage or insurrection against each other." They also agreed to "abide by the present Military Armistice Agreement . . . not use force . . . not undertake armed aggression against each other . . . carry out steps to build up military confidence and realize arms reduction . . . carry out exchanges . . . in various fields such as science and technology . . . literature and the arts . . . [and] permit free correspondence . . . and visits between dispersed family members."[12]

In addition, on December 18, after the removal of nuclear weapons from South Korea, President Roh Tae-woo announced, "As I speak, there do not exist any nuclear weapons whatsoever, anywhere in the Republic of Korea."[13] After this announcement, North-South negotiations on the nuclear issue were held at Panmunjom on December 26, and in a positive move, the North declared its intention to sign the inspection agreement with the IAEA at an early date. As a result, on December 31, both sides agreed to a Joint Declaration on the Denuclearization of the Korean Peninsula. The North and South promised "not to test, manufacture, produce, receive, possess, store, deploy or use nuclear weapons" (this agreement was officially signed on January 20, 1992).[14] In the course of these negotiations, the South Korean side promised not to engage in joint US-South Korean military exercises (Team Spirit) in 1992 in return for inspections of North Korea's nuclear facilities at Yongbyon. President Bush visited Seoul early in the New Year and, at a meeting with President Roh, said he was "prepared to forgo the Team Spirit exercise for this year . . . if North Korea fulfills its obligation and takes steps to implement the inspection agreements."[15] On January 30, North Korea signed the nuclear inspection agreement with the IAEA.

Chinese-South Korean Diplomatic Normalization

Unlike the Soviet Union, which entered into normalizing diplomatic relations with South Korea with hardly even a backward glance at North Korea, China undoubtedly had some concern for the North.[16] The Soviet Union was trying to make a break with the past and open up a new era; by contrast, it may have seemed to China, who thought becoming like the USSR and Eastern Europe would be disastrous, that North Korea, as now one of the few remaining socialist states, was sharing its own fate. Thus, in November 1989, when Kim Il Sung visited China, Deng Xiaoping himself went to North Beijing Station to meet him. And, on March 14, 1990, before mutually establishing trade offices with South Korea, General Secretary Jiang Zemin, who had become the top leader of the Chinese Communist Party after the Tiananmen Square incident, paid a visit to Pyongyang. Jiang let Kim Il Sung know that at this stage they were about to set up mutual trade offices with South Korea and told him, "It will probably be difficult to put off this matter much longer."[17] On October 4, 1991, after the North and South jointly became members of the UN, Kim Il Sung visited China and urged the Chinese not to be too hasty in normalizing relations with the South.[18] On their part, the Chinese leaders persuaded him to resolve the nuclear inspections issue in light of President Bush's decision at the end of September to withdraw tactical nuclear weapons.

With an eye on developments in the nuclear question and North-South relations, China moved slowly toward normalizing diplomatic relations with South Korea. As was discussed in Chapter 4, the issue of Chinese participation in APEC became an important theme heading into the APEC Ministerial Meeting to be held in Seoul in November 1991. As the host country, South Korea worked hard to let China, Taiwan and Hong Kong join APEC. Seizing the opportunity right after obtaining UN membership, South Korea brought about a meeting between China's Foreign Minister Qian Qichen and its own Foreign Minister Lee Sang-ock. And despite the fact that there were no diplomatic relations, Qian Qichen visited South Korea for the APEC Ministerial Meeting in November. The mass media in Seoul made a great to-do about the first visit to South Korea by a Chinese foreign minister, but at this stage Qian Qichen still made no reference to the possibility of diplomatic normalization.

It would not be until Lee Sang-ock's visit to China to attend the general meeting of ESCAP (the UN's Economic and Social Commission for Asia and the Pacific), held in Beijing the following April, that the Chinese side took the decisive step. At this meeting, Qian told Lee that they would like to enter into secret negotiations over normalization. China was probably moving ahead with relations with South Korea on the basis of the fact that progress had been made in North-South relations at the end of 1991 and the North had signed the nuclear inspections agreement with the IAEA. Preliminary meetings were subsequently held three times, and a joint communiqué on normalization was substantially agreed upon on July 29 and officially signed on August 24. During the period from the opening of secret talks until the agreement on the joint communiqué, important persons from China were also visiting North Korea. At roughly the same time as the ESCAP meeting, April 13–17, Yang Shangkun, president of the People's Republic of China, visited the DPRK. Ding Guangen, a member of the Politburo, visited in May, and Yang Baibing, secretary-general of the Central Military Commission, in June. On July 15, just before Chinese-South Korean normalization, Qian Qichen himself came. The role of Qian, who flew to Pyongyang in an air-force plane, was to notify the North that China was normalizing its relations with the South, the same role that Shevardnadze had once had. According to Qian's memoirs, "President Kim thought for a moment before he said that he had caught every word of my message. . . . In my memory, this meeting was the shortest of all the meetings President Kim Il Sung had had with a Chinese delegation. After the meeting, the DPRK did not give a banquet in our honor, contrary to what it had always done in the past."[19] The meeting must have been as cold as ice.

For China, this was a policy that would shock its sworn friend and ally North Korea. The first reason for it was, as has already been mentioned, to escape isolation after the Tiananmen Square incident. The second was to stabilize relations with the newly emerging industrial economy of South Korea in order to further its own openness and reform policies. In addition to these reasons, however, were we to cite one more motive, it would be the relationship with Taiwan. For a long time, Beijing and Taipei had each adopted the policy of severing ties with any country that had relations with the other. But, in November 1988, Taiwan changed this policy and began to approach other countries in the name of "flexible diplomacy." The Tiananmen incident in June 1989 had been advantageous for Taiwan, which was moving ahead with democratization. As a result, Taiwan established relations with Grenada, Belize and Liberia in the latter half of 1989; Lesotho, Guinea Bissau and Nicaragua in early 1990; and Central Africa in 1991. Considering that since 1971, the number of countries with diplomatic relations with Taiwan had been steadily declining, this was a sudden burst of movement toward expanded relations. Countries that had diplomatic relations with Taiwan had increased from 23 just before the Tiananmen incident to 29 at the end of 1991.

Sensing the threat from Taiwan's diplomatic initiatives, China reacted. The above-mentioned normalization of relations with Indonesia, Singapore and Brunei was partly a response to these Taiwanese moves. When China normalized relations with Saudi Arabia in July 1990, the Saudis severed their ties with Taiwan. When the three Baltic countries declared their independence from the Soviet Union after the abortive coup d'état in Russia in August 1991, China recognized their independence right away to prevent Taiwan from doing so, and established relations with all three of them in mid-September.[20] Early in 1992, Taiwan's diplomatic offensive was still making progress. In January, Taiwan established consular relations with Latvia, and in the spring, it became clear that talks were progressing with Niger.

This competition with Taiwan over the establishment of diplomatic relations was also behind the accelerated pace of China's negotiations with South Korea around this time. Although those relations themselves were important, just as important was the severing of South Korean-Taiwanese ties that would occur as a result. There would then no longer be any country in Asia that had diplomatic relations with Taiwan. In order to convince an unhappy North Korea, the Chinese authorities are reported as saying, "We need your help, because China has to respond to Taiwan's gaining recognition abroad."[21] This statement does not entirely seem to have been made merely as a face-saving measure on North Korea's behalf.

It should also be added that, from China's perspective, if normalization with South Korea might give the North a shock, the Chinese did not judge it to be a fatal one. As has already been noted, in contrast to the USSR, China carried out its rapprochement with South Korea in stages. It can also be seen to have kept pace with progress in North-South relations. As a result of the Agreement on Reconciliation, Nonaggression, and Exchanges and Cooperation between South and North Korea and the Joint Declaration on the Denuclearization of the Korean Peninsula, it probably seemed to China that there was no fear that normalizing relations with the South would destabilize the situation on the Korean peninsula. At the time, the chances were still good that the US and Japan would both normalize relations with the North. As long as the trend toward cross-recognition continued, China presumably thought that its rapprochement with South Korea would not cause any problems.[22]

It was not only North Korea that was shocked by the normalization of Chinese-South Korean relations. As a bastion of anti-Communism along with South Korea, Taiwan had a relationship with the South that could be described as one of kindred spirits on the front lines of the Cold War. It has become clear in recent years that, during the Korean War, Nationalist China sent more than 1,500 special forces and psychological warfare personnel to fight on the South Korean side.[23] But South Korea not only officially severed its ties with Taiwan as a result of normalization with China; it also made their relations much worse both substantively and psychologically. It had given Taiwan the impression that it was not going to cut its ties when it normalized relations with China, but, in fact, did so. In addition, it made the announcement only three days before those relations were to be established. It also caused problems by handing over Taiwanese assets to China. As a result, working-level relations between Taiwan and South Korea became very strained compared to what had happened when Japan normalized relations with China. In fact, for more than a decade after normalization, Taiwan refused to allow Korean Air Lines to fly to Taiwan.[24]

It should be added, however, that during the first phase of the normalization talks, China had asked South Korea to recognize that "Taiwan is an inalienable part" of China. In the joint communiqué that was ultimately agreed upon, South Korea stated that it "respects the Chinese position that . . . Taiwan is a part of China." The wording was similar to Japan's at the time that Japan and China normalized relations. There is still no accepted explanation as to why the wording ended up this way, but one plausible hypothesis is that it may have been a trade-off for not including in the joint statement the apology that South Korea sought from China for its participation in the Korean War.[25] During the negotiating process, the South Korean side raised the question of China's part in the Korean War and demanded that it state in the joint communiqué that such a thing would never occur again. In other words, it was a demand to include a reference to an "understanding of history" problem. China opposed this on the grounds that the issue raised was irrelevant to diplomatic normalization. As a result, South Korea withdrew its demand. On the other hand, the statement about Taiwan did not go the way that China demanded, and this theory suggests that there may have been some sort of relation between the two.

The Emperor's Visit to China

Having established relations with South Korea, in order to further improve the international environment, China also invited the Emperor of Japan to visit. The first to make such a request was Foreign Minister Qian Qichen while on a trip to Japan in June 1991.[26] He made the same request when Prime Minister Kaifu Toshiki visited China that August. A more formal invitation was made to Foreign Minister Watanabe Michio when he was in China in January 3–6, 1992. At this time, a visit to Japan by General Secretary Jiang Zemin had been agreed upon, and as a follow-up, Qian

Qichen invited the Emperor to China and specified the time, saying, "We would welcome a visit by Their Majesties this autumn on the occasion of the 20th anniversary of diplomatic normalization." Prime Minister Li Peng, too, told him, "We will ensure that Their Majesties, the Emperor and Empress, receive an enthusiastic welcome from the Chinese people and the Chinese government during their visit to China." Foreign Minister Watanabe replied positively to this request, saying he would "seriously consider" it. According to later reports, he had, in fact, promised at that time that the Emperor would visit, and the dates of October 22–27 had been proposed.[27]

Although Foreign Minister Watanabe had been positive about the Emperor's visit to China, arguments against it urging caution began to be heard within the LDP. Behind them was the realization that as a result of the Emperor's visit, discussions about responsibility for World War II might potentially arise in China in connection with the issue of Koreans who served as "comfort women" for Japanese soldiers, which was then becoming a problem in South Korea. As someone pointed out, "There is a concern that the Emperor will become involved in politics."[28]

Just around this time, on February 25, the Standing Committee of the National People's Congress adopted and enacted the Law of the People's Republic of China on the Territorial Sea and the Contiguous Zone. In it, the Senkaku Islands, to which Japan claimed territorial rights and which it effectively controlled, were named as Chinese territory along with Taiwan and the Spratly Islands. On the 26th, Saitō Masaki, the minister in charge of Political Affairs at the Japanese embassy in Beijing, delivered a verbal protest to the Chinese foreign ministry, saying "The Senkaku Islands both historically and under international law are unquestionably Japanese territory. The present measure is regrettable, and we demand that it be rectified." In Tokyo, as well, Owada Hisashi, the vice-minister for Foreign Affairs, protested to the Chinese ambassador to Japan, Yang Zhenya, "The Senkaku Islands are our country's inalienable territory, and we effectively control them. China's actions are extremely regrettable, and we demand that they be rectified."[29]

When the question was raised at a Chinese foreign ministry press conference held in Beijing on the 27th as to why, some 20 years after normalization, the Diaoyu (Senkaku) Islands had been included in the Law on the Territorial Sea, the foreign ministry spokesman replied, "A great amount of historical facts has proved the Diaoyu Islands belong to China. China's claim is also indisputable under international law. Consequently, the fact that China has reaffirmed its position in the Law on the Territorial Sea is irreproachable."[30]

China's announcement of the new maritime law had stirred up a backlash within the LDP and elsewhere. There was even speculation that an anti-Japanese offensive might be behind it. But subsequent statements by officials at China's Ministry of Foreign Affairs tried to somehow calm the matter down. On March 16, at a Sino-Japanese working-level consultation in Beijing, Vice Foreign Minister Xu Dunxin explained that "the present measure is part of a long-term consolidation of our laws. It is not a measure against any particular country, and we shall not take any new opportunity to promote this matter or attempt to adopt any new measures. In short, there is no change in our existing position; we do not want this to have an adverse effect on Chinese-Japanese relations."[31] Needless to say, the "existing position" had been stated by then Vice-Premier Deng Xiaoping on a visit to Japan in 1978, when he said, "I think that it is all right to shelve these issues for this moment."[32]

As to why the Senkaku/Diaoyu Islands were specifically cited in the Law on the Territorial Sea, there are reports of a split within China. According to these reports, the foreign ministry's Department of Treaties and Laws among others was opposed to naming them out of concern that if they were explicitly mentioned, it would provoke a reaction from Japan and worsen Sino-Japanese relations. As in the case of the Statement on the Territorial Sea in 1958, they argued that the phrase "Taiwan and the surrounding islands" would be sufficient. On the other side, the department in charge of the military's legal system and others insisted that the situation be spelled out plainly without any ambiguity as "Taiwan and its associated islands, including 'Diaoyu Islands.'" Ultimately, the hardliners got their way, and the "Diaoyu Islands" were explicitly mentioned.[33] In any event, there can be no doubt that this Law on the Territorial Sea strengthened arguments within Japan for caution about the Emperor's visit to China.

What strengthened these arguments even further was a movement occurring in China demanding reparations for war damages.

Some of the members of, and delegates to, the National People's Congress and the Political Consultative Conference were calling for the Japanese government to pay compensation for civilian losses. It was reported that a bill was going to be presented to the National People's Congress asking for USD 180 billion (nearly 23.8 trillion yen) in war reparations for Japan's invasion of China. On this matter as well, the Chinese government confirmed its existing position. On March 23, Foreign Minister Qian Qichen told a press conference, "The Chinese government has not altered its position on the question of war reparations, as clearly stated in the joint China-Japan communiqué of 1972 [in which the government renounced its demand for such claims]." But if the delegates to the National People's Congress call for civil compensation, they "have the right to table bills. The Congress secretariat is responsible for such proposals and will handle them in accordance with the relevant provisions and regulations," he said, indicating that he had no intention of trying to stop them.[34]

On April 6, General Secretary of the Chinese Communist Party Jiang Zemin visited Japan. It was the first visit to Japan by a head of the Chinese Communist Party since Tiananmen Square. At a meeting that day with Prime Minister Miyazawa, Jiang said, "The Chinese people sincerely wish to welcome the Emperor to China this year," repeating the request for an imperial visit. To this Prime Minister Miyazawa responded, "The government currently is seriously studying the matter. If the visit takes place to mark the 20th anniversary of China-Japan normalization, it would be extremely significant for the future development of friendly relations between the people of our two countries. We will continue to explore it seriously." On the 7th, Jiang met with the Emperor and extended the invitation to him directly. "China is looking forward to being able to welcome both Your Majesties to our country this fall."[35]

According to subsequent reports, Miyazawa told Jiang, "I will do my best to comply with China's wishes, but please give me a bit more time."[36] In order not to stir up opposition to the visit within Japan, however, the term he used in his statement was not "do my best" but "seriously study." In fact, as if to back up his concerns, the arguments for caution in regard to the imperial visit were intensifying within the LDP. At General Council meetings held three times on April 15, 16 and 21, some raised the possibility that the Emperor would be used for political purposes; others thought that the Emperor's first visit ought to be to South Korea rather than to China, where the political system was different.

The Chinese side may have decided that it was inadvisable to needlessly provoke such arguments in Japan. When Wan Li, the chairman of the Standing Committee of the National People's Congress arrived in Japan on May 25, he did not refer to the Emperor's visit during his meetings with the Japanese side.

China also demonstrated its consideration for the Japanese side in another area. Reactions to the PKO bill had become an major issue in Japan during May and June. The tone of Chinese statements on the subject had been roughly the same since 1991: it is a "delicate matter" and "we hope they will exercise caution." At the time of his visit in April, General Secretary Jiang Zemin, responding to Prime Minister Miyazawa who asked for China's understanding on the PKO bill, said, "The dispatch of Japanese military troops overseas is a very delicate issue. As a friend, China hopes that Japan will exercise utmost discretion" on this issue. He gave no response beyond this, however, although he also stated that he could "understand their use for disaster assistance."[37] In any event, at the time the PKO bill was in its final stages, without changing the tone it had used up to that point, China took an extremely restrained attitude. The statement of foreign ministry spokesman Wu Jianmin, at a regularly scheduled news conference on June 11, repeated the existing position. "Due to historical reasons, Japan's sending troops abroad is a very sensitive issue. The Chinese side has always hoped the Japanese government will act with prudence on this matter."[38]

Once the PKO law was passed and enacted, Prime Minister Miyazawa began to move toward a decision on the Emperor's visit. On June 17, on the matter of the imperial visit, he stated, "I think it is desirable for His Majesty to go there. We are now in a cooling-off period, so, while explaining the situation in China, we would like him to visit with the people's blessing." As to the "the cooling-off period," he did "not at all think" that it would "extend into next year" and expressed his hope that the visit would take place in the fall.[39]

Voices of opposition and discontent immediately arose from within the LDP in response to this statement, but after repeated attempts to persuade them, by mid-July, the secretary-general of the

LDP adopted the position that he would entrust the matter of the visit to the prime minister's judgment.

At this time, the Chinese side still seems to have been taking the utmost care not to provoke Japan. At a regularly scheduled press conference on July 16, a foreign ministry spokesman responded to the question, "If the Emperor of Japan visits China, will the Chinese government raise the issue of compensation for comfort women?" by saying, "We have made our views on the comfort women issue plain to the Japanese side through diplomatic channels and have asked them to deal with the matter seriously and appropriately. The Emperor's visit is a separate issue."[40] On the other hand, Prime Minister Miyazawa also avoided stirring up China, announcing on July 17 that he would not pay an official visit to the Yasukuni Shrine on August 15. When the LDP won a House of Councillors' election on July 26, Prime Minister Miyazawa personally began efforts to persuade party power brokers Nakasone, Kanemaru, Fukuda and others and also tried to convince senior LDP advisers at an informal discussion group on August 5. To counteract him, the side urging caution repeated their arguments in various venues. For that reason, Miyazawa, who had at first planned to get cabinet approval for the Emperor's visit on August 11, put off doing so. Perhaps out of consideration for those urging caution, on August 9, he made it clear that he would make a personal visit to the Yasukuni Shrine in the future. Having made these efforts, on August 10, he decided that the Emperor's visit would take place beginning October 22. After showing his concern for public opinion by holding meetings to hear the opinions of powerful men in the private sector both for and against the visit, he obtained cabinet approval for the Emperor's visit on August 25. In the official decision, however, the date was not October 22 as had been first announced, but had been changed to October 23. In China, the foreign ministry spokesman matter-of-factly announced the Emperor's visit and stated, "We believe that, through the joint efforts of both sides, this visit will be a complete success."[41]

Within Japan, debate continued as to what sort of statement the Emperor should make during his visit regarding the problems of the past; China took the position that that was for Japan to decide. During September and October, activities commemorating the 20th anniversary of Japan-China normalization were held one after another. During this period, statements that might be construed as critical of Japan were scarcely to be found in China. According to some reports, the Chinese leaders issued strict orders to public security agencies, news media and other relevant domestic organizations not under any circumstances to allow demonstrations, petitions or any other anti-Japanese statements or activities.[42]

On October 23, President Yang Shangkun said to the Emperor, "In modern history, Chinese-Japanese relations went through an unfortunate period, which brought untold suffering to the Chinese people. The past experience, if not forgotten, can serve as a good guide for the future. We agree that it is in the basic interest of the people of both countries to make clear the lessons of history."[43]

In response, the Emperor said, "In the long history of the relationship between our two countries, there was an unfortunate period in which my country inflicted great sufferings on the people of China. I deeply deplore this. When the war came to an end, the Japanese people, believing with a sense of deep reproach that such a war should never be repeated, firmly resolved to go the way of a peace-loving nation and deal with the reconstruction of our country."[44] Wu Jinan, head of the Japan Research Institute of the Shanghai Institute of International Studies, is reported to have rated the Emperor's speech positively, saying, "It frankly recognized that Japan 'inflicted great sufferings' on China in the past and, in so doing, made a clear distinction between victims and perpetrators.... I think it was a lucid statement."[45]

The Emperor's party subsequently left Beijing for Xian and Shanghai and returned to Japan on October 28.

Becoming a Great Power

From Deng Xiaoping's perspective, 1992, the year China established relations with South Korea and welcomed the Emperor of Japan, was the opportunity for China to recover from the harsh blow of the Tiananmen Square incident. Domestically, Deng once again raised the rallying cry of openness and reform. In January and February 1992, he visited Wuchang in Hubei Province, the special economic zones of Shenzhen and Zhuhai in Guangdong Province, and Shanghai, and issued the following manifestos:

We should be bolder than before in conducting reform and opening to the outside and have the courage to experiment. We must not act like women with bound feet. Once we are sure that something should be done, we should dare to experiment and break a new path. That is the important lesson to be learned from Shenzhen. If we don't have the pioneering spirit, if we're afraid to take risks, if we have no energy and drive, we cannot break a new path, a good path, or accomplish anything new. . . . [46]

There is nothing to worry about so long as we stress efficiency and quality and develop an export-oriented economy. Slow growth equals stagnation and even retrogression. We must grasp opportunities; the present offers an excellent one. The only thing I worry about is that we may lose opportunities. If we don't seize them, they will slip through our fingers as time speeds by.[47]

These speeches by Deng Xiaoping later came to be called the "Southern Tour Talks." They were a risk even for Deng, who had a formidable power base. There were still many conservatives who feared that turning China into a market economy would undermine Communist Party control. But Deng, who had not hesitated to suppress dissidents in Tiananmen Square, said let's boldly engage in openness and reform. The majority of the Chinese people thought that they could act boldly—as long as they confined themselves to the economy.

In fact, just a glance at the economic growth rate shows that in 1991, it was 8.2 percent and in 1992, 13.4, as compared to 4.4 and 4.1 percent in 1989 and 1990 respectively. The publication of World Bank and International Monetary Fund statistics for China's gross domestic product, calculated in terms of purchasing power parity (PPP), also had a great impact. The World Bank's statistics estimated that the Chinese GDP in PPP terms was close to USD 2 trillion. Since the GDP of China on an exchange rate basis was a bit less than USD 400 billion, the PPP estimate was actually five times larger. Multiply the PPP estimate by the economic growth rate, and it was even projected that China would become the world's largest economic power by the beginning of the 21st century; its economic strength would outstrip not only Japan's but even that of the United States.[48]

Not only was there talk of China's resurgence as a superpower; people also began to speak about the Chinese "threat."[49] Behind such talk was the expansion of Chinese military spending. National defense expenditures published by the government showed a nearly 15 percent annual increase since 1989. Since the perception was widespread that the government for-the-record spending did not reflect the true state of China's military strength, this actually made the published figures all the more significant. In other words, if the published figures only showed an increase of 15 percent, it raised concerns about how much the real military spending had risen. What is more, China showed a desire to purchase Soviet-made weapons being sold all at once at bargain-sale prices now that the Cold War had ended. Around 1992, rumors were rife that China was going to buy an aircraft carrier.[50] That same year, it bought 27 Sukhoi fighter jets from the USSR.

Actions by the Chinese government and statements by its naval personnel also attracted attention. As has already been noted, the Spratly and Senkaku Islands had been designated as Chinese territory in the Law of the People's Republic of China on the Territorial Sea and the Contiguous Zone promulgated in February 1992. Moreover, the importance of a navy and air force appeared frequently in statements and articles by military personnel. In the Chinese constitution, which was partially revised in 1993, "wealth and strength" (*fuqiang*) were cited as a national goal. For the Chinese people, who were aware that the history of the past 150 years had been one of repeated invasions by the Western powers and Japan, building a China that was wealthy and strong may not have been all that strange, but from the perspective of China's neighbors, that very goal was regarded as a sign of Chinese ambitions.

Nuclear Crisis on the Korean Peninsula

In the summer of 1992, when China normalized relations with South Korea, many people concluded that the situation on the Korean peninsula was, for the most part, heading in a healthy direction. At the end of 1991, the North and the South had accepted the Agreement on Reconciliation, Nonaggression, and Exchanges and Cooperation and the Joint Declaration on the Denuclearization of the Korean

Peninsula, and on January 30, the North and the IAEA signed the Safeguards Agreement. On April 8, the Supreme People's Assembly ratified the agreement, and on April 10, it took effect.

Given the situation within North Korea, however, these movements toward stabilization did not necessarily allow for optimism. The North Korean economy was now on the verge of bankruptcy. As mentioned earlier, during the Cold War, the North Korean economy had functioned on the premise that aid from China and the Soviet Union could be taken for granted. In the 1980s, the overwhelming majority of the North's industrial infrastructure—60 percent of its electric power, 30 percent of its steel, etc.—had been built with Soviet aid.[51] In addition, North Korea, which did not produce crude oil, was almost totally dependent on China and the USSR for its crude oil supply. During the 1980s, it annually imported 500,000 to a million tons from the Soviet Union and a million to 1.5 million tons from China.[52] North Korea relied on China and the Soviet Union for energy as well as other assistance in general. What is more, although they were all in the same camp during the Cold War, because of the China-Soviet split, it was effective for North Korea to play China and the USSR off against each other and gain favorable conditions for paying back its loans, etc. Moreover, energy was sold at a "friendship price," and it did not have to be paid in hard currency.

This all changed with the normalization of Chinese-Soviet relations, which occurred around the time the Cold War ended. Between 1990 and 1991, both China and the USSR demanded payment not through barter transactions but in hard cash. As a result, trade with the Soviet Union plummeted, and it also contracted with China. In 1991–92, North Korea was forced to reduce its oil consumption by between a quarter to a third.[53] According to Bank of Korea estimates, North Korea's GDP had had negative growth since 1990.

If there were any way to rescue North Korea from this economic dilemma, it was via the cross-recognition that China had hopes for, i.e., improved relations with the United States and Japan, and the precondition for this was to dispel suspicions about the North's nuclear ambitions. In mid-May 1992, a group led by Hans Blix, director-general of the IAEA, inspected North Korea's nuclear-related facilities. Then, from May 25 to June 5, an IAEA inspection team conducted inspections in the North. The IAEA subsequently carried out inspections in July and September, but conversely the results only raised more doubts. The analysis of a small amount of plutonium that the inspection team had acquired contradicted the North's claims that it had separated plutonium only once in 1990. It became clear that the plutonium separation process had likely been carried out three times in 1989, 1990 and 1991. Other doubts were raised as well.[54]

In January 1992, epoch-making direct talks between the United States and North Korea were held in New York. The representative on the US side, Under Secretary of State Arnold Kanter, demanded of Secretary Kim Yong Sun of the Korean Workers' Party that North Korea observe the International Safeguards Agreement; not export missiles; destroy any chemical and biological weapons; promote dialogue and reconciliation with the South; not engage in terrorist activities; and cooperate in searching for and returning the bodies of US soldiers who had died during the Korean War.[55] In return, Kim Yong Sun asked the US to promise that talks between the US and the North would continue. The US side responded that the results of the present round would not be put into writing and, without promising future talks, implied that if North Korea kept its promises, the future likelihood for such talks was good.[56] Since North Korea signed the Safeguards Agreement with the IAEA right afterwards on January 30, there was probably some significance to these US-North Korean contacts. But when the IAEA inspections conducted in the spring of 1992 raised further suspicions, US-North Korean relations came to a standstill.

The Japanese-North Korean talks had been suspended during 1991; early in 1992, the sixth round was held in Beijing between January 30 and February 1, and the seventh in May 13–15. During the seventh round, the North Korean side claimed that all the nuclear inspection issues had been resolved, but the Japanese side called upon the North to steadily implement the Joint Declaration and the Safeguards Agreement. This was precisely the time when China's normalization of its relations with South Korea was gaining momentum. As was previously discussed, Qian Qichen visited Pyongyang in July to tell the North that China was establishing relations with the South. Ambassador Nakahira Noboru, who was in charge of the

Japanese-North Korean negotiations on the Japanese side at the time, surmised the following:

> In August 1992, South Korea and China normalized relations. North Korea probably never imagined that China, its only supporter and friend, would enter into diplomatic relations with the South. I suspect it was then forced into the position of having to hastily reexamine its entire foreign policy, even shelving its normalization talks with Japan. As proof of this, the seventh Japanese-North Korean talks had been in May 1992, but despite our urgent requests, the eighth round was held six months later in November.[57]

And, at the eighth round in November, when the Japanese side raised the subject of "Lee Un Hae" (the name given by North Korea to Taguchi Yaeko, who had been kidnapped in 1978), the North Koreans unilaterally broke off the negotiations. Japanese-North Korean talks did not resume until the year 2000.

In the latter half of 1992, as suspicions raised by the IAEA's inspections deepened, there was a change of administrations in both the United States and South Korea. President Bush was defeated in the November election by the Democratic Party candidate Bill Clinton, and Kim Young-sam won the presidential election in South Korea that December. A number of important events were decided in the period of confusion resulting from these changes in government. One of these was the announcement at the beginning of October 1992 that the US and South Korea were preparing to hold the US-South Korean military exercises, Team Spirit, in 1993.[58] Behind this decision was the fact that the Roh Tae-woo administration, which had had hopes for North-South contacts, had become increasingly mistrustful of North Korea. The Joint Declaration on Denuclearization, which the North and South had agreed upon at the end of 1991, provided for mutual nuclear inspections to be carried out not by the IAEA, but by setting up a South-North Joint Nuclear Control Commission. In early 1992, however, North Korea rejected mutual inspections by the joint commission on the grounds that they constituted a double inspection on top of those by the IAEA.[59] It was discontent over this that led South Korea to resume Team Spirit. On October 31, President Roh said that as long as the threat from North Korea existed, he had no choice but to proceed with Team Spirit,[60] and President-elect Kim, who had won the December presidential election, announced that he would suspend Team Spirit only on the condition that the North accept mutual inspections.[61]

In response, North Korea warned that if Team Spirit resumed, it would halt all further contacts between the North and the South.[62] When Chinese-South Korean normalization came into effect in the summer of 1992, the Chinese side expected that North Korean talks with the US and Japan would move ahead. But, in fact, after the US-South Korean decision to resume Team Spirit, the North's relations with the US made no progress, North-South contacts also came to a halt, and Japanese-North Korean talks, too, hit a reef.

One other important event that took place in late 1992 was the new satellite photographs of the area in and around Yongbyon that the US handed over to the IAEA and that increased suspicions even further. On February 25, 1993, the IAEA Board of Governors examined the satellite photos that the American government had agreed to make public and reached the decision to ask for a "special inspection" of two facilities that had become the focus of suspicions. A special inspection is an inspection requested of a facility that the country concerned has not reported. On March 9, Team Spirit began. On the 12th, North Korea made public its response to the IAEA request; it was withdrawing from the Non-Proliferation Treaty, it announced. According to this announcement,

> The United States together with south [*sic*] Korea has resumed the "Team Spirit" joint military exercises, a nuclear war rehearsal, threatening the DPRK, and [has] instigated some officials of the IAEA Secretariat and certain member States to adopt an unjust "resolution" at the meeting of the IAEA Board of Governors on 25 February 1993 demanding us to open our military sites that have no relevance at all to the nuclear activities.

Because this was a violation of North Korean sovereignty, an interference in its internal affairs and "a strong-arm act designed to . . . strangle our socialist system," it declared that it was being forced "to withdraw from the Treaty on the Non-Proliferation of Nuclear Weapons (NPT)" in order to protect "its supreme interests."[63] The provision for withdrawal from the NPT (Article X) states as follows:

> Each Party shall in exercising its national sovereignty have the right to withdraw from the Treaty if it decides that extraordinary events, related to the subject matter of this Treaty, have jeopardized the supreme interests of its country. It shall give notice of such withdrawal to all other Parties to the Treaty and to the United Nations Security Council three months in advance. Such notice shall include a statement of the extraordinary events it regards as having jeopardized its supreme interests.

In short, the withdrawal would officially take effect on June 12, three months after the notice of withdrawal. Was there a way to get North Korea to retract the withdrawal before then? That was the task facing the international community. But neither the Clinton administration nor the Kim Young-sam administration, both of which had just come into office, had been able to put together a countermeasure.

The first to make a move was North Korea. Having pushed the situation to the brink, it unveiled a negotiating strategy that it would subsequently repeat over and over again to make its demands.[64] At the beginning of June, it sent a negotiating team to the United States, headed by First Vice-Minister of Foreign Affairs Kang Sok Ju, to carry on talks with Assistant Secretary of State Robert Gallucci. State Department official Kenneth Quinones, who had to achieve a breakthrough in talks that had almost immediately stalled, carried on lengthy discussions for three days with three North Korean delegates in a 42nd Street coffee shop in New York City. As a result of these coffee shop negotiations, official discussions were held just before the deadline, and an agreement was finally reached on June 11.[65] The US agreed to give North Korean security assurances and to continue official talks in exchange for North Korea's agreement to "defer" withdrawing from the NPT.

When the second round of US-North Korean talks began in July, North Korea asked the US to provide it with light-water reactors, and in return it would destroy its existing nuclear facilities. It was an astonishing request. A state suspected of being in violation of international law, instead of making an effort to dispel such suspicions, was saying that if international society had any doubts, since it would be destroying the cause of those doubts, in return they should supply it free of charge with something even more efficient. The focus of suspicions was the so-called graphite-moderated reactors that the North had developed. Although plutonium separation to make an atom bomb was easy with them, they were far inferior as a source of electric power supply. By contrast, separating plutonium to make a bomb was thought to be hard with a light-water reactor, but its electrical generating capacity was far greater than what North Korea presently had. In the sense of impeding the development of nuclear weapons, providing the North with light-water reactors had a certain logic to it, but it could not help but produce an enormous moral hazard. Unless the international community had the means of confirming that North Korea's nuclear-weapon-building capacity had been eradicated, this was a deal that benefited only North Korea.

After North Korea "deferred" its withdrawal from the NPT, 1993 passed without any major progress. In the summer of 1993, the IAEA was able to carry out limited inspections, but not the special inspection. North Korea demanded that the US call off Team Spirit, end economic sanctions and hold the third round of US-North Korean talks. These talks did not go as expected, and in the meantime the North-South dialogue also broke off. Kim Young-sam, who had become president in 1993, was annoyed. He voiced his dissatisfaction on various occasions about the US-North Korean talks, fearing that the South was being left out and believing it was his prerogative to decide whether Team Spirit went ahead or not.

The IAEA assessed what it should do based on its mandate and set February 21, 1994 as the date for the resumption of inspections of the nuclear facilities at Yongbyon. North Korea accepted IAEA inspections to a limited extent, refusing to allow measurements to be taken at a plutonium reprocessing facility, which the IAEA regarded as crucial. As a result, the IAEA pulled out its inspection team on March 15 without completing inspections and issued a statement that its suspicions had not been dispelled. And at a special meeting, the IAEA voted to refer the problem to the UN Security Council.[66] Immediately afterwards, the North Korean side made a statement that dramatically exposed the tensions on the Korean peninsula to the entire world. At a working-level meeting of the North and South at Panmunjon on

March 19, the head of the North Korean delegation Park Yong Su said, "Seoul is not far from here. If a war breaks out, it will be a sea of fire."[67]

On March 31, the UN Security Council issued a presidential statement urging the North to allow the completion of inspections, but the North refused. At the beginning of April, North Korea made a statement that again shocked the world. It announced that it would be replacing the nuclear fuel rods in its 5-megawatt experimental nuclear power reactor without IAEA supervision. IAEA Director Blix expressed concern that if the North went ahead with the replacement of the fuel rods as planned, it would be impossible to check whether the North had diverted them to military use in the past. What further heightened these fears was that if the estimated 8,000 fuel rods were removed and reprocessed, a considerable quantity of plutonium could be separated from them. In addition to previous suspicions, there were fears that North Korea would now proceed to full-scale possession of nuclear weapons. On May 8, the North, in fact, began extracting the nuclear fuel rods.

As the extraction continued, the view in Washington hardened that sanctions must be imposed in response. But if sanctions went into effect, judging from the North's "sea of fire" statement, the possibility was undeniable that a war might actually occur. In mid-May, the Secretary of Defense reported to President Clinton the estimated costs of a war on the Korean peninsula: "52,000 US military casualties, killed or wounded, and 490,000 South Korean military casualties in the first ninety days, plus an enormous number of North Korean and civilian lives, at a financial outlay exceeding $61 billion."[68] In mid-June, the Clinton administration was on the verge of taking the first step toward sanctions, which might give rise to the danger of such a war, as well as sending reinforcements to prepare for military action.

What prevented this crisis from turning into a full-scale war was the visit of former President Jimmy Carter to North Korea. North Korea had sent him an invitation much earlier. The US State Department had advised Carter that a visit to North Korea would be inappropriate, and up until then Carter had gone along with their advice. This time, however, he visited the North as a "private citizen" in the hopes of being of some use. Right around this time (the morning of June 16, Washington time), a meeting was being held at the White House to make the final decision on the North Korean nuclear weapons

Former President Carter and President Kim Il Sung (June 17, 1994).
Photo: Kyodo News

development issue. While they were discussing whether to adopt
sanctions or further expand and strengthen their military presence,
a telephone call came in that Kim Il Sung had made an agreement with
Carter to "freeze" his nuclear development plans. At first, the Clinton
administration had doubts about the meaning of the "freeze." It was
disconcerted by Carter's acting on his own initiative without prior
consultation and suspected that he was being taken in by the North.
A "freeze" didn't mean a "freeze" if the North were free to do whatever it pleased with the extracted fuel rods. It demanded confirmation
that this "freeze" meant that the North was not going to reprocess the
spent fuel rods that had already been taken out or load new ones in
the 5-megawatt reactor. Carter was angry at being asked for confirmation of these new conditions, but the North readily accepted Carter's
request for confirmation on these points. It, too, was probably not
eager to intensify the crisis any further.[69]

Chairman Kim Il Sung died in July 1994; that October, the
US-North Korean Agreed Framework went into effect, and the North
Korean nuclear development issue was for the moment settled. The
outline of the agreement is as follows:

- The US will organize an international consortium to cooperate in the project to replace the DPRK's graphite-moderated

reactors with light-water reactor power plants with a total generating capacity of approximately 2,000 megawatts by a target date of 2003. It will provide up to 500,000 tons of heavy oil annually to the DPRK while the light-water reactor project is being completed.

- The DPRK will freeze its graphite-moderated reactors until the light-water reactor project is complete, and during this period, the IAEA will be allowed to monitor this freeze. Once the light-water reactor project is completed, the DPRK will dismantle its graphite-moderated reactors and related facilities.
- The two sides will move toward full normalization of political and economic relations.
- The US will provide formal assurances to the DPRK against the threat or use of nuclear weapons by the US.
- The DPRK will consistently take steps to implement the North-South Joint Declaration on the Denuclearization of the Korean Peninsula.
- The DPRK will engage in North-South dialogue.
- Both sides will work together to strengthen the international nuclear non-proliferation regime. The DPRK will remain a party to the Treaty on the Non-Proliferation of Nuclear Weapons (NPT) and will allow implementation of its safeguards agreement under the Treaty.
- When a significant portion of the light-water reactor project is completed, but before delivery of key nuclear components, the DPRK will come into full compliance with its safeguards agreement with the IAEA, including special inspections.[70]

With this Geneva agreement, for the time being, the North's nuclear weapons development issue moved out of its critical phase, but from the Japanese perspective, the situation gave rise to an alarming lesson. Because Japanese domestic politics were in upheaval while this crisis was going on, few even in political circles had been completely aware of the seriousness of the North Korean problem. Just at the crucial moment, when one wrong move and, for the first time since the Korean War, war might break out on the Korean peninsula, the Hata administration had been formed after Prime Minister Hosokawa resigned, and it would spend all its time dealing with frictions within the ruling coalition. At the time, Tanaka Hitoshi, director of the Policy Coordination Division of the Foreign Policy Bureau in the Ministry of Foreign Affairs, wrote an article for the *Gaikō Fōramu* (Journal of Japanese perspectives on diplomacy).

> It is definitely not easy for Japan to deal with issues on the Korean peninsula. For its own unique reasons, Japan probably cannot help but make agonizing decisions in any number of situations. What must be clearly understood, however, is that all these problems have to do with Japan's own national security and that Japan must uncomplainingly accept the results of the choices that it makes. If North Korea reaches the point of possessing nuclear weapons, Japan will be directly threatened by them. If chaos occurs on the Korean peninsula, it will inevitably spill over into Japan. In an emergency on the Korean peninsula, Japan must rely heavily on the US for its security, but if Japan cannot maintain an adequate cooperative alliance with the US, won't the US wonder whether Japan is a country worth protecting?[71]

Looking back on this time ten years later in a conversation with Tahara Sōichirō, a prominent journalist, Tanaka was even more forthright.

> TANAKA Deputy Chief Cabinet Secretary Ishihara [Nobuo] had a simulation done as to what would happen if North Korea invaded Seoul. In this simulation, when they checked to see how much preparation Japan had made. . . .
>
> TAHARA They hadn't actually made any?
>
> TANAKA Exactly. That was totally exposed.
>
> Where would the hundreds of American fighter jets flown in from the US mainland to protect South Korea and Japan be based? Who would protect Japan's nuclear power generators, which might be a possible target of attack? Would the police force be enough? Could the Self-Defense Forces be mobilized? Then, since it was assumed there would be hundreds of thousands of refugees swarming in, the job of screening them would be needed to check whether there were any spies among them.

But who would do such a job and what procedures should they follow? These sorts of questions had never been asked before.[72]

In the end, the situation did not take a turn for the worst, and the Murayama Cabinet emerged out of a coalition between the LDP and the Japan Socialist Party. Murayama Tomiichi, head of the Socialist Party, did a complete about-face on what had been the Socialist Party platform up until then, supporting the constitutionality of the Self-Defense Forces and accepting the US-Japan Security Treaty. With the head of the Socialist Party in power, these fundamental constitutional issues hovering over postwar Japan dissolved politically. But those in the Ministry of Foreign Affairs and the Defense Agency (as well as those in the US military negotiating with Japan) had become painfully aware of the inadequacy of the Japanese security system should a crisis occur in Japan's neighborhood. The 1994 Korean peninsula crisis became a strong incentive to reexamine US-Japan guidelines and draw up the Act Concerning the Measures for Peace and Safety of Japan in Situations in Areas Surrounding Japan (1999).

Chapter 6

The "History" Flare-up and Strains in Japan-China Relations

History Issues

In Japan's relations with Asia, the problem of "history" is inescapable. Japanese colonization of the Korean peninsula and Taiwan, its invasion of China in the 1930s, its occupation of countries in Southeast Asia during World War II—these are all indisputable facts. And, for that reason, virtually all of Japan's foreign relations right after the war involved diplomacy as part of a postwar normalization process. Moreover, given the fact of a right-wing/left-wing split on views of history within Japan itself, these problems were also prominent domestic issues that had to do with the very identity of the Japanese people.

It was in the 1980s, however, that "history" began to emerge frequently as a diplomatic issue in international relations, and it evolved into an even greater problem from the 1990s into the 21st century. The issue of perceptions of history had, of course, been raised at the time of both the Treaty on Basic Relations between Japan and South Korea in 1965 and Japanese-Chinese diplomatic normalization in 1972. There had also been instances such as Zhou Enlai's forceful protest when Prime Minister Tanaka Kakuei apologized for the "*meiwaku*" (*mafan* in the Chinese translation, meaning close to "bother") Japan had caused.[1] Long after the texts of the peace treaty and diplomatic normalization were agreed on, however, "history" has increasingly flared up as a diplomatic issue.

Perhaps once the Cold War was over and peace grew more normal, demands became stronger to rectify past wrongs. When national security issues arising from geopolitical conflicts are serious, it makes it quite difficult, at least among friendly countries, to raise past problems. On the other hand, the advance of democratization in Asian countries and the increasing diversification and liberalization of their societies may have given rise to opportunities for individuals who had suffered in the past to try to right those wrongs. It is only natural that people who had been forced to keep their mouths shut under authoritarian regimes would want to bring up these issues as democratization made headway. The aging of the victims themselves was probably also a factor in raising history-related problems.

The first major problem in the perception-of-history issue was the "textbook controversy" in the summer of 1982.[2] In late June, several newspapers in Japan reported that during the screening of high-school textbooks for that academic year, the wording in the section on modern history was being changed from "invasion" to "advance";[3] on the basis of this report, the South Korean media demanded that the government protest to Japan. Some three weeks later, China also started charging Japan of "falsifying" history, and the Chinese foreign ministry issued a formal protest to the Japanese Embassy on July 26. During the following weeks, the *People's Daily* and other Chinese media carried stories critical of Japan almost every day. Perplexed by the extraordinarily strong criticism from China, which Japan had not experienced since the normalization of relations in 1972, and having already reached an agreement with China on the visit of Prime Minister Suzuki to Beijing in September, the Japanese government decided to adopt a conciliatory attitude toward its neighbors by expressing its views in a statement by the chief cabinet secretary on August 26.

1. The Japanese Government and the Japanese people are deeply aware of the fact that acts by our country in the past caused tremendous suffering and damage to the peoples of Asian countries, including the Republic of Korea (ROK) and China, and have followed the path of a pacifist state with remorse and determination that such acts must never be repeated. Japan has recognized, in the Japan-ROK Joint Communique of 1965, that the "past relations are regrettable, and Japan feels deep remorse," and in the Japan-China Joint Communique, that Japan is "keenly conscious of the responsibility for the serious damage that Japan caused in the past to the Chinese people through war and deeply reproaches itself." These statements

confirm Japan's remorse and determination which I stated above and this recognition has not changed at all to this day.

2. This spirit in the Japan-ROK Joint Communique and the Japan-China Joint Communique naturally should also be respected in Japan's school education and textbook authorization.[4]

This statement calmed the controversy down. Later, however, it was reported that the original report in June that "invasion" was being changed to "advance" was false.[5] Adding to the furor over this false report was criticism of the government from within Japan for allowing foreign interference in "domestic politics," i.e., the content of textbooks.

Deng Xiaoping clearly intended to show the Japanese that they were the ones responsible for the history problem. On August 10, he said that Japan's Ministry of Education "provided a very good opportunity for education. Since we have not raised the history issue for many years, it is good to have this problem now. Our children should not only know friendship but also know the history."[6] Deng and other Chinese leaders simultaneously launched a "Patriotic Education Campaign" to educate young Chinese that China would not have achieved true independence without the Communist Party, which, in their view, had played the most important role in defeating the Japanese. Now that the Party criticized Chairman Mao for his role during the Cultural Revolution and embraced Deng's "reform and opening," which virtually negated the Marxist-Leninist ideology of centralized economic planning, the historical role of the Communist Party during the "anti-Japanese war" was a valuable source of its legitimacy in China. The Japanese attempt to disavow its history of aggression against China indeed offered a good opportunity to educate young Chinese who had experiences only of friendship with Japan.[7]

The next history issue to become a major controversy were the visits of prime ministers to the Yasukuni Shrine. For a long time after the war, a prime ministerial visit to the Yasukuni Shrine had become almost de rigueur. On the one hand, however, critics within Japan had asked for a stop to these visits on the grounds of the "separation of religion and government"; on the other, there were strong appeals, primarily from organizations representing families of the war dead, to make them "official visits" on behalf of the state. This became a diplomatic issue in 1985, when Prime Minister Nakasone convened a panel of experts to consider ways of making it possible to pay an official visit to Yasukuni as prime minister. On the basis of their recommendation, he did so on August 15, 1985, the 40th anniversary of the end of the war. On hearing of Nakasone's visit, the Chinese government made a formal protest, but it was on September 18 when the inflammatory nature of this issue became apparent: anti-Japanese demonstrations took place at Peking University and elsewhere. The Chinese government took issue with the visit because of the enshrinement there of Japanese military and civilian leaders who had been designated Class A war criminals by the Military Tribunal for the Far East.[8] Worrying that the controversy would worsen the position of his close friend General Secretary Hu Yaobang, Nakasone called off subsequent visits.[9]

But the cessation of these visits provoked great discontent among supporters of visits to the shrine. Class A war criminals had been enshrined there in the autumn of 1978, a fact that had become clear in the spring of 1979. Even after that, Japanese prime ministers had visited the shrine, albeit unofficially. Why, some wondered, had this become a problem now? It is not clear why China started to raise this issue in 1985. One factor may have been the increasing criticism of Hu Yaobang for his reformist policies. Hu Yaobang and Nakasone visibly showed their friendship despite Nakasone's wide-spread reputation as a nationalist. The "official" status of Nakasone's visit to Yasukuni may have given Hu's enemies in China an opening that made him vulnerable to attack: why do you attach importance to this Japanese nationalist who pays tribute to the imperialists who perpetrated atrocities in China? Hu frankly told Japanese visitors a few months later that "the memory of the Eight-Country Aggression [the alliance formed to suppress the Boxer Rebellion] has faded recently since 85 years have passed, but only 40 years have passed since the Second Sino-Japanese War. We won't be able to calm down about it for another 40 or 50 more years. Among students, there are those who call me a member of the pro-Japanese clique."[10] Nakasone understood Hu's problem and decided not to visit the shrine the next year. To the dismay of Nakasone, Hu Yaobang lost power subsequently in any case.

Whether or not the termination of visits was motivated by Nakasone's friendship toward Hu, the symbolic significance of the Yasukuni visit had become more or less crystalized; if subsequent Chinese leaders did not criticize Japanese leaders visiting the shrine, they were regarded as members of the "pro-Japanese clique" excusing Japanese imperialists. To the right-wing nationalists in Japan and those who had worked hard to make it possible for prime ministers to make an "official visit" to the shrine, not doing so became a symbol of accepting foreign interference in Japan's domestic and spiritual affairs.[11]

The Comfort Women

The "comfort women" were "those who were forced to provide sexual services to officers and men of the former Japanese military at 'comfort stations' during wartime in the past."[12] Although efforts to discover the historical facts concerning "comfort women" have continued among historians since about the 1970s, not much attention had been paid to this problem until the 1980s since no former "comfort women" had made their traumatic experiences public. In 1982, the *Asahi Shimbun* reported that a former Japanese soldier, Yoshida Seiji, confessed that he personally had forcibly rounded up girls on Jeju Island. Over the course of a week in the early summer of 1943, he and ten fully armed Japanese soldiers rounded up 200 young Korean women, he said.[13] This report did not attract much attention in South Korea at the time, though Yoshida published a book in 1983, entitled *Watashi no sensō hanzai: Chōsenjin kyōsei renkō* (My war crimes: the forced conscription of Koreans), which essentially repeated and amplified his stories in the *Asahi Shimbun*.[14]

After democratization in the late 1980s, however, a number of non-governmental organizations in South Korea started investigating this issue, and in the summer of 1991, a former comfort woman came forward, agreed to be interviewed under her real name and criticized the Japanese government. The *Asahi* published stories citing Yoshida's experiences both before and after this former comfort woman spoke out. In December, three former Korean comfort women filed a lawsuit in the Tokyo District Court. On January 11, 1992, the *Asahi* reported the existence of a document that indicated the involvement of the military in the recruitment of comfort women.[15] Although "involvement" here meant such activities as the establishment and supervision of comfort stations, the report was taken by the South Korean media to have proven an extreme level of "coercion," including such cases as those that Yoshida had claimed to have taken part in. Moreover, many reports in both South Korea and Japan confused the Women's Volunteer Corps, which was an organization to mobilize young women for labor in factories, with organizations recruiting comfort women, and further inflamed public anger in South Korea with the image of young girls forcibly conscripted under the name of the Women's Volunteer Corps.[16]

Prime Minister Miyazawa Kiichi, who was visiting South Korea on his first overseas trip, responded to the criticisms of President Roh Tae-woo, by saying, "Judging from eyewitness accounts, reports and documents on this subject, it is undeniable the Japanese army was in some way or other involved in recruiting comfort women and operating [comfort stations]. I wish to express my remorse and apologize from the bottom of my heart for the indescribable suffering the people of South Korea endured,"[17] and he promised that his cabinet would look into it.

The subsequent investigation, the results of which were reported by Chief Cabinet Secretary Katō Kōichi in July 1992, revealed that "the Government had been involved in the establishment of comfort stations, the control of those who recruited comfort women, the construction and reinforcement of comfort facilities, the management and surveillance of comfort stations, the hygiene maintenance in comfort stations and among comfort women, and the issuance of identification as well as other documents to those who were related to comfort stations."[18] Since Katō also mentioned that the inquiry had not discovered any documents concerning the methods of recruitment, the media considered the investigation unsatisfactory. But President Kim Young-sam, who succeeded Roh Tae-woo in February 1993, stated on March 13 of that year, "We do not plan to demand material compensation from the Government of Japan. Compensation will be undertaken using the budget of the ROK government from next year. Doing so will undoubtedly make it possible to pursue a new ROK-Japan relationship by claiming the moral high-ground."[19]

The Japanese government conducted interviews with 16 former comfort women in late July. The major purpose of the hearings was not a rigorous investigation of the facts but to show the Japanese government's serious intention to "deeply understand their feelings," and therefore no attempt to cross-check their statements was made. In fact, the draft of the statement based on the inquiry had virtually been completed on the basis of in-depth consultation with the South Korean government.[20] The statement made by Chief Cabinet Secretary Kōno Yōhei on August 3, 1993 read as follows:

> As a result of the study which indicates that comfort stations were operated in extensive areas for long periods, it is apparent that there existed a great number of comfort women. Comfort stations were operated in response to the request of the military authorities of the day. The then Japanese military was, directly or indirectly, involved in the establishment and management of the comfort stations and the transfer of comfort women. The recruitment of the comfort women was conducted mainly by private recruiters who acted in response to the request of the military. The Government study has revealed that in many cases they were recruited against their own will, through coaxing, coercion, etc., and that, at times, administrative/military personnel directly took part in the recruitments. They lived in misery at comfort stations under a coercive atmosphere.
>
> As to the origin of those comfort women who were transferred to the war areas, excluding those from Japan, those from the Korean Peninsula accounted for a large part. The Korean Peninsula was under Japanese rule in those days, and their recruitment, transfer, control, etc., were conducted generally against their will, through coaxing, coercion, etc.
>
> Undeniably, this was an act, with the involvement of the military authorities of the day, that severely injured the honor and dignity of many women. The Government of Japan would like to take this opportunity once again to extend its sincere apologies and remorse to all those, irrespective of place of origin, who suffered immeasurable pain and incurable physical and psychological wounds as comfort women.
>
> It is incumbent upon us, the Government of Japan, to continue to consider seriously, while listening to the views of learned circles, how best we can express this sentiment.
>
> We shall face squarely the historical facts as described above instead of evading them, and take them to heart as lessons of

history. We hereby reiterate our firm determination never to repeat the same mistake by forever engraving such issues in our memories through the study and teaching of history.[21]

South Korea's foreign ministry expressed its appreciation of the Statement because it admitted the overall "coercive nature" of the recruitment and management of comfort women and stated Japan's apology clearly. The director-general of its Asian Affairs Bureau, Yu Byung-woo, stated that "it is the position of our government that it will not raise this issue as a diplomatic issue between South Korea and Japan." However, a *Dong-A Ilbo* editorial insisted that the sentiment of the Korean people differed from that of their government.[22] In Japan, voices were raised in support of some kind of material measures for the victims. When it came to what ought to be done, however, this involved very difficult legal problems. In the case of South Korea, for example, both governments had stipulated in the Agreement Concerning Claims and Economic Co-operation, concluded at the time of diplomatic normalization, that these issues had been "settled completely and finally."[23]

What complicated the matter even further was that it became clear that the statement of Yoshida Seiji, the former Japanese soldier who had confessed to forcibly conscripting Koreans to serve as comfort women, was of dubious credibility.[24] As a result, this gave rise in Japan to the opinion, especially among right-wing nationalists, that the statements by Prime Minister Miyazawa and Chief Cabinet Secretary Kōno had all been made on the basis of false evidence and thus were unnecessary and inappropriate. According to this view, since Yoshida's testimony was a fabrication, the government should assume that no "forced conscription" (*kyōsei renkō*) had taken place unless hard evidence was found. On the other hand, such criticism of the Kōno Statement in Japan was taken as a denial of all kinds of coerciveness and attracted even more anger in South Korea and elsewhere. As we shall discuss in Chapter 11, the *Asahi Shimbun* in 2014 retracted all stories based on Yoshida's testimony as fabrications and expressed its regret that it had confused the Women's Volunteer Corps with comfort women. However, the committee appointed that year to review the drafting process of the Kōno Statement concluded that there had been no prior assumption of "forced conscription" on the Japanese side. But this was a later development after many more acrimonious controversies over the comfort women issue.

Political Upheaval and History

Japan in 1993 was in the midst of political upheaval. Kanemaru Shin, the biggest power broker in the LDP after the death of Tanaka Kakuei, was arrested for tax evasion in March 1993, and thereafter politics became very fluid. An anti-Miyazawa group within the LDP headed by Ozawa Ichirō joined the opposition when it staged a vote of non-confidence. The vote passed, and Miyazawa dissolved the Diet in response. The LDP lost its majority in the general election though it retained a plurality. Ozawa managed to form a coalition consisting of seven non-LDP and non-Communist parties, and Hosokawa Morihiro, a popular former governor of Kumamoto Prefecture, the 14th head of the Hosokawa clan (a famous daimyō family) and a grandson of Prince Konoe Fumimaro,[25] became prime minister.

As the head of the first non-LDP government since 1955, Hosokawa attempted to make a difference in foreign policy by more forcefully coming to terms with Japan's own history. After becoming prime minister only three days after the Kōno Statement, he made statements on his own understanding of history which went further than any made before. At a press conference on August 10, he was asked what he thought about the past war. "I myself believe it was a war of aggression, a war that was wrong," he said, and in his general policy speech on August 23, he went on to say:

> I believe it is important at this juncture that we state clearly before all the world our remorse at our past history and our renewed determination to do better. I would thus like to take this opportunity to express anew our profound remorse and apologies for the fact that past Japanese actions, including aggression and colonial rule, caused unbearable suffering and sorrow for so many people and to state that we will demonstrate our new determination by contributing more than ever before to world peace.[26]

Prime Minister Hosokawa may have judged that by openly acknowledging his own sense of responsbility, it would make it easier to conduct his foreign policy without being entrapped in controversies with Japan's neighbors. When he visited China in March 1994 and met Premier Li Peng, for example, he said, "I express our apologies and profound remorse for the fact that Japan's aggressive actions and colonial rule in the past caused unbearable suffering to the peoples of Asia. Based on this remorse for our past history, Japan is working to establish even friendlier ties with China with a view to the future." At the same time, he made some significant demands on China. First of all, he asked for Chinese cooperation in dealing with the situation in the Korean peninsula, which had become extremely tense. "The international community has come to the end of its patience with the delaying tactics of the Democratic People's Republic of Korea [North Korea]," he said. Because there are "fears that the decisions discussed these past several weeks will come to nothing, China has an important role to play." Secondly, Prime Minister Hosokawa drew attention to the four fundamental principles of Japan's ODA related to the military spending trends of recipient countries and expressed his concern about the increase in China's military expenditures. He also told President Jiang Zemin that he particularly hoped China would exercise "self-control on nuclear testing."[27]

Before achieving much in foreign policy, however, Hosokawa was involved in serious in-fighting within the non-LDP coalition and resigned in April. The major achievement of the Hosokawa Cabinet was the adoption of a new election law for the lower house introducing 300 single-member constituencies and 200 members from proportional representation districts, replacing the old system of multiple member constituencies; under this new electoral system Japanese politics was to face new dynamics in the coming decades as we shall see in the subsequent chapters. After the resignation of Hosokawa, the coalition agreed to ask Hata Tsutomu, a moderate leader who had left the LDP with Ozawa, to succeed him. Immediately after the formation of the Hata Cabinet, however, the Japan Socialist Party left the coalition because of differences of opinion with Ozawa over the coalition management, making the Hata government a minority cabinet. As if to show the conflict-ridden nature of the government, challenges to the previous prime ministers' position on history erupted.

Nagano Shigeto, who had been appointed Minister of Justice in the Hata Cabinet, made the following problematic statement in May 1994:

I think it is incorrect to define that war as a war of aggression. The aggressive acts, various damage, cruel behavior and other trouble made in war are absolutely wrong, and war itself is an absolute evil. However, was what is known in Japan as the Greater East Asian War fought with the aim of aggression? On the verge of destruction, Japan rose up in order to survive. We were thinking seriously about liberating colonies and establishing the Greater East Asian Co-Prosperity Sphere. The various foreign powers that created that situation were the problem. The aim of the war itself was basically permissible and correct at that time.

I think the Nanjing Incident is a fabrication. I went to Nanjing immediately afterwards. That kind of thing is an evil that accompanies any war, and it is correct to say that it is absolutely wrong. I suppose you could call that an act of aggression, but Japan was not trying to make that Japanese territory and did not occupy it.[28]

On May 5, President Jiang Zemin expressed his displeasure with this statement when he met with Hara Bunbei, president of the House of Councillors, in Shanghai. On the same day, the Chinese foreign ministry called in Minister Matsumoto Kōichi of the Japanese Embassy in Beijing demanding an explanation and requesting a "sincere and serious response" to the matter. Prime Minister Hata immediately described Nagano's statement as "inappropriate," and on the night of the 7th, he accepted Nagano's resignation and in effect fired him as Minister of Justice.

In his policy speech on May 10, Prime Minister Hata himself said, "I recognize anew that Japan's acts of aggression and colonial rule caused unbearable suffering and sorrow for many people, and out of profound regret, I will make every effort in my power not only to convey this recognition to future generations but to build a bright future for the Asia-Pacific region on a foundation of peace. This, I believe, is the path Japan ought to take from now on."[29]

After the Hata Cabinet was virtually forced to resign en masse in June, Japanese politics underwent another dramatic turn of events.

The LDP asked its long-time political enemy, the Japanese Socialist Party, to join it in forming a coalition; Murayama Tomiichi, head of the JSP, became prime minister; and an administration came into being that would have been unthinkable in the past. Many wondered what the Socialist prime minister would do with respect to the Self-Defense Forces and the Japan-US Security Treaty, both of which the Socialist Party had long criticized as unconstitutional.

Prime Minister Murayama did a complete about face in regard to the two pillars of Japan's security policy. He bit the bullet and declared that the SDF was constitutional and that he would solidly maintain the Japan-US alliance. But, like Hosokawa, he attempted to take a different stand on other issues, one of which was history. In his policy speech of July 18, he said, "As we approach the 50th anniversary of the end of World War II, I recognize anew that Japan's actions, including aggression and colonial rule, caused unbearable suffering and sorrow for many people of this region. I express my sense of deep remorse and will make every effort to build a peaceful world on the determination never to go to war again."[30] As he recalled 18 years later, "it was abnormal for the head of a minority party to become prime minister. So I was not likely to serve for any length of time. However, given this opportunity to be appointed prime minister, I wanted to do something that only a Socialist could do."[31]

Different interpretations of Japan's modern history, however, emerged from within the Murayama Cabinet, too. On August 12, Sakurai Shin, head of the Environment Agency, said, "I don't believe that [Japan] went to war intending to fight a war of aggression. Parties of war often cause a lot of trouble even if they meant well so it is necessary to apologize for the whole thing. But we shouldn't deal with the issue from the view that Japan alone was bad." As a result of the war, he went on to say, the countries of "Asia gained independence from colonial rule, and education flourished, resulting in a high literacy rate. It gave rise to a vigorous economic revival and led to the revitalization of the Asian people."[32] Sakurai retracted his statement immediately that same day, but the fire had been lit. Prime Minister Murayama criticized the statement as "inappropriate."

At a press conference on August 13, a Chinese foreign ministry spokesman made the following comment.

We regret that in a short period of time Japan's cabinet has again brazenly made remarks which distorted historical facts. International society has already drawn its conclusions on the history of aggression by Japanese militarists. Adopting a correct attitude towards history is an important basis of Chinese-Japanese relations. We hope that the Japanese government will attach a high degree of importance to this issue and avoid disturbing the normal development of friendly and cooperative ties between China and Japan.[33]

As a result, the Socialist Party and others requested Sakurai's removal, and on the 14th, Prime Minister Murayama accepted his resignation and effectively forced him out of the cabinet. In quick succession, the Hata Cabinet and the Murayama Cabinet had removed one of its ministers as the result of different "understandings of history."

Having been tripped up in these ways by the history issue from the moment of his new cabinet's inception, however, Prime Minister Murayama and the Socialist Party, who wanted to do what "only Socialists could do," now tried to get the Diet to enact an "apology resolution" on Japan's aggression and colonial rule for the following year, 1995, the 50th anniversary of the end of the war. The opposition New Frontier Party also sought an "anti-war resolution" in the Diet. But it was not easy to get members of the three ruling parties to agree on the contents. In the LDP, powerful forces stubbornly opposed including an "apology" in the resolution, and doubts also arose about whether it was even desirable for the Diet to arbitrarily decide on an "understanding of history," which was by its very nature so diverse. Finally, in June 1995, the text agreed upon by the three ruling parties, in the form of a "resolution to renew the determination for peace on the basis of lessons learned from history," read as follows:

On the occasion of the 50th anniversary of the end of World War II, this House offers its sincere condolences to those who fell in action and victims of wars and similar actions all over the world.

Solemnly reflecting upon many instances of colonial rule and acts of aggression in the modern history of the world, and recognizing that Japan carried out those acts in the past, inflicting pain and suffering upon the peoples of other countries, especially in Asia, the Members of this House express a sense of deep remorse.

We must transcend the differences over historical views of the past war and learn humbly the lessons of history so as to build a peaceful international society.

This House expresses its resolve, under the banner of eternal peace enshrined in the Constitution of Japan, to join hands with other nations of the world and to pave the way to a future that allows all human beings to live together.[34]

This resolution eliminated as much as possible any wording that might pose problems, causing discontent both among its proponents because it was not a straightforward apology and among its opponents because any resolution had been made at all. At the time this resolution came up for a vote in a plenary session of the House of Representatives on June 9, members of the New Frontier Party, whose demands that the resolution be amended had not been accepted, boycotted the session, and nearly 50 members of the LDP also failed to attend. The resolution passed, nevertheless, but because of the confusion in the lower house, the session in the House of Councillors ended without the proposal being put to a vote. Seeing the difficulties in the drafting process of the resolution, Prime Minister Murayama once again strengthened his resolve to issue his own statement on history that would be much clearer than the Diet resolution.[35]

Japan can say it has influence in the international community only because it has a presence in Asia as a member of Asia. The relationship with the United States is important, but, after all, it is only because Japan has a presence in Asia, that the US considers Japan important. Without it, Japan is reduced to being just an isolated island nation no one cares about. In order for Japan to be a country with a significant presence in Asia in the future, we have to attach importance to relationships based on trust with other Asian countries. That's the reason I thought the Prime Minister's Statement was necessary.[36]

In July, Murayama ordered Tanino Sakutarō, chief of the Cabinet Councillors' Office on External Affairs, to draft the Prime Minister's

Statement to be issued on August 15. While Tanino worked on the draft in consultation with several historians,[37] another problematic statement was made by a member of the cabinet, which had been reshuffled on August 8. When Minister of Education Shimamura Yoshinobu was asked at a press conference immediately after the cabinet shuffle whether the last war had been a war of aggression, he replied, "War is a matter of one side attacking another and someone wins, the other loses; so whether it was aggression or not is a matter of point of view. Isn't it the case that the stronger side wins and gets to call the loser aggressive? If Japan alone had been so, that would be a matter to investigate thoroughly, but there are lots of precedents all over the world. If we think we did something wrong at all, it is more forward-looking to make amends and repayment in the form of international contributions."[38]

This statement immediately caught the mass media's attention, and in fact Shimamura himself retracted it right away. Although Prime Minister Murayama gave a Shimamura a "serious warning," this time he did not ask for his resignation. But given this type of statement, Murayama must have felt that it was all the more important to make his views as clear as possible. The Murayama Statement decided on by the cabinet on August 15 read:

> During a certain period in the not too distant past, Japan, following a mistaken national policy, advanced along the road to war, only to ensnare the Japanese people in a fateful crisis, and through its colonial rule and aggression, caused tremendous damage and suffering to the people of many countries, particularly to those of Asian nations. In the hope that no such mistake be made in the future, I regard, in a spirit of humility, these irrefutable facts of history, and express here once again my feelings of deep remorse and state my heartfelt apology. Allow me also to express my feelings of profound mourning for all victims, both at home and abroad, of that history.
>
> Building from our deep remorse on this occasion of the 50th anniversary of the end of the war, Japan must eliminate self-righteous nationalism, promote international coordination as a responsible member of the international community and, thereby, advance the principles of peace and democracy. At the same time,

as the only country to have experienced the devastation of atomic bombing, Japan, with a view to the ultimate elimination of nuclear weapons, must actively strive to further global disarmament in areas such as the strengthening of the nuclear non-proliferation regime. It is my conviction that in this way alone can Japan atone for its past and lay to rest the spirits of those who perished.[39]

A spokesman for the Chinese foreign ministry welcomed these words and said, "We've taken notice of Prime Minister Murayama's statement on behalf of the Japanese government on the occasion of August 15. We consider it a positive gesture on the part of the Japanese government to deeply reflect upon the history of colonial rule and aggression in the past and to apologize to the Asian people."[40]

South Korea, too, took note of Japan's response to the issues related to the understanding of history. But the South Koreans did not find the Murayama Statement completely satisfactory. President Kim Young-sam commented that although it "was a big step forward compared to the past," in light of Shimamura's comments, it was still not adequate. When, on October 5, Prime Minister Murayama stated in a plenary session of the House of Councillors that the Treaty of Annexation between the Empire of Japan and the Empire of Korea [of August 22, 1910] had been signed in a legally valid way, South Korean public opinion erupted, and the South Korean government protested to Japan. On October 16, the South Korean National Assembly unanimously passed a resolution demanding that Japan admit that the Treaty of Annexation had been invalid from the outset. Then, in November 1995, it became clear that Etō Takami, director of the Management and Coordination Agency, had said at the beginning of October that "Japan had also done some good things during its colonial rule in Korea," and Japanese-South Korean relations once again became tense. Ultimately Etō resigned.[41]

As we have already noted, the comfort women issue was a difficult matter for the Japanese government to deal with legally. On the other hand, the feeling was growing stronger within the Murayama administration that it would like to do something. In addition, there were those among the general public who were concerned about the comfort women issue and increasingly feared that the victims, who were growing older, would never actually receive compensation in their lifetime if they pursued the route of legally seeking reparations from the Japanese government. Out of these concerns was born the idea of taking some real steps separate from state redress in a narrow sense. The Murayama Cabinet accepted this broader initiative, and on June 14, 1995, it announced that it was setting up The Asian Peace and Friendship Foundation for Women (the Asian Women's Fund), in which it would provide compensation to former comfort women with funds from the general public and invest government funds for operating expenses and for a project to provide welfare and medical care to former comfort women.[42] University of Tokyo professor Ōnuma Yasuaki, one of the proponents of setting up the Fund, called for the cooperation of many Japanese citizens in an article in the *Yomiuri Shimbun*.

It is easy to criticize the government's plan. But if we reject it, what cabinet will compensate the former comfort women and in what way? As long as there is no real, specific alternative, rejecting this plan is tantamount to rejecting compensation for comfort women itself.[43]

In order to facilitate the activities of the Fund, the government set aside 480 million yen from the FY1995 budget, and the initial appeal for donations from the public was made on July 18. These donations reached 133.75 million yen by the end of 1995 and ultimately 565 million yen by 2002.[44] The government disbursed 510 million yen for medical and welfare support projects in addition to 4.8 billion yen for the Fund's operational costs.[45] Through this Fund, 285 former comfort women from the Philippines, South Korea and Taiwan were given "atonement money" and a "letter of apology" from the Prime Minister. In addition, 79 former comfort women from the Netherlands were acknowledged and provided with medical and welfare services. Welfare support for the elderly was carried out in Indonesia until 2007, and when that ended, the Asian Women's Fund was dissolved. In South Korea, the Fund's activities did not proceed smoothly. Prominent NGOs supporting the "comfort women" fundamentally rejected the Fund as not reflecting the formal and legal responsibility of Japan. Adding trauma to the original trauma of the comfort women, those who accepted the atonement money and letter of apology from the prime minister came under public attack for debasing themselves by taking the money.[46] Seeing this terrible development, the Fund decided to terminate its activities in Korea in 2002.

The Taiwan Strait Crisis

The democratization movement begun under Chiang Ching-kuo in Taiwan was entrusted to the leadership of Lee Teng-hui, who became chairman of the Kuomintang and president of the Republic of China. Lee, whom Shiba Ryōtarō once characterized as having "features that seemed to have been chiseled from a great tree which had just been cut down in the mountains,"[47] was at first thought not to have much political power. But he steadily gained authority within the Kuomintang, and in March 1990, having been reelected president by the National Assembly, he announced that he was convening a National Affairs Conference to initiate the "constitutional reform" that students demanding democratization had hoped for.[48] Although there was no strictly legal basis for the Conference, which brought together representatives of the people, it was, nevertheless, able to set the direction for reform. On the issue of representatives for life, a meeting of the Justices of the Constitutional Court worked out a "constitutional interpretation" that would terminate their tenure by the end of 1991, and the problem was finally settled. In April 1991, the National Assembly decided on "additional provisions" to the constitution to promote democratization and voted to abolish the "Temporary Provisions Effective During the Period of Communist Rebellion." With this, the legal basis for a dictatorial system premised on a "civil war" with the Communist Party finally disappeared. In December of that year, the National Assembly was entirely elected, and in December 1992, so was the Legislative Yuan, the real legislative body. March 1996 saw direct elections of the president, the head of state. The democratization of Taiwan, both in name and in reality, was heading toward completion.

The abolition of provisions that were appropriate only in times of "civil war" had enormous significance. The People's Republic of China was now no longer regarded as the "enemy" in a civil war. But if it was not the enemy, what relation did the Republic of China have with the People's Republic of China?[49] Up until then, according to the Taiwanese legal system there was "one China" (as was also the case with the People's Republic of China), and within this one China there was an ongoing civil war. But if the present situation was not one of "civil war," what was it? Was China really one? The opposition Democratic Progressive Party was blunt. A democratized Taiwan was Taiwan. Naturally, it ought to be independent and regain membership in the United Nations.

It goes without saying that these trends in Taiwan could not be ignored on the mainland. The "Message to Compatriots in Taiwan" had been issued in the name of Ye Jianying, then chairman of the Standing Committee of the National People's Party, on January 1, 1979, at the time Chinese-US relations were normalized, and ever since, the Taiwan question was one of the most important issues for the China of Deng Xiaoping, which was promoting openness and reform. Along with the return of Hong Kong and Macau, the unification of Taiwan with the "homeland" was regarded as a matter of great importance in overcoming the history of shame China had endured since the Opium Wars. In September 1981, Ye Jianying unveiled a fairly concrete proposal for Taiwan called the "Nine Principles." The most important point in the mainland's thinking about Taiwan after unification, as it later unfolded, was to go with "one country, two systems" based on the recognition of the "one China" principle. Since China was one, the idea of two Chinas, one on the mainland, one on Taiwan, was absolutely unacceptable. In other words, Taiwanese independence could never be tolerated. But if Taiwan were to accept this principle, China would be flexible in its thinking about "one country, two systems" for post-unification Taiwan and would allow it a high degree of autonomy as a special administrative district.

Had it been Chiang Kai-shek's Taiwan, there would have been no problem about accepting the principle of "one China." The point of conflict between Chiang Kai-shek and Mao Zedong had been which of them would rule over "one China"—that had been the reason they were fighting a "civil war." But now that the civil war was over, the "one China" principle was not something that could be so easily accepted by Taiwan, which had democratized and whose islander majority wanted to establish their own identity.

That does not mean, however, that there had been no talks whatsoever between the mainland and Taiwan. In April 1993, a meeting was held in Singapore between Wang Daohan (the former mayor of Shanghai), head of the People's Republic of China's Association for Relations Across the Taiwan Straits, and Koo Chen-fu of the Taiwan-based Straits Exchange Foundation. Again in January 1995, China presented a plan proposing mutual visits by heads of state and the holding of talks aimed at unification, and Lee Teng-hui gave a speech by way of an answer to this.

In the spring of 1995, however, when President Lee went to the US to attend commencement exercises at his alma mater, Cornell University, the situation took a dangerous turn for the worse. Although the Clinton administration refused to issue President Lee a visa, the Congress, which welcomed democratization in Taiwan, almost unanimously passed a resolution through both the Senate and the House of Representatives welcoming President Lee to the US. Under pressure from Congress, the Clinton administration issued President Lee a visa, and he came to the US.[50] Fearing that the Lee visit would set a precedent and that he would be able to go anywhere in the world, China searched for a hardline response. It was also undesirable for China that the Democratic Progressive Party candidate, who advocated Taiwanese independence, win in the general elections scheduled for March 1996. Perhaps to prevent this from happening, China carried out missile tests in the Taiwan Strait in July 1995 and conducted naval exercises at the time of Taiwan's Legislative Yuan election in December of that year. Then, just before the presidential elections in March 1996, it carried out both missile tests and naval maneuvers. Right before the elections, the Clinton administration, apprehensive about these activities, sent two aircraft carriers to the vicinity of Taiwan in preparation for any untoward event. For the first time since 1958, a US-Chinese military confrontation appeared to have become a matter of strategic reality.

But, in fact, it was just the psychological aspect of this crisis that was great. Militarily, China did not have the capability to carry out a full-scale invasion of Taiwan, and, indeed, it probably had no intention of engaging in military operations. Its aim seems to have been a psychological threat, but the effect of that was lowered by the sending of American aircraft carriers. As a consequence, the result of the elections was at best ambiguous from China's perspective. The fact that the Democratic Progressive Party candidate did not win was a plus for China, but Lee Teng-hui easily won reelection. Since the New Party,

The US aircraft carrier *Independence* during exercises at sea east of Taiwan (March 16, 1996). Photo: Kyodo News

which favored unification and openly opposed Taiwanese independence, had no prospects of winning, China's threats seem to have had the result of making a considerable number of Democratic Progressive Party supporters switch sides and vote for President Lee. Although Lee Teng-hui had not clearly stated that he supported Taiwanese independence, given the circumstances up to then, Lee could hardly have been a desirable presidential candidate from China's perspective.

The Japanese Reaction

The Taiwan Strait crisis was also a major source of concern for Japan. Prime Minister Hashimoto Ryūtarō, who took office in January 1996 after the sudden resignation of Prime Minister Murayama, strongly urged self-restraint at a Japanese-Chinese summit meeting at the time of the Asia-Europe Meeting (ASEM). "Tensions in the Taiwan Strait are rising, and I strongly hope for a peaceful solution. I wish that both parties concerned will act in accordance with this idea." In response, Premier Li Peng replied, "It is true there are tensions on both sides of the Taiwan Strait, but China's plan for peaceful reunification and 'one country, two systems' is unchanged," and, in turn, he requested Hashimoto that "Japan handle the issue of a possible visit of Taiwan's President Lee Teng-hui to Japan on the basis of the 'one

China' principle" (meaning that Japan should not allow Lee to visit Japan).[51]

Hashimoto's request had no impact whatsoever on China's actions. Four days later on March 5, China announced that the People's Liberation Army would conduct missile testing from March 8th to the 15th. In response, Foreign Ministry Press Secretary Hashimoto Hiroshi said in Japan that day that "the heightening of tensions in the Taiwan Strait is undesirable for the peace and stability of East Asia,"[52] and on the 6th, Katō Ryōzō, head of the Asian Affairs Bureau, summoned Counselor Zheng Xianglin of the Chinese Embassy in Japan and urged self-restraint, saying that "the increase of tensions in the Taiwan Strait is undesirable for the peace and stability of East Asia." Counselor Zheng replied, "Military exercises are necessary and normal to protect our sovereignty and territory. Some Taiwanese leaders who insist on independence are causing the tensions."[53] And so, on March 8, the missile tests were carried out as scheduled. Since one of the two missile impact areas was a few dozen kilometers from the Okinawan island of Yonaguni, commercial airliners headed to Southeast Asia from Japan were forced to avoid the area.

Prime Minister Hashimoto said, "I think [testing] is [a step] in an unfortunate direction," and Chief Cabinet Secretary Kajiyama Seiroku stated that the missile tests have had "quite a strong impact on the territory of Japan. Since they are over international waters, it is problematic what we can say by way of protest, but because of the serious effect they have had on air routes, navigation and fishing, we ask for self-restraint on these matters."[54] Because testing missiles over international waters was not itself contrary to international law, however, the response of the Japanese government was limited. "Since they are over international waters," Prime Minister Hashimoto also said, "they are not of a nature that we can protest. We have great concerns, but that is all. We can't go any further."[55] Outside the government, however, criticism of China was strong; Katō Kōichi, secretary-general of the LDP, said, "This is a problem that may have an impact on our country's safety. We want them to stop these exercises immediately."[56]

Because China pushed ahead with its live-fire war games in the Taiwan Strait off Fukien Province on the 12th, harder-line opinions began to be voiced in Japan. At a Foreign Affairs Committee meeting in the House of Representatives, Prime Minister Hashimoto reiterated that he had "very strong concerns." On the 12th, Yamasaki Taku, chairman of the LDP's Policy Research Council, said, "In response to the developing situation, which has a deleterious impact on our country's national security, I want to dig down deep and begin exploring measures including emergency legislation on national security," and announced he was referring the issue to the LDP's Research Commission on Security.[57] Within the LDP, some felt Japan ought to take steps such as freezing yen loans to China, while others condemned the Ministry of Foreign Affair's response for not being strong enough. While this was going on, it was reported that the ministry was preparing plans to postpone bilateral negotiations on the fourth yen loan package scheduled to begin in mid-March.[58] Hot on its heels followed a report that the ministry had begun a study to explore ways of "freezing" part of the fourth yen loan package.[59] Also reported was the decision (of foreign ministry authorities) that "it is necessary to convey our deep concerns and feelings of anxiety about Chinese-Taiwanese relations without having a serious effect on Japan-China relations," and comments (by ministry sources) that "depending on the direction China takes, there is a need for Japan to send a stronger signal than just a 'request for self-restraint.'" Although Foreign Ministry Press Secretary Hashimoto Hiroshi denied on March 15 that there was any truth to such a study, he left the impression that it might be a future possibility: "We will respond by making a comprehensive judgment of various factors and circumstances."[60]

Despite this reaction from Japan, China went ahead as scheduled with its military maneuvers, and upon hearing from Japan about the proposal to freeze the yen loans, its only reaction was that "the Taiwan issue is a Chinese internal matter. No country can intervene in any way."[61] Because China's policy of "verbal attack and military intimidation" (*wengong wuxia*) toward Taiwan was its most important policy, neither Japan's appeals for self-restraint nor the veiled threat to reexamine yen loans had much influence.

The Japanese response, however, may have been far stronger than the Chinese side had expected. Foreign Minister Qian Qichen, who visited Japan right after the Taiwan Strait crisis, in effect told Foreign Minister Ikeda Yukihiko, "There was a strong reaction from the United States, but aside from the US, the strongest reaction was

Japan's. We are aware of the historical circumstances behind the formation of the US-Japan Security Treaty, but we hope that it will not be inconsistent with the development of sound relations between China and Japan. Although we do not advocate any change in economic and trade relations at the private level between Japan and Taiwan, we are opposed to contacts between governments taking place."[62] The observation that the Japanese took a hardline on the Taiwan problem may have strengthened Chinese concerns about Japan's attitude after the signing of the Japan-US Joint Declaration on Security in April 1996. On the other hand, it is undeniable that China's "verbal attack and military intimidation" policy, which was totally impervious to criticism from the US and Japan, had an very large impact on Japanese public opinion and on Japanese policy makers, especially in the LDP, and strengthened support for the Japan-US Joint Declaration right afterwards.

China's Nuclear Testing

Along with the Taiwan problem, the focus of the Japanese public's anti-Chinese criticism was its nuclear testing. After China's nuclear tests in August 1995, the Japanese government took steps to freeze all grant aid to China except humanitarian assistance and demanded that China stop any further testing and sign the Comprehensive Nuclear-Test-Ban Treaty (CTBT). Early in 1996 as well, at a foreign ministers' meeting held between Ikeda Yukihiko and Qian Qichen on February 3, Ikeda noted that France had announced at the end of January that it was halting its nuclear tests and said, "We hope that China will stop any further testing."[63] When he met Qian again during the latter's visit to Japan immediately after the Taiwan Strait crisis, he asked for his cooperation in reaching an early agreement on the CTBT, and, when China requested an exception for small-scale nuclear explosions for peaceful uses, he pointed out that "the idea of a small-scale nuclear explosion is unacceptable in international society."[64]

At this time within Japan, the calls, already amplified by the Taiwan Strait crisis, were getting stronger and stronger for Japan to actually freeze yen loans if China conducted any more nuclear tests. The Chinese side stepped up its reaction against such a move. But although there had been no room for compromise on the Taiwan

issue, studies seem to have been under way in China about showing some degree of flexibility on nuclear testing. There was even
an effort to show some consideration with regard to Japan. China's
nuclear policy may also have been under review, and perhaps the
Chinese decided it was not beneficial to exacerbate anti-Chinese
sentiments in Japan any further.

Of course, that does not mean that China put a halt to its scheduled nuclear tests; they were held on June 8 and July 29. But at the
time of the June 8 test, it took steps to brief Japan on the testing in
advance. On June 3, Wu Dawei, acting Chinese Chargé d'Affaires to
Japan, met with reporters at the Japan National Press Club in Tokyo
and attempted to win Japanese understanding by making the following statement:

> I am aware that recently the Japanese media have indicated great
> concern about the Chinese nuclear test issue. The Japanese gov-
> ernment also indicated their disagreement with last year's nuclear
> tests. There are as well some among the Japanese people who have
> shown a strong reaction to these tests. We worry that this matter
> will have a negative impact on Chinese-Japanese relations. In fact,
> from the perspective of the Chinese government and the Chinese
> people, nuclear testing is unavoidable. Although this should not
> have a negative impact on Chinese-Japanese relations, unfortu-
> nately, the actual result is the opposite of what we had hoped.[65]

Although Wu fully understood the Japanese people's "special
feelings" on the nuclear issue, "at the same time we hope that the
Japanese people will also understand China's position on the matter."
At the time of the nuclear test on June 8, he made it clear that China
would conduct one more nuclear test and announced that after that
it would declare a "moratorium" on any further testing.

The response of the Japanese government was one of "regret," but
it did not go so far as to take any hardline measures such as stopping
yen loans. Foreign Minister Ikeda protested to Wu Dawei that "it is
extremely regrettable that the People's Republic of China conducted
another nuclear test today, despite repeated appeals by Japan for ceas-
ing nuclear testing." As for the grant aid that had been frozen, "We
must have the understanding and support of the people. Because the

tests have been repeated, we will have no choice but to continue the freeze." On yen loans, however, Prime Minister Hashimoto stated, "We must bring China back into the international community on [the nuclear] issue. Stopping yen loans is the opposite of doing so," thereby making it clear that he did not want to link the two issues.[66]

On July 29, China once again conducted a nuclear test and announced a "moratorium." The Japanese government response to the test was the same in being one of "regret"; as for the moratorium, Foreign Minister Ikeda said "We hope they show us with their actions." With China's halting of its nuclear testing, however, the Japanese side had no further issues on which to criticize China. Thereafter, it became a matter of the timing needed to reverse the steps that had been taken. First, there was the grant aid that had been frozen; at the end of July, Vice-Minister Hayashi Sadayuki said, "Since the nuclear testing has just ended, we are not in the mood [to resume] grant aid immediately." Although not regarded as "sanctions," a postponement of the negotiations on the fourth yen loans, which were being "studied" at the time of the Taiwan Strait crisis, had in fact been implemented. The Japanese government had said it was not freezing yen loans, but since no discussions whatsoever had been held on the implementation of 40 projects over three years worth a total value of 580 billion yen, this amounted to de facto "sanctions." When to begin talks on yen loans and resume grant aid would become a later task for Japan's China policy.

Yasukuni Visits and the Building of a Lighthouse in the Senkakus

July 29, 1996, the day that China conducted its last nuclear test, was Prime Minister Hashimoto's birthday, and on that day, he paid a visit to the Yasukuni Shrine. Before becoming prime minister, he had served as president of the Japan War-Bereaved Families Association as well as the head of the Diet Members' Group for Visiting the Yasukuni Shrine, and had frequently made visits there, including the "official visit" during the time of the Nakasone Cabinet. After Hashimoto became prime minister, he is said to have had the intention of "making personal visits on occasions other than the day commemorating the end of the war and the regular festivals in the spring and fall." After the July visit, he said, "Up until the end of the war, when I was a second grader in elementary school, I would see off soldiers departing for the front. The set phrase at those times was '[If I die in battle] come visit me at Kudan [the location of the Yasukuni Shrine].' Those people never came home. I feel that the promise I made to them as a child is still in effect, and so I chose a personal day, my birthday, a day close to my heart [for the visit]." It is said that he wanted to pay his respects in particular to the soul of his "cousin" who had doted on him when he was a small child. In the same interview, he said, "Because my cousin said he would come back there [to Yasukuni] as he was heading off to war, in that sense, I also want to go on the date we received the official announcement of his death."[67] The day the official announcement of Hashimoto's cousin's death arrived was October 16.

Hashimoto was surely aware of the reaction the Chinese government would have if the prime minister of Japan paid a visit to the Yasukuni Shrine. And yet he may have thought if he avoided major festivals and "that day" (August 15), the problem would not be as great. The situation, however, did not proceed as Prime Minister Hashimoto thought it would.

Immediately on July 29, Chinese foreign ministry spokesman Cui Tiankai criticized it, saying, "We express out profound regret that Prime Minister Hashimoto Ryūtarō paid a visit to the Yasukuni Shrine on the morning of the 29th. Prime Minister Hashimoto's visit has hurt the feelings of all the people of Asia, including China, who suffered greatly at the hands of Japanese militarists. Japan must show its heartfelt remorse for its past history of aggression and by real actions that it is walking the path of peaceful development."[68] Later, on August 11 and August 15, when four cabinet members paid visits to Yasukuni, criticism in the Chinese media reached the same levels as in 1985. The analysis of Beijing Broadcasting on August 13 was that "the dark clouds of militarism are hanging heavily in the Japanese sky,"[69] and the *People's Daily* on August 16 carried an article that stated, "Japan's reactionary view of history must end."

For China, Prime Minister Hashimoto's visit was in itself an important issue, but if that had been all, the criticism might not have been quite so great. The reason it stoked fears was that China seems to have thought the Yasukuni visit, the building of a lighthouse in the Senkaku Islands by a Japanese political organization that had taken place a few days earlier and the Japan-US Joint Declaration on Security, which America and Japan had agreed on in April 1996, were somehow all interconnected.

On July 14, seven members of the right-wing political group, the Japan Youth Society, built a lighthouse on Kitakojima, one of the Senkaku Islands. The solar-battery-operated lighthouse, approximately five meters high and made of a light aluminum alloy weighing about 210 kilograms, had a beam that, it was said, could be seen 30 kilometers out to sea.[70] The Japan Youth Society tried on July 25 to get permission for this lighthouse to be recognized as an official navigational signal, making the request to the Ishigaki Coast Guard of the Eleventh District Coast Guard Headquarters in the name of local fishermen.[71] Damaged by high winds and rain during Typhoon No. 9, the lighthouse was left leaning at a 45-degree angle, and the Society temporarily withdrew its request on August 8. But on September 9, it once again erected a lighthouse on Kitakojima that was said to be as high and have the same capacity as the previous one but was twice as strong. The following day it applied again to the Ishigaki Coast Guard for permission to be officially designated as a navigational signal in the name of interested local residents.[72] This political group had once before in 1988 set up a lighthouse in the Senkakus on the west coast of Uotsuri-jima and applied for permission for it in 1989. Because it fulfilled the necessary conditions for a lighthouse, the government was about to recognize it in 1990, but because of opposition from Taiwan and China, it shelved the application. This time, the UN Convention on the Law of the Sea had just gone into effect on July 20, and taking advantage of this opportunity, the Society was probably again pressuring the Japanese government to make clear its intentions regarding sovereignty over the Senkakus.

Hong Kong and Taiwan were more vociferous in their response to this matter than China was. On July 20, an organization of Taiwanese fisherman made plans to send out 200 boats and raise the ROC flag on Kitakojima. Because the first lighthouse had been destroyed, this attempt was put on hold for the moment. On September 4, however, a Hong Kong newspaper reporter and cameraman tried to land in the Senkakus and were prevented from doing so by a Japanese Coast Guard patrol boat. On September 15, a protest rally, around 10,000 strong according to the organizers' account, was held in Hong Kong, and in the second half of September, activists and journalists chartered a freighter and headed for the Senkakus. On September 26, four of the activists on board jumped into the sea in order to land on the island, and one of them, David Chan Yuk-cheung, died.

Compared to these activities in Hong Kong and Taiwan, the reaction in China at first was not all that intense. The response of Chinese foreign ministry spokesman Cui Tiankai on July 18 was that "the building of facilities on the islands by some Japanese arbitrarily is a serious encroachment of China's territorial sovereignty. We are paying close attention to this and demand that the Japanese government take immediate and effective steps to remove the undesirable influence that this has brought about."[73] The Japanese government's subsequent response was regarded by the Chinese as inadequate, however, and gradually their reaction changed to something sterner.

The first response from the Japanese government was made by Chief Cabinet Secretary Kajiyama Seiroku; he stated that in his personal opinion, "I insist that the territorial right [to the Senkakus] undeniably belongs to Japan. It is not the [government's] position to make any comment on legal matters."[74] As the reaction among Taiwanese fishermen and others grew stronger, Prime Minister Hashimoto ordered the Maritime Safety Agency (Japan Coast Guard), the police and other relevant agencies to prepare for "unforeseen events."[75] Again on September 13, Kajiyama repeated the government position that it had "neither the authority nor the ability to stop private individuals from acting in a place that belongs to them."[76] The reason why Kajiyama said that the government had no "authority" was because the island where the right-wing group tried to build a lighthouse was owned by a private citizen. Since these islands were returned from the United States in 1972 under the Okinawa reversion agreement, the three major islands that constitute the Senkakus had been privately owned.

The Japanese government's response that it was not in a position to get directly involved in this matter, in conjunction with Prime Minister Hashimoto's Yasukuni visit and the reaffirmation in April of the US-Japan Security Treaty, provoked very strong suspicions in China. The inference seems to have spread in China that there was a single, unified plan behind these three actions. The analysis of Beijing Broadcasting on August 13, for example, was that "right-wing politicians typified by Hashimoto . . . are trying to consolidate their own political position and win more right-wing votes by endorsing militarism."[77] And an article in the *People's Daily* on August 16 argued, "The tilt to the right of the Japanese government is becoming more blatant with every passing day. A narrow-minded nationalism is emerging; the policy views of some political parties are receding; the taboo of sending troops overseas has been broken; and the military alliance with the US has been strengthened. . . . Visits to the Yasukuni Shrine by some right-wing Japanese politicians are just the tip of the iceberg."[78] An editorial in the *People's Daily* stated, "It is by no means an accident that Japan is challenging China's sovereignty in the Diaoyutai [Senkaku] matter; it is the inevitable expression of the right-wing tilt of Japan's domestic government and an external show of force. In recent years, there has been a ceaseless stream of people in Japan who have tried to distort its history of aggression, beautify a war of aggression and plant the awareness of militarism in the Japanese people."[79]

On September 10, Chinese foreign ministry spokesman Shen Guofang stated the official position of the Chinese government on the matter, making it clear that China had lodged a protest with the Japanese government, and on the 11th, the Chinese Ambassador to Japan, Xu Dunxin, protested to the Ministry of Foreign Affairs. Ambassador Xu stated that "Both China and Japan at one time reached a joint recognition on the Diaoyutai issue; we temporarily shelved this problem and agreed to deal with it in the future. Now, the Japanese side is changing its original intention by accepting and allowing a free hand to the arbitrary actions taken by a Japanese group. The Chinese government strongly demands that the Japanese government steadily observe our mutual agreement, take immediate steps and avoid the negative impact and undesirable consequences that have been brought about by these actions, and ensure that another incident like this never happens again."[80]

The Chinese government, however, did not allow the anti-Japanese protests within China that were seen in Hong Kong and Taiwan. Activists like Tong Zeng who were seeking reparations for Japanese wartime aggression made plans for a protest in front of the Japanese Embassy in Beijing on September 18, but it was not allowed.

According to the foreign ministry spokesman, "Mr Tong Zeng has set out for the countryside to conduct technological research in his field of expertise."[81] It had no intention of having a showdown with Japan and probably feared that if it permitted anti-Japanese activities, they would spread to other, domestic issues.

In mid-September, the Japanese government, having seen the violent reactions in Hong Kong and Taiwan and observing the state of affairs in Beijing, where protest activities might also occur, tried to get on top of the situation. Following the precedent of 1990, it let the view be known that it would not authorize the lighthouse as a navigational signal. On September 24, Foreign Minister Ikeda met with his Chinese counterpart Qian Qichen and told him that the Senkakus "are an integral part of our country. Japan and China mutually recognize that this issue must not damage Japanese-Chinese relations as a whole. The Japanese government clearly states that it is neither involved in, nor does it support, the activities of the private group. It will deal prudently with the request for permission for the lighthouse,"[82] meaning that it would not be authorized. On October 4, Ikeda officially announced that the decision on this matter had been "deferred." The reason for doing so was a result of general considerations such as concern "for international relations and the safety of Japanese citizens abroad," and the fact that it was not "a building that complied with the government's intentions."[83] Although it had no direct legal relation to this incident, on October 3, the Hyogo Prefectural Police raided four sites belonging to the Japan Youth Society on the suspicion of violating the Sword and Firearms Control Law. On the same day, an adviser for the group was arrested on the same charge. In fact, the searches had the significance of making it clear that the Japanese government was not involved in the Society's activities in the Senkakus. China criticized the LDP for its House of Representatives' election campaign promise to call for Yasukuni visits and for its statement that the Senkakus were "Japan's integral territory." But in response, Prime Minister Hashimoto said on October 1, "That is a party decision; differences with government policy naturally occur. I have no intention of adopting such extreme measures as part of my foreign policy."[84]

On October 16, the anniversary of the day on which the notification of his cousin's death had been delivered, Prime Minister Hashimoto had hoped to make another visit to Yasukuni Shrine.

On September 26, it was reported that "someone close" to the prime minister had said that Hashimoto was "letting the Chinese side know in a way that they would clearly understand that he would not be visiting on that day."[85] On October 4, Hashimoto himself said, "I have always thought the visit was a personal issue, . . . but as long as I am prime minister, my actions must not invite misunderstandings or doubts against Japan; I must act more cautiously from now on," making clear his intention to forego any further visits during his tenure as prime minister.[86]

Improving Relations and Criticism over the Strengthening of the Japan-US Security Treaty

For the most part, around October 1996, Japanese-Chinese relations were headed toward improvement. China's fears of a single unifying trend behind Japan's hardline stance on Chinese nuclear testing, Prime Minister Hashimoto's Yasukuni visit, the Senkaku issue and the reaffirmation of the Japan-US Security Treaty may have been somewhat alleviated by the Japanese government's subsequent responses. Given Japan's extremely fluid political situation under a coalition government, the very idea that some sort of plot or unified plan among such divergent political phenomena was even possible bespeaks China's inadequate understanding of Japan's policy-making process. For the supreme leaders of China, however, who had neither the knowledge nor information to examine in depth the inner workings of Japanese policy decisions, it may not have been all that strange to think that there was some sort of "plot" behind Japan's words and deeds between the beginning of 1996 and September. Especially if they thought of Japan's policy-making as a mirror image of their own, the fact that the prime minister's visit to Yasukuni coincided with the building by a right-wing group of a lighthouse on a disputed island could only mean the existence of a calculated intention.

In any event, Japanese-Chinese vice-ministerial talks were held in Tokyo on October 29, and the two sides agreed to prioritize their relationship. Then, on November 23, while attending the APEC Ministerial Meetings in Manila, Foreign Minister Ikeda met with Foreign Minister Qian Qichen and let him know that talks would officially be held on the yen loans, the implementation of which had not yet been decided. By relaying the news about the opening of talks on the yen loans that had been subject to de facto "sanctions" in response to China's nuclear tests, the Japanese side was signaling its desire to improve relations. At the same time, Ikeda also indicated how much Japan valued China by telling Qian that during a speech right after the formation of the second Hashimoto Cabinet, the prime minister had placed relations with China as "important relations right along with the Japan-US relationship." In response to this Foreign Minister Qian said, "We take note of Prime Minister Hashimoto's clear statement on the importance of relations with China."[87]

After the meeting between the foreign ministers, President Jiang Zemin and Prime Minister Hashimoto met on November 24, and the trend toward repairing the relationship was confirmed. According to a Chinese report, Prime Minister Hashimoto said the following.

Japanese-Chinese relations, like Japanese-US relations, occupy a very important position in the foreign policy of Japan's new cabinet. The stable development of Japanese-Chinese relations is extremely important for the stability and development of the Asia-Pacific region, and both Japan and China bear an important responsibility for maintaining this. For that reason, the Japanese government wishes to do everything in its power to sincerely resolve the issues now facing us, to improve the Japanese-Chinese relationship and to move forward. Next year will be the 25th anniversary of the resumption of Japanese-Chinese relations, and we will develop the relationship between our two countries based on the Japan-China Joint Communiqué and the Treaty of Peace and Friendship.

The Japanese government acknowledges, profoundly regrets and sincerely apologizes for the fact that its colonial rule and aggression in the historical past caused great adversity to China and the countries of Asia. On this issue, the position of the new cabinet is in complete accord with that of the Murayama Cabinet. We also will not allow the revival of militarism in Japan, and on the basis of sincere remorse and increasing mutual trust, the Japanese government has made it clear that we must develop friendly relations with a view to the future.[88]

In response, President Jiang Zemin agreed to improve relations, saying, "Since the start of Japan's new cabinet, Prime Minister Hashimoto has made a number of comments giving importance to Chinese-Japanese relations, and we value this highly. We hope that the Japanese side will make further efforts so that its actions will correspond with its words." At this meeting, Prime Minister Hashimoto asked President Jiang to visit Japan, and Jiang asked Hashimoto to visit China.

Right after the meeting of the two leaders, beginning on November 27, negotiations were held in Beijing on the implementation of the yen loans, and an exchange of documents on the fourth yen loans for FY1996 took place on December 24. According to those same documents, the loans Japan was providing China for FY1996 amounted to a total of 170.511 billion yen for 22 projects in areas that included transportation, energy, environmental protection, communications and urban infrastructure. The conditions were repayment within 30 years with a 10-year grace period, and an interest rate of 2.3 percent per annum for general projects and 2.1 percent per annum for environmental protection projects.[89]

During Foreign Minister Ikeda's visit to China in March 1997, the Chinese side made even clearer its intention to improve relations. Ikeda signaled the Japanese side's desire for improvement by letting it be known that the grant aid which had been frozen was being resumed. In return, President Jiang Zemin and Premier Li Peng, without referring at all to the Senkaku issue, said that they "regarded very highly China's relationship with the US, Japan and Russia" and stated that there was no "zero sum" relationship among these three. At this meeting, it was decided that the Japanese prime minister and the Chinese premier would visit each other's country during 1997 and that President Jiang would visit Japan in 1998.

Despite this, what remained problems were those connected with the reaffirmation of the Japan-US Security Treaty. For Japan, this issue involved the country's long-term strategy and was not one in which China's preferences could play any part. In that sense, it was one on which complete agreement was nearly impossible given the geopolitical reality of the post-Cold-War era. In the summer of 1997, however, the issue became unnecessarily large when it became entangled in Japanese domestic politics.

It hardly needs saying that China was wary about the movement to reaffirm the Japan-US Security Treaty. It was well known there had been talk about the "China threat" in both the US and Japan. When the Japan-US Joint Declaration on Security was issued in April 1996 at the time of President Clinton's visit to Japan, China did not conceal its suspicions. On April 18, 1996, Chinese foreign ministry spokesman Shen Guofang said, "The security treaty between Japan and the United States is a bilateral, defensive arrangement formed by history and cannot go beyond its bilateral parameters. Any attempt to do so would give rise to complex factors in the regional situation. . . . If Japan increases its military and expands its defensive parameters, it will certainly be cause for vigilance and concern among Asian nations. China hopes that the Japanese government will adopt a cautious attitude on these issues."[90]

Although China indicated its wariness, it did not immediately ratchet up its anti-Japanese criticism. As we have already seen, it was after Hashimoto's visit to Yasukuni and the building of the lighthouse on the Senkakus by the Japan Youth Society that China's anti-Japanese criticisms intensified. As suspicions about Hashimoto's "tilt to the right" strengthened, the significance of the reaffirmation of the US-Japan Security Treaty became the source of intense misgivings. But, as has already been noted, the reaffirmation of the US-Japan Security Treaty formed the basis of Japan's post-Cold-War security policy, and its nature for the Japanese government was such that the purport of the Joint Declaration could not be changed simply because the Chinese government expressed its reservations. As a result, the only thing either side could do was for the Japanese to seek China's "understanding" on this issue and for the Chinese to continue to express their "concerns." Consequently, almost no mention was made of this issue at the meeting between Prime Minister Hashimoto and President Jiang, at which the move toward improved relations occurred.

But as the review of the Guidelines on Japanese-US Defense Cooperation agreed upon in the Joint Declaration got under way, the expressions of concern from the Chinese side once again became louder. What especially complicated the matter were the repeated statements by Japanese high officials whose views seemed to be different from one another. The one that started the problems off was a statement by LDP Secretary-General Katō Kōichi during a visit to China in July 1997. Katō met with Zeng Qinghong, head of the General Office of the Central Committee of Communist Party of China, Tang Jiaxuan, deputy secretary of Foreign Affairs, and Chi Haotian, minister of National Defense. During the meeting he reportedly said about the Guidelines review, "Frankly speaking, we're worried about what's going on in the DPRK [North Korea]. It's about what we should do to rescue Japanese when something happens and refugees cross the 38th parallel. . . . We didn't have China in mind," he insisted. Zeng Qinghong is said to have responded, "We are pleased by the Secretary-General's statement."[91] According to the *Asahi Shimbun* (July 18, 1997), Katō said that the Chinese side's understanding of the Guidelines was "still inadequate," and he acknowledged that he had been unable to fully dispel their concerns that the region the Guidelines applied to included the Taiwan Strait. On the 22nd, Katō met with Thomas Pickering, US Under Secretary of State for Political Affairs, and, according to the July 23 *Yomiuri Shimbun* (evening edition), he told him, "For China, the Guidelines are about the Taiwan issue. The Japanese and US governments need to work out how to deal with Taiwan before Prime Minister Hashimoto visits China." He is also said to have indicated that the US and Japan ought to confirm that the Taiwan Strait was not included in the region applicable to "the areas surrounding Japan" in the Treaty. The headline of the article reporting these comments was "US-Japan Should Confirm 'Taiwan Strait' Not Included in 'Areas Surrounding Japan,' LDP Secretary-General Katō Hints."

Criticism of this string of comments by Katō arose within Japan. Chief Cabinet Secretary Kajiyama, in particular, was critical, "It is better for deterrence if we don't put restrictions on particular areas. Undoubtedly, the Korean peninsula is more than 90 percent of the problem, but we ought not to say unconditionally that other regions are not."[92] At a subsequent LDP meeting, Katō explained that if it had been reported that he said "the Guidelines exclude Taiwan [from the regions to which the Treaty applies]," it was a mistake. Even when asked by the Chinese side, "I avoided answering by saying it is 'under consideration.'"[93]

The view still remained, however, that Katō's statements had been too considerate of China, and on August 17, Kajiyama made the following statement on a program on TV Asahi:

Originally the Japanese government left the area unrestricted. There is no question that the Korean peninsula occupies the larger part of our mind. But if we limited the area, it would raise the question whether other areas are different. [A war between China and Taiwan] naturally would be included. We have no intention of interfering in their internal affairs, but we would have enormous concerns if China were to try to take Taiwan by force. When we look at the Guidelines that are the basis for Japan-US security, how could we refuse to support American actions and say, "We won't do anything; we won't even give you a drink of water." The Japan-US Security Treaty wouldn't work effectively that way.[94]

Whether there were domestic political considerations behind Kajiyama's statement is not well known, but the Chinese media immediately reacted. The August 19 edition of *Xinhua News Agency* criticized Kajiyama for making "statements that threaten the sovereignty and safety of China."[95] The next day it also criticized the foreign ministry's Vice-Minister Yanai Shunji for saying that Kajiyama's statement represented the unified view of the Japanese government since 1960 and demanded that Japan "give up its absurd 'unified view.'"[96] The *People's Daily* of August 22 carried an editorial headlined "Serious Situation Damaging China-Japan Relations."

It does not seem, however, to have been the Chinese side's intention to use these comments to stop trying to improve China-Japan relations. On August 22, when Premier Li Peng was asked in Malaysia for his views on what Kajiyama had said, he replied, "These statements are a serious interference in Chinese internal matters. Taiwan is an integral part of China." But "we are just making clear our fundamental position"; on the whole, "China-Japan relations" are good, and "we hope to develop a normal, friendly and cooperative relationship with Japan because that is useful for regional peace and stability."[97]

Ultimately, as a result of Prime Minister Hashimoto's visit to China, which took place soon after this at the beginning of September, the two sides agreed to maintain the Japan-China relationship, even including the various issues surrounding the US-Japan Security Treaty. Throughout his visit Hashimoto showed his consideration for the Chinese side in his understanding of history, going to Shenyang and touring the September 18th Mukden Incident History Museum. He also rectified the confusion caused by Katō's and Kajiyama's statements on Japan's stance on the Guidelines and on Taiwan and conveyed to the Chinese side his government's policy on those issues. According to the Japanese media, Hashimoto told President Jiang Zemin, "The review of the Guidelines for Japan-US Defense Cooperation will carry through on its plans to move ahead while maintaining transparency. Our discussions are not conducted on the assumption of hypothetical situations that might occur in a specific country or region, including China. We plan to explain this to China once the process is complete. There will be no change in the framework of our Constitution, or in such positions as our exclusively defense-oriented policy and our three non-nuclear principles. . . . As for the Taiwan issue, Japan's consistent position is that we have no concept of 'two Chinas' and that we do not support Taiwan's independence."[98]

The review of the Guidelines was subsequently completed at the end of September, and the final report was made public. Although criticisms of it appeared in the Chinese media, these had no impact on moves to improve relations between the two governments. This became clear at the time of Premier Li Peng's visit to Japan, which took place in November. On Japan-US security, Li stated, "The Chinese government and the Chinese people have great concerns about the Japan-US Security Treaty. The Treaty ought to be defensive, and the positions on the Taiwan issue in the China-Japan Joint Communiqué and the Peace and Friendship Treaty must be maintained"; he refrained from making any further comment. When Prime Minister Hashimoto expressed his intention to actively push ahead with a Japanese-Chinese security dialogue, Li agreed saying, "An exchange of views in the security area is very important; we agree in principle on an invitation for Minister of National Defense Chi Haotian to visit Japan."[99]

Chapter 7

The Asian Financial Crisis

The Baht Crisis

When the Thai Central Bank announced in July 1997 that it was switching to a floating exchange rate system for the Thai baht, in quick succession financial crisis spread throughout Asia.[1] It was not just the baht; the currencies in Indonesia, the Philippines, South Korea and elsewhere dropped precipitously. Not only did the economic growth achieved by the "East Asian miracle" easily go into reverse; it became clear that the governments and societies in several countries were quite fragile.

Thailand, where the crisis began, was emblematic of Asian economic growth during the 1980s and 1990s. Having built the foundations for economic development on developmental authoritarianism and achieved democratization in the process, it was hailed as an "economic miracle." Along with other East Asian countries with authoritarian regimes—Park Chung-hee's South Korea, Marcos's Philippines, Suharto's Indonesia, etc.—ever since Prime Minister Sarit Thanarat had come to power as the result of a coup d'état in 1957, Thailand had made developmental authoritarianism the basis for economic growth. But the subsequent government process was characterized by a gradual movement toward democracy following cycles of "coup d'état—promulgation of a constitution—formation of political parties—general elections—parliamentary government—political crisis—coup d'état."[2]

As the result of a clash between the government and a pro-democracy movement in October 1973 (the Student Uprising), the military regime was overthrown, and a party government lasted for a while after that, but on October 6, 1976, a coup d'état took place after the army had brutally suppressed the pro-democracy movement (the Thammasat University Massacre). As it was subsequently impossible to return to a strong military dictatorship, a government that might be called a "semi-democracy" was launched under a new constitution in 1978.[3] The administration that in 1980 made Army General Prem Tinsulanonda prime minister lasted eight years, and in 1988, Chatichai Choonhavan, the first civilian leader in years, came to power. It was during the administrations of Prem and Chatichai that the Thai economy made enormous strides.

As a result of the rise in the yen exchange rate after the Plaza Accord of September 1985, enormous amounts of Japanese capital flowed into Southeast Asia, especially Thailand. Japanese ODA projects such as the Eastern Seaboard Development program (see Chapter 1) facilitated direct investment. This influx transformed Thailand's previous image as an exporter of agricultural products into that of an exporter of electrical appliances and other manufactured goods. Thanks to this investment boom, the Chatichai administration formulated a number of public works programs as well as plans for heavy and chemical industries such as petrochemical projects, integrated steel mills and a proposal to built its own automobile engine. But these huge projects led to vast amounts of corruption among key figures in the administration, and in February 1991, the army, led by General Suchinda Kraypayoon and others, staged a coup d'état and overthrew the government, signaling that the vicious cycle of Thai governments had not ended. Suchinda and others set about to make the diplomat Anand Panyarachun the prime minister of the provisional government, draw up a new constitution and hold general elections.

After the general elections of March 1992, however, huge anti-government protests erupted when, as a result of various twists and turns, Suchinda himself became prime minister. The situation got even worse when the army fired indiscriminately on crowds of demonstrators. As tensions mounted, the royal family, the stabilizer of last resort in Thai politics, intervened. In the middle of the night of May 20, King Bhumibol summoned Prime Minister Suchinda and the former governor of Bangkok, Chamlong Srimuang, the leader of the opposition, to the royal residence and advised them to resolve the conflict between government and anti-government forces through talks. As a result of the royal intervention, Prime Minister Suchinda resigned, and the situation calmed down. In September

1992, elections were held, and the Democratic Party came to power with Chuan Leekpai as prime minister. After the bloody incident in March, the Thai government finally headed toward stability. The government of Banham Silpa-Archa in 1995 was succeeded by Chavalit Yongchaiyudh in 1996, and there was a peaceful transfer of power, all as a result of general elections.

The post-1992 period of increasing democratization and government stability was, in fact, what brought about unprecedented economic growth in Thailand. In 1990, the per capita GDP was USD 1,528; in 1996, it had doubled to USD 3,040. In 1993, the World Bank published a report entitled *The East Asian Miracle* that cited Thailand and other East Asian countries as having good economic fundamentals.[4] More and more foreign capital flowed into Thailand. On top of that, the Thai government further liberalized capital transactions, and as a result, there was a massive influx of short-term capital with repayment dates of less than a year.

That does not mean, however, that the economy had no problems whatsoever. The financial crisis of 1997 did not occur out of the blue. But the arguments about its causes are complex, and there are many different theories. Competitiveness in the real economy may have been waning. In 1995, Paul Krugman provoked debate when he made the argument that because total factor productivity was not increasing in the East Asian countries, when investment stopped, their economies would also come to a standstill.[5] Others argued that economic growth in East Asia had many Asian characteristics, particularly those linked to structural corruption, i.e., "crony capitalism."

But since the triggers for the crisis were the exchange market and the financial market, it is hardly possible that there were not serious problems in both. From that perspective, the important facts are: (1) no matter what the cause might have been, Thailand in the mid-1990s had an enormous current account deficit; (2) this was financed by an enormous capital account surplus; and (3) the overwhelming majority of its capital transaction surplus flowed in in the form of short-term capital.

What proved decisive under these circumstances was what Yoshitomi Masaru and others have called "double mismatches."[6] The first of these was the "maturity mismatch" that was likely to occur when local banks raised short-term capital to finance long-term projects. The second was the "currency mismatch" that was likely to occur when the capital was raised in a foreign currency and then exchanged for local currency and allocated to local investments. For example, when short-term borrowing suddenly becomes impossible, if a bank has made only long-term loans, it cannot collect on those loans, and so repayment is no longer feasible. That is a "maturity mismatch." And, if the exchange rate of a country's currency suddenly drops, repaying foreign-denominated funds becomes extremely difficult for those banks which lent in the local currency. That is a "currency mismatch."

To sum up Yoshitomi Masaru's ideas in my own way:

> Once economic expansion, which has been financed by vast amounts of short-term loans from foreign banks denominated in foreign currencies, begins to move in the opposite direction, the value of the assets on the local banks' balance sheets falls as the result of an economic recession or the collapse of a bubble. This precipitates a withdrawal of foreign bank loans, causing a deficit in the country's capital balance as a whole and a drop in its foreign reserves. At this point, international speculators and others mount a short-selling offensive, and the currency authorities, forced to use their foreign reserves in order to maintain a fixed exchange rate, watch these reserves get lower and lower. If these authorities ultimately decide that they cannot maintain the fixed rate system, the currency depreciates. But the depreciation in the exchange rate produces a currency mismatch, causing the debts of local banks and companies to balloon and forcing them into insolvency. On the other hand, the same withdrawal of foreign bank loans ensnares local banks in a liquidity deficit as a result of the maturity mismatch. The deterioration of the local banks' balance sheets further exacerbates the withdrawal of foreign bank loans, and those balance sheets get worse and worse. Thus, a vicious cycle occurs: the more foreign loans are repatriated the worse local bank balance sheets get. This spirals out of control, as the currency continues to depreciate and the worsening of balance sheets becomes unstoppable. The currency does not simply fall; it goes into free fall.[7]

This was precisely the scenario that occurred in Thailand between 1996 and 1997. Beginning around 1996, international speculators repeatedly short-sold the baht, which continued to maintain a fixed exchange rate, but the attack on May 13, 1997 was devastating. According to the memoirs of Japan's Vice-Minister of Finance for International Affairs Sakakibara Eisuke,

> May 13, 1997 was when an enormous concerted attack on the Thai baht began, unlike anything that had ever happened before. On this one day, the volume of baht-dollar transactions exceeded USD 6 billion, and everyone in the market was selling. It wasn't just the hedge funds; American and European financial institutions and almost everyone else in the market were in a rush to sell. Only the Thai Central Bank and other currency authorities were buying.
>
> One factor that precipitated this attack was an analysis by the big American brokerage Goldman Sachs at the beginning of May, which spread the rumor that the baht was about to be devalued. The intervention of the Thai authorities on May 13 actually amounted to USD 6.3 billion on that one day. Even with major currencies like the yen and the dollar, it is rare for an intervention to exceed USD 5 billion in a single day. An intervention of USD 6.3 billion in the market for the baht, a single local Asian currency, was indeed astonishing.[8]

The Thai currency authorities made desperate efforts to defend the baht and managed to overcome this crisis. But having most likely used up virtually all their foreign currency reserves in the defense of the baht, they announced on July 2 that they were moving to a floating exchange rate system. In itself the move to float the currency may, of course, have been a rational policy decision. But the markets took the Thai authorities' announcement as a "declaration of defeat." The sell-off advanced even further, and the expectation was formed that the baht would continue to go down. The exchange rate, which had been 24.5–25.5 bahts to the dollar, fell to the 30 bahts to the dollar level by the end of July. With that, what Yoshitomi has described as a vicious cycle began to spiral out of control. What is more, the Thai situation did not remain in Thailand. The same sort of "double mismatch" existed in other countries as well.

On July 11, the Philippine Central Bank moved to a floating exchange rate system for the peso. That same day, Indonesia expanded the fluctuation margin for the rupiah. On July 14, Malaysia floated the ringgit. And on August 14, Indonesia, too, finally moved the rupiah to a floating exchange rate system. By September, the values of these currencies were down by 20 to 30 percent of what they had been before the crisis.

The immediate crisis, however, seemed to be in Thailand. Desperate to raise foreign capital, on July 29, Thailand appealed to the International Monetary Fund for help. After negotiations, an IMF-sponsored meeting of "Friends of Thailand" was held in Tokyo on August 11. Ultimately a package was put together to which the IMF committed USD 4 billion, the World Bank 1.5 billion, the Asian Development Bank 1.2 billion, Japan 4 billion, etc., for a total of USD 17.2 billion. On August 21, however, the Thai Central Bank announced that futures contracts for the coming year amounted to USD 23.4 billion. This further accelerated the baht sell-off in the markets, and the baht continued to fall until January 1998.[9] Furthermore, the IMF package applied the same prescription it had made to other countries that had previously become enmeshed in currency crises and demanded that the Thai government put into effect sweeping austerity measures. As a result, economic activity contracted even further.

While the economy was in crisis, it would be fair to say that the government functioned pretty well. Inevitably, criticism of Prime Minister Chavalit intensified. But the government's response was that of a law-abiding parliamentary system. In short, at the beginning of November, Prime Minister Chavalit announced his resignation, and as a result of a coalition in the National Assembly, former Prime Minister Chuan, head of the largest opposition party, came to power. Despite Thailand being in a state of crisis, the birth of the Chuan administration took place legally; even the stock markets felt good about the new government, and prices rose. Extremely faithful to the IMF's prescription, the Chuan administration introduced austerity measures and grappled with economic reform, so much so, that it might even have gone into overkill. The economic growth rate in 1997 had been a negative 1.8 percent; in 1998, it was a negative 10.4 percent.[10]

But somehow or other the government functioned during the economic crisis. It might be noted that on August 15, at the very height of the crisis, a draft constitution, which for the first time had been drawn up through a democratic process, was presented to the National Assembly. A new Constitution Drafting Assembly consisting of 99 popularly elected representatives submitted it. The National Assembly adopted the constitution on September 27, and it went into effect on October 11.[11]

The Fall of the Suharto Regime

By contrast, in Indonesia, the economic crisis subsequently gave rise to a serious political and social crisis. When the baht crisis happened in July, very few would have predicted that Indonesia would succumb to a severe economic crisis, let alone a political one. Government finances were balanced, there was no inflation, and the country had achieved an annual growth rate of 7 to 8 percent. When the economic crisis struck, the government of Indonesia was the authoritarian system under President Suharto that had lasted for nearly 30 years. Indonesia is a country of more than 17,000 islands that extends nearly 5,100 kilometers from east to west, longer than the distance between New York and San Francisco, and where there are more than 300 ethnic groups speaking some 200 to 400 different languages. The Netherlands had ruled over this vast diversity of people and places as the "Dutch East Indies," but the person who unified it and established it as the independent country of "Indonesia" was Sukarno, the founding father. After Sukarno fell from power at the time of the September 30th Movement of 1965 under circumstances that are still not entirely clear, the person who seized control was Suharto, the leader of the army; he was the one who made Indonesia into what was called the most stable authoritarian regime in Asia. As the leading political figure in Southeast Asia, he was a driving force behind the development of ASEAN, and in APEC he brought to fruition the Bogor Declaration promoting free trade in Asia and the Pacific in 1994.[12]

Although the Suharto regime was considered stable, not surprisingly, its contradictions had become obvious with the passage of 30 years. As long as Suharto remained healthy, no one ever dreamed that the Suharto regime might cease to exist, but every time one heard that Suharto was going to be reelected president again, as one might expect, there was a sense that perhaps he had been around too long. The Suharto regime, which had started as a military government, had ultimately changed into a dictatorship, and this caused vested interests and power to be concentrated on the Suharto family. As a result, the nation's armed forces, which functioned as the country's stabilizing force, and the Golkar (Suharto's support group) both turned into organizations noted for their excessive flattery of the Suharto family.[13] While most people said resignedly that the Suharto regime would last, in reality, it was steadily being hollowed out.

It must be added, however, that the decisions the Indonesian government took after the baht crisis seemed to have been sound. It was rational to float the Indonesian rupiah. The range of depreciation between July and August was not all that great. And in October, when Indonesia requested assistance from the IMF, it seemed to show its intention to move toward economic reform.

But the situation subsequently deteriorated. Emergency aid totaling USD 36 billion was agreed on at the Friends of Indonesia meeting at the end of October, but the conditionality imposed by the IMF at that time caused severe shocks both economically and politically. From an economic perspective, the IMF's demands for structural reform were inappropriate in many ways. In the midst of ongoing financial uncertainty, it demanded extreme fiscal restraint. But it did live up to the expectations of political forces both inside and outside Indonesia calling for democratization. Suharto's sons were involved in some of the unnecessary projects that the IMF demanded be stopped, and the Suharto family also had interests in some of the 16 banks that had been ordered to suspend operations. Just at that moment, Suharto's health deteriorated; he was forced to miss the ASEAN summit meeting scheduled for December, and the political situation in Indonesia became opaque.

In the midst of this disquieting political situation, the government's draft budget was announced on January 7, 1998, and this would plunge the economy into the abyss in the coming months. This budget, based on the excessively optimistic projection that the exchange rate would be 4,000 rupiah to a dollar, was an increase of more than 32 percent over the previous year, far from the fiscal belt-tightening demanded by the IMF. The markets reacted in unison, and the exchange rate reached 10,000 rupiahs to the dollar. The US and the IMF sent senior officials to Indonesia demanding that the draft budget be revised. As a result, the Indonesian government acceded to all of the IMF's demands for a large-scale review

President Suharto and IMF Managing Director Camdessus (March 15, 1998).
Photo: Reuters/Kyodo News

of the draft budget and President Suharto's family business. The photograph of President Suharto signing the agreement with IMF Managing Director Michel Camdessus watching over him as if looking down from above was carried by the media around the globe, conveying the impression to the world that the Suharto regime had finally capitulated to the IMF.

But economic conditions did not improve at all. The markets did not believe the Suharto government's efforts were genuine. As prices soared, protest demonstrations and the looting of food and daily necessities were taking place everywhere. On March 10, presidential elections were held as scheduled, and since there was no opposition candidate, Suharto won his seventh election. The cabinet list that the president subsequently announced once again betrayed the expectations of the international community and those within the country hoping for reform. Many members of the new cabinet were close Suharto allies and family members.

On May 4, the raising of prices for gasoline, electricity and other public utilities sparked demonstrations and rallies primarily at universities throughout the country protesting the rate hikes, criticizing the family business and demanding that Suharto step down.

From May 5 on, protest rallies and demonstrations spread outside college campuses and onto the streets; anti-Suharto riots as well as violence and looting aimed at ethnic Chinese and others occurred. Some of the security forces used live ammunition, and people were killed. On May 14, the city of Jakarta was temporarily without a government. Support for Suharto in the administration's inner circle fell, and on the 20th, General Wiranto, commander of the Indonesian armed forces, announced that he could no longer support him. US Secretary of State Madeleine Albright said in a speech, "Now he has the opportunity for a historic act of statesmanship."[14] On May 21, President Suharto announced his resignation, and Vice President B.J. Habibie came to power. After 32 years, what had once been called the most stable authoritarian rule in Southeast Asia had come to an end.

The Crisis in South Korea

Indonesia was not the only other place to be affected by the financial crisis. South Korea faced a particularly serious situation. According to the memoirs of Japanese Vice-Finance Minister Sakakibara Eisuke,

> It was on September 22 that George Soros informed me that South Korea was a problem. From that time on, in fact, banks first in America and Europe and then in Japan quickly began to withdraw their loans. During the two months from the end of September to the end of November, foreign debt in South Korean banks actually fell by USD 12.3 billion. The South Korean Central Bank tried somehow to stop the deterioration of the banks' financing from leading to a crisis in the entire financial system by depositing foreign reserves in the banks, but because the foreign reserves at the end of September only amounted to USD 21.1 billion, by the end of November, they were driven to the point where, if the capital outflow continued to accelerate, there was no way of knowing what the financing for the month would be.[15]

Problems in the South Korean economy had surfaced at the beginning of 1997, and more than 40 listed companies went bankrupt during that one year. In particular, the managerial crisis at the Kia

Group, whose core business was Kia Motors, the number two auto maker in the domestic market, aroused deep anxiety among South Koreans, who had bought into the myth that government-supported conglomerates could not go bankrupt.[16] That year was the final year of President Kim Young-sam's term in office, and politically, the second half of the year was all about the presidential elections. The candidates for president were Lee Hoi-chang of the ruling party, Kim Dae-jung of the opposition party and Lee In-je, who had broken with the ruling party just before the election. In addition to the split in the ruling party camp, the economic crisis probably worked in Kim Dae-jung's favor. He won 40.3 percent of the vote, defeating Lee Hoi-chang with 38.7 percent, and secured the office of president. This was the first time that a ruling party candidate had ever been defeated in a South Korean presidential election.

During the presidential elections, the South Korean economy had continued to worsen; on November 21, the Kim Young-sam administration asked the IMF for USD 20 billion in emergency assistance. This request for aid was taken by the markets as conceding defeat, however, and the Korean won plummeted instead. An aid program was finally agreed upon on December 3, and the total sum reached USD 55 billion: 21 billion from the IMF, 10 billion from the World Bank, 4 billion from the Asian Development Bank, 10 billion from Japan, 5 billion from the US, etc. Despite this, however, there was a sell-off of the won, which dropped from 1,166 won to the dollar to 1,533 won to the dollar. South Korea's foreign reserve holdings plummeted to such dangerous levels that the G7 issued an emergency statement.

Kim Dae-jung, who had just been elected president, declared that he would thoroughly implement the agreement with the IMF, and before he took office on February 25, he cooperated with the Kim Young-sam administration and in rapid succession adopted reform measures. Although the subsequent management of the economy came to be known as the "IMF Rule," the fact that Kim Dae-jung, who could well be called the symbol of the country's pro-democracy movement, had called on the Korean people to endure hardships was a powerful factor in rescuing South Korea from the crisis. According to a public opinion poll conducted by Gallup South Korea on January 10, 82.9 percent of respondents said they were glad that Kim had been elected president.[17] In 1998, at every international meeting he attended, President Kim appealed to the heads of government from around the world to invest in South Korea.

The Crisis in Malaysia

Malaysia, too, was hugely affected by the baht crisis. Between the start of the crisis and August 1998, the value of the Malaysian currency, the ringgit, plummeted by 40 percent from 2.5 to 4.2 ringgits to a dollar. During the same period, the price index for the Kuala Lumpur stock exchange also plunged from 1012.8 to 302.9. Thirty companies listed on the exchange went bankrupt between February and August 1998.[18]

For Malaysian Prime Minister Mahathir, who was never hesitant to criticize the countries of Europe and America, this crisis must have had quite an impact. Ever since he took office in 1981, Prime Minister Mahathir had resorted to highhanded measures to manage domestic criticism of his government, but what had vindicated his authoritarian rule were the results—economic growth. With a territory that spans the Malay peninsula and Sabah and Sarawak on the island of Borneo and with a complicated demographic consisting of 65 percent Malay, around 25 percent of Chinese descent and 6 percent of Indian origin, but where the Chinese minority is economically powerful, Malaysia has always had sensitive ethnic issues. After the bloodshed resulting from race riots on May 13, 1969 (the 13 May Incident), the ethnic issue became extremely sensitive, and the so-called Bumiputera, or sons of the soil, policies that gave preferential treatment to Malays were consistently adopted.[19] After Mahathir took power, these complex social conditions along with Mahathir's own personality helped to strengthen his authoritarian rule. But, now, the Asian crisis had greatly shaken the economy that was the basis for its legitimacy.

Unlike Thailand, Indonesia and South Korea, however, Mahathir did not ask the IMF for assistance. He, too, was forced to freeze the construction of large-scale projects that would require imports of vast amounts of capital. But having reviewed his economic policies since the beginning of 1998, Mahathir did not adopt the austerity measures that the IMF had recommended to other countries and instead decided on a policy package that called for the expansion of total demand and restrictions on capital transactions. The policy that the Malaysian government adopted on September 1, 1998 is summed up by journalist Hayashida Hiroaki as follows:

> In addition to instituting a Central Bank licensing system on all ringgit transactions between non-residents (foreign companies, etc.), there was also a licensing system for ringgit transfers from non-residents to residents (domestic companies, etc.). It was forbidden, for one year, to take out of the country the foreign currency obtained by selling Malaysian stocks and ringgit-denominated assets that non-residents had bought. Residents, too, were limited to taking no more than 10,000 ringgits out of the country. At the same time, a fixed exchange rate of 3.80 ringgits to a dollar was introduced. The administration also embarked on a substantial expansion of government spending and a reduction of high interest rates.[20]

On the one hand, the aim was to expand aggregate demand at home by Keynesian policies to deal with the worsening economy, while putting a stop to short-term capital transactions to prevent invested capital from flowing out of the country. The latter policy came as a thunderbolt to foreign hedge funds and others that dealt in short-term capital transactions, and many of them suffered losses as a result. Because Prime Minister Mahathir himself had repeatedly said since the start of the crisis that hedge funds were the culprits behind it, as soon as the restrictions on capital transactions were announced, there was an outpouring of criticism of Malaysia especially from the US and Europe. They were denounced as a mistaken economic policy that went against the tide of globalization.

At that very moment, the rivalry within Malaysia between Mahathir and Deputy Prime Minister Anwar Ibrahim, whom Mahathir had named to be his successor, assumed serious proportions in regard to the handling of the crisis. Anwar is said to have called for the strict economic reforms that the IMF and others were recommending. The friction between the two was not simply a conflict over policy; it had all the makings of a power struggle, and the day after Mahathir announced the restrictions on capital transactions, he announced Anwar's dismissal. Then, in the early hours of September

21, the Malaysian police arrested Anwar on suspicion of violating the Maintenance of the Public Order Act. The prosecution subsequently indicted him on a charge of aberrant sexual behavior (homosexuality). Anwar was ultimately sentenced to six years in prison for abuse of authority and nine years for sodomy.[21] The fall of Anwar was regarded as an all-too-blatant attempt on Mahathir's part to crush an opponent, and Malaysia provoked criticism, primarily in the American and European media, for promoting an anti-democratic government, on the one hand, and for its illiberal, anti-globalization economy.

On the economic side, Mahathir's "irregular" restrictions on capital transactions were a success. Supported by the settlement of the worldwide crisis between the end of 1998 and 1999 and a buoyant US economy, the Malaysian economy steadily recovered. A year later, restrictions on overseas remittances of profits on stock sales were unconditionally eased, and yet no massive capital outflow occurred. But while Mahathir's economic policies succeeded in averting a crisis, Malaysia's budget deficit worsened, and, on the political side, this led to political demands at home for a freer system. Mahathir remained in office until 2003 and voluntarily handed power over to his successor, Abdullah Badawi. Under Prime Minister Badawi, the modes of authoritarian control formed in Mahathir's time gradually moved toward greater freedom.

Japan and the Asian Financial Crisis

At first glance, the Japanese economy in 1996, which had been in recession since the collapse of the bubble economy in 1991, seemed to be in very good shape. The economic growth rate from January to December of that year was at 3.6 percent, the highest it had been since the bubble burst. Prime Minister Hashimoto Ryūtarō, who came to power in January 1996, took advantage of this growth rate and tried to implement fiscal and other long-term reforms. At the time, Japan's budget deficit had already climbed to 5 percent of GDP. The national and local deficit balance was 450 trillion yen, Hashimoto said, the equivalent of each and every Japanese citizen, including infants and the elderly, being in debt to the tune of 3.5 million yen.[22] His first step in restoring government finances was to raise the consumption tax. The House of Representatives' election held on October 20, 1996 had been the first to be held under the system of single-seat constituencies with proportional representation, which had been introduced as an important item of political reform in 1994. Hashimoto campaigned on the promise of raising the consumption tax the following April from 3 percent to 5 percent, and defeated Ozawa Ichirō's New Frontier Party, which said it would keep the tax as it was. In April 1997, the consumption tax was in fact raised to 5 percent, special tax cuts were abolished, and politically these moves did not become a major problem. The Japanese people supported the Hashimoto government's course of fiscal consolidation. Since the opposition camp at the time was in disarray because of a split in the New Frontier Party among other things, the Hashimoto administration was fortunate to have smooth sailing. In the election for the leader of the LDP in September 1997, Hashimoto was reelected by acclamation. The economy was already showing signs of weakness, but the government continued to hold the view that "business is picking up."

Japan's response when the Thai baht crisis struck in July 1997 was, therefore, exactly that of an economic superpower. When Thailand asked the international community for help, Japan presided over the Friends of Thailand meeting in Tokyo and promised to contribute USD 4 billion, the same amount as the IMF. As a result of its energetic efforts at the Friends of Thailand meeting, the idea arose in the Ministry of Finance to set up an "Asian Monetary Fund" in order to deal even more aggressively with financial crises like this in Asia. According to Sakakibara's memoirs,

> We concluded that we should ride the wave that had crested at the Friends of Thailand meeting and accelerate it even further by immediately proposing the establishment of such a fund at the general meeting of the IMF and the World Bank in Hong Kong scheduled for September 23–24. Thinking back on it now, the plan was much too hasty, and the failure to lay the groundwork with China and the US was a fatal flaw, but I felt at the time we were being carried along by the momentum and went for it right off the bat.[23]

The plan is said to have begun being discussed within the Ministry of Finance sometime around September 1996 as a way to deal with future crises.[24] But discussions were strictly limited to ministry experts in charge of international finance. After the baht crisis, studies started in earnest, and Japan began to lay the groundwork for creating a "USD 100 billion fund centered on ten Asian countries and regions, China, Hong Kong, Japan, South Korea, Australia, Indonesia, Malaysia, Singapore, Thailand and the Philippines."[25] But the fact that the US was not included in the plan as well as the fact that the AMF, although cooperating with the IMF, would also be able to act independently of it, incurred American criticism. To counter these efforts to set up an AMF, the view even spread primarily in the European countries and the US that Japan was trying to create a fund of this sort in order to cozy up to the "crony capitalism" of Asia's authoritarian regimes. Having been left out in the cold, the US at first reacted strongly, and Deputy Secretary of the Treasury Lawrence Summers stiffly began his protest to Vice-Minister Sakakibara with the words, "I thought you were my friend." Not only was there a fierce reaction to the fund from the US, China didn't support it either, and in the end the plan came to a nothing. Japan later changed its response to that of cooperating with the IMF in dealing with each individual crisis.

As for the reason the US was opposed, one possibility that has been mentioned is that "it took [the fund] as a Japanese challenge to American hegemony in Asia."[26] But another theory suggests that "the US and the IMF did not understand the depth of the Asian currency crisis."[27] Since they believed that the baht crisis was a uniquely Asian phenomenon of "crony capitalism," they concluded optimistically that the crisis would be confined to Asia and that there was no need for the special framework that Japan was proposing. In fact, the crisis went beyond Southeast Asia and spread worldwide.

Meanwhile, dark economic clouds were also beginning to hover over Japan. The deflationary policies begun in April steadily drove the economy into recession, and the situation noticeably deteriorated at Japanese financial institutions, which were weighed down by bad debts. Just then the Asian financial crisis occurred. To begin with, Japanese banks had been the largest providers of short-term funds to East Asian countries. When these banks along with banks from Europe and elsewhere began to withdraw their funds en masse, the financial crisis can be said to have begun. According to Kuroda Haruhiko, who was then director-general of the International Bureau in the Ministry of Finance,

> But they were caught in a trap of their own devising and were strangling themselves with their own hands. Because they were rapidly withdrawing their money, the currency crisis in these countries just became more and more serious, and the loans they had made went from bad to worse. As Japanese banks strangled themselves in this way, it caused confidence in them, already greatly shaken with the collapse of the bubble economy at home, to sink much lower.[28]

On November 3, Sanyo Securities, one of Japan's second-tier securities companies, filed for protection under the Corporate Rehabilitation Law and went bankrupt.

> Sanyo Securities was a mid-level brokerage and a participating member of the money market. In the Japanese money market, not only banks but mid-level and higher securities companies also take part and deal in short-term funds. It was in this money market that Sanyo Securities went bankrupt, and the first default on financial obligations in the postwar period occurred. . . . Up until then no one ever dreamed a default would occur there. . . . But because it had happened in Japan's money market, where no one imagined this sort of thing could possibly occur, soon financial institutions at the regional bank level and below were no longer supplying funds to the money markets, and the supply of funds stopped almost completely, except to a very few city banks. And so the big banks, which were wholly dependent on the money market for their ordinary short-term funds, were at a loss as to what to do. The Japanese banking world had been backed into a corner.[29]

On November 17, when merger talks with the Hokkaido Bank came to a dead end, the Hokkaido Takushoku Bank declared bankruptcy. Then, on November 22, the distinguished firm of Yamaichi Securities, one of Japan's big four brokerages, was forced to go out of business. In the case of the bankruptcy of Yamaichi Securities, not only was

Yamaichi itself unable to raise funds from the money market because of a scandal, its main bank could not do so either, and ultimately it was impossible to save Yamaichi. As Kuroda Haruhiko recalls, "There has never been a time before or since that I had the feeling of crisis as I did then. The following year, 1998, the Long-Term Credit Bank of Japan and the Nippon Credit Bank went bankrupt, but the crisis of November 1997 was much closer to a real crisis than that was."[30]

At that very moment, on November 28, 1997, the Diet passed the Fiscal Structural Reform Act, aimed at making national and local fiscal deficits less than 3 percent of GDP by 2003 and reducing the issuance of deficit-financing government bonds to zero. It was a bill that deserves to be called the finishing touch to the Hashimoto administration's fiscal consolidation plans. This hyper-austere bill was approved just at the time when financial institutions were going bankrupt one after another and the flow of money was coming to a standstill. Ultimately, the economic growth rate for fiscal 1997 (April 1997 to March 1998) was minus 0.7 percent, the first negative growth rate since the first oil shock 23 years earlier.

Since the budgetary process for 1998 was based on the Fiscal Structural Reform Act, even the budget that passed in March 1998 was incredibly austere. At that point in the spring of 1998, the crisis was over in Thailand, but was deepening in South Korea and Indonesia. With crisis throughout Asia and growing concern about the financial situation of its own economy, Japan was strengthening the impression that it would, of all things, continue to adopt deflationary policies. Some even compared Prime Minister Hashimoto to US President Herbert Hoover, who had taken deflationary measures after the worldwide stock market crash in 1929. In fact, on April 3, the US television network NBC superimposed a picture of President Hoover over that of Hashimoto for the latter's failure to come up with effective economic policies.[31] In April, after the budgetary process had ended, a revised stimulus budget was hastily drawn up; this may have been the only way of getting it through the Diet, but it reinforced the impression that neither Japan nor the Hashimoto administration was capable of managing the economy as the situation demanded.

Of course, that does not mean that the Hashimoto administration did not engage at all in Asian diplomacy. In March 1998, when conflict arose between the IMF and the Suharto regime over economic reforms, Prime Minister Hashimoto made a hasty trip to Indonesia to get Suharto to cooperate with the IMF, and Suharto agreed.

In May, India and Pakistan shocked the world by conducting nuclear tests. Immediately after India's test, the Japanese government sent a special envoy (Noboru Seiichirō, head of the Cabinet Councillors' Office on External Affairs) to Pakistan and asked for self-restraint, but that request went unheeded. The Japanese government conveyed to both sides Japan's position that nuclear testing was unacceptable and extremely regrettable and took steps to stop new grant aid and yen loans to both countries. For Japanese, the Indian and Pakistani nuclear tests were an issue related to their national identity, one that left them no choice but to oppose. But even though India and Pakistan were Asian countries, at that time, the distance between Japan and India and Pakistan was still as far away as ever. Indeed, one reason Prime Minister Hashimoto took clear economic sanctions against the two South Asian countries in such a short time was that there were no vested interests in Japan prepared to challenge the country's anti-nuclear identity and oppose them. It must be added, however, that Japanese economic sanctions did not change either country's attitude.

Ultimately, the LDP was only able to win 45 seats in the House of Councillors' election in July 1998, far fewer than the 61 seats it had had before, and Prime Minister Hashimoto was forced to resign. After his resignation, the person who took power was Obuchi Keizō, the head of the LDP's largest faction, the Heisei Research Council (the old Takeshita faction). Because Kajiyama Seiroku, who belonged to the same faction, suddenly announced his candidacy, that meant there were two candidates from the same faction. When Koizumi Jun'ichirō also announced his intention to run, the election for the LDP presidency became a three-way race. Although Kajiyama and Koizumi were highly popular with the general public, there were 366 LDP members in both Houses of the Diet and 47 representatives from the prefectures for a total of 413 votes. Obuchi got 225 votes and won the election.

Obuchi, however, who had not done much to gain attention up to then, had the image of being someone who lacked charisma and had simply come to power through his steady work in the largest LDP faction. Internationally as well, the assessment in *The New York Times*

(July 13 edition) definitively summed it up by saying that Obuchi had "all the pizazz of a cold pizza." The support rate for his cabinet at first hovered around the 20 percent level.[32] But when he dared to select an important figure like former Prime Minister Miyazawa Kiichi to be his Minister of Finance, it signaled that he wanted to do something about the economic crisis both at home and abroad.

What the Obuchi administration came up with to deal with the Asian crisis was the New Miyazawa Initiative. The plan, which was announced at an IMF annual meeting in October 1998, was "a package of support measures totaling USD 30 billion, of which USD 15 billion will be made available for the medium- to long-term financial needs for economic recovery in Asian countries, and another USD 15 billion will be set aside for their possible short-term capital needs during the process of implementing economic reform."[33] The medium- to long-term financial needs envisioned were:

(1) Supporting corporate debt restructuring in the private sector and efforts to make financial systems sound and stable;
(2) Strengthening the social safety net;
(3) Stimulating the economy (implementation of public undertakings to increase employment); and
(4) Addressing the credit crunch (facilitation of trade finance and assistance to small- and medium-sized enterprises).

These measures were aid that would be useful for countries that had overcome the short-term crisis, but they also sent the message that, even though its own economy was in very bad shape, Japan was prepared to provide large-scale assistance; as a result, the estimate of the Obuchi government rose in Asia.

In a policy speech that Obuchi himself had given in Singapore in May 1998 when he was foreign minister, he had said, "Economic crisis has its heaviest impact on the poor, the aged, the disabled, women and children, and other socially vulnerable segments of the population," and he designated the issues related to them as "human security" concerns.[34] After he became prime minister, he developed this line of thought even further, and in a policy speech in Vietnam in December 1998, he described the second major task that needed to be carried out after the New Miyazawa Initiative as follows:

The second area where our efforts are needed is "placing emphasis on human security." "Human security" is a concept that takes a comprehensive view of all threats to human survival, life and dignity and stresses the need to respond to such threats. The economic crisis confronting the Asian countries today has been a direct blow to their socially vulnerable—the poor, women and children, and the elderly—threatening their survival and dignity. We need urgently to implement measures for the socially vulnerable who are affected by the Asian economic crisis. Japan will continue to address this area utilizing its official development assistance and multilateral frameworks such as APEC.

At the same time, even in times of economic crisis, we should not forget cooperation on medium- and long-term problems such as environmental degradation, narcotics and international organized crime which need to be addressed if we wish to protect human survival, life and dignity. Japan has decided this time to contribute 500 million yen (USD 4.2 million) for the establishment of the "Human Security Fund" under the United Nations so that international organizations concerned can provide support in a flexible and timely manner to projects that are to be implemented in this region.[35]

The reputation of the Obuchi administration in the countries of Southeast Asia slowly rose. The *Far Eastern Economic Review*, reporting on Prime Minister Obuchi's visit to Hanoi, wrote "Japan is back." According to the same article "What makes the Hanoi announcement different from Tokyo's past rhetoric on regional cooperation is that, this time, Japan came armed with cold cash and concrete proposals." The same article quotes Thai Foreign Minister Surin Pitsuwan as saying, "The Japanese want to show leadership, which has been conspicuously missing from the US." According to the article, although the prevailing impression of Japan among the people of Southeast Asia had been that "Tokyo is sitting on the margins of the economic crisis licking its own economic wounds," the change in Japan had attracted attention.[36]

Chapter 8

East-Asian Regionalism and Japan

ASEM

One development that came to command much attention as a result of the Asian financial crisis was the rise of East-Asian-oriented regional frameworks, specifically the framework centered on the summit meetings known as ASEAN+3. As has already been examined earlier, such a plan had been proposed right after the start of APEC but had never materialized—Prime Minister Mahathir of Malaysia's idea for an East Asia Economic Caucus (EAEC). But the United States, particularly the Bush administration, was strongly against the plan, and partly for that reason, Japan, too, was extremely cautious, and the other ASEAN countries were also not all that keen. The EAEC, it was said, would split Asia and the Pacific down the middle; it was a plan to form a "non-white club" that discriminated against "white" countries. It was also interpreted as an attempt at "closed regionalism." As a result, the plan was essentially shelved and never made much progress.

Even before the Asian financial crisis, however, groups that consisted of roughly the same countries as postulated in the EAEC plan had come to be formed, albeit without as clear an intention as Dr Mahathir's. The Asia-Europe Meeting (ASEM) offered a first such occasion. Faced with the explosive growth of the East Asian economies in the early 1990s, Europe became aware that its East Asian strategy had failed to keep up with the times. And so in July 1994, the European Commission proposed a "New Asia Strategy." That September, the EU's "New Asia Strategy" was explained to the Asian side at an EU-ASEAN Ministerial Meeting held in Karlsruhe, Germany. In response, Prime Minister Goh Chok Tong of Singapore, while on a visit to France in October, suggested holding a meeting of European and Asian heads of state.[1] In a speech at the Institut Français des

Relations Internationales, Goh "noted that Apec bridged North America and East Asia, while North America and Europe also had substantial ties. What was missing in the tripolar economic world was the link between Europe and East Asia."[2] At this stage, the proposal was clearly Goh's; he said he would need to sound out the feelings of the countries at the APEC Summit to be held later at Bogor. Prime Minister Goh proposed this Europe-Asia summit even more clearly at the end of January 1995 in a speech to the annual World Economic Forum in Davos. By February, according to Singapore's Foreign Minister S. Jayakumar, there was already an "ASEAN consensus on a Europe-Asia summit."[3] On January 27, just before Prime Minister Goh made his speech at the World Economic Forum, he had consulted with Vice-Premier Zhu Rongji of China and received his support.[4] Even before this, there were reports that the presumptive participants on the Asian side would be the countries of ASEAN as well as Japan, China and Korea, the same members as for the EAEC.[5]

What further advanced the implementation of the Asia-Europe Meeting was an ASEAN Senior Officials Meeting held on March 18. At this meeting, ASEAN is said to have decided on the basic plan of holding the first summit meeting in Thailand between February and April 1996.[6] It was also reported that Singapore argued for including Australia and New Zealand among the countries participating on the Asian side, but, "in view of EU circumstances negative to the participation of both countries," the Asian side would in fact be the countries hypothetically assumed for the EAEC plan.[7]

At just the same time as the ASEM preparatory meeting, another meeting with possible links to the EAEC was being proposed—that of ASEAN economic ministers and those from Japan, China and South Korea planned to be held in Phuket, Thailand, at the end of April 1995. When Japan's MITI and ASEAN held a meeting in Chiang Mai in the fall of 1994, Deputy Prime Minister Supachai Panitchpakdi of Thailand had suggested it to MITI Minister Hashimoto Ryūtarō, but because such a meeting would be made up of the hypothetical members of the EAEC, Hashimoto was cautious and indicated that Japan would be willing to participate if Australia and New Zealand did, but that if they did not, it would be difficult for Japan to do so.[8] On April 10, word came from Thailand that ASEAN could not reach a consensus on the participation of Australia and New Zealand, and so Japan decided not to attend the meeting. In response to Japan's decision, South Korea took the position that it would not attend if Japan was not there, and since the meeting would be meaningless if only China attended, the host country Thailand abandoned plans for an ASEAN, Japanese, Chinese and South Korean economic ministers meeting.[9]

At the beginning of May 1995, an EU-ASEAN Senior Officials Meeting was held, and it formally agreed to launch the Asia-Europe Meeting. The main topic at issue at this meeting was the membership of ASEM. Although the European side showed a willingness to have Hungary, Poland and the Czech Republic participate, it was more problematic on the Asian side. ASEAN's assumption was that the members would be the then-six ASEAN countries, Vietnam, which would become a member of ASEAN in July, Japan, China and South Korea. As an ASEAN working paper said, "for Asia, the most important consideration is to include dynamic economies which have contributed to the region's prosperity and growth." There was also a report at the time that, in addition to the above countries, Hong Kong, Taiwan, New Zealand and India indicated they wanted to take part.[10] Ultimately, the participating countries agreed on at this meeting were the 15 members of the EU and, as had been assumed all along, ten Asian countries—six ASEAN countries and Vietnam, Japan, China and South Korea.

Japan reportedly voiced its opposition to these candidates. At a preparatory meeting held in Brunei on July 31, 1995, Japan is said to have presented the Singapore foreign minister, who was chairing the meeting, with a paper requesting the inclusion of Australia and New Zealand on the Asian side. According to this report, Indonesia and Singapore supported Japan's view, but Malaysia opposed it on the grounds that Australia and New Zealand "do not share our Asian values."[11] On July 31, ahead of the ASEAN Regional Forum (ARF) meeting beginning on August 1, the foreign ministers of the now-seven ASEAN countries, Japan, China and South Korea attended an informal lunch. Foreign Minister Kōno Yōhei of Japan proposed that "Australia and New Zealand ought to be added to the ten countries," but Foreign Minister Abdullah Badawi of Malaysia argued flatly against it. Foreign Minister Kōno said that he was "well aware of the ASEAN tradition of valuing consensus" and did not insist.[12] Although the Phuket meeting had not taken place because Japan refused to attend, Japan did not make the participation of Australia and New Zealand a condition for its participation in ASEM. The members of ASEM on the Asian side here were virtually identical to the hypothetical members of the EAEC.

Hereafter, Japan became less negative about meetings consisting of ASEAN, Japan, China and South Korea. In conjunction with an APEC Ministerial Meeting held in Osaka in November 1995, the economic ministers of six of the ASEAN countries (Vietnam did not attend), Japan, China and South Korea held an unofficial two-hour lunch on the 19th. The topic was consultation about ASEM.[13] The aborted economic ministers meeting at Phuket materialized, albeit at an informal luncheon in Osaka.

Thus, in early 1996, the Asian side was holding further preparatory meetings on ASEM. On February 2–3, the foreign ministers of the seven ASEAN countries, Japan, China and South Korea met at Phuket, and a meeting of the economic ministers from the same countries was held in mid-February. The heads of state on the Asian side gathered in Bangkok on February 29 and held a summit meeting of the ten Asian countries before the ASEM banquet. Although the host country Thailand categorized it as only a "preparatory meeting for the Asian side," here for the first time in history the leaders of the proposed countries of the EAEC had the opportunity to meet in the same room.[14] As part of the bigger framework of ASEM, a de facto East Asian summit was brought about, as it were, through the back door. But this "back door" East Asian summit meeting which came into existence through the ASEM framework was, in fact, an organization capable of dealing with far more comprehensive issues than had been envisioned for the EAEC. As their names imply, APEC and Mahathir's proposed EAEC were frameworks that dealt with economic matters; by contrast, there were no rules restricting the topics brought up at ASEM. It was a framework in which both political and cultural issues could also be considered. At this stage, however, a multinational East Asian framework had yet to be formed head-on.

The Birth of ASEAN+3

As we have seen from the analysis thus far, the reason the EAEC proposal did not proceed as Prime Minister Mahathir had expected was that Japan, fearing American opposition and the fallout therefrom, had not been all that enthusiastic about it. But with the arrival of the Clinton administration, the US position on the EAEC was not as hostile as the Bush administration's had been. Even during the preparatory stages of ASEM, the US did not have any noticeable reaction. Although Japan continued to maintain the desirability of a framework that allowed Australia and New Zealand to participate, the idea of creating an East Asian framework was gaining strength even within Japan. Unlike 1990–91 when Prime Minister Mahathir had first put forth his proposal, APEC was now well established as a solid multinational framework. At the 1994 Ministerial Meeting in Bogor, APEC announced the long-term goal of free trade among the APEC membership and drew up the Osaka Action Agenda to implement it at its Osaka meeting in 1995. Although Japan did not take the initiative in this East Asian regional plan, as Foreign Minister Kōno showed by his concession on the Asian participants in ASEM, it had no choice but to go along with what ASEAN proposed.

That said, Japan was not regarded as being enthusiastic about the East Asia concept. In that sense, as the following developments show, it is rather ironic that the catalyst for the ASEAN+3 Summit was the Hashimoto administration. Although the first meeting of the leaders of the ASEAN countries plus Japan, China and South Korea took place in December 1997 at the time of the ASEAN informal summit in Kuala Lumpur, it had been Prime Minister Hashimoto Ryūtarō's visit to Southeast Asia in January of that year that had got the ball rolling. That does not mean, of course, there had been no hints in advance. At the time of the ASEAN Summit in Bangkok in December 1995, Singapore's Prime Minister Goh Chok Tong, with Thailand's support, proposed holding an informal ASEAN summit meeting in a year and a half's time and inviting East Asian leaders from outside the region.[15] And at the end of November 1996, when asked whether the leaders of Japan, China and South Korea would be invited to the informal ASEAN summit the following year, Prime Minister Mahathir, too, replied that an "invitation was possible."[16]

Prime Minister Hashimoto's visit to Southeast Asia, however, was what made the ASEAN side begin to think seriously about inviting the leaders of Japan, China and South Korea to the

Prime Minister Hashimoto and Prime Minister Mahathir shaking
hands in the Prime Minister's Office, Kuala Lumpur (January 8,
1997). Photo: Kyodo News

ASEAN informal summit. On January 7–14, 1997, Prime Minister
Hashimoto visited Brunei, Malaysia, Indonesia, Vietnam and Singapore and appealed for a strengthening of Japanese-ASEAN relations.
In the policy speech that he made in Singapore on the 14th in particular, he set forth what came to be known as the "Hashimoto Doctrine"—the three pillars of Japan's policy, he said, were closer and
more frequent dialogues between Japan and the leaders of ASEAN,
multilateral cultural cooperation and joint efforts to deal with global
issues.[17] As part of the closer dialogue with regional heads of state, in
every country he visited Prime Minister Hashimoto proposed that
the leaders of Japan and ASEAN hold regularly scheduled summit
meetings. Although each of these leaders supported the proposal
in principle, they were cautious about giving a definite response.[18]
There were concerns in Southeast Asia about what impact it would
have on China if ASEAN held regular summit meetings just with
Japan.[19] In Kuala Lumpur, Prime Minister Mahathir would only say
to Prime Minister Hashimoto that "a policy of friendship is better
than a policy of containment" toward China.[20]

Mahathir may have thought that Hashimoto's proposal of an
ASEAN+1 was a lucky windfall. Thereafter, in discussions within

ASEAN, Mahathir reportedly suggested holding top-level talks not just between ASEAN and Japan, but with the three countries of Japan, China and South Korea.[21] When Prime Minister Mahathir paid an official visit to Japan in late March 1997, he told a press conference in Tokyo that at the end of the year he would "like to hold a summit meeting of ASEAN, Japan, China and South Korea after the ASEAN summit and then have an ASEAN-Japan summit."[22] Subsequently, the foreign ministers of ASEAN, who had gathered in New Delhi for a Non-Aligned Foreign Ministers Conference at the beginning of April, held an informal meeting and agreed on this issue. Thai Foreign Minister Prachuap Chaiyasan conveyed the results to Parliamentary Vice-Minister for Foreign Affairs Kōmura Masahiko, who visited Thailand on April 28. The message's substance was the same as what Prime Minister Mahathir had said in Tokyo: on December 16, right after the ASEAN informal summit meeting to be held on December 14–15, a summit meeting between ASEAN and Japan would be held as well as a summit consisting of ASEAN, Japan, China and South Korea.[23] On May 31, a special meeting of ASEAN foreign ministers convened in Kuala Lumpur and officially decided that in addition to the ASEAN informal summit meeting in December, there would be an ASEAN, Japan, China and South Korea summit, followed by a summit between ASEAN and Japan and one between ASEAN and China.[24] The Hashimoto Doctrine aimed at creating ASEAN+1 had ultimately contributed indirectly to the establishment of ASEAN+3.

The Special Meeting of the ASEAN Foreign Ministers on May 31 might be called a crowning moment for ASEAN. Among the decisions made at this meeting, far more important than the one to invite the heads of Japan, China and South Korea, was the one to admit Laos, Cambodia and Myanmar as members. In the 30th year since five countries had founded it in 1967, ASEAN had been able to add to its membership the three other countries of Indochina along with Vietnam. This was the moment when ASEAN became, in name and in fact, the Association of Southeast Asian Nations. According to Satō Kōichi, "With the creation of ASEAN 10 in sight and the invitation of the leaders of Japan, China and South Korea, ASEAN was also intent on displaying its international influence."[25] Needless to say, at the very moment that the ASEAN foreign ministers were optimistic about the future, their economies were beginning to head down the road to crisis. In addition, in Cambodia, which had just been admitted as a member, the situation was worsening. Although Cambodia had continued to experience difficulties even after peace had been achieved, the divisions between First Prime Minister Norodom Ranariddh and Second Prime Minister Hun Sen intensified, and in mid-June 1997, armed clashes broke out between the forces of the two men. Fighting also occurred at the beginning of July, and ultimately, Cambodia alone was unable to become a member of ASEAN that year.

Beyond the merely symbolic significance of ASEAN+3, what gave it real meaning in terms of practical consequences was the East Asian financial crisis discussed in the previous chapter.[26] After the baht crisis in July 1997, the financial crisis struck country after country, and the economies of Indonesia and South Korea fell into extreme disarray. The historic summit to celebrate ASEAN's 30th anniversary as well as the meeting that included the leaders of Japan, China and Korea, Dr Mahathir's dream, were held in the midst of economic upheaval. The oldest of the ASEAN leaders, President Suharto, did not come because of political unrest in Indonesia, and of the three leaders invited from Japan, China and South Korea, President Kim Young-sam of South Korea was unable to attend because of his country's economic problems and the impending presidential elections (scheduled for December 18) so Prime Minister Koh Kun attended instead.[27] Before the Asian financial crisis, the aim of the summit had been a rosy-colored survey of ASEAN's prospects as it headed into the 21st century, but, it, in fact, assumed the guise of an emergency meeting to deal with the crisis. In terms of content, however, although "ASEAN Vision 2020" outlining the future image of ASEAN was presented at the informal summit, no quick policy fixes for overcoming the crisis were presented either at this meeting or at ASEAN+3. In that sense, one would have to say that the meetings failed to live up to expectations.

Still, the ASEAN+3 summit meeting on December 14, 1997, was an epoch-making event in the context of East Asian regionalism. This meeting, at which Prime Minister Hashimoto Ryūtarō participated from Japan and President Jiang Zemin from China, was the very first summit of East Asian nations. For Prime Minister Mahathir of Malaysia, who chaired the meeting, a summit consisting of the members of his proposed EAEC had been realized. It would be fair to say that his long-cherished wish had come true. But at this meeting, the heads of Japan and China both disagreed with arguments for a closed direction for East Asia. "Let us join forces without excluding anyone," President Jiang said. And Prime Minister Hashimoto talked about "cooperating for the political stability of the region." Both Jiang and Hashimoto were said to be reluctant when Mahathir asked that ASEAN+3 meet on a regular basis.[28]

The Institutionalization of ASEAN+3

By 1998, the Asian financial crisis had not subsided. As we saw in the previous chapter, the crisis was not confined to the economy but had political and social repercussions as well.

With the East Asian situation still in turmoil, on August 3, 1998, the Vietnamese government, which was hosting the ASEAN Summit that year, announced it was inviting the leaders of Japan, China and South Korea to the summit meeting in December.[29] From the perspective of ASEAN, which was aiming to shake itself free from the financial crisis, it was necessary to secure aid from the countries of the world and from Japan. And from Japan's perspective, it was necessary to respond to criticisms, primarily from the US, about its economic policies since the crisis broke out. President Clinton's visit to China from late June to early July and his criticisms of Japan's economic policy while there had been especially shocking. They gave the impression that, while China had made a commitment not to devalue the renminbi, Japan was not doing anything. Moreover, the fact that Clinton spent more than a week in China without even making a stopover in its ally Japan caused consternation. The US, it was said, had gone from "Japan bashing" to "Japan passing" and then on to "Japan nothing." The opportunity to make its presence felt in Asia was therefore welcome in Japan. President Kim Dae-jung, too, welcomed an ASEAN, Japanese, Chinese and South Korean summit meeting. With the economy at home in bad shape, he was seeking an opportunity to show his leadership on the world stage and attract global investment to South Korea. The ASEAN+3 framework had use value for China as well, in the opposite sense from Japan. It was a propitious opportunity to convey to ASEAN the magnitude of the Chinese presence that the Clinton visit had revealed.

It was against this background that on October 2, an Asian economic mission from Keidanren (the Japanese Federation of Economic Organizations) met with Prime Minister Phan Van Khai during a visit to Vietnam, and its chairman Imai Takashi handed him a personal letter from Prime Minister Obuchi Keizō stating that he would attend the ASEAN Summit that December in Hanoi. By that time, China and South Korea, too, were leaning toward accepting the invitation.[30] Thus, on December 16, right after the ASEAN Summit, an ASEAN+3 Summit attended by the leaders of Japan, China and South Korea once again took place. Prime Minister Obuchi Keizō attended from Japan, Vice President Hu Jintao from China, and President Kim Dae-Jung from South Korea. The meeting was held after the ASEAN Summit on the morning of the 16th, and at it Prime Minister Obuchi disclosed that Japan would shortly be putting into place a "New Miyazawa Initiative" totaling USD 30 billion mainly in yen loans in order to overcome the economic crisis in ASEAN. Vice President Hu proposed that the deputy finance ministers and deputy governors of the central banks of ASEAN, Japan, China and South Korea meet at irregular intervals to discuss financial issues. He also indicated his desire that ASEAN+3 summits continue.[31] President Kim of South Korea proposed setting up an "East Asian Vision Group" of knowledgeable people who would consider a mid- to long-term vision for East Asia.[32]

The fact that meetings with the same framework had been held for two consecutive years was the first step toward institutionalization. At the first meeting, there had been some uncertainty about holding any further meetings. The second meeting in Hanoi, though, it is fair to say, confirmed both that the ASEAN+3 framework existed and that it was taken for granted that a third meeting would be held. Hu Jintao's suggestion to make use of the ASEAN+3 framework for sectoral meetings and its approval guaranteed the former. And as for the latter, the agreement to hold an ASEAN-Japan-China-South Korea summit whenever there were formal or informal ASEAN summit meetings guaranteed its continuation.[33] President Kim's proposal to set up a Vision Group and its approval also bespoke an acceptance of the latter premise: the Terms of Reference for establishing the Vision Group stated that it should submit its report at the 2001 summit meeting.[34]

As for sectoral activities, on March 18, 1999, ASEAN and Japan-China-South Korea held a meeting of deputy finance ministers and deputy central bank governors in Hanoi and agreed to strengthen the monitoring of short-term capital, which had been the immediate trigger of the currency crisis.[35] Hu's proposal was thus the first to be realized. On April 30, an ASEAN+3 Finance Ministers Meeting was held in Manila and agreed to expand the use of the yen to strengthen market stability and economic relations, and Japan indicated that it would include Vietnam in its New Miyazawa Initiative.[36]

President Joseph Estrada of the Philippines, which was hosting the ASEAN informal summit (and the ASEAN+3 Summit) in 1999, was a vocal advocate for building an East Asian framework. At a symposium held in Tokyo in June (the fifth "Future of Asia" international conference sponsored by the *Nihon Keizai Shimbun*), he set forth a plan for an "East Asian common currency" with a view to regional economic integration, despite the unlikelihood of such a proposal being accomplished in the short term. In order to build the ASEAN+3 framework, South Korea, too, sent former foreign minister Han Sung-joo, a professor at Korea University, to Japan and all the other ASEAN+3 countries to ask for their cooperation in setting up at an early date the East Asian Vision Group that President Kim had proposed.[37]

By the fall, the host country of the Philippines started to make extremely ambitious proposals. At the beginning of October, its Undersecretary for Foreign Affairs Lauro Baja expressed his hope that the ASEAN+3 would develop into a new consultative body and that this "new body would also become a forum for sharing political and security concerns."[38] Foreign Secretary Domingo Siazon sought an enhanced role for it on the economic front and spoke of the possibility of a "framework that in future would also evolve into a free trade zone and a common currency."[39] At subsequent discussions, however, what was decided took the form of "promoting [enhanced dialogue] by stages in various areas, based on the existing methods of discussion and cooperation" without reaching any agreement on the plan to establish a new "consultative body."[40] It should be mentioned, however, that for the first time, ASEAN+3 also agreed to draw up a "joint statement" covering several areas. This was a movement in the direction of binding each country's policies: ASEAN+3 would not be a meeting at which the heads of state merely met; it would produce a declaration of consensus in the form of a joint communiqué.

In addition, the finance ministers and central bank governors of ASEAN+3 met in Manila on November 25 before the summit and agreed to promote a plan for "regional support mechanisms."[41]

Having incorporated various new functions in this way, the ASEAN+3 Summit Meeting opened on the evening of November 26 and issued its first joint communiqué on November 28. Entitled a "Joint Statement on East Asia Cooperation," it indicated that the areas ASEAN+3 ought to deal with were the "economic and social fields" and the "political and other fields"; under the former, it cited economic cooperation, monetary and financial cooperation, social and human resources development, scientific and technological development, cultural and information areas and development cooperation, while under the latter it noted transnational issues and the political-security area.[42] As for the issues of a common currency and security, it did not make the advances that President Estrada had ambitiously hoped for,[43] but even so, the comprehensive nature of ASEAN+3 had become clear. At this meeting, as well, at Japan's suggestion, it was agreed that a meeting of the ASEAN+3 foreign ministers would convene at the time of the ASEAN Post Ministerial Conference in 2000.[44] In this way, further ministerial-level meetings in addition to those on the financial side came to be established for ASEAN+3.

The Taepodong Shock and Kim Dae-jung's "Inclusion Policy"

While a framework for East Asian regionalism was advancing in the form of ASEAN+3, in Northeast Asia, a complicated interplay of tension-producing trends and efforts to relieve those tensions was going on. The source of the tension-producing trends once again was North Korea.

Following the Framework Agreement in the fall of 1994, the Korean Peninsula Energy Development Organization (KEDO) was set up in March 1995. Although negotiations on the details of its implementation, as usual, encountered rough going, operations finally began in August 1997. Although the Framework Agreement and KEDO had been expected to end the crisis on the Korean peninsula, these hopes were premature. First, the floods that hit North Korea in the summers of both 1995 and 1996 caused terrible famines there. The US, South Korea, Japan and surrounding countries were suddenly confronted with a North Korea requesting food aid rather than a militarily threatening country. While North Korea was seeking food aid, however, under the excuse of still being in mourning after Kim Il Sung's death, a puzzling state of affairs continued in its political system; strange behavior outside the country drew attention as well. In April 1996, there were incursions into the demilitarized zone, and that summer, a submarine infiltrated the coast of South Korea.

As for relations between Japan and the North, Chairman Kim Il Sung's willingness to resume talks had been conveyed to the Japanese government by former President Carter, who had settled the 1994 crisis. Having been sounded out in this way, a joint investigating commission from the three ruling coalition parties visited the North on March 30, 1995, and unofficial talks were held at the department chief level, but no real progress was made. During this period, Japan declared in June 1995 that it would supply 300,000 tons of rice as aid for the North Korean food crisis and promised an additional 200,000 tons in October.[45] The Kim Young-sam administration in South Korea did not welcome Japan's efforts to re-open normalization talks as the North was reluctant to proceed with negotiations with Seoul. In any event, the food aid did not lead to progress in Japanese-North Korean relations.

What was also shocking for most Japanese was the abductee issue, the kidnapping of Japanese citizens by North Korea. In the 1970s and 1980s, people in all parts of Japan had gone missing in mysterious ways. As the families and close associates of these missing persons searched for their whereabouts, suspicions arose among them that they might have been kidnapped in Japan by North Korea. Without any conclusive evidence, they continued their difficult campaign on behalf of the kidnapping victims; then, a person who had fled from the North to the South testified that someone who appeared to be Yokota Megumi, who had disappeared in 1977, had been sighted in North Korea. In February 1997, questions about the Yokota Megumi incident were raised in the Diet, and thereafter the abductee issue emerged as what might well

Taepodong test launch (August 31, 1998).
Photo: Kyodo News

be called the biggest issue in Japanese-North Korean relations.

In addition, in the summer of 1998, suspicions about North Korea deepened even further. Serious misgivings arose that the North might be in violation of the Framework Agreement. An enormous underground facility thought to be for the purpose of developing nuclear weapons was discovered in Kumchang-ri 40 kilometers northwest of Yongbyon. Then, on August 31 almost immediately after the discovery of this underground facility, without any warning, the North conducted a test of its Taepodong-1 missile over Japanese air space. The Japanese media and public opinion were stunned by the fact that North Korea possessed the capability to launch missiles that had the entire territory of Japan in their range. Although it had become clear from the Nodong missile test in 1993 that the western half of Japan was within North Korean missile range, there was no comparison to the shock the Taepodong missile test inflicted on the Japanese people.

The magnitude of this shock manifested itself in two measures taken by the Japanese government. The first was to take steps to delay entering into the agreement on funding KEDO; and the second was to make the decision to develop its own information-gathering satellite. As facilitating KEDO involved the US and South Korea, Japan unilaterally delaying funding could not help but create friction with those two countries. The development of its own intelligence satellite, too, had been regarded as difficult in terms of both cost and expertise and had even been thought to be open to question in terms of Japan's official stance on the peaceful use of space. After the Taepodong shock, however, even the opposition parties called for an indigenous information-gathering satellite, and on December 22, the cabinet decided to enter into such a project.[46]

The period in which the North's Taepodong missile sent shock waves throughout Japan was also one in which the Kim Jong Il regime in North Korea finally clearly revealed itself. After the death of Kim Il Sung in 1994, the North was said to have gone into a long period of "mourning," and it was unclear what sort of government it was going to have. In October 1997, when the three years of mourning ended, Kim Jong Il assumed the office of General Secretary of the Korean Workers' Party. And on September 5, 1998, the first session of the Tenth Supreme People's Assembly—the first since Kim Il Sung's death—was held and revised the constitution. The position of "Eternal President" was posthumously bestowed on Kim Il Sung, and the chairman of the National Defense Commission, which Kim Jong Il had assumed, was declared the "highest post of the state."

Through 1998 into 1999, the situation between the US and North Korea once again resembled a war of nerves. Opposing the investigation of Kumchang-ri that the US was demanding, the North, without acknowledging the suspicions, demanded that, if there were an inspection, it should be compensated for it. When the US refused to provide compensation, tensions heightened, but ultimately the North accepted the "visit" of American experts to the facility in May 1999. All that was discovered during the visit was an enormous hole. On the other hand, it was learned that North Korea was making preparations to test the Taepodong missile again. Japan, which had frozen its participation in negotiations to fund KEDO when the Taepodong missile had been tested a year earlier, had lifted the freeze at the end of that year, but the view arose in Japan that it would have to reconsider its financial cooperation to KEDO if a missile test were repeated. Ultimately, as a result of talks in Berlin between the US and the North, North Korea indicated that it would not launch any missiles while negotiations with the US were going on.

After the US and North Korea had reached some sort of agreement, the Kim Dae-jung administration in South Korea stepped up its "inclusion policy" (the "sunshine policy") toward the North. On January 20, 2000, Kim Dae-jung officially proposed holding a North-South summit. After several rounds of secret talks, it was announced on April 8 that such a summit would be held in June. In the final stages, the summit was delayed a day and opened on June 13. On the 15th, the two leaders agreed on the following items:

1. The South and the North have agreed to resolve the question of reunification independently and through the joint efforts of the Korean people, who are the masters of the country.
2. For the achievement of reunification, we have agreed that there is a common element in the South's concept of a confederation and the North's formula for a loose form of federation. The South and the North agreed to promote reunification in that direction.
3. The South and the North have agreed to promptly resolve humanitarian issues such as exchange visits by separated family members and relatives on the occasion of the August 15 National Liberation Day and the question of unswerving Communists serving prison sentences in the South.
4. The South and the North have agreed to consolidate mutual trust by promoting balanced development of the national economy through economic cooperation and by stimulating cooperation and exchanges in civic, cultural, sports, health, environmental and all other fields.
5. The South and the North have agreed to hold a dialogue between relevant authorities in the near future to implement the above agreements expeditiously.

President Kim Dae-jung cordially invited National Defense Commission Chairman Kim Jong-il to visit Seoul, and Chairman Kim Jong-il will visit Seoul at an appropriate time.[47]

In October 2000, President Kim Dae-jung was awarded the Nobel Peace Prize for bringing about the North-South Summit.

Improvements in Japanese-South Korean Relations

Japanese-South Korean relations were quite unsettled during the Kim Young-sam administration. There had been a strong reaction within South Korea to Diet debates about the understanding of history and the statements of Japanese politicians during the time leading up to the 50th anniversary of the end of World War II. Intense anti-Japanese sentiments also made themselves felt over the islands known as Takeshima, which Korea calls Dokdo.[48] When it became clear that South Korea was proceeding with plans to build a wharf facility there, in February 1996, Foreign Minister Ikeda Yukihiko declared that, "Takeshima is Japan's inherent territory historically and legally in international law."[49] South Korean public opinion objected strongly, calling this statement "absurd," and President Kim Young-sam refused to receive a courtesy call by a Japanese delegation from the ruling coalition. Ultimately, when President Kim and Prime Minister Hashimoto attended ASEM in March 1996, they reached an agreement to discuss the Takeshima territorial issue separately from the exclusive economic maritime zone issue and negotiations on a fisheries agreement.[50] In order to improve the rocky relations between two countries, Prime Minister Hashimoto visited South Korea in late June 1996 and held a summit meeting on Jeju Island with President Kim. Just before this summit, on June 1, the board of directors of the Fédération Internationale de Football Association (FIFA) decided that Japan and South Korea would jointly host the 2002 World Cup. Both heads of state highlighted the decision to co-host the World Cup and made a show of friendship. But discussions between the two countries over the signing of the fisheries agreement continued to encounter difficulties, and in the end there was no dramatic improvement in Japanese-South Korean relations while Kim Young-sam was in office.

President Kim Dae-jung, who succeeded him, showed a strong desire to build a new relationship with Japan. A report issued by his transition team on February 17, 1998, noted that the Kim Young-sam administration's policy toward Japan had combined an "emotional-level approach" and a "blind, hardline response."[51] On the understanding of history issue, Kim Dae-jung stated in April that he highly appreciated postwar Japan's "adherence to its peace constitution with its firm determination to maintain world peace and never repeat its mistakes" as something that the South Korean people should regard as a positive.[52]

In response to Kim Dae-jung's attitude toward Japan, Prime Minister Obuchi made the political decision to sign the still pending new fisheries agreement on September 25, just before President Kim Dae-jung was to visit Japan. On this visit, President Kim confronted Japan with a challenge: if Japan made an official apology in writing, he would never raise the history issue again. In response to President

Prime Minister Obuchi and President Kim shaking hands at the Akasaka State Guest House in Tokyo (October 8, 1998). Photo: Kyodo News

Kim's commitment not to broach that topic again, Prime Minister Obuchi agreed to put a clear apology in writing.[53]

The outcome of the October 8 summit was the Japan-Republic of Korea Joint Declaration that said, "Looking back on the relations between Japan and the Republic of Korea during this century, Prime Minister Obuchi regarded in a spirit of humility the fact of history that Japan caused, during a certain period in the past, tremendous damage and suffering to the people of the Republic of Korea through its colonial rule, and expressed his deep remorse and heartfelt apology for this fact." In response, "President Kim accepted with sincerity this statement of Prime Minister Obuchi's recognition of history and expressed his appreciation for it. He also expressed his view that the present calls upon both countries to overcome their unfortunate history and to build a future-oriented relationship based on reconciliation as well as good-neighborly and friendly cooperation."[54]

In his speeches both at the banquet at the Imperial Palace and to the Diet, President Kim did not, in fact, refer to "colonial rule" but emphasized a future-oriented Japanese-South Korean relationship. And on postwar Japan, he said he "highly appreciated the role that Japan has played for the peace and prosperity of the international community through its security policies, foremost its exclusively defense-oriented policy and three non-nuclear principles under the postwar Japanese Peace Constitution, its contributions to the global economy and its economic assistance to developing countries, and other means." He also revealed plans to open South Korea to Japanese popular culture, which had previously been banned.

Jiang Zemin's Visit to Japan

As a result of the Taiwan Strait crisis in 1996, China's hardline stance had had an impact worldwide, and from the latter half of that year, the Chinese were making efforts to improve relations with major countries. Jiang Zemin, who had become the most powerful man in China both in name and in fact after the death of Deng Xiaoping on February 19, 1997, became assertive in promoting foreign and domestic policies under his own leadership.

The task immediately facing Jiang was the handover of Hong Kong (or, from the Chinese perspective, its reunification) on July 1, 1997. Hong Kong was the symbol of territory sliced away by imperialism, and in terms of maintaining the legitimacy of Chinese Communist rule, nothing could replace being able to get it back by peaceful means. During his tenure the last British governor of Hong Kong, Chris Patten, had reformed the electoral system for the Legislative Council and tried to promote democratization in Hong Kong. But China objected to these moves, and after reunification it dissolved the Legislative Council and set up a new one. The post-unification Hong Kong Special Administrative Region was to be ruled by an indirect electoral body by which the Hong Kong elite chose people who would not go against China's wishes.

The second diplomatic task Jiang Zemin had to grapple with was improving relations with the United States. From late October to early November 1997, Jiang visited the US and held a summit meeting with President Clinton. At this meeting US-Chinese relations were given the status of a "constructive strategic partnership." Clinton's visit to China took place after that, from June 23–July 3, 1998. For

China the foremost achievement of this visit was that it got Clinton to state the Three No's—No independence for Taiwan, No two Chinas or one China-one Taiwan, and No Taiwanese membership in international organizations. China also raised its standing in the international community by advancing relations with Russia and by living up to its commitment not to devalue the renminbi at the time of the Asian financial crisis.

As part of this diplomatic charm offensive, President Jiang Zemin was scheduled to visit Japan in the summer of 1998. For China, Jiang's visit to Japan was an important event not only in terms of its Japanese policy but also for its foreign policy as a whole. The enthusiasm for this visit could be felt in April when China had Vice President Hu Jintao make an advance visit to Japan. Vice President Hu not only held meetings with Prime Minister Hashimoto Ryūtarō and Foreign Minister Obuchi Keizō, but he also tirelessly met with the leaders of every sector of Japanese society. "This will be the first visit to Japan by the President of the PRC," he said. "We are confident that this historically significant meeting will inevitably push Chinese-Japanese relations to a new level."[55] Against the background of improved relations with major countries such as the US and Russia, if relations with Japan, too, were stabilized, it would create an advantageous environment for Chinese diplomacy. As a third document after the 1972 China-Japan Joint Communiqué and the 1978 Treaty of Peace and Friendship, the Chinese were appealing to the Japanese side to draw up a joint statement setting forth the future course of Japanese-Chinese relations and cooperation for the 21st century. Wary that China would try to include Taiwan or other problematic issues, the Japanese side was slow to respond, but when the Chinese side agreed in principle to the Japanese counterproposal that a "forward-looking statement on Japanese-Chinese relations in the 21st century" would be acceptable, Japan agreed at the beginning of July to draw up a joint statement.[56]

The situation did not turn out the way China expected, however, on several fronts. First, in the early part of 1998, Japan succumbed to what might be called its worst economic conditions in the postwar period (see Chapter 7). During the Asian financial crisis in 1997, the Japanese economy, too, had fallen into recession. Because of the mismanagement of the economy, the LDP lost heavily in the July

House of Councillors' election, and Prime Minister Hashimoto stepped down. Having from the outset worked out its plans for Jiang's visit on the assumption that the Hashimoto administration would continue, the Chinese now had to contend with a new administration, the Obuchi Cabinet. The public support ratings for the just-created Obuchi administration were especially low, and it was even reported that there was some ambivalence about how "seriously" China should deal with the Obuchi government.[57] The second unexpected situation were the enormous floods that struck China that summer. It was not just the Yangtze that flooded; floods in the northeast also caused massive damage. As a result, the Chinese government informed the Japanese government on August 21 that it was postponing the visit of President Jiang, which had been scheduled to begin on September 6. There was speculation within Japan, though, that the prime reason for the postponement was doubt about the stability of the Obuchi Cabinet; there was other speculation as well, including that it was due to Japan's refusal to accept the Three No's that China was asking for in regard to Taiwan during the preparatory stages of drafting the joint declaration. Although the facts are unclear, there is no doubt that the flooding was serious.

Another unexpected event for China was that the postponement of Jiang's visit meant that the visit of President Kim Dae-jung took place first, and, as has already been examined, the history issue between Japan and South Korea was, after a fashion, resolved. Watching the "results" of Kim Dae-jung's visit, there emerged a determination in China that a similar statement of "remorse and apology" had to be written into the joint declaration being drafted for the time of President Jiang's visit.[58] Since "history" had been referred to in the text with South Korea, the Japanese side began to realize that it would be impossible not to refer to "history" in some form or other in the text with China as well. Within the LDP, however, there had been objections even to the contents of the Japan-Republic of Korea Joint Declaration. Opposition was strong against putting into writing once again the "understanding of history," especially toward China, in light of the 1972 Japan-China Joint Communiqué, which already stated that Japan "is keenly conscious of . . . and deeply reproaches itself" for the damage it caused, not to mention the Emperor's speech during his visit to China in 1992.[59]

On the Chinese side, the idea arose that the exact wording in the Japan-South Korea Joint Declaration, which Japan had accepted, should be put into the joint declaration between Japan and China, while on the Japanese side, the idea arose that this time it did not want to be forced to include such wording. As a result, the task of drawing up the joint declaration turned into a symbolic game as to which words would or would not be included. What became key for the Japanese side was whether or not to put in the words "aggression" and "apology," and for the Chinese side just how "future-oriented" its stance would be. The Japanese understanding was that the reason "colonial rule" and "apology" had been inserted in the Joint Declaration with South Korea was that President Kim Dae-jung had promised not to rehash the history issue. Consequently, when Prime Minister Obuchi realized there would be strong objections within the LDP, in order to incorporate "aggression" and "apology" into the joint statement, he seems to have tried to get assurances that the Chinese side would not bring up the "history problem" again. According to the recollections of Kōmura Masahiko, who was foreign minister in the Obuchi Cabinet, "The reason Japan apologized in writing to South Korea was that Kim Dae-jung promised that if we did so, the Korean side would be future-oriented and not broach the history problem again. Jiang Zemin refused to make any such promise. And so we didn't do so with China."[60]

President Jiang's visit to Japan finally took place from the 25th to the 30th of November. The first visit in history to Japan by a Chinese head of state, it included conferring with Prime Minister Obuchi, attending a banquet at the Imperial Palace, giving a commemorative address at Waseda University, meeting with important persons in the financial and political world and even touring the Tohoku and Hokkaido. But apart from the welcome he received everywhere he went, for the first visit by a Chinese head of state, Jiang's visit failed to generate much excitement. The reason was that the work of drawing up the joint statement had clearly been a failure, and, perhaps as a result, everywhere President Jiang went, he stubbornly referred to the "history problem."

The final adjustments to the joint statement took place between Foreign Minister Kōmura and Foreign Minister Tang Jiaxuan, who came to Japan just ahead of President Jiang. During this fine-tuning process, the Japanese side agreed to accept the wording that the Japanese-Chinese War had been "aggression" and to include its "deep remorse" in the joint statement, but it refused to insert the "apology" that the Chinese side was demanding and let the Chinese know that Prime Minister Obuchi would like to express the apology verbally to President Jiang. Foreign Minister Tang reluctantly agreed to this, but said, "Because President Jiang belongs to a different generation, I'm not sure whether this will be good enough."[61]

President Jiang Zemin was clearly not satisfied with this. At the summit meeting with Prime Minister Obuchi on the evening of the 26th, Jiang is said to have spent almost the entire time talking about the history problem and Taiwan. In the account published in the newspapers, Jiang Zemin said, "I am opposed to the opinion that the problem of history has been sufficiently discussed so there is no need to discuss it further. For China the problems of history and Taiwan are at the root of Chinese-Japanese relations and cannot be side-stepped. This does not mean being obsessed with the past, but that properly understanding and dealing with these two issues will clear the way to the future. Friendship and cooperation constitute the mainstream of the 2000 years of Chinese-Japanese history. In recent times, Japanese militarism launched aggressive wars that inflicted suffering on the Chinese people. Prime Minister Murayama [Tomiichi] and other leaders have made statements that they would never allow a revival of Japanese militarism, and China appreciates this. Although sometimes words and deeds have been the exact opposite of this, I hope that you will review the lessons of history and enlighten the people. That is my advice as a neighbor."[62]

In response, Prime Minister Obuchi said, "There was a very unfortunate relationship between Japan and China for a certain period in the past. The Prime Minister's Statement in 1995 expressed a sense of acute remorse about our country's aggression and colonial rule during a period in our past, and declared our sincere feelings of apology. The Japanese government expresses once again its remorse and apology to China on this occasion."[63] This statement by Prime Minister Obuchi, in short, constituted the verbal expression of "apology."

If the joint document, which came to be called the "Japan-China Joint Declaration: On Building a Partnership of Friendship and Cooperation for Peace and Development," had been signed right after the summit, perhaps the negative impression of President Jiang's visit to Japan might not have spread as much as it did. But, in fact, since too much time was spent on the history problem, it took a long time to translate other parts of the text into Chinese, and so it was five hours after the meeting ended before the text was released. What is more, the two leaders did not sign the document. As a result, there was considerable speculation up until the Joint Declaration was issued as to why an "apology" had not been written into it and why the document had not been signed.

The relevant part of the Joint Declaration that was ultimately published is as follows:

> Both sides believe that squarely facing the past and correctly understanding history are the important foundation for further developing relations between Japan and China. The Japanese side observes the 1972 Joint Communique of the Government of Japan and the Government of the People's Republic of China and the 15 August 1995 Statement by former Prime Minister Tomiichi Murayama. The Japanese side is keenly conscious of the responsibility for the serious distress and damage that Japan caused to the Chinese people through its aggression against China during a certain period in the past and expressed deep remorse for this. The Chinese side hopes that the Japanese side will learn lessons from the history and adhere to the path of peace and development. Based on this, both sides will develop long-standing relations of friendship.[64]

As President Jiang Zemin said in the summit meeting that he was opposed to the view that "the problem of history has been sufficiently discussed so there is no need to discuss it further," he does not seem to have been prepared to make a firm commitment not to play the history card again if an "apology" had been written into the text. The result of this was a game of symbol trading: the Japanese side would not give a written "apology" but only a verbal one. And, since that was the case, China probably decided not to praise postwar Japan in the Joint Declaration as President Kim Dae-jung had done. The official reason the Joint Declaration was not signed was that there had never been any intention of doing so.

In order to demonstrate his dissatisfaction with the Joint Declaration, President Jiang brought up the history issue on several occasions during his visit. He did so during his formal response to the Emperor at the banquet at the Imperial Palace and again at the meeting with business leaders. His speech at Waseda University was entitled "Taking History as a Mirror, Opening to the Future," and in it he noted that as a result of the Japanese-Chinese War, "35 million Chinese soldiers and people were killed or injured, [and] economic losses were in excess of 600 billion dollars."[65] Whatever President Jiang's intentions may have been, within Japan, these observations did not generate much sympathy from the Japanese public.

Up until this point, whenever the Chinese side criticized Japan about the history problem, there had been statements or deeds on the Japanese side to attract such criticism such as denials of aggression or visits to the Yasukuni Shrine. This time there had been none. Instead, Prime Minister Obuchi made an "apology," albeit a verbal one, and even though the Chinese side was dissatisfied with the Joint Declaration, it included the term "aggression" in writing for the first time. In this context, the fact that the leader of China insistently made statements about the "history problem" was incomprehensible to most Japanese, and many of them were offended by it.

Within China, too, the assessment of Jiang Zemin's visit to Japan was by no means enthusiastic. Officially, it was uniformly regarded as a "success," but the *People's Daily*, for example, did not carry the full text of the Joint Declaration.

Thus, the first visit in history of a Chinese head of state to Japan left an extremely bad aftertaste. But a cool-headed analysis of the agreements that were actually concluded between the two countries would show that many of them were positive. By comparison with the Joint Communiqué and the Treaty of Peace and Friendship, the Joint Declaration was not confined to bilateral relations but made clear to the whole world that Japan and China were cooperating. That point is even clearer in the joint press statement the two governments released, which listed 33 specific items of cooperation. They also agreed on a plan for exchange visits by 15,000 young people between FY1999 and FY2003. Furthermore, the Japan side made known its decision to provide loans of 390 billion yen during the latter two years of the fourth yen-loan round.

From Prime Minister Obuchi's perspective, Kim Dae-jung's visit to Japan had been a great success. Jiang Zemin's visit had been rocky, but it had not been a failure as far as Obuchi was concerned. The Japanese people were left with the image of Obuchi as someone who did not easily say yes to Jiang's hardline approach. Internationally as well, *The Economist* (December 12, 1998), for example, said that Japan's refusal to bow to China's demands for an apology and on Taiwan should be welcomed.[66] The American columnist Jim Hoagland, too, observed, "[Obuchi's] elegant apology for Japanese crimes to South Korea's democratically elected president, Kim Dae Jung, . . . set the stage for his principled refusal of the same concessions to the Communist Party boss Jiang."[67] After receiving this international praise, Obuchi visited Vietnam in December to take part in the ASEAN+3 Summit. There he confirmed his commitment to the New Miyazawa Initiative to deal with the Asian financial crisis and laid out his ideas about "human security."

Japan-China-South Korea Cooperation

Although it had been expected at first that China's policy vis-à-vis Japan after President Jiang Zemin's visit would be strained, and there were even signs that that would be the case, no serious situation actually occurred. Some sort of reappraisal seems to have been taking place within China on how to repair Chinese-Japanese relations after President Jiang's visit. In the first half of 1999, in particular, as deliberations in the Diet progressed on the "Surrounding Situations" Bill (measures to ensure peace and prosperity in areas around Japan), there were fears that Chinese criticism might intensify, but it did not really do so to any great extent.

Thereafter, the biggest challenges in Chinese diplomacy were how to handle the bombing of Serbia, which NATO had begun in connection with the Kosovo Conflict, and, on the other hand, how to expedite China's membership in the World Trade Organization. On the NATO bombings, China argued that the bombing of Serbia without a UN resolution was a violation of sovereignty; in April, Premier Zhu Rongji visited the US to protest the bombings and attempt to persuade the Americans to help bring about Chinese membership in the WTO. But the US turned a deaf ear to China's protests against the NATO bombings, and even Zhu's visit failed to win the Clinton administration's clear support for China's WTO membership. Meanwhile, the Chinese Embassy in Belgrade was bombed in May by a NATO plane, and when that event occurred, the anti-American mood in China suddenly spiked.

While these tensions were arising in its relations with the US, China presumably made the decision to leave its policies toward Japan unchanged and not make matters any worse than they already were. On May 21, when the Japan-US Defense Cooperation Guidelines-related bill was expected to be passed in the Diet, Foreign Minister Tang Jiaxuan said, "After the bill is passed there will be no change in our Japan policy. . . . China is not that juvenile; it will propose what it ought to propose and be indignant about what it ought to be indignant about, but the policies between the two countries ought to proceed from a broader perspective."[68]

As a result, Prime Minister Obuchi's visit to China, which took place in July, went off without a hitch. The Chinese side did not raise the history problem. In regard to the Guidelines-related law, Premier Zhu, who met with Prime Minister Obuchi, demanded once again that Taiwan be removed from the ambit of US-Japanese security, though he confined himself to saying that he had "listened to Prime Minister Obuchi's careful explanation, but we want you to prove your words with actions."[69] At the same time as Obuchi's visit to China, bilateral talks between Japan and China on the latter's membership in the WTO also reached an agreement.

While the Obuchi administration's diplomatic policy was gradually getting on track, its support rating at home was rising as well. Japan was to host the G8 Summit in 2000, and so on April 29, 1999, Obuchi announced that the 2000 Summit would be held in Okinawa. Because all the previous summits in Japan had convened in Tokyo, this was regarded as a new departure. Both from the perspective of the smooth working of the US-Japan alliance as well as to lighten the burden on the people of Okinawa, about which he had had a personal concern,[70] not to mention from the standpoint of the importance of Japan's relation with Asia, he thought there would be symbolic significance in holding the summit there.

Obuchi probably also assumed that his administration would be long-lived. To formulate a vision for Japan in the 21st century, he launched a commission at the end of March 1999 on "Japan's Goals in the 21st Century," headed by Kawai Hayao, director of the International Research Center for Japanese Studies. This commission, which was divided into five subcommittees to explore various issues facing Japanese society, presented its report to Prime Minister Obuchi in January 2000. Although the subtitle of the report was "The Frontier Within," the themes cited in regard to international relations called for "enlightened national interest" and the promotion of "neighborly relations" with countries in Japan's immediate vicinity.[71]

For Obuchi, one stage on which "neighborly relations" were played out was the ASEAN+3 Summit, which was held in the Philippines in November 1999, just before the report was completed. Obuchi called on China and South Korea to hold three-way leadership talks. Kim Dae-jung agreed and so did China. Up until then, the three leaders of Japan, China and South Korea had not conferred together. At Obuchi's initiative this summit was held in Manila in the form of a "breakfast meeting."

Because the breakfast meeting was held in the short space of a single hour, it was effectively limited to discussing economic cooperation. But both Premier Zhu Rongji and President Kim Dae-jung said they appreciated Prime Minister Obuchi's initiative, and when he proposed that the leaders of the three countries meet on a regular basis, President Kim agreed saying, "I would like to see this continue." Premier Zhu did not give the proposal his clear support but limited himself to saying, "It is desirable for East Asia's views to be conveyed to the international community by having our three countries build cooperative relations."[72] The leaders of the three countries met again in 2000, and the trilateral summit meeting became an established custom.

It would be against this background of trilateral cooperation and Asia-centered diplomacy—"neighborly relations"—that Obuchi would hold the summit in Okinawa, or so he must have thought. In January he visited Cambodia, Laos and Thailand; in February he attended the general meeting of the United Nations Conference on Trade and Development (UNCTAD) in Thailand, the first Japanese head of state to do so in 21 years, and gave a speech about dealing with economic disparity between the advanced countries and the developing world at the Kyushu-Okinawa Summit. Although it ultimately never materialized, Obuchi explored the possibility of inviting China to the G8 summit. But he himself was unable to preside over his own summit. On April 2, 2000, Obuchi suddenly fell ill and lost consciousness; he was hospitalized and died on May 14.

Chapter 9

Enter Koizumi

The Birth of the Koizumi Administration

Because Obuchi Keizō had suddenly fallen ill, Secretary-General Mori Yoshirō of the Liberal Democratic Party hastily succeeded him as prime minister. Since Obuchi was in a coma during the transfer of power, it was described as a "closed-door selection," and, thus, from the very outset, the Mori administration suffered from low support ratings. Prime Minister Mori, though a person of unrivaled sensitivity to interpersonal relationships, also made many careless public remarks that incited attacks from the mass media. In any event, he had never imagined he would become prime minister, and as he himself wrote in his memoirs, when he was put in charge of the administration, "I felt that once I sorted out the situation [after Obuchi's death], somehow I would have to hand the position over to the next person."[1] He did not intend to introduce many initiatives of his own.[2]

The major task of Mori's foreign policy was to ensure the success of the Okinawan G8 summit meeting that Obuchi had planned. Mori did add a small touch of personal preference, though; he invited presidents Thabo Mbeki of South Africa, Olusegun Obasanjo of Nigeria and Abdelaziz Bouteflika of Algeria to Tokyo and arranged a meeting with the G8 leaders a day before they left for Okinawa. As this event indicated, Mori himself had an interest in Africa and visited the continent in January 2001; at the World Economic Forum in Davos right afterwards, he made a policy speech primarily on African issues. In the summer of 2000, he also had visited India and indicated his interest in restoring relations with New Delhi after India's nuclear tests in 1998 by referring to the Japanese-Indian relationship as "strategic." But these initiatives remained one-shot efforts; because of political unrest, the Mori administration did not last long.

In November 2000, former LDP Secretary-General Katō Kōichi and others asked Prime Minister Mori to step down; turmoil ensued when they agreed to approve a vote of non-confidence called for by the opposition parties (the Katō rebellion). Although the non-confidence vote was defeated, early the following year, support for the Mori Cabinet dropped even further. In February 2001, the Ehime Maru, a training ship belonging to Uwajima Fishery High School in Ehime Prefecture, was hit by a US nuclear submarine off Hawaii and sank. Public opinion reacted indignantly upon learning that after hearing the news, Prime Minister Mori resumed playing golf, and his cabinet's support rating fell to 9 percent. Mori finally decided to step down in March. According to his memoirs, "There was a House of Councillors' election in the summer of 2001. We had to win the election. If my resignation could become an opportunity to bring about a popular new cabinet, then the election would work out all right, I thought. At that time, of course, I had Koizumi in mind."[3]

Four candidates ran in the LDP presidential election that took place after Mori announced his resignation: Hashimoto Ryūtarō, Koizumi Jun'ichirō, Asō Tarō and Kamei Shizuka. In the election that year, each of the 346 LDP Diet members had one vote, and the prefectural branch chapters had three each, making a total of 487 votes being contested. Thus, the commonsense view was that the will of the Diet members would be decisive, and, as the leader of the largest faction, former Prime Minister Hashimoto Ryūtarō seemed to be most powerful.[4] But the results of the primary elections conducted in the prefectural chapters were overwhelmingly for Koizumi. The LDP members who participated in the primaries were fed up with the "old way" of selecting leaders and were attracted by Koizumi, a lone wolf determined to "break up the LDP."[5] Although Koizumi had long been regarded as a single-issue politician only arguing for the privatization of the postal service, he increased his stature as a potential leader of the party after his failed candidacy in the 1998 LDP presidential election; the public found his blunt manner attractive and saw him as somebody who could make a difference. The fact that another blunt speaker, Diet member Tanaka Makiko, the very popular daughter of former Prime Minister Tanaka Kakuei, supported Koizumi helped, too. As Iijima Isao, Prime Minister Koizumi's executive secretary, says, "Ms Tanaka was unmistakably a driving force behind the birth of Koizumi's presidency."[6] Ultimately, at the election in which the Diet members participated, Koizumi won by a landslide. The Koizumi Cabinet, which was formed on April 26, had unprecedentedly high support ratings among the citizenry. In an opinion poll taken by the *Yomiuri Shimbun*, the support rate was 87 percent and 78 percent in an *Asahi Shimbun* poll, the highest ratings ever.

The Absence of a Foreign Policy

The biggest tasks facing the Koizumi administration were the privatization of the postal service and economic reform. He showed his intention to tackle reform by appointing Professor Takenaka Heizō of Keio University as Minister of State for Economic and Fiscal Policy and making full use of the Council on Economic and Fiscal Policy set up at the time of the Mori Cabinet. Domestic policy was the centerpiece of the Koizumi administration.

By comparison, foreign policy was not an area to which Prime Minister Koizumi particularly attached much importance. His indifference to foreign policy was demonstrated by his appointment of Diet member Tanaka Makiko to be his Minister of Foreign Affairs.[7] Setting aside Ms Tanaka's self-perceptions, a glance at her subsequent words and actions reveals that she was clearly not a prudent choice to be Japan's foreign minister.[8] At the beginning of May, she canceled a meeting with an important visiting American official just before it was scheduled to occur and showed on various occasions including in Diet debates that she was not fully informed on international affairs.

In January 2001, a scandal had occurred over the misappropriation of public funds by foreign ministry employees, and in connection with this, public disapproval mounted over the make-up of the foreign ministry. There was growing criticism that the ministry bureaucracy was arrogant and did not conduct diplomacy that at all reflected Japan's national interests. When Foreign Minister Tanaka took office, she concentrated most of her energy on rectifying this situation and roundly criticized the ministry's leaders. In fact, rather than carrying out real reform, she spent most of her time personally feuding with the ministry's upper echelons. Why Prime Minister Koizumi appointed Foreign Minister Tanaka is not entirely clear, but some think that the appointment was a reward for the support she had given him in the LDP presidential election, since her own public popularity was even greater than Koizumi's.[9] "It was said to be what she wanted, but I don't know whether that's true or not," the prime minister's Executive Secretary Iijima recalls,[10] but there is probably little doubt that Ms Tanaka herself wanted the post of foreign minister. And for quite some time, the Japanese mass media, especially the television stations, extravagantly praised her for confronting the leaders of the foreign ministry. Judging from the mass media's reaction, there is surely no doubt that she contributed to the administration's high support ratings right after it was formed. Be that as it may, there is also no doubt that her appointment was made with a view to domestic politics and not from the perspective of her abilities as foreign minister.

The antagonism between Foreign Minister Tanaka and the ministry leadership lasted for a long time. Finally, in January 2002, the question arose as to whether Diet member Suzuki Muneo had applied undue pressure on the Ministry of Foreign Affairs; Foreign Minister Tanaka's and Permanent Vice-Minister Nogami Yoshiji's statements in the Diet at the time were different. The Diet was thrown into confusion, and the foreign ministry was paralyzed. To restore order in Japan's foreign policy bureaucracy, Prime Minister Koizumi fired both Tanaka and Nogami. As always, the mass media, especially television, supported ex-Foreign Minister Tanaka, and the ratings for the Koizumi Cabinet subsequently fell. Prime Minister Koizumi finally recognized the devastating consequences of keeping Ms Tanaka as his foreign minister.

The second thing which signaled that Prime Minister Koizumi gave higher priority to domestic politics than to foreign policy was the pledge he made at the time of the LDP presidential election to visit the Yasukuni Shrine on August 15. Former Prime Minister Hashimoto Ryūtarō, who was one of the opposing candidates in that election, had served as head of the Japan War-Bereaved Association, but because his visit to Yasukuni in 1996 had strained Japanese-Chinese relations, he had taken the position that he would not visit the shrine as prime minister. In reference to the visit he had once made, former Prime Minister Hashimoto said, "As a result, it turned into big trouble, and I stopped. . . . Naturally, I want to go. But I just think it's better not to cause a disturbance."[11] From Koizumi's perspective, it may have seemed a major coup to garner the support of the War-Bereaved Association for himself. According to the memoirs of Nonaka Hiromu, who was then a Hashimoto supporter:

> At the time of the presidential election, Koizumi for the first time said he would visit the Yasukuni Shrine. He did so because he was aware of Hashimoto's local chapter votes. The War-Bereaved Association and the Military Pensioners' Federation, which wanted the prime minister to go to the Yasukuni Shrine, had been close to Hashimoto up to then. When Koizumi said he would visit the shrine on August 15, he was trying to steal their votes from Hashimoto.[12]

As Nonaka saw it, Koizumi's statement was effective because "the War-Bereaved Association and the Military Pensioners' Federation are the two pillars of the LDP membership," he said. It is not known, of course, whether that statement determined the outcome of the presidential election. There were many other factors. It is not clear either if Koizumi's promise to visit the shrine was motivated solely by his need for the votes of Yasukuni supporters. Koizumi had been critical of the way the shrine visit had been treated as a diplomatic issue; in his view, paying respect to the 200 million war dead was the prime minister's duty. In any case, doing something that a veteran politician like Hashimoto could not do must have got Koizumi's adrenaline going.[13]

As August 15 approached, the media speculated wildly on whether or not he would actually pay a visit to the Yasukuni Shrine. China openly warned that a visit would damage relations between Beijing and Tokyo. Ultimately, he decided to go two days earlier on August 13. The Chinese media were furious. But this might not have been all that bad a decision from the perspective of domestic politics. In the public opinion polls taken immediately afterwards, the majority favored the prime minister's Yasukuni visit on August 13. But as the result of that visit, in the second half of August, it was absolutely impossible to foresee what sort of diplomacy Japan would be pursuing in East Asia.

The 9/11 Terrorist Attacks

Right afterward, on September 11, 2001, the world drastically changed. As a result of terrorist attacks on the heart of America, the focus of global diplomacy was on the US war on terror. The parameters of foreign policy—the structural conditions for it—were sharply redefined from that day on. All the minutiae of previous dealings with the United States were shelved, and the relationship with America of virtually all the countries in the world was now defined by how quickly, how clearly and how specifically to support the US in the war on terrorism. Every country's foreign policy converged on this point. It would have been impossible for the Koizumi administration in Japan to be an exception.

Most of those in charge of Japanese policy wanted this time to avoid at all costs a repeat of the Gulf Crisis of 1990. During the Gulf Crisis and Gulf War in 1990–91, the Kaifu administration had been slow to take specific steps, devoting time to legal issues such as the interpretation of the constitution and doling out Japan's response bit by bit. Despite the fact that Japan ultimately contributed USD 13 billion to the war, the world, and especially the United States, had little regard for the Japanese effort. This "Gulf trauma" was a decisive factor in the Koizumi government's 9/11 policy.

Although the "Gulf trauma" overshadowed everyone involved in foreign policy, it alone cannot explain the speed of the Koizumi administration's response. The decisiveness of Prime Minister Koizumi himself was very significant. During a short visit to the United States in June, Koizumi met President Bush, and they found in each other a friend with the right chemistry. Koizumi must have felt that this was the time to help his newly found friend. On September 19, he announced his three-point basic policy as well as seven measures to be taken immediately. These included: the Self-Defense Forces would provide medical care, transport and logistics to the US and others acting against terrorism; Japan would send Self-Defense Force naval vessels to gather intelligence; and it would supply emergency aid to Pakistan and India. In addition, Prime Minister Koizumi himself paid a personal visit to the US, met with President Bush on September 25 and declared that, as a member of the coalition, Japan would not hesitate to provide its utmost cooperation and assistance and "make all possible contributions that do not require the use of force." As for discussions over legal fine points, the decision to allow Maritime Self-Defense Forces, etc., to participate would have been difficult without the Prime Minister's decision to brazen the matter out with an appeal to "common sense." In a short time, he had spelled out the necessary policies to give the US Japan's full support, presented the Anti-Terrorism Special Measures Law to the Diet to carry out these policies and saw it enacted by the end of October. As a result, the Maritime Self-Defense Forces were engaged in refueling activities for the American military in the Indian Ocean.

The firm decision to support the United States was a diplomatic home run, cementing the friendship between Koizumi and Bush. Thereafter, there were many situations in which Koizumi's foreign policy was helped by the trust this decision had earned him from the Bush administration.

The 9/11 attacks were also a major test for China and South Korea. In China, right after 9/11, anti-American sentiments cropped up on the Internet in the form of assertions that the US had it coming, but the Chinese government itself immediately made its relationship with the US clear. In siding with the US, it also tried to improve relations with Japan, which had been in limbo after Koizumi's visit to the Yasukuni Shrine. The events of 9/11 reset Chinese diplomacy. In South Korea, too, there was no dissent about adjusting the Japanese-Korean relationship in the face of the emergency in its relations with the US.

Prime Minister Koizumi also wanted to reset Japan's relations with its neighbors; it was agreed that he would visit China on October 8 and South Korea on the 15th. China accepted Koizumi's visit because, in any event, the prime minister would later be attending the APEC meetings in Shanghai that China was hosting, and it decided it wanted to avoid having the first meeting between the two countries' leaders take place there.[14] The Chinese side is also said to have asked that during his visit, Koizumi visit Lugouqiao (the Marco Polo Bridge), the site of the military clash in 1937 that brought Japan and China into a full-fledged war. The prime minister accepted, and on the 8th, he made a day trip to Beijing, visited the Marco Polo Bridge and expressed his "heartfelt apology" to the victims of the Japanese-Chinese war. President Jiang Zemin showed his appreciation of the prime minister's "apology" by saying that the "phase of tension between the two countries has been relaxed through today's meeting." On the other hand, "Japanese militarist war criminals are enshrined at Yasukuni. Visits there by Japanese leaders are a serious problem," and he told Koizumi not to go there again. Koizumi did not respond to this.[15] During this visit, Prime Minister Koizumi also asked for China's understanding in regard to Japan's cooperation in the war on terror. While noting that the people of Asia were wary, given the post-9/11 situation, the Chinese leaders did not raise any serious objections to Japanese activities that included the Self-Defense Forces. The Anti-Terror Special Measures Law was subsequently enacted, and Japan decided to send Self-Defense Force ships to the Indian Ocean. Although China expressed its misgivings, it avoided making any major protest.

Japanese-South Korean relations had been steadily moving forward. A future-oriented relationship had been agreed on during President Kim Dae-jung's visit to Japan in 1998, and since then, the history question had not been brought up to any great extent; moreover, the two countries were jointly hosting the 2002 Soccer World Cup. However, the Yasukuni controversy occurred at the time the Koizumi administration took office in 2001, and the authorization of textbooks by the Committee to Draw up a New History Textbook had also become a problem. The committee's membership included historians critical of the "masochistic view of history," and the South Korean government and media were concerned that the new textbooks would deny Japan's responsibilities for its aggression and colonial rule. Nevertheless, at the summit meeting between the two countries' leaders, President Kim, though critical, was not harsh; he suggested that the Yasukuni issue might be solved if Japan built a new memorial facility for its war dead.

As for relations with the US, the Koizumi government's support for the war against Iraq in the spring of 2003 was yet another important plus factor. That does not mean that support for the Bush administration on the Iraq War was high in Japan. Nevertheless, at the start of the war, the Koizumi Cabinet made clear its firm support for the Bush government. In the context of Japanese-US relations, as well as from President Bush's personal perspective, this probably also strengthened the perception that Koizumi ranked alongside Tony Blair of Britain—or just behind him—as America's staunch friend.

After 9/11, the foreign policy of support for the US up to the Iraq War made the management of Japan-US relations very easy. Since the collapse of the bubble economy in the 1990s, serious economic frictions between the US and Japan had altogether ceased to exist, and for that reason, it seemed unlikely that economic matters themselves would become major problems. But any number of minor economic issues did exist, for example, the ban on American beef imports as a result of mad cow disease (BSE=Bovine Spongiform Encephalopathy) and the slump in sales of GM and other American automakers. Neither became major political issues at the heads-of-state level. In connection with the reorganization of US forces, negotiations at the working level on the removal and reorganization of US bases in Japan (especially those in Okinawa) made little progress, but it was possible to avoid these, too, from becoming politicized.

Koizumi's approach to North Korea, which we discuss below, could have caused tensions with the United States, but the US made no public opposition to it. It is not clear when, and to what extent, the US was notified about the Koizumi administration's secret contacts with the North, but at the end of August 2002, when Koizumi's visit to North Korea was suddenly announced, it is hard not to imagine that serious frictions in Japanese-US relations would have arisen had it not been for the friendliness of the Koizumi-Bush relationship.[16]

The Visit to North Korea

If one were to cite the successes of Koizumi's foreign diplomacy, his policy vis-à-vis North Korea ranked next to his US policy. The shock and horror that many Japanese felt about North Korea's abduction of Japanese nationals were further reinforced by the "facts" that North Korea revealed to Prime Minister Koizumi when he visited Pyongyang on September 17, 2002. Much of that shock and anger was directed toward Japanese foreign policy and added more fuel to criticisms of the Ministry of Foreign Affairs. The sentiment was widely expressed that it was because Japan's foreign policy had been so spineless in its dealings with North Korea that the horrific facts about the kidnapping of Japanese citizens had not come to

The two prime ministers shaking hands after the signing of the
Joint Japan-DPRK Pyongyang Declaration (September 17, 2002).
Photo: Kyodo News

light much earlier. Even though the Koizumi administration did not
entirely solve the abduction issue, nevertheless, there is no doubt
that it made the situation far better than it had been. Subsequent
diplomatic negotiations and the Prime Minister's second visit to the
North succeeded in bringing back to Japan at least all the abductees
and their families that North Korea said were still alive.

Although relations with North Korea had been chilly since the
Taepodong missile launch in August 1998, in April 2000, for the first
time in seven and a half years, the ninth Japan-DPRK normalization
talks were held in Pyongyang, and opportunities for contact slowly
increased. That year North Korea became a member of ARF (the
ASEAN Regional Forum), and at this meeting, for the first time in
history, talks were held between the foreign ministers of Japan and
the North, Kōno Yōhei and Paek Nam Sun. After these talks, the
tenth round of normalization talks was held at the end of August
and the eleventh in Beijing in October. During these three rounds of
talks, North Korea emphasized the issue of settlement for the past,
which included the payment of huge amounts of "compensation,"
while the Japanese side asked for clarification about the Japanese
abductee issue and raised the matter of the North's missiles. At this
stage, however, there was no prospect of reaching an agreement.

The situation began to make headway in 2001 after 9/11. A North Korean later known as "Mr X" approached the Ministry of Foreign Affairs and sometime around October entered into secret talks with Tanaka Hitoshi, director-general of the Asian and Oceanian Affairs Bureau. In December 2001, however, a gun battle occurred between a North Korean spy ship and Japanese Coast Guard patrol boats; the Korean vessel sank, and the talks stalled.

At the beginning, those among Japan's highest leaders who were receiving reports on these secret talks were Prime Minister Koizumi, Chief Cabinet Secretary Fukuda Yasuo, Deputy Chief Cabinet Secretary Furukawa Teijirō and, in the Ministry of Foreign Affairs, only Vice-Minister Nogami Yoshiji. The fact that such information was not conveyed to Foreign Minister Tanaka gives some idea of how the prime minister began to view his foreign minister at that time. (After Tanaka and Nogami were fired, Foreign Minister Kawaguchi Yoriko and Vice-Minister Takeuchi Yukio received these reports.) The instructions that Prime Minister Koizumi gave to Director-General Tanaka were as follows:

- Get North Korea to admit to the truth about and apologize for the kidnappings and provide information about the abductees.
- With regard to the "settlement for the past," get the North to waive its property claims from before and during the war and resolve the matter through economic cooperation using the "Japan-South Korea formula."
- Not acknowledge either publicly or privately the amount of economic cooperation.[17]

It was in July 2002 that North Korea accepted these principles. Even in public, North Korea's attitude toward Japan was softening. At the time of the ASEAN Regional Forum meeting, which was held in Brunei on July 31, ministerial-level talks were held between Foreign Ministers Kawaguchi Yoriko and Paek Nam Sun, and North Korea agreed to specifically refer to a "humanitarian issue" (i.e., the abduction issue) in the joint statement released after their meeting. At the time of the talks between Kōno and Paek the previous year, the North had refused to accept these words.[18]

Seeing the North's position, Prime Minister Koizumi decided to go to North Korea himself. At the director-general-level meetings held in Pyongyang August 24–26, the prime minister's desire to visit the North was made known to the North Korean side, which indicated they would welcome such a visit. On August 30, Chief Cabinet Secretary Fukuda announced that the prime minister would visit North Korea on September 17.

All those involved, including Koizumi himself, had no idea what sort of information the North would provide on the abduction issue. According to the prime minister's executive secretary, Iijima Isao, Koizumi was determined. "I'm going to get results with my own hands; I'm taking a risk in the event things don't go well. But it's impossible to make a breakthrough in Japanese-North Korean relations unless the two heads of state meet."[19] On the other hand, among those involved in the Ministry of Foreign Affairs, the expectation was that the conditions were now in place for a normalization of relations with North Korea. This turned out to be wishful thinking.

Just ahead of the morning summit meeting on September 17, the North Korean side brought the Japanese shocking information. Though five of the kidnapping victims were still alive, eight others were already dead, including Yokota Megumi, who had become the symbol of the abductees. There was a heated exchange over the abduction issue at the morning session. During the noon break, some on the Japanese side aired the view that if Kim Jong Il did not apologize for the kidnappings, they ought to go home without signing the joint statement that had already been prepared. Whether the North was wiretapping these discussions is not clear, but at the afternoon meeting, Chairman Kim Jong Il apologized saying,

> I would like to take this opportunity to apologize straightforwardly for the regrettable conduct . . . . I will not allow that to happen again. . . . It is my understanding that this incident was initiated by special mission organizations in the 1970s and 1980s, driven by blindly motivated patriotism and misguided heroism. . . . I believe there were two reasons behind the abduction of Japanese citizens. First, the special mission organizations wanted to obtain native-Japanese instructors of the Japanese language. Second, the special mission organizations hoped to use abductees

to penetrate into "the South." . . . Those who were responsible were punished. This kind of thing will never be repeated.[20]

Prime Minister Koizumi accepted Kim Jong Il's apology and signed the Pyongyang Declaration. The contents are as follows:

Both leaders confirmed the shared recognition that establishing a fruitful political, economic and cultural relationship between Japan and the DPRK through the settlement of [the] unfortunate past between them and the outstanding issues of concern would be consistent with the fundamental interests of both sides, and would greatly contribute to the peace and stability of the region.

1. Both sides determined that, pursuant to the spirit and basic principles laid out in this Declaration, they would make every possible effort for an early normalization of the relations, and decided that they would resume the Japan DPRK normalization talks in October 2002.
Both sides expressed their strong determination that they would sincerely tackle outstanding problems between Japan and the DPRK based upon their mutual trust in the course of achieving the normalization.

2. The Japanese side regards, in a spirit of humility, the facts of history that Japan caused tremendous damage and suffering to the people of Korea through its colonial rule in the past, and expressed deep remorse and heartfelt apology.
Both sides shared the recognition that, providing economic co-operation after the normalization by the Japanese side to the DPRK side, including grant aids, long-term loans with low interest rates and such assistances as humanitarian assistance through international organizations, over a period of time deemed appropriate by both sides, and providing other loans and credits by such financial institutions as the Japan Bank for International Co-operation with a view to supporting private economic activities, would be consistent with the spirit of this Declaration, and decided that they would sincerely discuss the specific scales and contents of the economic co-operation in the normalization talks.

Both sides, pursuant to the basic principle that when the bilateral relationship is normalized both Japan and the DPRK would mutually waive all their property and claims and those of their nationals that had arisen from causes which occurred before August 15, 1945, decided that they would discuss this issue of property and claims concretely in the normalization talks.

Both sides decided that they would sincerely discuss the issue of the status of Korean residents in Japan and the issue of cultural property.

3. Both sides confirmed that they would comply with international law and would not commit conducts threatening the security of the other side. With respect to the outstanding issues of concern related to the lives and security of Japanese nationals, the DPRK side confirmed that it would take appropriate measures so that these regrettable incidents, that took place under the abnormal bilateral relationship, would never happen in the future.

4. Both sides confirmed that they would co-operate with each other in order to maintain and strengthen the peace and stability of North East Asia.

Both sides confirmed the importance of establishing co-operative relationships based upon mutual trust among countries concerned in this region, and shared the recognition that it is important to have a framework in place in order for these regional countries to promote confidence-building, as the relationships among these countries are normalized.

Both sides confirmed that, for an overall resolution of the nuclear issues on the Korean Peninsula, they would comply with all related international agreements. Both sides also confirmed the necessity of resolving security problems including nuclear and missile issues by promoting dialogues among countries concerned.

The DPRK side expressed its intention that, pursuant to the spirit of this Declaration, it would further maintain the moratorium on missile launching in and after 2003.

Both sides decided that they would discuss issues relating to security.[21]

As can be seen from a reading of the Pyongyang Declaration quoted here, on the whole, it included contents that were favorable to Japan. Particularly advantageous to Japan was the North's agreement to continue normalization talks in basically the same form as the Japan-South Korean normalization talks in 1965. Although the refusal to include any mention of the abduction issue in the document provoked discontent on the Japanese side, nevertheless, the fact that Kim Jong Il himself had apologized was an enormous change from what had been the North Korean attitude up to then.

What caused North Korea to change its position in this way is an important question. But as is usually the case with North Korean issues, its internal affairs are completely opaque. If one were to hazard a guess, they may conceivably have thought they had to improve their international standing by improving relations with Tokyo and thus influencing US-North Korean relations, which at the time were making no progress, or even deteriorating. The Bush administration, which came into office in 2001, held the view that the Clinton administration's North Korean policy had been too conciliatory; it criticized past policies and made no attempt to propose new ones. Not only that, in President Bush's State of the Union address in January 2002, he named North Korea along with Iran and Iraq as part of the "axis of evil." Once before when the Soviet Union was about to normalize relations with South Korea, and the North appeared isolated, North Korea had approached Japan and arranged for Kanemaru to visit (see Chapter 2). This time, since relations with the US were not improving at all, the North Koreans' acceptance of plans to normalize relations with Japan may perhaps be regarded as an attempt to make progress in their relations with the US.

Even if North Korea had had such intentions, though, events did not proceed as they had planned. The North Korean revelation about the abductees incensed the Japanese public. It was too shocking, and what is more, the North did not seem to have revealed all the facts. As for further talks that would lead to diplomatic normalization in the foreseeable future, the feelings of the Japanese people made such talks impossible.

Koizumi's visit to North Korea was distinct from the way Japanese diplomacy had often been practiced up to then; it was the result of negotiations so secret that they even surprised its ally, the United States. Information about the visit was passed on to the US a mere three days before it was officially announced by the chief cabinet secretary. Although this caused considerable discontent among the Americans in charge of the day-to-day handling of Japanese affairs, President Bush showed his understanding about the North Korean trip when Koizumi visited the US on September 12 just before going there.

However, the intelligence on North Korea that the US had gathered up to then contained much cause for concern. Despite the fact that the North had consented to the Agreed Framework in 1994, fears were mounting that it was going ahead with its uranium enrichment program. Although under the Agreed Framework, graphite-moderated reactors had been shut down, suspicions were raised that the North was proceeding with uranium enrichment, using technology it had received from Pakistan, and was thereby once again engaged in making nuclear weapons.

At the beginning of October, when Jim Kelly, Assistant Secretary of State for East Asian and Pacific Affairs, visited Pyongyang, and when he asked whether or not a uranium enrichment program existed, the North Koreans involved admitted that it did. Although North Korea later claimed that there was no such program, the American side concluded that the North was indeed enriching uranium. The results of Kelly's visit were made public on October 16, causing a chain reaction that at once returned the North Korean situation to what it had been in 1993 and 1994.

On October 20, Secretary of State Colin Powell in an interview on US television expressed his opinion that the Agreed Framework with North Korea was null and void. On November 14, the directorate of the Korean Peninsula Energy Development Organization (KEDO) met and warned North Korea that if it did not immediately give up its entire nuclear weapons program, it would freeze heavy-fuel-oil aid from the US from December on. North Korea did not respond, and ultimately the supply of heavy oil from the US was suspended. Because of this, North Korea claimed that the US was in violation of the Agreed Framework, and on December 12, it announced it was reopening and immediately resuming construction on the related nuclear facilities that had been frozen under the Agreed Framework. On the 21st, it removed the seals from most of the monitoring devices that the IAEA had installed on its graphite-moderated reactor in Yongbyon. On the 26th, it shipped around a thousand nuclear fuel rods to this reactor. On the 27th, it announced that it had decided on three things: (1) to expel the IAEA inspectors who were already there; (2) complete the nuclear power plant that it had stopped building; and (3) reopen the Radio-chemistry Research Institute, which was believed to be a reprocessing plant for plutonium extraction. At the beginning of the year, on January 10, 2003, North Korea announced it was immediately withdrawing from the Non-Proliferation Treaty and revoking the Safeguards Agreement (on nuclear inspections). That North Korea had, in fact, reactivated one of its graphite-moderated reactors was confirmed by the US at the end of February. The entire framework that had been put in place to resolve the crisis in 1994 was now in ruins.

As North Korea proceeded to break each provision in the Agreed Framework one after another, the Bush administration took no steps to prevent the North from doing so. This is a big puzzle. The reason for this may have been the firm position of the Bush inner circle that the administration would not make any deal with the North and their belief that the Agreed Framework was not worth defending. Or perhaps at the time, with their heads full of plans for the Iraq War which would begin in March 2003, they may not have fully explored policies to counter these moves by the North. That will be a topic for future historical research.

As North Korea moved further and further away from the Agreed Framework, relations between Japan and the North also worsened. Just around the time that the Japanese government was receiving Assistant Secretary of State Kelly's report that North Korea had admitted to having a uranium enrichment program, the Japanese government tried to facilitate a temporary return to Japan for the five abductees whose existence the North had admitted to. The North allowed the five to go home, saying that they were being "returned to Japan temporarily." On October 15, the return of Hasuike Kaoru, Okudo Yukiko, Chimura Yasushi, Hamamoto Fukie and Soga Hitomi became a reality. Because the American government announced the results of Kelly's visit on October 16 US time, it was two days before tensions between the US and the North would begin in earnest. Within the Japanese government, there was a fierce debate over whether or not Japan should send the five abductees back to North Korea as promised.[22] Prime Minister Koizumi supported the opinion of Deputy Chief Cabinet Secretary Abe Shinzō that they should not be sent back, and on October 24, Chief Cabinet Secretary Fukuda announced that the five would not be returning. North Korea criticized the Japanese government for breaking its promise. On October 30, normalization talks between Japan and the North were held in Kuala Lumpur, Malaysia, but made no progress. The North Korean nuclear crisis subsequently became even more serious, and the Japan-North Korea relationship came to a standstill.

The situation began to change at the beginning of 2004. The precise details have not been made clear, but sometime around April, there was a report that if Prime Minister Koizumi visited North Korea again, the North would be willing to return the families of the abductees. On the basis of this report, the Ministry of Foreign Affairs negotiated with North Korea, and on May 22, Prime Minister Koizumi once again paid a visit to the North. While he was there, he promised 250,000 tons of food aid, and as a result, he returned to Japan with the five children of the Chimura and Hasuike families; subsequently, Soga Hitomi's husband, Charles Jenkins, and their two daughters also returned to Japan. There was much criticism of Koizumi's second North Korean visit within Japan. But from the perspective of the abduction issue, it must be rated a success since, thanks to this visit, Koizumi was at least able to bring home to Japan all the families of the abductees that North Korea claimed were still alive. It should be added, however, that North Korea's subsequent response to the abductee issue was extremely unsatisfactory. Although the North handed over the "remains" of Yokota Megumi, whom the North claimed had died, the results of DNA tests conducted by the Japanese side indicated there was an extremely high likelihood that they belonged to someone else. Thereafter, North Korea took the attitude that the abduction issue had been "settled."

ASEAN+3 Materializes

Compared to the time when the Cold War ended, several regional cooperative frameworks had already come into existence in Asia in the year 2000. Of these, however, APEC was losing momentum because, among other things, Japan and the United States in 1998 had different views on how to liberalize trade.[23] The ASEAN Regional

Forum (ARF), too, was unable to make much substantial progress in its original plan to move from confidence building to defense exchanges and then to conflict resolution. By contrast, the ASEAN+3 framework, begun at the end of 1997, began to attract more attention from the countries in the region.

ASEAN+3 cooperation had a tangible dimension, particularly on the financial side. On March 24, 2000, deputy finance ministers and Central Bank deputy governors from the ASEAN+3 countries met at Bandar Seri Begawan, Brunei, and agreed to look into creating a framework for financial cooperation with a view to establishing a new fund to make provisions against any future economic crisis.[24] The initial step they agreed to discuss was a currency swap mechanism. Against a background of fear that the ASEAN financial crisis might happen again, the Japanese Ministry of Finance took the initiative and drew up a plan that this time China came to support.[25] The ASEAN+3 Finance Ministers Meeting on May 6 agreed to start negotiations to create a network of bilateral currency swap agreements. This plan came to be called the Chiang Mai Initiative, as this meeting took place at Chiang Mai, Thailand. At this session, the ASEAN+3 finance ministers also agreed to convene every six months and keep an eye on East Asian economic trends.[26]

At this moment, yet another new sectoral forum was added to the ASEAN+3. On May 2, its first Economic Ministers Meeting was held at Yangon, where it was agreed, among other things, to standardize the rules for e-commerce and expand the agreement for promoting investment.[27] At the end of July, the ASEAN+3 foreign ministers met, and Foreign Minister Surin Pitsuwan of Thailand, who served as chair, declared that ASEAN+3 was "already institutionalized."[28] At the end of August, it was also reported that an ASEAN+3 agricultural ministers meeting would be created within the year.[29] On October 7 at Chiang Mai, the ASEAN+3 Economic Ministers Meeting was already being held for the second time.[30]

Thus, the 2000 ASEAN+3 Summit was clearly shaping up to be the chief among a number of cabinet-level meetings unlike anything that had happened before. At this summit, which was held on November 24, members thrashed out such topics as the future nature of free trade in the region and the need for ASEAN+3 to evolve into an "East Asian Summit." Following up on his earlier idea for an "East Asia Vision Group," President Kim Dae-jung of South Korea proposed establishing an "East Asia Study Group" to promote East Asian cooperation from a practical viewpoint, and the ASEAN+3 Summit agreed to have the group explore plans for free trade and investment as well as the feasibility of an East Asian Summit.[31] Though the occasion was the ASEAN+3 Summit, the term "East Asia" was front and center. And because Chinese Premier Zhu Rongji at a meeting of ASEAN and Chinese heads of state had proposed exploring plans for an Chinese-ASEAN free-trade area, discussions expanded into the possibility of a free-trade zone for the entire East Asian region.[32]

A meeting among the leaders of Japan, China and South Korea, which had occurred at the time of the ASEAN+3 meeting in 1999, took place once again. Premier Zhu of China had been cautious, but when he visited Japan in October and Prime Minister Mori proposed the meeting, he replied, "That's very good. Let's do it."[33] When the Japanese, Chinese and South Korean summit meeting was held on the morning of November 24, President Kim proposed that the trilateral summit be held on a regular basis, and this time Premier Zhu immediately consented; it was agreed to hold regular meetings from then on.[34]

By 2001, ASEAN+3 cooperation in various sectors was making progress. In May 2001, the economic ministers held their third meeting in Siem Reap and their fourth in September in Hanoi. Also in May, the first meeting of labor ministers was held in Kuala Lumpur, and the first meeting of agriculture ministers in Medan. Among these sectoral discussions, the finance ministers' Chiang Mai Initiative was the first to bear fruit. On the occasion of the ASEAN+3 Finance Ministers Meeting at Honolulu in May, the monetary authority of Japan agreed to conclude bilateral currency swap agreements with its counterparts in South Korea, Thailand and Malaysia; it was reported that negotiations between Japan and China and between Japan and the Philippines were also under way.[35] As other countries concluded their bilateral swap agreements one by one, the network became denser and more multilateral. A full-fledged multilateral network of swap agreements was agreed upon in 2009.

From early 2001 on, however, signs could be seen that the center of political leadership in the ASEAN+3 cooperation development process was shifting from South Korea and Japan to China.

President Kim Dae-jung of South Korea had been unable to maintain the momentum that had led to the summit talks between the North and the South in the spring of 2000. As the result of his inability to advance North-South relations as he had hoped, criticism mounted within South Korea, and his support ratings fell. As we saw in the previous chapter, in Japan, Prime Minister Mori, who had succeeded Prime Minister Obuchi after the latter fell ill in the spring of 2000, failed to increase his domestic support; between late 2000 and early 2001, his ratings were at their lowest ebb, and he was finally forced to resign in April. Prime Minister Koizumi, who came to power after him, had phenomenal popular support, but diplomacy was not a matter of top priority for him. By fulfilling his promise to visit the Yasukuni Shrine, relations with China and South Korea stalled. Nor did he seem to have had much interest at all in Southeast Asia at the beginning of his administration. Thus, of the three countries, only China had a firm power base. Hitherto, the Chinese had not been particularly proactive when it came to the ASEAN+3 framework, though there had been circumstances in which they had passively promoted it by not opposing the initiatives of other countries. But now, with almost no moves coming from Japan and South Korea, the proposal for a China-ASEAN free-trade area that Premier Zhu Rongji had suggested was becoming the focus of attention.

The terrorist attacks on the United States on September 11, 2001, had an impact on ASEAN+3 relations. On the one hand, Japan enacted the Anti-Terrorism Special Measures Law and cooperated with the US, while, on the other, it searched for opportunities to rebuild its East Asian diplomacy. Prime Minister Koizumi hastily visited China and South Korea as a way of improving relations with Japan's nearest neighbors in the war on terror, and at the ASEAN+3 Summit as well, he worked hard to put together an anti-terror statement.[36] But at the ASEAN+3 meeting held on November 5, the ASEAN side's response was that there was no need to issue a new ASEAN+3 statement in addition to the one that the ASEAN Summit had already adopted, and so no ASEAN+3 statement materialized. It could be said that, having taken care of the terror issue at its own summit meeting, the ASEAN side made ASEAN+3 concentrate exclusively on economic issues.[37]

What attracted greater interest at the time of this meeting was the decision by China and ASEAN on the morning of November 6 to sign a free-trade agreement within ten years.[38] In response to a question at a press conference as to what Japan should do about the development of Chinese-ASEAN economic relations, implying that Japan was lagging behind China, Prime Minister Koizumi responded, "Japanese newspapers often take a masochistic view" and said that he welcomed a deepening of the Chinese-ASEAN economic relationship. But on the question on how he felt about talk of a free-trade area in East Asia, it "involves many difficult matters," he said, and showed no sign of taking the initiative in the economic area, concluding with the abstract statement that the only thing to do was to move "forward."[39]

The report of the East Asia Vision Group (EAVG), which President Kim Dae-jung had taken the initiative to establish, was presented at this summit meeting. The report made 57 recommendations, 22 of which were designated as "key." Among the latter were that they should aim at forming an East Asia Free Trade Area and that ASEAN+3 ought to evolve into an East Asian Summit.[40] The chair's statement summed up these two items as "bold yet feasible."[41] President Kim articulated the vision based on this report, and it was highly thought of in the local media.[42] But it did not strengthen his domestic political base, and South Korea took no further initiatives beyond this.

Prime Minister Koizumi is likely to have recognized the importance of Southeast Asian diplomacy as a result of attending the ASEAN+3 Summit. The Prime Minister and the Japanese government subsequently set out to reinforce Japan's relations with Southeast Asia. Koizumi visited Southeast Asian countries in January 2002 and made an important policy address in Singapore. In it he spoke of the need to make the best possible use of the ASEAN+3 framework with the aim of creating "a community that acts together and advances together," and he proposed an "Initiative for Japan-ASEAN Comprehensive Economic Partnership" to do so.[43]

From the beginning of 2002 on, the evolution of ASEAN+3 advanced through a three-way process with moves to deepen relations between China and ASEAN, moves to deepen relations between Japan and ASEAN and the discussions of the East Asia

Study Group. The deepening of Chinese-ASEAN relations, needless to say, took the form of activity to establish a free-trade area. At the ASEAN+China Summit held on the margins of the ASEAN+3 Summit in Phnom Penh in November 2002, the two sides agreed to sign a Framework Agreement on Comprehensive Economic Cooperation, and China offered to liberalize some sectors earlier than others ("early harvests").

Movements between Japan and ASEAN were centered around the Initiative for Japan-ASEAN Comprehensive Economic Partnership that Prime Minister Koizumi had proposed. Japan, which had signed an economic partnership agreement with Singapore, set up a study group under the chief cabinet secretary to consider the Initiative and explore future Japanese efforts. Consequently, at the ASEAN+Japan summit meeting in November, it was decided to reach bilateral agreements that contained free-trade elements between Japan and each of the ASEAN countries as soon as possible within the next ten years and to draw up a framework for a Comprehensive Economic Partnership by the 2003 summit meeting.[44]

Although it is true that these free-trade experiments between China and ASEAN and Japan and ASEAN advanced an essential aspect of East Asian cooperation, that does not mean they were representative of trends in the ASEAN+3 region as a whole. A more comprehensive policy review for ASEAN+3 was entrusted to the East Asia Study Group (EASG) to assess the East Asia Vision Group's report. The EASG operated as a gathering of senior-level ASEAN+3 officials.[45] The EASG report was presented and agreed to at the ASEAN+3 Summit in November. This document became the first official agreement that came to grips with specific policies for implementing ASEAN+3 cooperation. According to the report, having examined in detail all the East Asia Vision Group's recommendations and taken into consideration their importance and the feasibility of enacting them, the EASG was proposing 17 short-term measures and 9 medium- to long-term measures. The 17 short-term measures were ones that did not require significant funding and were thus easy for the member countries to agree to. By contrast, among the mid- to long-term measures were important ones like the proposals for an East Asian Free Trade Area and a regional financing facility, which required the specific agreement of the member states.

One other important theme that the EASG was particularly asked to consider was the feasibility of the "East Asian Summit" that the EAVG report had proposed. Without coming to any categorical conclusions, the report noted that the ASEAN+3 framework was ideal for moving the East Asian process forward; that an "East Asian Summit" was "a long-term desirable objective"; and that it must proceed in a way that was within the "comfort level" of the present ASEAN+3 and avoided the "marginalization" of ASEAN.[46]

In 2004, however, talk of an East Asia Summit[47] suddenly intensified. Malaysia, which was scheduled to chair ASEAN in 2005, indicated its intention to hold the first East Asia Summit in Kuala Lumpur in 2005. Then, China said it wanted to hold the second East Asia Summit in Beijing in 2007. Japan began sounding out Malaysia about co-hosting the first East Asia Summit. The ASEAN+3 Summit, as the name indicates, was a meeting of ASEAN. The East Asia Summit that was beginning to be discussed, however, had the potential for Japan and China to host the meeting. With such a possibility in sight and with both Japan and China beginning to make proposals that had all the makings of a leadership struggle, fears arose among the ASEAN countries that ASEAN would be marginalized. After a heated debate among ASEAN leaders, the ASEAN Summit held in Vientiane, Laos, in 2004 concluded that an East Asia Summit should be established. The ASEAN+3 Summit held immediately afterward consented to the ASEAN decision. No details of the East Asia Summit, its participants or modalities, however, were worked out at that time.

Ultimately, in the first half of 2005, in a study conducted primarily by ASEAN, it was agreed that the East Asia Summit would continue to be ASEAN-centered. The membership issue was contentious; some countries like Indonesia and Singapore wanted to include India, Australia and New Zealand while others like Malaysia and Thailand insisted on restricting the membership to the ASEAN+3 members. Japan supported the former, China, the latter. Finally, the ASEAN foreign ministers agreed on the three criteria for membership in the East Asia Summit: (1) being a dialogue partner of ASEAN; (2) being a signatory of the Treaty of Amity and Cooperation in Southeast Asia (TAC); and (3) having a significant cooperative relationship with ASEAN. India was the only country that fulfilled these criteria, but

New Zealand and Australia indicated their intention to sign the TAC; as a result, the three countries joined the EAS. Thus, in December 2005, the ASEAN Summit, the ASEAN+3 Summit and the first East Asia Summit were held in Kuala Lumpur.[48]

The Six-Party Talks

While the ASEAN+3 framework, as the name implies, was primarily centered on the ASEAN countries of Southeast Asia, the Six-Party Talks that emerged in 2003 were Northeast-Asian-centered. These meetings, attended by representatives of six countries—North and South Korea, the US, Japan, Russia and China—came about to deal with the North Korean nuclear weapon development problem, which was assuming dangerous proportions at the end of 2002. Back in 1988, President Roh Tae-woo of South Korea had proposed a Consultative Conference for Peace in Northeast Asia consisting of the same member countries, and in 1999, Prime Minister Obuchi had also proposed that these six countries meet, but neither of these plans materialized.

It was China that brought the meeting about in 2003. Vice-Premier Qian Qichen visited North Korea in March and suggested that the US, North Korea and China meet; these trilateral talks first took place in Beijing in April. Although the talks themselves bore no fruit, in compliance with the wishes of the US, South Korea and Japan, China made the effort to arrange for talks among all six countries, and after negotiating with each of the countries involved including North Korea, the first Six-Party Talks were held in August.

In retrospect, during the North Korean nuclear crisis in 1993–94, the Chinese had behaved as if it had nothing to do with them. By contrast, China in 2003 played the role of go-between with the US and North Korea and hosted the Six-Party Talks. During that decade, international conditions around China had changed, as had the diplomatic stance of China itself.

From the perspective of Chinese diplomacy, strengthening China's relations with the United States after 9/11 was an extremely important task.[49] President Jiang Zemin seems to have taken advantage of the nascent Bush presidency in early 2001 to try to give greater emphasis to US relations. But that April, a Chinese fighter jet collided off

Hainan Island with an American reconnaissance plane; the Chinese jet crashed, and the American plane landed on Hainan. This incident caused Chinese anti-Americanism once again to flare up. But since this was also the time that negotiations over China's membership in the World Trade Organization (WTO) were reaching a climax, the Chinese government could not help but seek to improve relations as quickly as possible. Thus, the fact that President Jiang, who had watched the 9/11 terrorist attacks on Phoenix Television, immediately telephoned President Bush to express his condolences was a sign of the importance that the Chinese government attached to the US. Even after China became a member of the WTO that November, that did not change.

In February 2002, President Bush visited China as well as Japan and South Korea. He gave a speech at Tsinghua University and emphasized the importance of democratization, but the outcome of the visit that mattered from President Jiang's perspective was the decision that the latter would visit the US in October. Moreover, Jiang Zemin wanted the meeting to take place not at the White House but at Bush's private residence in Crawford, Texas, presumably out of a desire to symbolize his particularly close relationship with the President. The Americans, who needed Chinese cooperation in the war on terror, accepted this, and the US-China summit was held in Crawford on October 25, right after North Korea had admitted its uranium enrichment program to Assistant Secretary of State James Kelly. At this meeting, Jiang Zemin revealed that he had told the North Koreans ten years earlier: "If a war were to break out as a result of North Korean mismanagement of its nuclear issues, we would simply continue on our path toward national development [and not get involved]. I need your understanding on this point."[50]

Thereafter, China came to make public its opposition to North Korea's development of nuclear weapons, and when President Putin visited Beijing in December, Jiang and Putin agreed to seek the denuclearization of the Korean peninsula and stated the importance of normalizing the relations between the United States and North Korea.[51] The following March, Vice-Premier Qian Qichen was sent to North Korea and urged the North to engage in a dialogue with the US; right before then, in February, China is said to have stopped sending oil via the China-Korea Friendship Pipeline for three days because of "technical difficulties."[52] As a result of these sorts of carrot-and-stick measures, three-party talks opened in Beijing on April 23. That does not mean, however, that North Korea was being cooperative; quite the contrary, it declared at this meeting that its reprocessing of nearly 8,000 spent nuclear fuel rods was "almost complete." And in the middle of the meeting, Li Gun, deputy director-general for North American Affairs, announced that the North already had "nuclear capability."[53]

At the National People's Congress in March 2003, Hu Jintao officially became President of China. He attended the G8 meeting held that year in St Petersburg as a guest and held a number of important bilateral meetings with other leaders. Through these meetings, he pursued the possibility of talks that would include Japan, South Korea and Russia in addition to the members of the three-party talks, which appeared to be getting nowhere. In August, he dispatched Deputy Foreign Minister Dai Bingguo to North Korea and the US, and succeeded in gaining North Korean consent to the holding of six-party talks.

Behind these Chinese diplomatic efforts was a position that consistently prioritized the United States. But we can also see in them the beginnings of a change in China's diplomatic orientation in the direction of multilateralism. For a long time after escaping its post-Tiananmen isolation, China had not been particularly enthusiastic about multilateral diplomacy. Even though it participated in APEC and ARF, it was extremely cautious and maintained a defensive posture. For China, the fear was probably strong that a multilateral forum would become a place where others would gang together and criticize China. The Chinese were even cautious about invitations to multilateral frameworks that might be beneficial to them. It was Premier Li Peng to whom Prime Minister Mahathir first proposed the EAEG, but China did not get on board. Again in 1997, China was negative about the AMF that Japan was calling for.

This tendency to shy away from multilateral diplomacy began to change at the end of the 1990s. One sign of this was ASEAN+3. During the process that led to the Chiang Mai Initiative, China was becoming more proactive than it ever had been in the past. In November 2001, it held a meeting to sign the China-ASEAN Free Trade Agreement, and in October 2003, it became a signatory to the Treaty of Amity and

Cooperation in Southeast Asia, the basic treaty among the ASEAN countries. Earlier, in April 1996, the heads of China, Russia, Kazakhstan, Kyrgyzstan and Tajikistan had met in Shanghai with the aim of strengthening trust among the regions on their borders; these countries were thereafter called the Shanghai Five, and it was China that actively attempted to get this to grow as a multilateral framework. Uzbekistan joined in June 2001, leading to the formation of an international organization called the Shanghai Cooperation Organization (SCO). Behind China's activism as seen in the Six-Party Talks is the accumulation of such initiatives in multilateral diplomacy.[54]

The Six-Party Talks, first held in Beijing on August 27, 2003, however, turned into a long-term process. A list of the meetings is as follows:

August 27–29, 2003	First Six-Party Talks
February 24–28, 2004	Second Six-Party Talks
June 23–26, 2004	Third Six-Party Talks
July 26–August 7, 2005	Fourth Six-Party Talks, First Session
September 13–19, 2005	Fourth Six-Party Talks, Second Session
November 9–12, 2005	Fifth Six-Party Talks, First Session
December 18–22, 2006	Fifth Six-Party Talks, Second Session
February 8–13, 2007	Fifth Six-Party Talks, Third Session
March 19–22, 2007	Sixth Six-Party Talks, First Session

There was a gap of nearly a year between the third meeting and the fourth; this was basically because North Korea refused to meet during the American presidential elections. After the reelection of President Bush, the US, too, showed no willingness to compromise; in testimony before Congress, Secretary of State-designate Condoleezza Rice called North Korea an "outpost of tyranny." In response, the North Korean foreign ministry officially stated in February 2005 that it had nuclear weapons.

The Fourth Six-Party Talks went on and on with a midsummer break in between, and in the second year since the talks began, a joint statement was agreed upon for the first time on September 19, 2005. In this statement, North Korea "committed to abandoning all nuclear weapons and existing nuclear programs and returning, at an early date, to the Treaty on the Nonproliferation of Nuclear Weapons and to IAEA safeguards," and "the United States affirmed that it . . . has no nuclear weapons on the Korean Peninsula and has no intention to attack or invade the DPRK with nuclear or conventional weapons." The US and North Korea promised in writing to take steps to normalize their relations, as did Japan and the North. In regard to these measures, "the Six Parties agreed to take coordinated steps . . . in line with the principle of 'commitment for commitment, action for action.'"[55]

Just before this joint statement was issued, however, the US Treasury Department alleged that the Banco Delta Asia (BDA) in Macau was involved in North Korean money laundering and prohibited all US financial institutions from having any dealings with that bank. The Macau government froze the North Korean accounts in the BDA. These steps hardened North Korea's attitude, and the situation became deadlocked once again. At the Fifth Six-Party Talks held in November 2005, no constructive steps were taken as the US clashed with North Korea, which pressed for resolution of the BDA issue while the Americans insisted it was a judiciary matter not a diplomatic one.

North Korea subsequently requested a bilateral meeting with the US, but the Americans refused. The North presumably turned once again to the diplomacy of brinkmanship. In July 2006, it conducted several ballistic missile tests including Taepodongs and finally its first nuclear test on October 9, 2006.

In the American midterm elections held right after this in November, the incumbent Republican Party lost badly. The American public had supported President Bush in the 2004 presidential elections, but as the situation in Iraq subsequently continued to worsen, many Americans judged that the Iraq War had been a mistake and delivered a harsh verdict on the Republicans. After this big election defeat, the influence of the neoconservatives within the Bush administration waned. President Bush dismissed Secretary of Defense Donald Rumsfeld and replaced Ambassador to the UN John Bolton. With this change in the Bush administration's overall stance and the Iraq stalemate, the calls of those demanding success in other areas strengthened. In its North Korean policy, there was a growing tendency to try to settle the situation through some sort of "deal." Such a move must have come as a surprise to Pyongyang, which might well have expected a tougher attitude from Washington after its nuclear test.[56] As a result, the Six-Party Talks reconvened in December 2006 after a little more than a year, and early in the new year, in February 2007, a "first phase action plan" was agreed on. It took time to resolve the BDA issue, and the plan did not go so far as to close North Korea's nuclear facilities, but finally in July 2007, the situation at last reached the point in which the nuclear facilities were shut down and IAEA inspectors had again returned to the North.

After North Korea was let off the hook for its announcement that it had nuclear weapons, its ballistic missile tests and its nuclear test, the situation returned to what it had been in October 2002; in that sense, the Six-Party Talks process failed to clearly demonstrate that it had been an effective means of diplomacy. Nevertheless, for some time thereafter relations between North Korea and the other members of the Six-Party Talks improved. The New York Philharmonic Orchestra even went to Pyongyang in February 2008. As usual in North Korea's international relations, this period of calm did not last. As the health of the Dear Leader deteriorated, North Korea began to display another round of erratic behavior.

Deteriorating Japanese-Chinese Relations

In East Asia, on the one hand, there was regional cooperation in the form of ASEAN+3, with ASEAN at its core; discussions aimed at an "East Asian community" were also progressing. On the other hand, in Northeast Asia, diplomacy centered on the Six-Party Talks was also under way to deal with the troubling North Korean problem. What was especially noticeable in both contexts was the deterioration in the Japanese-Chinese relationship.[57]

As has already been noted, after the 9/11 terrorist attacks, Prime Minister Koizumi went to China in October and visited the Marco Polo Bridge. At the Japanese-Chinese summit meeting at this time, Koizumi is said to have made no response to President Jiang Zemin's objections to his visit to the Yasukuni Shrine.[58] Quite possibly Jiang may have misinterpreted Koizumi's "unspoken reply." During the LDP presidential campaign Koizumi had created a stir by saying he would visit the shrine on August 15 but had compromised and gone two days earlier on August 13; he visited China, then went to the Marco Polo Bridge and apologized. President Jiang may well have

Prime Minister Koizumi at the end of his visit to the
Yasukuni Shrine (August 13, 2001). Photo: Kyodo News

thought that Koizumi had given up his visits to the Yasukuni Shrine.
The prime minister's subsequent actions up until the spring of 2002
were also highly desirable from President Jiang's point of view.

In the spring of 2002, Prime Minister Koizumi was invited to the
first Boao Forum for Asia, an international conference sponsored by
the Chinese government, and on April 12, he gave a keynote address
in which he stated that he did not accept the "China-as-threat idea"
and was praised by Premier Zhu Rongji and others. On April 18, the
Koizumi Cabinet approved the War Contingency Bills, but China
only went so far as to express its concern. While Japanese-Chinese
relations continued to mend, Koizumi suddenly paid a visit to the
Yasukuni Shrine on the morning of April 21. The 21st was the beginning of the shrine's annual spring festival, and after the visit, the
prime minister declared that he would visit the shrine once a year but
not in August. President Jiang was said to have been furious about the
prime minister's visit. The Chinese government immediately made
an official protest, but reports in the print media were restrained.
China announced, however, that it was postponing the visit to China
of Nakatani Gen, head of the Japan Defense Agency, as well as the
planned visit of Chinese naval vessels to Japanese ports to commemorate the 30th anniversary of diplomatic normalization.

Japanese-Chinese relations, which had soured after Koizumi's second visit to the Yasukuni Shrine, were greatly shaken by repercussions from the situation on the Korean peninsula. On the afternoon of May 8, 2002, five asylum-seeking North Korean men and women had tried to enter the Japanese consulate at Shenyang and were arrested by armed Chinese police inside the consulate compound. The Japanese government stressed that the arrest had taken place within the consulate compound and demanded an apology and a return to the status quo on the grounds that China had infringed the inviolability of its diplomatic premises. The Japanese foreign ministry's response to the incident had been clumsy, however, and public opinion at home was increasingly critical of both China and its own Ministry of Foreign Affairs. Still, anti-Chinese sentiments in Japan worsened considerably as a result. Events celebrating the 30th anniversary of Japanese-Chinese normalization were held in September 2002, but Prime Minister Koizumi did not visit China, and there was no visit by the Crown Prince and Princess despite the Chinese invitation extended by such prominent figures as Zhu Rongji and Li Peng.[59]

At the end of October 2002, at the Japanese-Chinese summit meetings held at the time of the APEC Summit at Los Cabos, Mexico, President Jiang met with Prime Minister Koizumi and is said to have asked him three times not to visit the Yasukuni Shrine. Koizumi did not say he would stop doing so.[60] Given Koizumi's personality, President Jiang's repeated requests at this time may have had the opposite of the desired effect and hardened the prime minister's resolve to visit the shrine. There was nothing Prime Minister Koizumi resented more than having someone lecture him about changing his policy. Ultimately, Koizumi visited Yasukuni once again in mid-January 2003.

The Hu Jintao administration that was formed in 2003 initially took several steps to improve relations with Japan.[61] Hu Jintao, who met Prime Minister Koizumi in St Petersburg, was grateful for the Japanese government's cooperation at the time of the SARS outbreak that spring. In addition to inaugurating the New Japan-China Friendship Committee for the 21st Century agreed upon with Koizumi, he had Foreign Minister Li Zhaoxing visit Japan in August and Wu Bangguo, chairman and party secretary of the Standing Committee of the National People's Congress, in September. At the time of Foreign Minister Li's visit, China revealed its policy not to require visas of Japanese nationals making trips of less than two weeks. The concept of "new thinking on Japan" propounded by Ma Licheng, an editorial writer for the *People's Daily*, and Professor Shi Yinhong of Renmin University of China, was being widely discussed; both argued for improving relations with Japan as a matter of strategic importance and suggested putting the history issue on the backburner. It was even speculated that the Hu administration might be considering a full-scale improvement in its relations with Japan.

Since there was no noticeable reaction from the Koizumi administration, however, the view intensified within China that the Hu government's policy toward Japan was too conciliatory. Moreover, in the summer and fall of 2003, a string of incidents took place that worsened the image of Japanese in China. In August, a leak of poisonous gas from an old Japanese army facility caused casualties in Qiqihar, Heilongjiang Province. And in September, a sex scandal occurred at Zhuhai, Guangdong Province, involving prostitutes and a group of around 300 employees from a Japanese firm. In October, after Prime Minister Koizumi met with Premier Wen Jiabao on Bali, Indonesia, he told the press corps accompanying him, "I think we understand each another" about the "visits to the Yasukuni Shrine."[62] As this statement seemed to imply the Premier "understood" these visits, Wen Jiabao is said to have lost face.[63] At the end of October 2003, a huge anti-Japanese riot erupted out of what had begun as a "short skit" by Japanese students at Northwest University in Xi'an City, a vulgar but innocuous skit misunderstood to imply Japanese arrogance.[64] The fact that the Hu administration was virtually unable to do anything to quell the riot may well have determined the direction of the intensifying anti-Japanese activities.

In a situation like this, Prime Minister Koizumi's visit to the Yasukuni Shrine on January 1, 2004, probably made the Hu administration feel it had no choice but to be passive in its policies toward Japan. From President Hu's perspective, it was a sensitive time in domestic politics, heading toward a complete transfer of power, but with former President Jiang Zemin still holding on to the position of chairman of the Central Military Commission. Thus, Hu was likely to have been unable to take bold policy steps vis-à-vis Japan. The fact that anti-Japanese heckling occurred during July and August 2004, the time of soccer's Asia Cup, was indicative of the worsening anti-Japanese feelings within China but also suggested that these sentiments had the backing of powerful political forces. The image of China in Japan, which had been intensely hurt by this incident, deteriorated even further with the incursion of a Chinese submarine into Japanese territorial waters in November (see Figure 2.1 in Chapter 2, p. 45).

The deterioration of bilateral relations peaked in April 2005, however, when huge anti-Japanese riots occurred across China. The trigger was a statement by UN Secretary General Kofi Annan on March 21, in which he suggested the possibility of Japan having a permanent seat on the UN Security Council if the UN reform he recommended was implemented. A huge campaign took place on the Internet in China and elsewhere to collect signatures protesting Japan's candidacy. The anti-Japanese movement spread from the Internet to the real world when Chinese protesters attacked a supermarket run by a Japanese company in Chengdu on April 2. Another anti-Japanese demonstration took place in Beijing on April 9, and some protesters stoned the Japanese Embassy. A puzzling slogan, "Down with the modern Li Hongzhang!" appeared. Just who was it who was being referred to as the present-day equivalent of the Qing dynasty politician who signed the Shimonoseki Treaty that settled the Sino-Japanese War of 1894? On April 16, a still larger demonstration took place in Shanghai, causing physical damage to the Japanese consulate. More puzzling still, the *Jiefang Ribao* (Liberation Daily) carried a commentary on April 25 stating that the "illegal demonstration that happened recently was not a patriotic action in any sense of the term, . . . and was an intrigue worked out behind the scenes." The commentary was withdrawn from the newspaper's website on April 28.[65]

Although a meeting of Japanese-Chinese foreign ministers took place in Beijing right afterwards and a summit meeting was held in Indonesia, subsequent relations between the two countries never returned to normal. In May, Vice-Premier Wu Yi, who was visiting Japan, canceled a scheduled meeting with Prime Minister Koizumi just before it was to be held and returned home. In terms of diplomacy at the heads-of-state level, relations between the two countries were in total deadlock.

Deteriorating Japanese-Chinese relations affected other aspects of Japanese diplomacy. The first of these was diplomacy at the

United Nations. Becoming a permanent member of the UN Security Council, it would be fair to say, was the dearest wish of Japan's Ministry of Foreign Affairs. Despite the fact that Japan's contribution to the UN's general budget was second only to that of the United States, there were many instances when Japan was not involved in important UN decisions; this was regarded as a serious diplomatic handicap. Particularly at the time of the Gulf Crisis at the beginning of the 1990s, Japan's inability to take part in the process of drawing up the Security Council resolution caused extremely strong discontent among the ministry's bureaucrats. Thus, Secretary General Kofi Annan's desire to reform the UN was judged to be an important plus for Japanese diplomacy. At the General Assembly meeting in September 2004, Koizumi personally declared Japan's strong desire to become a permanent member of the Security Council.[66]

The strategy of Japan's Ministry of Foreign Affairs was to join forces with the three countries of Germany, India and Brazil that also wanted new seats on the Security Council, get a resolution passed to reform the Council through an overwhelming majority of Asian and African countries in the General Assembly, and then press for reform of the Council among the existing permanent members. After accepting a report on Security Council reform by a "high-level committee," i.e., the Secretary General's advisory committee, the plan was to conduct a major campaign beginning in the spring of 2005.

This campaign did not work out, however. In February 2005, anti-Japanese feelings soared in South Korea when the legislature in Shimane Prefecture proposed a law to create a "Takeshima Day," in honor of the disputed islands that the South calls Dokdo; then, as noted above, large-scale anti-Japanese demonstrations occurred in China and had an enormous impact. In the midst of these huge displays of anti-Japanese sentiment at home, the governments of both China and South Korea expressed their opposition to Japan's becoming a permanent member of the Security Council. China, in particular, engaged in a diplomatic campaign throughout the world against Japanese permanent membership. As a result, even the countries in Southeast Asia that Japan had been relying on were clearly hesitant to express their support. Ultimately, the campaign to reform the Security Council, carried out primarily by the four countries of Japan, Germany, India and Brazil, was sent back to square one.[67]

The summer of 2005 in Japan, however, was totally devoted to domestic politics. Diplomatically, no progress whatsoever had been made from the time of the anti-Japanese demonstrations in China to Vice-Premier Wu Yi's cancellation of her meeting with Koizumi, and relations with South Korea had also cooled off after the anti-Japanese sentiments over Takeshima/Dokdo in March and President Roh Moo-hyun's declaration of a "diplomatic war" with Japan. But the Japanese economy was recovering, and interaction with China and South Korea at the business level was neither deteriorating nor stalled.

In the meantime, Prime Minister Koizumi was determined to realize his life-long political dream: privatization of the postal service. Equally determined were the opponents of his policy, including many members of his own party. In August, the House of Councillors failed to pass the bill as a result of opposition within the ruling LDP; the prime minister dissolved the House of Representatives and declared that he would relentlessly fight the resisting forces in the LDP. The election campaign from late August to early September attracted national attention, and the results of the September 11 vote were an overwhelming show of popular support for Koizumi. The successful candidates from the LDP and the Komeito who had backed him occupied more than two-thirds of the seats in the lower house.

This great victory on the home front, it was thought, would give the prime minister the opportunity to break the diplomatic deadlock, depending on how he handled it.[68] If, for example, Koizumi had announced in a general policy speech at an extraordinary session of the Diet in September that he was reviewing his foreign policy strategy, including for the moment stopping visits to the Yasukuni Shrine, there would have been a possibility that prospects for Japanese diplomacy would brighten considerably. Although the view might have arisen at home that he was bowing to pressure from abroad, even so, he could well have asserted that the diplomacy conducted by a prime minister who had just won such a huge mandate was not one that would yield to foreign pressures. Saying he was adjusting his policies in view of the "big picture" would have been sufficient.

In fact, however, after its big win in the House of Representatives election, the Koizumi administration did not adjust its foreign policy at all. On October 17, right after the postal privatization bill was passed in the Diet, Prime Minister Koizumi visited Yasukuni Shrine. This time he visited without wearing formal clothes and without entering the inner sanctuary. But, as a result of the visit, China decided that it would not hold any further meetings with Japan at the heads-of-state level. The Roh Moo-hyun administration in South Korea, too, froze summit-level interaction to a minimum. After his victory in the general election, Prime Minister Koizumi had promised he would resign once he had completed his term as head of the LDP in September 2006; both China and South Korea probably decided it would be difficult to "improve relations" while Koizumi remained in office.

The APEC summit meeting was held in November at Pusan, and the ASEAN+3 Summit and the first East Asia Summit were held in Kuala Lumpur in December. Up until then, the three countries had taken advantage of these multinational summit meetings to conduct separate talks between the heads of state of Japan and China and Japan and South Korea. After the October 17 visit to Yasukuni Shrine, however, China changed its stance and refused to hold any summit talks with Prime Minister Koizumi. Not only that, China took the position that it would also not hold meetings with Asō Tarō, who had succeeded Machimura Nobutaka as foreign minister. As the host country at the APEC summit meeting, South Korea held a Japanese-South Korean summit, but it was extremely formal. After that, it, too, adopted the policy of not holding heads-of-state meetings with Japan. The last phase of Koizumi diplomacy reached the anomalous state of affairs in which summit-level communications with Japan's Chinese and South Korean neighbors had broken off, a situation to be repeated again in the 2010s.

With no progress in political relations with China and South Korea in sight, Japanese diplomacy's only significance from early 2006 on was to bridge the gap to the next administration by maintaining good diplomatic relations in other areas. For the time being, priority was given to attempts to adjust relations with countries that had not formerly had close ties with Japan. Examples of this were Prime Minister Koizumi's visits from the end of April into May to Kenya, Ethiopia and Sweden, to Mongolia in early August and to Kazakhstan and Uzbekistan in late August. By visiting Yasukuni Shrine on August 15, 2006, Prime Minister Koizumi kept the promise he had made in the spring of 2001 to visit Yasukuni on "August 15." Although both China and South Korea criticized the visit, at this point in time, both countries were shifting their attention to how to deal with the next administration, and no major problems occurred as a result.

In retrospect, one positive policy in the Koizumi administration's Asian diplomacy was to promote East Asian regional partnership by developing friendly cooperative relations with the ASEAN countries. This approach was first revealed in a policy speech Koizumi gave in Singapore while on a tour of Southeast Asia in January 2002. In it the prime minister spoke of his hopes to create "a community that acts together and advances together" in East Asia. At the same time, he signed the Economic Partnership Agreement (a free-trade treaty) with Singapore and indicated his intention to conclude similar agreements with many other Southeast Asian countries. Later, in December 2003, Koizumi held a special Japan-ASEAN summit meeting in Tokyo that all the leaders of the ASEAN countries attended. In this process Koizumi himself clearly came to use the expression "East Asian community" and signaled that the formation of such a community would be a focal point of Japanese diplomacy.

The Koizumi administration, however, was unable to formulate a systematic policy to promote a diplomacy that would advance the ideal of an "East Asian community." What was key to economic partnerships with Southeast Asian countries was, first of all, the prompt signing of effective bilateral free-trade treaties. But in order for Japan to ask the Southeast Asian countries to reduce its high tariffs on manufactured products and other goods and make institutional improvements, it was necessary to "give" something in return, namely, abolish protection on agricultural products. Because Prime Minister Koizumi was virtually unable to touch the agricultural issue, in the end, progress was slow in the EPA talks between Japan and the Southeast Asian countries. Secondly, an East Asian community was not simply a matter of Southeast Asian diplomacy; cooperation among the +3 part of ASEAN+3—i.e., Japan, China and South Korea—was also indispensable. At previous ASEAN+3 Summits, at Obuchi's suggestion, the three heads of state held a breakfast meeting each time. And in 2003, they even drew up a joint statement. As has already been discussed, however, the Koizumi administration failed to iron out relations with China and South Korea and was unable to display sufficient leadership both in the context of ASEAN+3 and in the process of preparing for the East Asia Summit. At the time the first East Asia Summit was held in 2005, Japan, together with Indonesia and Singapore, advocated that the three countries of Australia, New Zealand and India should be added to ASEAN+3. But Malaysia, Thailand and China made the argument that the present membership was fine the way it was. While this debate was going on, tensions were rising in Japanese-Chinese relations, and, thus, even the difference of opinions as to which countries should participate in the East Asia Summit came to seem like a leadership struggle between Japan and China. Since the East Asia Summit was held at the request of Japan and others, that in itself was a success for Japanese diplomacy, but discussions ultimately did not go deeply enough into what this gathering was actually supposed to accomplish.

In any event, at the time of the ASEAN+3 Summit in December 2005, anomalously, no Japan-China-South Korea summit took place, nor were there any separate Japanese-Chinese or Japanese-South Korean meetings. By refusing to meet with the Japanese Prime Minister, China and South Korea may not have succeeded diplomatically, but in terms of Japan promoting an East Asian diplomacy, the Kuala Lumpur meeting in December 2005 was undoubtedly far from being a success for Japanese diplomacy.

Judging from the special features of his administration's policy decisions and their formation processes, what characterizes Koizumi diplomacy was that it was primarily determined by the prime minister when it came to matters that the prime minister himself focused on, but decision-making was siloed on matters that did not pique the prime minister's interest. US relations, North Korean policy and dealing with the Yasukuni Shrine issue were handled by the prime minister and his close associates. When it came to the Yasukuni issue, he alone made the decision; all other issues he delegated to the bureaucracy. And yet he did not allow bureaucratically formulated policies to interfere with the policies on which he focused; in terms of Prime Minister Koizumi's priorities, East Asian regional diplomacy, for example, took second place to the Yasukuni issue.

Nor did Koizumi show much interest in formulating a comprehensive strategy to guide the bureaucracy in handling the issues he delegated to it. In the first half of the Koizumi administration, a foreign relations task force was set up at the initiative of Chief Cabinet Secretary Fukuda Yasuo to receive advice, primarily from outside experts, on drawing up strategy. In 2002, its "Basic Strategies for Japan's Foreign Policy in the 21st Century" was presented to the prime minister,[69] but no steps seem to have been taken to implement these "strategies" sufficiently or effectively. Later, Secretary Ijima Isao, a confidante of Prime Minister Koizumi, wrote one volume of his memoirs on the Koizumi administration's domestic policy and another on its diplomacy, but there is no mention in either volume of the foreign policy task force and hardly any reference to an East Asian community. After the scandals involving the Ministry of Foreign Affairs at the beginning of 2001, reform of the ministry was carried out, but the prime minister did not take any special initiative even in organizational reform. As for the creation of a "Strategic Council on Diplomacy and National Security" proposed by the foreign policy task force's "Basic Strategies for Japan's Foreign Policy in the 21st Century," it was never even explored.[70]

Chapter 10

Six Prime Ministers in Six Years

Twisted Diets and Short-lived Administrations

As he had promised at the time of the general election in the summer of 2005, Prime Minister Koizumi finished his term as leader of the LDP and resigned as prime minister in September 2006. Thereafter, Japan entered an unstable period of domestic politics with six prime ministers taking turns in six years. The Japanese public gave its support to the then-opposition in every one of the four national elections from 2007 to 2012; the first such election, the July 2007 upper house election, brought about a "twisted" Diet (*nejire kokkai*), in which the ruling coalition lost control of the House of Councillors though it maintained a majority in the lower house. Two years later, the public's anger at the LDP had increased, and in the June 2009 lower house election, the opposition won overwhelming popular support, bringing about the first change of government since 1993. The public, however, did not support the Democratic Party of Japan, the new ruling party, for very long. The upper house election in July 2011 inflicted the same fate on the DPJ as it had on the LDP three years earlier, by "twisting" the Diet once again. Finally, in December 2012, the public clearly rejected the DPJ-led government and allowed an LDP-Komeito coalition to return to power, bringing Abe Shinzō, who had succeeded Koizumi, back again to the position of prime minister.

The public's erratic voting behavior may be explained by the existence of a large number of independent voters with no strong ties to any political party (*mutōhasō*). When asked about their party preferences in opinion polls, nearly 50 percent responded "none."[1] Judging the LDP performance poor, they shifted their support to the DPJ, and when they found the DPJ performance poor as well, they shifted back again to the LDP. The twisted Diets of July 2007–June 2009 and July 2010–December 2012 were brought about by such "non-party" voters and became the underlying factor behind the frequent changes of prime ministers. Since the constitution requires bicameral consent for the passage of most legislation, when the ruling party does not control both houses, gridlock can emerge. Since the lower house has the prerogative of appointing the prime minister, passing the budget and ratifying treaties, a prime minister can theoretically survive as long as his party secures a majority in the House of Representatives. In practice, however, once the opposition controls the House of Councillors, it can employ any number of parliamentary tactics to harass the ruling party. Issuing government bonds to finance budget deficits, for example, requires a special law; even if the budget does not require the consent of the upper house, it cannot go into effect unless the upper house passes a law to issue bonds. If the prime minister has a two-thirds majority in the lower house (as was the case of the LDP from July 2007 to June 2009), he can override dissent in the upper house and pass important legislation, but again, in practice, the opposition can engage in a series of delaying tactics to cause difficulties for the incumbent administration.

The Abe Administration: Setting about to Improve Relations with Japan's Neighbors

On September 26, 2006, Abe Shinzō, a grandson of former Prime Minister Kishi Nobusuke and a son of former Foreign Minister Abe Shintarō, at 52, became the youngest prime minister in Japan since World War II. As his policy goals, Abe called for a "departure from the postwar regime" at home and for "assertive diplomacy" abroad. Abe had accompanied Koizumi, whose deputy cabinet secretary he then was, on his visit to North Korea in 2002, and thereafter always maintained a hardline stance on the abduction issue. Indeed, that was a major reason for his high popularity. In addition, he supported Prime Minister Koizumi's visits to Yasukuni Shrine and was always critical of the conciliatory approach to Japan's near neighbors on other aspects of the history issue. It would be fair to say that he was a rising star among the nationalists who criticized the "masochistic view of history."

It was apparent, however, that if Abe adopted the same position as Prime Minister Koizumi on the Yasukuni Shrine, relations with

China and South Korea would not improve. By the end of the Koizumi administration, criticism about the stalemate in Japanese-Chinese and Japanese-South Korean relations had been mounting even from the United States. If relations with China and South Korea remained completely sclerotic at the start of the administration, US relations, which were the basis of Japanese diplomacy, might also be shaken. It was presumably because of considerations such as this that, despite it being an unsatisfactory decision among his nationalist supporters, Abe made it a policy not to state clearly whether he would or would not visit Yasukuni Shrine, or whether he had or had not done so.

The government of Hu Jintao in China, too, probably wanted to avoid a repeat of the anomalous situation that had existed with the Koizumi administration.[2] Though the power struggle within China was continuing, Hu now appeared to be controlling China's foreign policy more effectively; he had applied the catchword "harmony" (*hexie*) to his foreign policy since the end of 2005.[3] Hu seems to have concluded that China should improve relations with Tokyo only if Japan's prime minister did not visit the Yasukuni Shrine. At the beginning of August 2006, there was a report that Chief Cabinet Secretary Abe had secretly visited Yasukuni early on the morning of April 15.[4] In response Abe said, "I would like to continue to feel that I can express my sense of respect for those who died in the war and put my hands together and pray for their repose, but as long as visits to Yasukuni are made into diplomatic and political issues, I have no intention of saying whether I will or will not go, or whether I have or have not gone, to the Yasukuni Shrine."[5] China did not make any significant reaction to this report. On August 15, Prime Minister Koizumi visited Yasukuni Shrine, but Abe did not. That he did not, in fact, do so was likely an important signal to China.

At the same time that Abe won the LDP leadership election on September 20, he is said to have decided that once his administration took office, his first overseas visit would be to China.[6] On Abe's instructions, Vice-Minister for Foreign Affairs Yachi Shōtarō explored the possibilities with Chinese Deputy Foreign Minister Dai Bingguo, who was visiting Japan for the vice-ministerial comprehensive policy dialogue in late September.[7] Perhaps to advance the reconciliation process, Abe made a statement in the Diet that further dashed the nationalists' hopes. At a plenary session of the

House of Representatives on October 2, he said, "the government's perception of the last major war is, as indicated by the Prime Ministers' Statements on August 15, 1995 and 2005, that Japan, through its colonial rule and aggression, caused tremendous damage and suffering to the people of many countries, particularly to those of Asian nations."[8] The Prime Minister's Statement on August 15, 1995, the so-called Murayama Statement, was anathema to right-wing nationalists. Then, on the next day, Abe stated that "the government's basic position on the issue of the so-called comfort women is to accept the statement of Chief Cabinet Secretary Kōno on August 4, 1993."[9] Among right-wing nationalists, the Kōno Statement was the object of far more negative criticism than even the Murayama Statement. Thus, having arranged matters regarding the understanding of history in a way that would be impervious to criticism not just from China and South Korea but even from those in Japan suspicious of his right-wing tendencies, Abe set off on October 8 for China on his first overseas trip. The nationalists were furious, but the *Asahi Shimbun* and others that had openly feared Abe's right-wing leanings were left speechless, unable to criticize the Abe administration.

China welcomed Abe. The two countries issued the Japan-China Joint Press Statement in which both countries said they "would strive to build a mutually beneficial relationship based on common strategic interests" and agreed to work together to make the East China Sea a "Sea of Peace, Cooperation and Friendship."[10] The document contained so few references to "history" as to make one think that the imbroglio over history with the Koizumi government had never existed, though the two sides did agree to start a joint study of history in which historians of both countries would participate.[11] By establishing friendly relations with Prime Minister Abe, China indicated its willingness to try and revive relations that had been icy cold with the Koizumi administration and substantially improve Japanese-Chinese relations by the time of the Beijing Olympics in 2008.

After Prime Minister Abe left China and while on his way to Seoul, the next stop on his itinerary, North Korea conducted a nuclear test. In their reaction to the North's test, Japan and China were able to take a cooperative stance. Relations at the heads-of-state level between Japan and South Korea, however, did not improve as dramatically as they had between the leaders of Japan and China.

President Roh Moo-hyun continued to talk at length to Prime Minister Abe about the importance of the history question. Thus, there was no joint statement between Japan and the South, as there had been between Japan and China. But because Japanese-Chinese relations showed dramatic improvement, the atmosphere surrounding international relations was completely transformed for Japan. Almost all the foreign heads of state who subsequently met with Prime Minister Abe praised his dramatic visit to China.

Premier Wen Jiabao visited Japan in April 2007. In his speech to the Diet, which was also broadcast live in China, he said, "Since the normalization of diplomatic ties between China and Japan, the Japanese Government and leaders have on many occasions stated their position on the historical issue, admitted that Japan had committed aggression and expressed deep remorse and apology to the victimized countries. The Chinese Government and people appreciate the position they have taken."[12] Up to that point, the leaders of China had rarely acknowledged that the Japanese government had apologized to the victimized countries. No other speech had so clearly emphasized that Japan had apologized—and had expressed China's appreciation for it—as Wen's speech did. The Premier also went on to say, "China has received support and assistance from the Japanese Government and people in its reform, opening-up and modernization drive. This is something the Chinese people will never forget."[13] That a Chinese leader so openly stated his gratitude for Japanese aid to China, including ODA, is probably also worth special mention.

As the relationship with China improved, Prime Minister Abe made efforts to broaden the geographic scope of Japan's diplomacy. One target was India. When India conducted nuclear weapons tests in 1998, Japan suspended its economic assistance. But as the Indian economy grew, Japan began to find in India a promising market as well as a strategic friend located on the southern tip of the Eurasian continent. The first prime minister who attached a clear importance to India had been Prime Minister Mori, who visited India in August 2000. Japan resumed its economic assistance to India in October 2001,[14] and in the following years India became one of the largest recipients of Japan's ODA. Prime Minister Koizumi visited India in late April 2005. But it was Prime Minister Abe who for the first time since the end of the Cold War offered an expansive vision of the Japan-India relationship.

When he visited India in August 2007 to reciprocate Prime Minister
Manmohan Singh's visit to Japan in December 2005, he addressed the
members of the Indian parliament:

> My friends, where exactly do we now stand historically and geo-
> graphically? To answer this question, I would like to quote here
> the title of a book authored by the Mughal prince Dara Shikoh in
> 1655. We are now at a point at which the Confluence of the Two
> Seas is coming into being.
>
> The Pacific and the Indian Oceans are now bringing about
> a dynamic coupling as seas of freedom and of prosperity. A
> "broader Asia" that broke away geographical boundaries is now
> beginning to take on a distinct form. Our two countries have the
> ability—and the responsibility—to ensure that it broadens yet
> further and to nurture and enrich these seas to become seas of
> clearest transparence. . . .
>
> What I would like to convey to you, the representatives of
> the citizens of India, is that Prime Minister Singh and myself
> are steadfastly convinced that [the] "Japan-India relationship is
> blessed with the largest potential for development of any bilat-
> eral relationship anywhere in the world." We are also in perfect
> agreement that "a strong India is in the best interest of Japan,
> and a strong Japan is in the best interest of India."[15]

Another country Abe actively courted was Australia. In March,
Prime Minister John Howard visited Japan, and he and Abe signed
the Japan-Australia Joint Declaration on Security Cooperation. By
this joint declaration, Japan and Australia made clear their policy
of reinforcing cooperation with the United States, with whom they
were both allied. China began to express its wariness about Abe's
moves to strengthen relations with India and Australia, but did not
take any specific steps to change its policy toward Japan.

Abe was also conscious of the need to maintain good relations
with the ASEAN countries. At the ASEAN+3 Summit and the East
Asia Summit, postponed to January 2007 as a result of the typhoon
that hit the Philippines in December 2006, Prime Minister Abe suggested, among other things, establishing the Economic Research
Institute for ASEAN and East Asia (ERIA), which was eventually to

grow into ASEAN's premier research institution. He also announced the JENESYS Programme, a plan to invite 6,000 East Asian young people to Japan every year for the next five years financed by a 35 billion yen contribution from the supplementary budget.[16]

In addition to Prime Minister Abe's own diplomatic efforts such as these, Foreign Minister Asō Tarō, Abe's rival in the LDP leadership contest whom Abe had reappointed as Minister of Foreign Affairs, was also conducting his own vigorous diplomatic initiatives. At the end of November 2006, he made a policy speech entitled the "Arc of Freedom and Prosperity," suggesting a future focus of Japanese diplomacy. The arc of freedom and prosperity was a vast bow-shaped region stretching from Japan to Southeast Asia, South Asia, the Middle East, the Balkans and eastern and central Europe up to the Baltic Sea, where, according to Asō, the stirrings of freedom and democracy and a movement toward prosperity were occurring. Although Japan had given considerable assistance to this region before, from now on, he said, it would consciously become the "escort runner" on the road to democratization and prosperity for the countries there.[17]

Thus, as far as Asian diplomacy was concerned, the Abe administration's foreign relations had an energy that was in stark contrast to the stagnation of that of the Koizumi administration. In Abe's diplomacy, which dramatically improved relations with China and deepened the partnership with India, Australia and elsewhere, one could sense some sort of strategy. Despite this, however, Japan's diplomacy during the first year of Abe's administration had fragile foundations.

First, there were the problems inherent in the contradiction between the principles of his nationalist supporters and the diplomatic realities that Abe had to live with. To begin with, there is a kind of anti-liberal, anti-human-rights strain in right-wing nationalist ideas implicit in their statements justifying Japanese aggression and colonial rule. Extended to its logical conclusion, the right-wing nationalist ideology may even lead to a justification of Japan's anti-liberal prewar system, and so in this regard Prime Minister Abe could potentially be drawn into a confrontation with those value systems, American and otherwise, that emphasize freedom and human rights. In fact, as the very values that Abe emphasized in his diplomacy included freedom and human rights, the logical implications of his right-wing supporters' ideas were in direct contradiction with Abe's diplomacy. In a reply in the Diet right after he came to office, Abe tried to overcome this contradiction by saying he considered himself to have inherited all the government's existing views. To the extent that Abe was loyal to his long-time supporters, he could be vulnerable to what this contradiction might pose for the smooth execution of his diplomacy.

The second problem with Abe's diplomacy, as was the case with previous administrations, was its lack of coherence. The diplomacy of the Abe administration was energized by having a man of action like Asō as foreign minister. On the other hand, however, such activism raised doubts as to whether Japan's diplomacy was Abe's or Asō's. In a speech on administrative policy given to the Diet in January 2007, Prime Minister Abe said he would conduct a "Proactive Diplomacy . . . founded on three pillars: (a) strengthening partnerships with countries that share the fundamental values of freedom, democracy, basic human rights and rule of law, (b) creating an Asia that is open and rich in innovation, and (c) contributing to global peace and stability."[18] By contrast, in a speech on diplomatic policy given on the very same day, Foreign Minister Asō said that the "three pillars" of Japanese diplomacy thus far have been "the Japan-U.S. alliance, international cooperation, and taking our neighboring Asian nations seriously," but to these he would add a fourth one. "I would say it is essential for Japan to establish the fourth pillar, that is to create the 'Arc of Freedom and Prosperity,'" he stated.[19] According to Prime Minister Abe there were three pillars of Japanese diplomacy; according to Foreign Minister Asō, the arc of freedom and prosperity should be added to make four. In terms of content, the policy speeches given on the same day by the prime minister and the foreign minister of the same administration were decidedly odd.

As one of the Abe administration's plans, a panel was set up to create a "Japanese version of the National Security Council" to integrate diplomacy with national security policy, and it presented a report saying that such an integrated framework would be desirable. The very lack of unity in diplomatic policy within the Abe administration itself bespoke the need for such a council.

The third weak point of Abe's diplomacy was domestic politics. The Abe administration had started out with extremely high support ratings, yet right from the outset it was tripped up by personnel issues and was forced to replace people in several key posts. Misstatements by important cabinet members continued, and finally, the Minister of Agriculture, Forestry and Fisheries committed suicide because of a personal scandal. The response to problems involving the handling of pensions by the Social Insurance Agency was always late. As a result, the House of Councillors' election in July 2007 was a major defeat for the LDP, which lost its majority there to the opposition parties. Although Abe decided to continue to serve as prime minister and reshuffled the cabinet, dealing with the Diet was expected to become very difficult in the coming months.

But the biggest weak point was Abe's health. He had suffered from ulcerative colitis since high school, but after he became prime minister, under overwhelming stress, his health deteriorated. He also suffered from functional dyspepsia, and viral enteritis contracted abroad worsened the already bad conditions, forcing him to announce his resignation on September 12.[20]

The Fukuda Administration: Promoting Improved Relations with China

Hurriedly selected by the LDP to succeed Abe was Fukuda Yasuo, a son of former Prime Minister Fukuda Takeo and the chief cabinet secretary in the first three years of the Koizumi administration. His biggest challenge was how to continue Self-Defense Force operations in support of the war on terror in Afghanistan and elsewhere; it had been stress from this issue that had worsened Abe's illness and led to his resignation. The main activity of these operations, legally sanctioned by the Anti-Terrorist Special Measures Law, was the refueling of allied ships by MSDF ships in the Indian Ocean. But the law was due to expire in November, and the DPJ, now in control of the House of Councillors, made it clear that it would not support the refueling operation because it was not based on any UN resolution. Fukuda, who considered the continuation of the operation critical to maintaining Japan's international credibility as well as good relations with

Washington, felt it necessary to reach a compromise with the DPJ. Because the ruling coalition still maintained more than two-thirds of the seats in the House of Representatives, he could count on the lower house to override the upper house, but he did not want to take advantage of this except as a last resort. Having been informed that Ozawa Ichirō, president of the DPJ since March 2006, appeared interested in a grand coalition with the LDP, Fukuda entered into discussions with Ozawa in late October and early November. They agreed to form a grand coalition, but when Ozawa consulted with the other leading members of the DPJ, most of them were opposed; frustrated, Ozawa with his characteristic abruptness told them to forget it and called Fukuda to tell him do the same.[21] The lower house passed the new bill on November 13; the upper house, after prolonged deliberation, rejected it on January 11, 2008. That same day, the ruling coalition passed the bill with a two-thirds majority in the lower house; it was the first time since 1957 that the lower house had overridden the upper house.[22] Japan resumed its refueling mission in the Indian Ocean in February, four months after operations had ceased in November.

Fukuda accelerated the efforts to improve relations with China that Abe had begun. He visited China in December 2007, and after meeting with the Chinese leaders, he delivered a speech at Peking University calling on China to join Japan in "forging the future together." He then went to Qufu, the birthplace of Confucius, and when asked to display his calligraphic talent, he wrote with a big brush "Reanimate the Old and Create the New" (*wengu chuangxin*).[23] The following spring, President Hu Jintao came to Tokyo and concluded with Fukuda a "Joint Statement on Comprehensive Promotion of a 'Mutually Beneficial Relationship Based on Common Strategic Interests'" on May 7, 2008, in which the "Chinese side expressed its positive evaluation of Japan's consistent pursuit of the path of a peaceful country and Japan's contribution to the peace and stability of the world through peaceful means over more than sixty years since World War [II]."[24]

In his speech at Waseda University, Hu Jintao expressed Chinese appreciation of Japan's role in the modernization of China:

> The Japanese Government has played a positive role in China's modernization drive by making Japanese yen loans in support of

China's infrastructure construction, environmental protection, energy development and scientific and technological advancement. In addition, Japanese friends from various sectors offered warm-hearted help to China in its course of modernization. The Chinese people will always remember those Japanese friends who have devoted themselves to China-Japan friendship.[25]

The joint statement also expressed the agreement to "build a mechanism for the periodic exchange of visits by the leaders of the two countries, with the leader of one country visiting the other country once a year in principle; to convene summit meetings frequently, including holding meetings on the occasion of international conferences . . . ."

As a backdrop to this amicable relationship between Fukuda and Hu, both countries announced a significant agreement on the joint exploration of natural resources in the East China Sea on June 18, 2008. This agreement was a breakthrough since there were fundamental differences between the two countries on the EEZ (Exclusive Economic Zone) and the continental shelf in the East China Sea, Japan maintaining that its EEZ extends to the median line equidistant between the territories of the two countries; China insisting that its continental shelf extends to the Okinawa trough. Although the delimitation of maritime boundaries in the East China Sea had not been established between the two countries, China started seabed exploration at many sites east of the median line in the 1990s. One of them, which China called the Chunxiao oil and gas field ("Shirakaba" in Japanese), attracted Japanese attention in 2003 since its drilling activities were located just five kilometers east of the median line. The Japanese asked the Chinese government to provide information about the underground geological structure, pointing out that the oil and gas field might extend to the Japanese side; thus, the Chinese facility would be able to syphon Japan's share of oil and gas, Tokyo complained. Starting in October 2004, both sides engaged in a series of difficult consultations on possible cooperation in the East China Sea. These did not proceed smoothly given the strained political relations particularly after 2005. Hu Jintao's visit to Japan was a strong impetus to reach a compromise. The agreement of June 18, 2008, without touching on the delimitation of the EEZ and the continental shelf, indicated a geographically defined area in which both countries would select sites for joint development with the details to be decided through further consultation; in particular, it suggested the possibility of joint development of Shirakaba/Chunxiao.[26] Hu Jintao came to Japan again in July to attend the Major Economies Meeting on Energy Security and Climate Change held immediately after the G8 Summit, which Fukuda hosted. Fukuda attended the opening of the Beijing Olympic Games in August.

Another area of foreign policy Fukuda wanted to make progress in was the abduction problem with North Korea. Since the agreement that the Six-Party Talks in February 2007 finally arrived at had stipulated the resumption of normalization talks between Japan and the North, both countries had held a working consultation in Hanoi in March 2007, but at that time North Korea simply declared that the abduction issue had already been resolved. The next meeting, held in Ulan Bator the following September just before Prime Minister Abe's abrupt resignation, did not produce any results, but only confirmed that the issue North Korea attached importance to was the "settlement of the past" while Japan was eager to resolve the abduction issue. Prime Minister Fukuda appears to have felt the need to offer incentives to North Korea; on the occasion of extending sanctions against North Korea in April 2008, he had Chief Cabinet Secretary Machimura Nobutaka announce that "if North Korea takes concrete steps toward the resolution of various issues including the abduction problem, nuclear weapons and missile deployment, after comprehensive consideration we could end our sanctions partially or entirely."[27] The meeting between the two sides took place in Beijing on June 11 and 12, and this time Pyongyang did not repeat its usual statement that the abduction problem had already been resolved. The Japanese negotiator, Saiki Akitaka, director-general of the Asian and Oceanian Affairs Bureau, told the press, "The meeting had a constructive atmosphere, and we had in-depth discussions on very important issues including the abduction issue. Both sides agreed on a basic understanding of how to proceed with the DPRK-Japan relationship. It was a productive discussion."[28] Japan offered to lift part of the sanctions if North Korea agreed to implement a re-investigation of the remaining abductees and missing persons. Since North Korea had submitted its nuclear plans to China in accordance with the agreement made in the

Six-Party Talks, the United States announced its intention to remove North Korea from the list of "State Sponsors of Terrorism" in June. At the next round of talks between Japan and North Korea in early August, North Korea agreed to establish a "re-investigation" committee. In Saiki's words, "if North Korea makes a big step, Japan will make a big step; if it makes a small step, we will make a small step."[29]

Pyongyang made no steps. A few days after Fukuda announced his resignation as prime minister on September 1, North Korea revealed its intention to wait and see what the approach of Japan's next administration's would be. Nor did it move forward even after the United States removed it from the State Sponsors of Terrorism list in November. It launched long-range missiles in April 2009, and conducted its second nuclear weapons test the following month. As Kim Jong Il's health faltered, North Korea entered the unpredictable period of succession.

Why did Fukuda decide to resign? Despite his positive performance in diplomacy, Fukuda also had serious difficulties at home. In the twisted Diet, the opposition in control of the upper house used all legally possible tactics to thwart his administration, refusing consent to important appointments, including that of the Bank of Japan governor, postponing deliberation on important bills and finally passing a censure motion against Fukuda himself in the upper house, though such a motion is not legally binding. Unfortunate incidents continued to occur; poisonous dumplings were found among those imported from China; an American serviceman was arrested for assaulting a girl in Okinawa; an MSDF Aegis-equipped destroyer hit and sank a fishing boat off Tokyo Bay. The approval rate of the Fukuda Cabinet, which had been more than 50 percent in September 2007, plummeted to somewhere around 20 percent by April 2008. Because almost three years had passed since the previous general election that gave the LDP-led coalition a two-thirds majority, a general election had to be called by late August 2009. Fukuda could wait until then hoping for a rebound in his approval rate; or he could dissolve the Diet and call a general election immediately. Calm, cool-headed and objective, Fukuda decided not to take either course. His answer was to hand over his position to Asō Tarō. Fukuda calculated that Asō, a flamboyant and popular grandson of Yoshida Shigeru, could dissolve the Diet immediately after becoming prime minister and call a general election. Because Asō's popularity was higher than his own, he could provide the LDP with a much better chance in the election than Fukuda could.[30]

Based on his solid performance in diplomacy, Fukuda had talked about his long-term vision for Asia in a speech delivered in May 2008:

> Coming into my mind is the image of a developing Asia that is forming a network of countries for which the Pacific Ocean is an "inland sea." . . . Whose "inland sea" is this, exactly? Clearly, it is an inland sea for Japan and the countries of ASEAN, yet also one for North and South America and for Russia . . . . It is most certainly an inland sea for China and the nations of Indochina as well as Australia, and New Zealand, and in my view this sea also continues beyond India to connect to the nations of the Middle East.[31]

Fukuda stepped down without doing much to realize this broad notion of an "inland sea," as had been the case for Abe, who resigned immediately after he expressed a similar vision in his "confluence of the two seas" speech in India.

The Asō Administration: Portents of Turbulence Ahead in Japanese-Chinese Relations

Asō did not call a snap election after all. Something that Fukuda did not anticipate when he announced his resignation happened between then and the time Asō was appointed prime minister on September 24: the bankruptcy of Lehman Brothers. In the subsequent months, the world faced a serious economic downturn. On October 27, the Nikkei Average sank to 7,162 yen, its all-time low since the collapse of the bubble economy.[32] What Alan Greenspan described as a "once-in-a-century" crisis required a series of international measures. President George W. Bush asked Asō, the G8 chair, to help form a new framework later to be known as the G20. The fate of the economy overwhelmed politics.

In the meantime, partly because of gaffes by his cabinet members as well as his own and largely as a result of public disappointment about what appeared to be the LDP's poor performance, the approval rating of the Asō Cabinet plummeted; by early 2009 it was below 20 percent. No matter when the general election was called, the results appeared certain: the historic defeat of the LDP. In fact, when the election took place in late August, the DPJ won 308 seats while the LDP secured only 119, far less than half the 300 that it had had before the election.

Asō appeared to have found in foreign policy a space in which he could more usefully serve the country. Despite the increasingly confusing domestic political scene (or perhaps because of it), Asō set aside time to attend important international conferences and to visit important foreign partners. He visited China to attend the 30th anniversary of the Japan-China Peace and Friendship Treaty and made an official visit to China in April 2009.

But probably a more significant diplomatic achievement of the Asō administration was the Trilateral Summit among Japan, China and South Korea in Fukuoka on December 13, 2008, held independently from the ASEAN+3 Summit for the first time in history. As was previously mentioned, the Trilateral Summit first took place in 1999 at the initiative of Japanese Prime Minister Obuchi as an informal breakfast meeting among the leaders of the three countries at the time of the ASEAN+3 Summit, and had been held on the sidelines of the ASEAN+3 Summit ever since. In October 2003, the three countries issued a Joint Declaration on the Promotion of Trilateral Cooperation. In 2004, the foreign ministers of the three countries agreed on an "Action Strategy on Trilateral Cooperation" covering more than 20 areas of cooperation in economic, cultural and people-to-people exchanges, and political and security issues. Though China refused to hold a trilateral summit with Koizumi in 2005, with the coming of the Abe administration, the Trilateral Summit resumed at the ASEAN+3 Summit in 2007. Now, the three countries agreed to hold a Trilateral Summit independently from ASEAN-related meetings. In Fukuoka, the three leaders—Asō, Wen Jiabao and Lee Myung-bak—agreed to hold this type of independent Trilateral Summit once a year, rotating the host country, while continuing to meet at ASEAN-related meetings. They also issued an action plan for trilateral cooperation to expand the areas of cooperation beyond those in the Action Strategy.

The improvement of Japan's relations with its immediate neighbors that Abe had initiated appeared to be on track. A sign of future turmoil emerged just before the Trilateral Summit, however. On the morning of December 8, five days before Premier Wen Jiabao came to Fukuoka, two Chinese ships belonging to the State Oceanic Administration intruded into Japan's territorial waters around Uotsuri-jima, one of the Senkaku Islands. In response to Japan's protest, the Chinese foreign ministry spokesman asserted that they were conducting "normal patrol operations in an area under Chinese jurisdiction."[33] China had sent ships to these waters once before in 2006, but at that time it justified the operation as a "normal maritime scientific investigation." In addition to its verbal claims of sovereignty, China now began to demonstrate its capacity to control the waters they claimed as their own. Why Beijing decided to send these ships just before the First Trilateral Summit is a puzzle. The commander of the operation may have given the order without permission from Beijing, some speculate.[34] In any case, this incident was a harbinger of the coming upheaval in Japanese-Chinese relations. The approach taken by Hu Jintao and Wen Jiabao to improve relations with Japan was about to be turned upside down.

The Hatoyama Administration: A Vision for an "East Asian Community"?

Aside from being rich, Hatoyama Yukio and Asō Taro, grandsons of former prime ministers, Hatoyama Ichirō and Yoshida Shigeru, had another thing in common: making statements without being sufficiently briefed by their staff. Gaffes damaged Asō's popularity and contributed to the defeat of the LDP. But Asō's statements often were misleading and/or insensitive out of a desire to be humorous; he rarely strayed away from the main line of established policies. Hatoyama, in contrast, was always serious, seriously making statements that could potentially negate the policies of his own party and administration. His problem had to do with not calculating the full implication of his words, or even not caring to do so.

His most significant statement in this category was his campaign promise to relocate the US Marine Corps' Futenma Air Station outside of Japan, or at least outside of Okinawa Prefecture. Ever since the American occupation ended there in 1972, Okinawa, a prefecture composed of small islands in the southwestern part of Japan, has continued to bear a much heavier burden than other prefectures in terms of the number of American military facilities: some 75 percent by area are found in Okinawa. Futenma, now surrounded by a heavily congested urban area, is the symbol of Okinawa's burden. After the horrible rape of a girl by US servicemen in 1995 and the subsequent anti-US base activities in Okinawa, Japan and the United States agreed to move the Futenma facilities elsewhere. After considering various alternatives, the LDP government and the US came to the consensus in 2006 that a place called Henoko, Nago City, in Okinawa was an appropriate choice. Lending an ear to the many voices of dissent in Okinawa, the DPJ wrote in its manifesto that it would "propose the revision of the Japan-US Status of Forces Agreement [and move] in the direction of re-examining the realignment of the US military forces in Japan and the role of US military bases in Japan."[35] Okada Katsuya, secretary-general of the DPJ during the campaign and later foreign minister in the Hatoyama administration, recalled that this phrase was intentionally made vague because of the difficulties involved in the Okinawa problem. Hatoyama, president of the DPJ, paraphrased this into a promise to "move [Futenma] out of the country, or at least out of Okinawa."[36]

The expectations of the Okinawan people heightened. Now that the prime minister himself had promised, surely this time the base would be moved out of the prefecture. Neither Hatoyama's foreign minister, Okada, nor his defense minister, Kitazawa Toshimi, however, believed such a move would be possible.[37] Though he originally designated the end of December as the deadline for finalizing his plans, aware of the opposition from his ministers, Hatoyama postponed the deadline until May, another signal that raised Okinawan expectations; the prime minister must have secret plans to realize his promise, it was thought. An opponent of the base's relocation to Henoko was elected mayor of Nago in January 2010. Those in Okinawa who had argued that the relocation to Henoko was the only realistic way to reduce the burden on Futenma lost credibility.

After futile attempts to find a better alternative, Hatoyama gave up in May, saying "the more I learned, the more I realized that deterrence is maintained by our alignment not just with the Marines but with all American forces. Call me shallow. I accept this."[38] Stunned, many DPJ supporters realized that their prime minister knew few of the basic facts of Japan's security. Disappointed, many Okinawans realized that they had once again been betrayed.

Another idea Hatoyama stressed, though eventually more innocuous, was the call to create an "East Asian community." As this book has demonstrated, efforts at community-building in East Asia already had a long history. ASEAN, APEC, ASEAN+3, the East Asia Summit and the Trilateral Summit among Japan, China and South Korea had followed a different path from European integration but had achieved a certain level of cooperation. Prime Minister Koizumi had already used the concept of an East Asian community in his parliamentary speeches. Whether he was aware of this or not, Hatoyama presented his vision of an "East Asian community" as if it had been a new idea. What did he mean when he wrote in *The New York Times*:

> We must not forget our identity as a nation located in Asia. I believe that the East Asian region, which is showing increasing vitality, must be recognized as Japan's basic sphere of being. So we must continue to build frameworks for stable economic cooperation and security across the region.[39]

Some suspected he was trying to create a regional framework that excluded the United States; when Hatoyama met with Hu Jintao in New York on September 21, he proposed building an East Asian Community minus the US.[40] Because he mentioned a "currency union" in Asia and argued that "the structures required for the formation of a regional bloc are already in place," he may have contemplated transforming ASEAN+3 or other schemes into much stronger institutions. Among the various regional institutions, however, the only one that Hatoyama made some impact on was the Trilateral Summit among Japan, China and South Korea. At the two summits he attended (October 2009 and May 2010), he argued for establishing a project to promote university-level student exchanges, which became one of the legacies of Hatoyama's community-building in East Asia.[41] Dubbed CAMPUS Asia (Collective Action for Mobility Program of University Students in Asia) by the South Korean government, the project was launched in April 2010, and ten pilot programs involving 27 universities in the three countries were adopted in late 2011. Under CAMPUS Asia, more than 2,000 students from the three countries have experienced university life at campuses in Japan, China and South Korea.[42] The third Trilateral Summit held in Jeju, South Korea, on May 30, at which the establishment of a Trilateral Cooperation Secretariat in 2011 was agreed on, would be Hatoyama's last appearance on the diplomatic stage.

The approval rate of the Hatoyama cabinet, as high as 70 percent at its inception, fell to 20 percent, the same level as the previous LDP administration in its final days. Like the LDP government, the DPJ also began to worry about their prospects in the upcoming House of Councillors' election scheduled for July. Hatoyama stepped down on June 2, and Kan Naoto took over.

The Kan Administration: Domestic Stagnation, Natural Disaster and Mindanao Peace Negotiations

Kan, a politician who had emerged out of the citizens' movement, had held a cabinet post in the Murayama Cabinet and most recently served as finance minister in the Hatoyama Cabinet. As finance minister, he was involved in difficult international negotiations to find a solution to the Greek crisis, and he heightened awareness about the critical state of Japan's own financial situation: the accumulated government debt exceeded 200 percent of GDP, a much higher percentage than that of Greece. Since his approval rate was high, more than 60 percent, and thinking perhaps that it would be better to shift the political agenda away from the Futenma problem and a financial scandal involving Ozawa Ichirō, the DPJ's secretary-general who resigned his post at the same time as Hatoyama, he discussed the need to raise the consumption tax to 10 percent from the current 5 percent. Although he was successful in shifting the agenda, this was a risky decision since all the previous prime ministers who had proposed raising taxes before an election had lost.

The result of the House of Councillors' election on July 11 was a disaster for the DPJ. The DPJ won 44 seats while the LDP held 51. As a result, the ruling coalition lost its majority in the upper house; the Diet was again twisted, this time causing the DPJ-led coalition to suffer for its mismanagement. Critics of Kan within the DPJ became more vocal; they argued that Kan should take responsibility for the defeat. Kan persisted. Just as Asō had found in foreign policy a place to demonstrate his competence, Kan also tried to use diplomacy to prove his worth.

On August 10, Kan made a statement commemorating the 100th anniversary of Japan's annexation of Korea. To establish a better relationship with South Korea, and to show that the DPJ government was different from the LDP government, Kan stated:

> I would like to face history with sincerity. I would like to have [the] courage to squarely confront the facts of history and [the] humility to accept them, as well as [the] honesty to reflect upon the errors of our own. Those who render pain tend to forget it while those who suffered cannot forget it easily. [For] the tremendous damage and sufferings that this colonial rule caused, I express here once again my feelings of deep remorse and my heartfelt apology.[43]

In order to back up his statement symbolically, he promised to "transfer" cultural documents including some of the "Royal Protocols of the Joseon Dynasty" that had been brought to Japan during Japanese colonial rule and that South Korea had demanded be returned. President Lee Myung-bak expressed his appreciation in a telephone conversation after Kan made the statement. It appeared that the prime minister might fare well in international relations. As it turned out, he had to face rough sailing there too.

On September 7, a Chinese fishing boat entered Japanese territorial waters near the Senkakus. When the Japanese Coast Guard demanded it leave, the fishing boat intentionally collided with the Japanese patrol ships. The Coast Guard arrested the captain and brought him to Ishigaki Island. When seven Chinese had landed on Uotsuri-jima in 2004, the Okinawa Police had arrested them but then immediately expelled them to China as their act was deemed the minor crime of violating the immigration law. This time, however, the Coast Guard considered the captain's act an "obstruction of the performance of their public duties," a much heavier violation of the law, and detained him.

China reacted promptly and harshly; it demanded through the Japanese ambassador that the captain be released immediately. As his detention lengthened, China announced it was stopping cabinet-minister-level contacts and canceling many people-to-people exchanges, including a concert by a Japanese pop group. It also restricted visits by Chinese tourists to Japan, discontinued negotiations on increasing commercial flights between the two countries, detained four Japanese on charges of "taking photographs in a military district" and terminated the export to Japan of "rare earth," critical materials for electronic and magnetic products for which Japan was almost 100 percent dependent on China. Perplexed and frightened by these seemingly disproportionate Chinese reactions, Japan sent the captain back to China on September 24.[44] The Kan administration was criticized for kowtowing to China.

It is not clear why China's reaction escalated so rapidly. The DPJ had shown a much more positive attitude to China than the LDP did. Hatoyama had attached importance to Japan's relations with China; Ozawa Ichirō accompanied by 143 DPJ Diet members visited China in December 2009; the DPJ government made special arrangements at short notice to bring about Vice President Xi Jinping's meeting with the Emperor; and the DPJ leaders all declared that they would not visit Yasukuni Shrine. China had responded positively to these conciliatory gestures; it had arrested the person responsible for the poisonous dumplings in March 2009, and Wen Jiabao expressed his willingness to proceed with the June 2008 agreement to promote joint exploration in the East China Sea.

The strong Chinese reaction in September, however, may be attributed not to its attitude to the DPJ but to the change in its self-perception: its recognition of itself as a great power and the resultant reorientation in its foreign policies.[45] After the Lehman shock, China's economic growth successfully continued, and its GDP was about to surpass Japan's. China had now clearly become a great power while the relative power of the United States was on the decline; it was high time to revise Deng Xiaoping's dictum, "conceal our capacities" (*taoguang yanghui*).[46] China did indeed reveal its capacities and in so doing frightened the Japanese, its other neighbors and the world.

The DPJ government under Kan tilted more clearly to the United States, particularly after the Senkaku uproar. The US welcomed such a tilt; when Foreign Minister Maehara Seiji visited in late September, US Secretary of State Hillary Clinton assured Maehara that the US-Japan alliance applied to the Senkaku Islands.[47] The Defense Program Guidelines, revised under the DPJ government in December 2010, did not change the basic orientation of Japan's defense and emphasized the need to "deepen and develop" the alliance with the United States while pointing out the need to upgrade the protection of remote islands.[48]

Another signal that showed Kan's tilt toward the United States was his interest in the Trans-Pacific Partnership (TPP). The TPP had originally been a free-trade negotiating framework, started by Singapore, Brunei, New Zealand and Chile in 2006, which aimed to eliminate virtually all trade barriers. When the United States, Australia, Peru and Vietnam participated in it in early 2010, it became a focus of attention in Asia-Pacific economic community-building. Prime Minister Kan, in his Diet speech on October 1, stated:

> We will look into participating in such negotiations as those for the Trans-Pacific Partnership agreement and will aim to build a Free Trade Area of the Asia-Pacific. With a view toward making the East Asian Community a reality, I want to open our country to the outside world and move forward with concrete steps of negotiations as much as possible.[49]

Japan's participation in the TPP, however, was not realized during the DPJ governments. Not just TPP, many important policies appeared to be getting nowhere. Part of the reason for the mess was the LDP's strong, almost nasty, opposition to the DPJ in the twisted Diet; the LDP pulled no punches in getting revenge for the suffering it had experienced during the previous twisted Diet. But another reason for the political gridlock was the lack, or inadequacy, of internal coordination within the DPJ; in-fighting had, in fact, become the norm in policy and personnel matters. Furthermore, the personal conflict between Kan and Ozawa Ichirō intensified especially after Hatoyama joined Ozawa in an attempt to oust Kan from the DPJ leadership. By the beginning of March 2011, the Kan government was on the verge of collapse.

What saved the Kan government momentarily was the mega earthquake that devastated Eastern Japan on March 11. The tsunami triggered by the earthquake destroyed huge areas along the Pacific coast and killed nearly 20,000 people; it also crippled the nuclear power plant in Fukushima. The disaster demonstrated both the strengths and weaknesses of Japan. Earthquake-related technology had proven its excellence: very few modern structures collapsed; no Shinkansen trains derailed. Local communities maintained law and order despite being physically devastated. Well-trained children escaped from schools before the tsunami engulfed their alma maters. But critical weaknesses were revealed by the meltdown of the nuclear reactor in the Fukushima No. 2 power plant; Japan lacked both plans and concrete measures to cope with a crisis whose magnitude exceeded normal assumptions. Some even argued that Fukushima revealed the worst aspects of Japanese organizations on a par with what resulted in the Japanese wars of the 1930s and 1940s.[50]

The Japanese were fortunate in receiving support from all over the world. The US forces immediately started "Operation Tomoda-chi" (Friends) with 24,500 personnel, 24 ships, and 189 aircraft;[51] together with the SDF, American soldiers rescued devastated victims. All together, 24 countries and regions sent rescue and medical teams to Japan. Assistance and donations came in from 169 countries and regions. Donations made through the Red Cross amounted to 100 billion yen.[52] The people of Taiwan donated 18 billion yen in total.[53] All the developing countries in Asia extended financial and material support. With the donation from Kandahar, Afghanistan, its mayor sent the message, "I know this amount is miniscule for a country like Japan but this is a token of the gratitude of the people of Kandahar."[54] Following the Fourth Trilateral Summit held in Tokyo on May 22, both Premier Wen Jiabao and President Lee Myung-bak visited Fukushima to encourage the victims of the tsunami and the nuclear-power-plant crisis. Japan-South Korea relations appeared quite good, and Japan-China relations seemed to be improving.

The political ceasefire did not last long, however. The approval ratings of the Kan government fell below 30 percent, and the in-fighting within the DPJ continued. Betting on a split in the DPJ, the opposition staged a vote of non-confidence in the lower house. In order to avoid passage of the vote, Kan proposed a compromise to his opponents in the DPJ; he would step down once he fulfilled important responsibilities, he told them. Believing that Kan would resign soon, his adversaries within the DPJ did not agree to the non-confidence vote. With the rejection of the vote, Kan appeared ready to carry on much longer than his opponents were prepared to tolerate. Another round of in-fighting started in the ruling party. Since a vote of non-confidence cannot be held twice in the same Diet session, Kan's position appeared secure. But the biggest headache for Kan was that the budget could not pass the Diet without cooperation from the opposition in the upper house to pass the bill to finance it by issuing deficit bonds. For the LDP and Komeito it was risky to keep opposing the bond-issuing bill in the midst of reconstruction from the March 11 disaster. They struck a deal with the DPJ to the effect that if Kan stepped down, they would help pass the bill. With this compromise, Kan was forced to resign.

Though few in Japan's political circles noticed during this politically chaotic period, Japan played an important role in bringing about peace to an area of an important Asian country: Mindanao, the Philippines. At the request of the Philippine government and the Moro Islamic Liberation Front, Japan offered a site for a secret meeting between President Benigno Aquino III and MILF Chairman Murad Ebrahim at a hotel in Narita on August 4, 2011.

Muslims had populated Mindanao since the 14th century, but Christians had started to migrate there during the American colonial period and after independence. As many Christians flowed into Mindanao, conflicts with the Muslim population increased. In the late 1960s, the Moro National Liberation Front (MNLF) rose up in armed rebellion to create an independent Moro National Republic. Peace talks had been held on and off since then. The MNLF and the Ramos government in 1996 agreed to form the Autonomous Region of Muslim Mindanao (ARMM) government. Those opposing the MNLF formed a new organization, the MILF, to continue armed struggle. Since the ARMM government under the MNLF turned out to be ineffective and corrupt, the MILF increased its influence and engaged militarily with the Philippine government. The Estrada government intensified its attack on the MILF in 2000, resulting in a huge number of internally displaced persons.

President Gloria Arroyo resumed peace talks with the MILF through the mediation of Malaysia. On the basis of these talks, an International Monitoring Team (IMT) was formed in 2004, to which Malaysia and Brunei sent military personnel. When socio-economic development was added to the IMT's mandates in 2006, Japan decided to send a civilian expert to the IMT from the Japan International

Cooperation Agency (in the subsequent years, Norway, the EU and Indonesia also sent personnel to the IMT). To back up its participation in the IMT, Japan provided a comprehensive aid package known as J-BIRD (Japan-Bangsamoro Initiatives for Reconstruction and Development) to the areas under the control of the Philippine government and the area under MILF control. After a setback in 2009, an International Contact Group (ICG), consisting of the UK, Japan, Turkey, Saudi Arabia (after 2011) and four international NGOs, was established to support the peace process. Under J-BIRD, Japan extended assistance to build schools, community facilities, agricultural facilities, vocational training centers and other human-resource development projects. Japanese experts were seconded to the IMT to coordinate J-BIRD projects with both the ARMM government and MILF, cultivating reliable personal networks.

When President Aquino took office, he decided to breathe new life into the peace process and felt the need to establish communications with the MILF leadership. Manila and MILF agreed to direct contacts between the highest leaders, but the MILF was very sensitive about the location of the summit. In their view, Japan was desirable because only Japan was party to both the IMT and the ICG and because its IMT experts as well as embassy staff had proved themselves reliable. Japan agreed to offer the two sides a place to meet. At the signing of the peace accord with the MILF in March 2014, President Aquino thanked Japan for the meeting, which had been the critical turning point in the move toward peace.[55]

The Noda Administration: Rocky Relations with China and South Korea

Noda Yoshihiko, 54, was elected prime minister on August 30. A son of a former SDF serviceman, Noda became the first prime minister from the Mastushita Seikei Juku (The Matsushita Institute of Government and Management), an institution that Matsushita Kōnosuke, the founder of Panasonic, established in 1979 to educate future political leaders in Japan. Without wealth or dynastic political networks, Noda had kept on speaking on a soapbox in front of a railway station in his constituency almost every morning until he became finance minister in the Kan government. Modest, low-profile, conciliatory, he adopted an almost LDP-like management style in domestic politics. Unlike Hatoyama or Kan, Noda listened very carefully to the bureaucrats and sometimes sought advice from people like Nakasone Yasuhiro. But the difficulties resulting from the twisted Diet and the DPJ's second nature—in-fighting—remained the same.

Noda's diplomatic debut was his speech at the United Nations General Assembly on September 23. Japanese prime ministers' speeches there had become a kind of self-introduction; a new prime minister took the podium every year. Before he gave the UN speech, Noda met with US President Obama on September 21. Pressed by Obama as to Japan's participation in TPP, Noda promised to reach a domestic consensus as early as possible. Since the United States was the host of the APEC meeting to be held in November, Noda wanted to reach a conclusion by then. However, opposition to Japan taking part in TPP was widespread.

Chairman of JA-Zenchu (Japan's Central Union of Agricultural Co-operatives) Banzai Akira expressed his opposition to TPP, declaring that "participation in TPP is incompatible with the rebirth of Japanese agriculture." JA-Zenchu sent a petition to the speakers of both houses to oppose Japan's participation in TPP; a petition can only be made if introduced by Diet members, and this time JA-Zenchu made public the introducers' list of 356 Diet members from both the ruling and opposition parties. Despite the mounting opposition, Noda announced his intention to "enter into consultations with the countries concerned at the coming APEC meeting with a view to participating in the TPP negotiations."[56] The protesters against TPP, however, successfully persuaded broader segments of society to oppose the government's attempt to join the negotiations. Noda was unable to overcome this opposition while he was in office.[57]

Another round of international conferences that Prime Minister Noda attended that autumn were the ASEAN-related meetings in Bali, Indonesia—the ASEAN+3 Summit on November 18, the ASEAN+Japan Summit on the same day and the East Asia Summit on November 19. On the sidelines of these meetings, he met with the president of a country long one of the most secluded from the rest of the world: Myanmar. Since the democratization movement had been brutally suppressed in 1990, Myanmar had been under military rule. Although Aung San Suu Kyi was awarded the Nobel Peace Prize in

1991, she had been under house arrest until 1995. Suu Kyi was again put under house arrest in 2000 and released in 2002 only to be detained the following year.

ASEAN accepted the membership of Myanmar in 1997. But to many members of ASEAN, especially the democratic ones, Myanmar had become something of an embarrassment. In response to their demands to show at least some signs of change, the government of Myanmar decided on a "Roadmap to Democracy" in 2003. The ASEAN Summit held in Laos in 2004 agreed on the creation of an ASEAN Community by 2015 consisting of a security community, an economic community and a social-cultural community. The agreement to build a security community included the goal of "achiev[ing] peace, stability, democracy and prosperity in the region," and its Annex listed several activities to promote "a just, democratic and harmonious environment" including "strengthening democratic institutions and popular participation"; "strengthening the rule of law and judiciary systems, legal infrastructure and capacity building"; and "enhancing good governance in public and private sectors."[58] Myanmar accepted this agreement but was not able to implement the Roadmap promptly. Though 2006 was Myanmar's turn to act as chair of ASEAN, probably persuaded by other members, Yangon withdrew to avoid the embarrassment of having no dialogue partners at the meetings.

The United States tabled a UN Security Council resolution to censure Myanmar in 2006, which was vetoed by China and Russia. Just before the vote on the UNSC resolution was taken, the Myanmar government released political prisoners, including participants in the 1988 movement, who immediately organized a protest demonstration criticizing the government for its mismanagement of economic policy. The military suppressed the protest but went ahead with drafting a new constitution as stipulated by the Roadmap. The draft was adopted in February 2008 and approved by a national referendum in May. Finally, after 14 years in the making, a new constitution was enacted.

As stipulated in the constitution, a general election was held in November 2010, but its results failed to reduce international skepticism about Myanmar's movement toward democracy; Suu Kyi was still under house arrest, and her party, the National League for Democracy (NLD), boycotted the election. Six days after the election, however, Suu Kyi was released. General Thein Sein, former prime minister from 2007 to 2011, was elected president by the Assembly of the Union on March 30, 2011. Contrary to expectations, Thein Sein took strong initiatives in implementing political reform and economic liberalization.

By the time Noda met with Thein Sein, the NLD had agreed to participate in the bi-election scheduled to be held on April 1, 2012, a move Noda welcomed. He sent Foreign Minister Genba Kōichirō to Myanmar in December 2011 to explore the possible resumption of large-scale economic cooperation. After the bi-election, monitored by teams of international observers, that resulted in a landslide victory for the NLD, President Thein Sein visited Japan on April 21, 2012. One of the obstacles to resuming economic assistance to Myanmar was the accumulated arrears from the loans that Japan had extended over the past decades (502.4 billion Japanese yen in principle, interest and overdue charges). Japan offered the combination of a concessional bridge-loan and a substantial amount of debt cancellation, to which Thein Sein agreed.[59] Noda explained Japan's ODA policy to Myanmar as efforts "to spread the dividends of democratization, national reconciliation and economic reforms," consisting of three pillars: "assistance for improvement of people's livelihood, assistance for capacity building and the development of institutions to sustain the economy and society, [and] assistance for the development of infrastructure and related systems necessary for sustainable economic development." One project in particular that attracted Thein Sein was the "Yangon Thilawa Development Initiative," intended to transform the area south of Yangon into a modern center of manufacturing, a project reminiscent of Thailand's Eastern Seaboard project of the 1980s.

Noda was also eager to improve relations with Japan's close neighbors, South Korea and China. But new conditions that he had not anticipated thwarted his hopes. On August 30, 2011, the very same day that Noda was appointed prime minister by the Diet, the Constitutional Court of South Korea issued the following decision:

In this case, the Court found unconstitutional the respondent's failure to resolve, under Article III of the "Agreement between Japan and the Republic of Korea Concerning the Settlement of Problems in Regard to Property and Claims and Economic Cooperation," the dispute over the interpretation of whether the damage claims filed by the complainants against Japan, in their capacity as comfort women, have been rendered null and void by Article II Section 1 of the same Agreement.[60]

Here, the "respondent" was the ROK government and the "complainants" were 64 former "comfort women" and their support groups. Article II Section 1 of the 1965 Agreement cited above confirms that such problems "have been settled completely and finally." The ROK government had expressed its view in 2005 that the problems of Korean residents in Sakhalin, Korean victims of atomic bombs, and comfort women had not been resolved by the Agreement, while the government of Japan maintained that all those problems had been "settled completely and finally." The South Korean Court ruled, however, that it was unconstitutional for the ROK government not to resolve these differences under Article III, which stipulates that any dispute concerning the interpretation of the Agreement "shall be settled primarily through diplomatic channels" and that any dispute which cannot be settled that way shall be settled through arbitration. Since the Court found that the South Korean government had not made sufficient efforts to pursue the steps stipulated in Article III, the administration of President Lee Myung-bak was now forced to engage in negotiations with the Japanese government on an issue that had been dormant as a diplomatic controversy for almost a decade.

On December 14, supporters of the former comfort women placed a bronze statue of a girl (representing a comfort woman) in front of the Japanese Embassy in Seoul. During his visit to Kyoto four days later, President Lee Myung-bak raised the issue at a meeting with Prime Minister Noda. Noda repeated the Japanese government's official line that the legal issues concerning the comfort women had been settled by the 1965 Agreement. But Lee pointed out that "this is an issue of national emotion and feelings first and law second. . . . Unless Japan takes sincere measures," he said, "a second and a third statue will be erected." Lee must have felt that Noda's response was legalistic and spent more than 40 minutes of the hour-long meeting on this issue.[61] Noda was puzzled by this sudden emotional burst of anger from someone whom he considered a pragmatic businessman-turned-politician and who had been more or less silent on this issue since he became president in 2008. According to Noda, on his first visit to Seoul that October, when he delivered some of the cultural documents that Kan had promised to hand over to South Korea the previous year, President Lee had told him, "Previous presidents and administrations attempted to raise their popularity by attacking Japan on historically important dates when the management of domestic politics became difficult. I will not do such a thing. . . . Korea-Japan relations thus far always repeat the pattern of starting off with a good ambiance at the beginning of a new administration, then turning bad at the end. I don't want to do that."[62] In any event, what President Lee meant by "sincere measures" had never been clarified.

When Japanese Vice Foreign Minister Sasae Ken'ichirō visited Seoul and sounded the South Korean government out about a possible package deal reported to have consisted of (1) an apology conveyed by the Japanese ambassador directly to former comfort women, (2) a statement by the prime minister expressing his apology to former comfort women, and (3) support to former comfort government, the Lee government rejected it on the grounds that it was "not clear about legal responsibility."[63] Frustrated by the lack of satisfactory responses from Tokyo, President Lee decided to show his anger in August 2012 by becoming the first South Korean president to land on the disputed island of Takeshima (Dokdo in Korean). When the possibility of a visit by the Japanese Emperor to South Korea was raised, President Lee said, "Although [the Emperor] wants to visit Korea, I have told Japan he can only do so if he visits [the graves of] those who died in independence movements and apologizes to them from his heart. . . . He need not come if he [only] brings words of 'deepest regret' (tsūseki no nen)."[64] As there was no real possibility then of the Emperor's visit, President Lee's words were troubling even to those Japanese who generally had friendly views of South Korea. Japan recalled its ambassador from Seoul; Noda wrote a letter of protest, which the South Korean government returned unopened; Japan declared it was preparing to go to the International Court of Justice over the

Takeshima issue. Relations between Tokyo and Seoul appeared to have hit rock bottom.

Why did President Lee compound a difficult relationship already troubled by the comfort women issue by adding the territorial problem and his comments about the Emperor? With his approval rate very low by 2012, he may have resorted to the practice that he told Noda the previous year he would not engage in: attacking Japan to prop up public support. But his term was to end by early 2013, and he was prohibited by the constitution from running again. Lee was also reported as saying, "The influence of Japan in international society is not what it once was."[65] He might have believed that South Korea no longer needed to heed Japan very much anymore. Or, he might have simply been angry at Japan and Noda.

Another development Prime Minister Noda did not foresee was Governor of Tokyo Ishihara Shintarō's plans for the Senkaku Islands. Of the five islands that constitute the Senkakus, Taishō Island was owned by the government, and the four other islands were owned by private citizens. Of those four, Kuba had been rented to the government since the islands were returned in 1972 from the United States, which had used it for military exercises. As a result of several attempts by Japanese nationalists to build physical structures on the privately owned islands and the subsequent Chinese reaction, the government entered into an agreement with the landlord to rent the remaining three islands in 2002 so that, with the right of lease, it would be able to prevent unpredictable activities in the islands, including those by the landlord. This government policy of doing nothing on the islands caused frustration among right-wing nationalists, one of whom was Ishihara. On April 16, he announced in a speech at the Heritage Foundation in Washington, DC, that "the metropolitan government of Tokyo is planning to buy these islands."[66] Vice Governor of Tokyo Inose Naoki solicited public donations to fund the purchase,[67] and money rolled into the metropolitan government's account, reaching a total of 1.47 billion Japanese yen by early September.[68] Seeing this, Prime Minister Noda realized that should the islands be owned by the Tokyo Metropolitan Government, the central government would not be easily able to control what Ishihara and his right-wing friends might do. He therefore came to believe that it would be much better for the central government to buy the islands. When Noda's decision was leaked to the press on July 7, China reacted strongly, sending three ships belonging to the China Fisheries Law Enforcement Command (FLEC) to the territorial waters around the Senkaku Islands. On August 15, seven activists from Hong Kong landed on Uotsuri-jima. On August 19, ten Japanese raised Japan's national flag on the same island. In more than 20 cities in China, anti-Japanese protesters took to the streets. On August 27, two cars stopped Ambassador Niwa Uichirō's car, and a man ripped off the Japanese flag.[69]

As tensions rose, Noda held a secret meeting with Ishihara on August 19. As Noda recalls:

> If the metropolitan government bought [the islands] and made dramatic changes such as building a harbor and stationing personnel there, we could not predict how China would respond. In the meantime, day by day donations were pouring into the account that the metropolitan government had set up. The more I thought about it, the more I realized that the central government had better buy them as soon as possible. . . . I had a secret meeting with Governor Ishihara on August 19. . . . I will not reveal specific details of our conversation. But that evening I became convinced that ownership of the islands by the Tokyo Metropolitan Government would be disastrous for Japanese-Chinese relations.[70]

According to Sunohara Tsuyoshi, who conducted in-depth interviews with many of the players involved, during the secret meeting on August 19, Ishihara told Noda that "if building a harbor in the Senkakus brings about a war with China, so be it. Japan could win a conventional war."[71] Horrified, Noda ordered his staff to intensify talks with the landlord and finally obtained his agreement in early September.

The Chinese reaction to the "nationalization" of the islands was harsher than it had been to the arrest of the captain in 2010. When Noda approached Hu Jintao at the APEC Summit in Vladivostok on September 9, 2012 to express his condolences to the victims of the earthquake that had recently taken place in Yunnan, Hu Jintao without looking Noda in the eye told him bluntly, "Nationalization of Diaoyu Dao is absolutely unacceptable." "This is a matter of a change in land ownership, not a change in territoriality," responded Noda.[72] On September 10, the Japanese cabinet decided to purchase the islands. Chief Cabinet Secretary Fujimura Osamu explained, "The acquisition and ownership of the Senkaku Islands is a transfer of property rights to the land, part of our country's territory, from the previous owner to the government. It will not create any problem with other countries."[73]

Anti-Japanese protests took place in such cities as Beijing, Shanghai, Guangzhou and Weihai on September 11. On the following Saturday, September 15, anti-Japanese demonstrations took place in more than 40 cities throughout the country. Huangdao JUSCO, a supermarket owned by a Japanese chain, was surrounded by 3,000 protesters, some of whom stormed into the supermarket and ransacked the shop: goods worth 200 million Chinese yuan were destroyed. Toyota and Honda auto dealers were set on fire. On Sunday, demonstrations spread to more than 80 cities. On the following day, September 18, the 81st anniversary of the Mukden Incident of 1931, anti-Japanese protests engulfed more than 100 cities in China.

The waters surrounding the Senkaku Islands saw a dramatic rise in Chinese activity. On September 14, six ships belonging to the China Marine Surveillance (Zhongguo Haijian, CMS) entered the territorial waters around the Senkakus, the first time that as many as six Chinese government ships had entered these waters. On September 18, ten CMS ships and two ships from the China Fisheries Law Enforcement Command (FLEC) appeared off the territorial waters, and three of the CMS ships entered the waters. By September 19, four more ships joined the Chinese flotilla.

China also started to wage a war of words against Japan at the United Nations. Foreign Minister Yang Jiechi stated in his speech to the General Assembly on September 27:

Diaoyu Dao and its affiliated islands have been an integral part of China's territory since ancient times. China has indisputable historical and legal evidence in this regard. Japan seized these islands in 1895 at the end of the Sino-Japanese War and forced the then Chinese government to sign an unequal treaty to cede these islands and other Chinese territories to Japan. After the Second World War, the Diaoyu Dao islands and other Chinese territories occupied by Japan were returned to China in accordance with the Cairo Declaration, the Potsdam Proclamation and other international documents. By taking such unilateral actions as the so-called "island purchase", the Japanese government has grossly violated China's sovereignty. This is an outright denial of the outcomes of the victory of the world anti-fascist war and poses a grave challenge to the post-war international order and the purposes and principles of the Charter of the United Nations. The moves taken by Japan are totally illegal and invalid. They can in no way change the historical fact that Japan stole Diaoyu Dao and its affiliated islands from China and the fact that China has territorial sovereignty over them. The Chinese government is firm in upholding China's territorial sovereignty. China strongly urges Japan to immediately stop all activities that violate China's territorial sovereignty, take concrete actions to correct its mistakes, and return to the track of resolving the dispute through negotiation.[74]

Kodama Kazuo, Japan's deputy permanent representative to the United Nations, took the floor and made the following rebuttal:

- The Government of Japan made a Cabinet Decision in January 1895 to formally incorporate the Senkaku Islands into the territory of Japan, while the island of Formosa and the islands appertaining or belonging to it were ceded to Japan in accordance with the Treaty of Shimonoseki which was signed in April 1895. Therefore it is clear that such an assertion that Japan took the islands cannot logically stand at the outset. In any case, from 1885, surveys of the Senkaku Islands had been thoroughly conducted by Japan. Through these surveys, it was confirmed that the Senkaku Islands had been not only uninhabited but had shown no trace of having been under the control of China. Based on this confirmation Japan formally incorporated the Senkaku Islands into the territory of Japan.
- Japan renounced the territorial sovereignty over the Island of Formosa (Taiwan) and the Pescadores ceded by China after the Sino-Japanese War, in accordance with Article 2(b) of the San Francisco Peace Treaty. However, it was made clear that the Senkaku Islands were not included in "the Formosa and the Pescadores", by the fact that the United States actually

exercised administrative rights over the Senkaku Islands as part of the "Nansei Shoto (South West Islands)" in accordance with Article 3 of the San Francisco Peace Treaty, and the Islands were explicitly included in the areas whose administrative rights reverted to Japan in 1972.

- It has only been since the 1970s that the Government of China began making its own assertions on territorial sovereignty over the Senkaku Islands, which constitute Japan's inherent territory. Until then, they had never expressed any objections to Japan, nor did they protest the fact that the Islands were included in the area over which the United States exercised administrative rights in accordance with Article 3 of the San Francisco Peace Treaty.[75]

Without touching on the specific points made by Kodama, Ambassador Li Baodong, China's permanent representative to the UN, asserted, "What he said is utterly nonsense," and continued:

The recent so-called "island purchase" by the Japanese government is nothing different from money laundering. Its purpose is to legalize its stealing and occupation of the Chinese territory through this illegal means and to confuse international public opinion and deceive people in the world. This action of Japan constitutes a serious encroachment upon China's sovereignty, and intends to continue and legalize the result of Japan's colonial policy. It is an open denial of the outcomes of victory of the world anti-fascist war, and a grave challenge to the postwar international order and the purposes and principles of the Charter of the United Nations.[76]

What Ambassador Li meant by "money laundering" is not entirely clear, but if it means an attempt to give a legal facade to an activity regarded by China as an infringement on its claim to sovereignty, Japan has been engaging in this type of "money laundering" since the 1970s when China started to claim sovereignty over these islands. Before the 1970s, Japan and the United States had engaged in similar activities many times, and China made no protests. Since the 1970s, Japan continued to accept the landlord's property rights; it concluded a lease contract with the landlord in 2002; it arrested Chinese who landed on these islands. Why the act of buying the land from a private citizen at this point in time became a particular source of extreme indignation was not entirely clear. Minister Yang demanded Japan "take concrete actions to correct its mistakes." But if the Japanese government were to sell the islands back to the original landlord, that too would be a purely domestic legal act. Would it not be a further instance of "money laundering"? It was also not clear why China suddenly referred to the purchase as something that "poses a grave challenge to the post-war international order and the purposes and principles of the Charter of the United Nations." If this act could be characterized in this fashion, there had been many previous occasions when China could have, but didn't, indulge in similar rhetoric. Why resort to it now?

China could have appealed to the International Court of Justice. But it did not show any signs of going to The Hague. As Chief Cabinet Secretary Fujimura mentioned, the purchase of the islands by the Japanese government was a purely domestic legal act that did not affect any country's international legal claims including Japan's and China's. Just as President Lee Myung-bak's visit to Takeshima did not affect Japan's international legal claim to that island, the "nationalization" of these islands would not affect China's international legal claim until the dispute was resolved by diplomatic agreement or by such means as the International Court of Justice. If China had said nothing, on the other hand, its silence could have been interpreted as having accepted Japan's act as legitimate, and so as long as China continued to maintain its claim of sovereignty over the islands, it was important to repeat its sovereignty claim. In this sense, Minister Yang and Ambassador Li were right to voice their protests, though they could have used somewhat less emotional rhetoric.

What China did was not limited to verbal rebukes, however; by repeatedly sending government ships into Senkaku waters, it began to make significant challenges to Japan's effective control of the area. As the Figure 10.1 below indicates, the frequency of Chinese intrusion into the territorial waters and the number of ships involved dramatically changed in September 2012. How can we explain this change in maritime behavior coupled with the extreme indignation shown in the street protests as well as the diplomatic attacks on Japan?

No. of vessels identified within the territorial sea (total/month) (■)

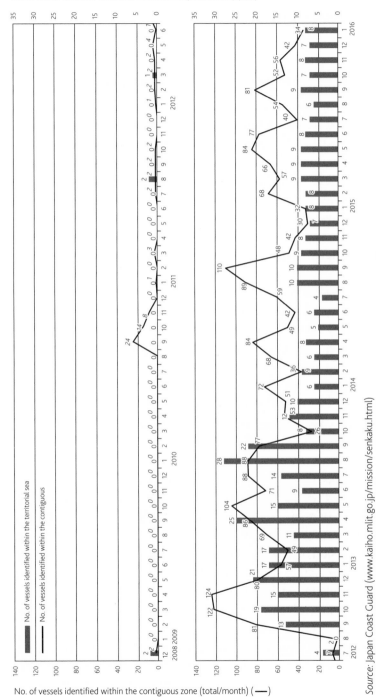

No. of vessels identified within the contiguous zone (total/month) (—)

Source: Japan Coast Guard (www.kaiho.mlit.go.jp/mission/senkaku.html)

Figure 10.1 The Numbers of Chinese Government and Other Vessels that Entered Japan's Contiguous Zone or Intruded into Territorial Sea Surrounding the Senkaku Islands

Some Chinese leaders may have concluded that Noda, with Ishihara's help, was actually attempting to make dramatic changes to Japanese activities on the islands; perhaps they may have suspected that Noda was going to do exactly what Noda feared Ishihara would do. Ishihara revealed on August 24 that he had met with Noda secretly, and he again referred to the secret meeting in his press conference on August 31.[77] On the surface, then, the prime minister appeared to be collaborating with Ishihara, or at least it was not unreasonable to suspect that Chinese analysts, at least some of them, might so conclude. Japanese diplomats conveyed to their Chinese counterparts that it would be much better to manage the islands issue moderately under national government ownership than under Ishihara's control. At least some Chinese diplomats may have seen the point. Chinese leaders were faced with two hypotheses: Noda the collaborator with Ishihara and Noda the conciliator with China. In the end, the former may have seemed more persuasive; hence, the decision was made to take the toughest possible action against Japan.

Another explanation that does not necessarily contradict the above is based on China's rising capability as a maritime power. China naturally resented Japan's effective control of the islands. As we have seen, it had specified Diaoyu Dao as its territory in its 1992 Law on the Territorial Sea. At that time, however, it was a purely legislative act; China had neither the capability to wield effective control over the islands nor the intention of challenging Japan. Along with the rapid buildup of the military, China increased and modernized its maritime surveillance ships; between 2000 and 2012, it launched about twenty 1000t-class patrol vessels.[78]

The two ships that entered the territorial waters to conduct "normal patrol operations" in 2008 were both built in 2005. Now that its capability had increased, the Chinese leaders may have decided to use it. Japan's decision to "nationalize" the islands may have been the trigger (if not the pretext) to start an operation that had long been planned. It was a risky operation, however, as its ships might collide with those of Japan, which was always prepared to monitor its own territorial waters. The Chinese leadership may have concluded that now that China surpassed Japan in terms of GDP, it was time to flex its muscles.

Volatility in Chinese domestic politics may also have been a factor. The summer of 2012 was a delicate period of political transition.

Xi Jinping was eventually selected general secretary of the CCP and chairman of the Central Military Committee at the 18th Party Congress in November, but the succession process may have been complex. Although the annual Beidaihe conference, attended by retired party leaders including Jiang Zemin, seems to have agreed on Xi's succession, the decision may have been preceded and followed by intense power struggles among the leaders. The fate of Bo Xilai, who along with Xi had been regarded as a potential candidate to succeed Hu Jintao, was the focus of attention. Bo's wife was charged with the murder of an Englishman and given a suspended death sentence on August 20.[79] In late September, the Chinese Communist Party decided to strip Bo Xilai of his membership.[80] Just before the Party Congress, *The New York Times* reported on the huge wealth accumulated by the family of Wen Jiabao after he became premier.[81] These tense political conditions seem to have motivated most political players to play it safe by getting on the bandwagon of anti-Japanese rhetoric.

In Japan, Prime Minister Noda was facing another issue in domestic politics: the consumption tax. He was convinced that it was his mission to find a way to rectify Japan's budget deficits; he believed that an increase in the consumption tax was absolutely necessary. But under the twisted Diet, unless he had the consent of the LDP, passing any tax-related bill was next to impossible. Noda had several meetings with LDP President Tanigaki Sadakazu, who demanded Noda promise to dissolve the Diet if the LDP gave its consent to the bill to raise the consumption tax. In the meantime, a group of the DPJ politicians led by Ozawa split the party in disagreement over the consumption tax issue. Noda told Tanigaki that once the bill passed both houses, he would call an election "soon." The bill to raise the consumption tax passed the Diet on August 10. With the next general election pending, the LDP once again selected Abe Shinzō as president and prepared for the election. The election of the lower house took place on December 16. The approval rating for the Noda Cabinet was about 30 percent in October, not as low as it had been for Kan or Asō or Abe before their respective elections.[82] The results, however, were the same: a disastrous defeat for the DPJ.

Chapter 11

Abe's Come-back

"I am back," said Abe Shinzō to the audience in Washington, DC, when he visited the United States two months after becoming prime minister for the second time in December 2012; "and so shall Japan be," he promised.[1] Since he left office because of illness five and a half years earlier, Japanese politics had been on a roller coaster ride; the Japanese economy was suffering from persistent deflation and steadily falling prices, and GDP growth had been minimal. Indeed, Japan's GDP was surpassed by that of China in 2010. Relations with China and South Korea had reached their nadir. American specialists on East Asian policy were asking, "Does Japan desire to continue to be a tier-one nation, or is she content to drift into tier-two status?"[2]

During this same period, Abe appeared to be a spent horse. Few anticipated that he would have a second chance to return to a leadership position in Japanese politics. Yoshida Shigeru had served two separate terms as prime minister, but that was an exceptional case during the American occupation period. No one had served twice as prime minister since then. Abe, who resigned in disgrace, had not attracted much media attention as a viable candidate to represent the Liberal Democratic Party against the Democratic Party of Japan. However, he was able to maintain three types of followers. His constituency in Yamaguchi Prefecture was rock solid in support of its political prince. He regained the support of nationalists by resuming the rhetoric he had refrained from using when he was in power.[3] And a small number of non-ideological, middle-of-the-road LDP power brokers saw in Abe the leadership potential to carry out the strategic and pragmatic actions needed to revive the LDP. In addition, Abe received a great assist from medical science; thanks to newly available drugs, he regained his health. Suga Yoshihide, one of the power brokers who supported Abe, persuaded the hesitant former prime minister to run again for the presidency of the LDP.[4] The election in September 2012 was a neck-and-neck race among five candidates with no one gaining a clear majority vote, resulting in a run-off between Abe and Ishiba Shigeru, a former minister of defense. Abe won. Thus began the unprecedented come-back of a once failed prime minister.

Abenomics

Abe appeared to have learned many lessons from his failure during his first administration and from the failures of the subsequent DPJ governments. Although the December election was a landslide victory for the LDP and Komeito coalition, the votes the LDP received were not a sign of support for the LDP but of dismay and disappointment with the DPJ. The coalition regained a two-thirds majority in the lower house, but the next upper house election was just around the corner, scheduled to take place in July. Unless the LDP government was able to demonstrate its competence, the voters might repeat their behavior of 2007 and 2010 and "twist" the Diet once again. The DPJ did not have a majority in the upper house, but neither did the LDP-Komeito coalition. Since only half the seats were being contested in the upcoming election, the coalition had to win big in order to gain a majority.

Abe could not afford to make mistakes this time in his cabinet appointments; in his first administration, scandals involving cabinet members had damaged the reputation and integrity of the government. He also had to avoid the mistakes that the DPJ government repeatedly made: in-fighting over important policy issues. Abe appointed LDP heavyweights to important cabinet posts: Asō Tarō his deputy prime minister and finance minister, Kishida Fumio foreign minister, Hayashi Yoshimasa agriculture minister, Ishiba Shigeru minister in charge of reinvigorating the rural area, and Suga Yoshihide, who had persuaded Abe to run again, chief cabinet secretary. Abe had to deliver results as quickly as possible. He could not afford to waste time by getting involved in contentious issues. The policy focus he chose was the economy.

In order to rebuild the Japanese economy, Abe announced the "three arrows" of what would come to be known as "Abenomics"—"bold monetary policy, flexible fiscal policy, and a growth strategy that encourages private sector investment"—in his speeches to the Diet in January and February.[5] Abe wanted the first arrow to be visibly effective. Advised by such prominent economists as Yale emeritus professor Hamada Kōichi and former Ministry of Finance official Honda Etsurō, Abe was convinced that the economic policy mistakes of previous administrations stemmed from the fact that all tried to achieve fiscal consolidation by cutting the budget and raising taxes without attending to the troubles caused by deflation. Given the widespread expectation of falling prices, households and businesses naturally deferred consumer spending and investment. Cutting public spending and raising taxes in a situation like this would further shrink the economy and decrease prices, decelerating consumption and investment in the private sector even faster. This deflationary spiral, Abe concluded, had to be broken. Because the interest rate was already virtually zero, the only policy option the government had left, Hamada and Honda advised, was to have the Bank of Japan set an "inflation target" and engage in a radical quantitative easing of the money supply. Setting an official target for raising prices, along with the influx of huge quantities of money, could change the private sector mindset from deflationary to inflationary with the expectation that consumers would spend more and business would invest more.

To realize this policy change, Abe appointed Kuroda Haruhiko, president of the Asian Development Bank, to be the new governor of the Bank of Japan in March. Under Kuroda's leadership, the BOJ announced the introduction of "quantitative and qualitative monetary easing" on April 4 and declared that, in order to achieve a two percent inflation target, "it will enter a new phase of monetary easing both in terms of quantity and quality."[6] The economic indicators had already begun to pick up even before the BOJ's announcement. The Nikkei average had risen 21 percent since the birth of the Abe Cabinet; the yen depreciated 8.6 percent in the same period; Honda announced its highest global sales in April.[7] The approval rate for the Abe Cabinet jumped from 62 percent in late December to 76 percent in late April.[8]

40th Anniversary of ASEAN-Japan Association

On the foreign policy front, Abe targeted areas where he could achieve positive results: Southeast Asia and the United States. For the former he took advantage of the fact that 2013 marked the 40th anniversary of Japan's association with ASEAN, which had started in 1973 with the establishment of a rather modest forum on synthetic rubber. Immediately after the formation of the cabinet, Abe sent Finance Minister Asō to Myanmar (January 2–3) and Foreign Minister Kishida to the Philippines, Singapore, Brunei and Australia (January 9–12). Abe himself visited Vietnam, Thailand and Indonesia (January 16–19). Although Abe had to cut short his stay in Indonesia because of a terrorist attack on an oil plant in Algeria, the victims of which included Japanese, during the trip he outlined the following "five principles" of Japan's ASEAN policy:

(1) Protect and promote together with ASEAN member states universal values, such as freedom, democracy and basic human rights;
(2) Ensure in cooperation with ASEAN member states that the free and open seas, which are the most vital common asset, are governed by laws and rules and not by force, and to welcome the United States' rebalancing to the Asia-Pacific region;
(3) Further promote trade and investment, including flows of goods, money, people and services, through various economic partnership networks, for Japan's economic revitalization and [the] prosperity of both Japan and ASEAN member states;
(4) Protect and nurture Asia's diverse cultural heritages and traditions;
(5) Promote exchanges among the young generations to further foster mutual understanding.[9]

Supporting Myanmar, which was accelerating the process of liberalization under President Thein Sein, was an important policy that Abe inherited from the Noda Cabinet. The Abe administration boosted its support by increasing Japan's ODA to Myanmar in an amazingly wide range of areas. In late January, it implemented debt relief worth 198 billion yen.[10] As Prime Minister Noda had promised the previous year, Japan agreed to cancel both overdue charges (176.1 billion yen) and the principal (12.5 billion yen).[11] In addition to extensive grant aid and technical cooperation, Japan agreed to extend very concessional yen loans worth 50 billion yen to three projects: a regional development project for poverty reduction in seven states and seven regions in Myanmar; a project to rehabilitate and upgrade the power supply infrastructure; and an infrastructure development project in the Thilawa area, a large riverside district south of Yangon to be developed into a major industrial park.[12]

Prime Minister Abe visited Myanmar in late May 2013, the first such visit by a Japanese prime minister in 36 years. In July, he visited Malaysia, Singapore and the Philippines. In October, he went to Bali, Indonesia, to attend the APEC summit and to Brunei to attend ASEAN+3, the East Asia Summit and the ASEAN+Japan Summit. In November, he became the first Japanese prime minister to visit Cambodia and Laos in 13 years. After visiting all the ASEAN member states during the year, on December 14, 2013, Abe hosted a special summit in Tokyo commemorating the 40th anniversary of Japan's association with ASEAN, which all the ASEAN heads of state attended. The summit approved a "Vision Statement on ASEAN-Japan Friendship and Cooperation" and issued a joint statement entitled "Hand in hand, facing regional and global challenges."[13] Abe also announced that Japan would extend two trillion yen's worth of ODA to the ASEAN countries over the coming five years mainly with the aim of "enhancing connectivity" and "narrowing the development gap."[14]

The US Alliance and TPP

The United States had always been the most important foreign country for Abe. But to solidify Japan's relations with the US, Abe believed that both the economic and security relationship with Washington had to be improved. Both involved major domestic controversies; economic and trade liberalization could alienate Japan's agricultural interests, the LDP's traditional election machine; upgrading security relations could necessitate making a controversial law to protect intelligence secrets and revising the government's interpretation of the right of collective self-defense. Abe decided to plunge into economic matters first. Despite the LDP's unremitting opposition to the Trans-Pacific Partnership when the DPJ was in power, Abe was convinced that the proposed

trade agreement among Pacific Rim countries was absolutely necessary to buttress Abenomics. He did his best to draft the LDP campaign platform in the December election in a way that would leave
open the possibility of Japan's participation in TPP. The platform
listed several conditions for joining the TPP negotiations, the most
critical of which stated that "the LDP opposes participation in these
negotiations, if the government enters them on the assumption of
'tariff elimination without sanctuary' (*seiiki naki kanzei teppai*),"
i.e., the removal of all tariffs with no exceptions whatsoever.[15] After
appointing Hayashi Yoshimasa, an internationalist, his minister of
agriculture, Abe persuaded many of the opponents of TPP within
the party to soften their views. When he met President Barak
Obama in Washington in late February, Abe successfully persuaded
Obama to agree to the following sentence:

> Recognizing that both countries have bilateral trade sensitivities,
> such as certain agricultural products for Japan and certain man-
> ufactured products for the United States, the two Governments
> confirm that, as the final outcome will be determined during the
> negotiations, it is not required to make a prior commitment to uni-
> laterally eliminate all tariffs upon joining the TPP negotiations.[16]

Abe insisted that this statement guaranteed Japan's participation
without committing the country to "tariff elimination without sanctuary." Based on this, Abe announced Japan's intention to participate
in the TPP negotiations on March 15. This was a risky decision as
many opponents of TPP in the LDP argued that such participation
could have an adverse effect on the upper house election.

As it turned out, the coalition of the LDP and Komeito won the
election on July 21 and secured a majority in the upper house. Abe
took the risk of joining the TPP negotiations before the election and
won. But in retrospect, Abe was right in doing so because it had
been the LDP that had opposed TPP while the DPJ prime ministers
had been its proponents. Thus, TPP could not become an election
issue since the DPJ was not able to oppose it. In addition, just seven
months after the DPJ government's collapse, voters still remembered
its poor performance and finally stopped punishing the incumbent
government no matter which party it was.

With the victory in the upper house election, Abe achieved a solid political base unprecedented since the beginning of the 1990s. The coalition now had a two-thirds majority in the lower house and a majority in the upper house. As long as the Komeito continued to be the coalition partner, the prime minister would have no difficulty passing any bill. Now Abe was able to engage in controversial law-making, with that one proviso: with the Komeito on his side, Abe was all powerful; without it, Abe could rely only on the LDP's simple majority in the lower house since it did not have a majority in the upper house. The Komeito, on the other hand, could not easily take advantage of its swing position on every issue; if it did so, it could undermine the LDP, but it would also lose its role as the coalition party. Abe now began a delicate game with the Komeito on three important issues concerning Japan's national security and international relations: passing the Act on the Protection of Specially Designated Secrets; revising the constitutional interpretation of the right of collective self-defense; and drafting the prime minister's statement commemorating the 70th anniversary of the end of the Second World War.

Abe believed that the first two, the secrecy protection act and the re-interpretation of the collective self-defense right, were critical to making the Japan-US alliance more effective in an increasingly tense international environment. North Korea with its nuclear capability and ballistic missiles appeared more unpredictable than ever; after the death of Kim Jong Il in December 2011, the North under his son, Kim Jong Un, conducted a long-range missile test just before the formation of the Abe Cabinet in December 2012 and a nuclear weapons test in February 2013. China was constantly expanding its military forces, sending its government ships to the Senkaku area as well as to the South China Sea. Japan obviously had laws to punish the leaking of confidential information by civil servants and others who had access to it. But there were no special laws to protect high-level confidential information and impose severer punishment on those who disclosed state secrets. The government reasoned that unless Japan was equipped with a more effective system for protecting confidential information, it would become difficult to increase information- and intelligence-sharing with the United States. Abe also believed that it was necessary to revise the constitutional interpretation of the collective self-defense right in order to add more credibility to the Japan-US alliance. But the Abe government decided to submit the secrecy protection act first to the Diet as it was expected to be less controversial. Most of the media reacted negatively, however; since it was difficult to explain what constituted "specially designated secrets," the media critical of Abe inflamed public concern. Seventy percent of the respondents to a poll said that they had concerns about the bill. The approval rate of the Abe Cabinet declined to 47.6 percent in early December, a month-over-month drop of more than 10 percent.[17] The ruling parties had majorities in both houses and secured passage of the bill. The approval rate did not continue to decline.

A bill that did not attract the attention of the media and the public also passed the Diet around this time, the bill to establish a National Security Council in Japan. This was an idea that Abe had promoted during his first administration but, as a result of his resignation, had failed to achieve. Abe had long been aware of the need for comprehensive analysis of intelligence as well as for the integration of Japan's international and security policies. He felt this necessity acutely in January when he had to face the terrorist attack on the oil plant in Algeria in which many Japanese were killed. With the passage of the NSC law, Japan established a central decision-making apparatus in the Prime Minister's Residence with a fairly strong secretariat. He appointed Yachi Shōtarō, a former vice-minister of foreign affairs who had worked closely with him in his first administration, to be the first head of the NSC secretariat. In December, the NSC drafted Japan's first National Security Strategy as distinguished from the Defense Program Guidelines, the 2013 version of which was approved together with the first NSS.

A far more controversial and unpopular measure that Abe sought was the revision of the interpretation of Article 9 of the constitution with respect to the right of collective self-defense. Article 9 stipulates that "land, sea, and air forces, as well as other war potential, will never be maintained," but Japan had established the Self-Defense Forces in 1954 based on the interpretation that Japan as a sovereign state naturally had the right of self-defense and that the constitution did not prohibit the government from maintaining the minimum necessary forces to exercise that right. The issue then became what constituted the "minimum necessary forces." During subsequent Diet deliberations, the interpretation that the Cabinet Legislation Bureau (CLB) developed was that the dividing line between the minimum necessary forces and forces beyond the minimum was derived from the distinction between the right of individual self-defense and the right of collective self-defense. The right of collective self-defense allows countries to protect friendly countries even if they themselves are not attacked. The forces to carry out such protection, the CLB reasoned, went beyond the minimum necessary requirements, and hence the exercise of the right of collective self-defense was not allowed under the Japanese constitution.

Many constitutional scholars did not agree with this government interpretation and insisted that the SDF was simply unconstitutional: Japan should not possess military forces without first revising the constitution. A minority, however, argued that Article 9 did not prohibit forces for self-defense, individual or collective; it only prohibited aggressive wars. From their viewpoint, the government interpretation was too restrictive. Since neither viewpoint was backed by a political majority, the SDF had continued to exist on the basis of this government interpretation. The LDP has always insisted that it would be better to revise the constitution, but it has never won a two-thirds majority in both houses, which is the requirement for proposing a constitutional amendment. As a governing party, the LDP had embraced the CLB's interpretation as a compromise. During the Cold War, it did not raise practical problems because it was unthinkable that the Soviet Union would attack the US military near Japan without attacking Japan too. After the end of the Cold War, however, as North Korean threats increased, contingencies that might require joint US-Japan action even when Japan itself was not technically attacked became conceivable, if not very likely. Should such contingencies occur, however, many experts and politicians began to worry that if Japan were to refuse to support the US, the United States would be unwilling to fulfill its alliance obligations to protect Japan. Abe Shinzō was one of them.

Abe therefore set up an expert panel to tackle this issue in his first administration, but before the panel produced a proposal, Abe resigned. Now, in his second administration, Abe asked virtually the same experts to come up with a proposal. In May 2014, the panel proposed a wholesale revision of the constitutional interpretation by adopting what had for a long time been the viewpoint of the minority constitutional scholars; it argued that the constitution does not prohibit the exercise of individual and collective self-defense nor does it prohibit Japan from participating in UN-sanctioned operations even if they require the use of force. Komeito, however, did not accept this wholesale re-interpretation and insisted that the change be a minimal one.

After lengthy consultations between the LDP and Komeito, Abe decided to go along with Komeito, that is, to make a minimal amendment without denying the basic logic of the original interpretation that justified the SDF. Thus, the cabinet decision, made on July 1, 2014, after repeating that "Article 9 of the Constitution cannot possibly be interpreted to prohibit Japan from taking measures of self-defense necessary to maintain its peace and security and to ensure its survival" and that the "'use of force' to the minimum extent necessary to that end is permitted," stated the following:

> [T]he Government has reached a conclusion that not only when an armed attack against Japan occurs but also when an armed attack against a foreign country that is in a close relationship with Japan occurs and as a result threatens Japan's survival and poses a clear danger to fundamentally overturn people's right to life, liberty and pursuit of happiness, and when there is no other appropriate means available to repel the attack and ensure Japan's survival and protect its people, use of force to the minimum extent necessary should be interpreted to be permitted under the Constitution as measures for self-defense in accordance with the basic logic of the Government's view to date.[18]

In other words, the requirement of "the minimum extent necessary" was the same, but it now included at least some types of the exercise of the right of collective self-defense. In addition to revising the constitutional interpretation of the collective self-defense right, the cabinet decision required many pieces of legislation to fill the legal gaps that might occur under the current legal system. Therefore, the government prepared a package of legislation and submitted it to the Diet in 2015. The opposition labeled the package "war legislation" and accused the Abe government of making laws that would enable Japan to start a war. A constitutional scholar invited by the LDP to the Diet testified that he considered the legislation "unconstitutional." Rare street demonstrations occurred in front of the Diet during the summer. The approval ratings of the cabinet polled by various media declined to somewhere around 40 percent during the same period. Facing this rise in popular opposition, however, the coalition of the LDP and Komeito did not back down. The bills passed the Diet on September 19, 2015. Government officials in the United States, Australia, the Philippines and the UK explicitly welcomed the legislation.[19] The spokesman for the South Korean foreign ministry commented that "Japan should firmly stick to the spirit of the pacifist Constitution . . . and implement (its defense policy) with transparency so that it will contribute to regional peace and stability."[20] The Chinese foreign ministry commented that the legislation would make "the international community question whether Japan is going to drop its exclusive defense policy and deviate from the path of peaceful development," and demanded that Japan "learn hard lessons from history, . . . take seriously the security concerns of its Asian neighbors, stick to the path of peaceful development, [and] act with discretion on military and security issues."[21] North Korea accused the legislation of being an "evil law worked out to pave the way for invading other countries."[22] Chinese and South Korean reactions to the security legislation were rather moderate; this was mainly because, as we shall see, by September 2015, both Japan-China relations and Japan-South Korea relations had greatly improved from the serious tensions of the previous few years.

History and Territory

When Abe assumed power again in December 2012, both China and South Korea made no effort to conceal their suspicions about Abe's ideological orientation. In a departure from previous patterns, China did not send a congratulatory telegram to Abe,[23] and the South Korean media depicted him as an extreme rightist.[24] This was partly because while in disgrace Abe repeated statements popular among his right-wing supporters; he was grateful to those who had continued to be loyal to the failed prime minister. During the campaign for the LDP presidency in September 2012, Abe stated that "it was a matter of greatest regret that I did not visit Yasukuni Shrine when I was prime minister" and that "the Kōno Statement [on the comfort women issue] should be reviewed and replaced by a new statement."[25] On October 17, Abe visited Yasukuni as president of the LDP and repeated the phrase he had made six years before, "it would be better not to say whether or not I will visit the shrine when I become prime minister."[26] Just a few days after the inauguration of his cabinet, in response to a question about the Murayama Statement on Japan's role in the Second World War, he revealed his intention to write a "future-oriented statement that would be appropriate for the 21st century"; as for the Kōno Statement, he responded that after consulting with experts, his chief cabinet secretary would make the policy of the cabinet clear.

Tensions in the East China Sea continued. On December 13, 2012, an aircraft belonging to China's State Oceanic Administration entered Japanese territorial airspace near Uotsuri-jima, and Japan's Air Self-Defense Force scrambled eight F15 fighters and an E2C early warning aircraft in response. In a concerted manner four Chinese Marine Surveillance ships entered Japan's territorial waters on the same day.[27] Chinese civilian and military aircraft started flying frequently within Japan's air defense identification zone in late December, although none of them entered Japanese airspace. Japan's Defense Minister Onodera Itsunori revealed in a press conference on February 5 that the Chinese frigate *Wenzhou* had locked its weapons-targeting radar on a MSDF helicopter on January 19, and that another Chinese frigate, the *Lianyungang*, did the same on the *Yudachi*, an MSDF destroyer, on January 30. "These acts were very unusual," Onodera said, adding, "One step in the wrong direction could have pushed things into a dangerous situation."[28] Asked if the Chinese foreign ministry had been unaware of the radar lock-on, China's foreign ministry spokeswoman responded after a six-second silence "it is all right for you to understand so." Three days later, China's defense ministry completely denied the Japanese accusation on its website, saying that the naval vessels' radar had "maintained normal observational alertness, and [that] there was no use of fire-control radar," and accusing Japan of "deliberately creating a tense atmosphere and misleading international opinion."[29] Onodera and Prime Minister Abe insisted that Japan had evidence that fire-control radar had been used against

Japanese ships and called for resumption of negotiations to establish a maritime communication mechanism to prevent accidental confrontations.[30] The Japanese government did not pursue this issue much further, however, partly because of the nuclear weapons test that North Korea conducted on February 12; China's cooperation was essential for getting a UN Security Council resolution to apply effective sanctions against Pyongyang.

In the meantime, Abe started to explore the possibility of improving relations with Beijing. When Xi Jinping assumed the presidency of the People's Republic of China in March, Abe sent him a congratulatory telegram; in remarks made in London, Abe emphasized that "China is an important country for Japan, and I am always ready to have a summit meeting with President Xi Jinping." By the spring of 2013, the number of Chinese tourists to Japan was approaching the level of the previous year, and bureaucratic contacts on economic issues had become easier.[31] On the other hand, eight CMS ships had intruded into the territorial waters around Uotsuri-jima, the largest number of Chinese ships ever, and China refused to hold the annual China-Japan-South Korea Trilateral Summit in the spring.[32] In June, Abe sent Special Adviser to the Cabinet Yachi Shōtarō to China to explore the possibility of a meeting between Abe and Xi.[33] Another Special Adviser to the Cabinet, Iijima Isao, based on contacts he made during his visit to China in July, stated that a summit would take place "in the not-too distant-future."[34] The *China Daily*, however, reported that a Chinese authority had denied such a possibility as "not true and . . . fabricated" and said that Japan should "stop using empty slogans" and "take concrete measures to improve strained ties."[35] On August 12, the 35th anniversary of the signing of the Treaty of Peace and Friendship between Japan and China of 1978, *Xinhua* asserted that "Sino-Japanese relations are approaching their lowest ebb since normalization, and the responsibility resides solely with the Japanese side."[36]

On the occasion of the G20 Summit in St Petersburg that September, Abe approached Xi immediately before the summit meeting and held a conversation with him for several minutes. Since Chinese Vice-Minister of Foreign Affairs Li Baodong had stated beforehand that there were no plans to hold a summit meeting with Japan, saying "how could we arrange a meeting when there is no basis for dialogue," Abe's approach appeared to take Xi by surprise. Not wanting to repeat such an unexpected encounter, China made it very clear that there was no possibility of a bilateral summit with Japan at the APEC Summit to be held in Bali, Indonesia, in October; perhaps to avoid a foreign-minister-level meeting, Chinese Foreign Minister Wang Yi canceled his participation in the APEC Foreign Ministers Meeting.[37] What the Chinese meant by "concrete measures" needed to overcome the impasse between the two countries was not revealed, but the central issue appeared to be whether Japan would admit the existence of a "territorial dispute" over the Senkakus. The Abe government appeared ready to acknowledge that a "diplomatic issue" but not a "territorial issue" existed.[38] In any case, President Xi Jinping did not want to have a bilateral meeting with Prime Minister Abe Shinzō in the autumn of 2013.

Neither did President Park Geun-hye of South Korea, a daughter of Park Chung-hee, the third president of the ROK and a very controversial authoritarian ruler who helped realize the "Miracle of Han River"—South Korea's rapid economic growth. Although her father was known for his close relationship with Japan after concluding the Treaty on Basic Relations between the two countries in 1965 despite strong street protests in Seoul, Park Geun-hye, strong-willed and always dead serious, could not afford to be considered overtly pro-Japanese even to protect her father's achievements. Her father had good relations with Japan not because he liked Japan but because he wanted the South to become strong.

When both Park and Abe won their respective elections in December 2012, Abe, a grandson of Prime Minister Kishi Nobusuke who had been a good friend of Park Chung-hee, must have thought that he could establish a similar relationship with Park Geun-hye. One of his first diplomatic initiatives was to send his special envoy, Nukaga Fukushirō, a former finance minister and chairman of the Japan-Korea Parliamentarians' Union, on January 4, to congratulate her on her victory. Park told Nukaga that "she was pleased that Abe had sent a special envoy at an early time." When Nukaga asked her to visit Japan soon, she responded positively and promised to consider it.[39] Japan's foreign ministry, which had been prepared to bring the case of Takeshima to the International Court of Justice after President Lee Myung-bak visited the disputed island, decided not to do so at this moment as a friendly diplomatic gesture to Park's incoming government.[40]

President Park, however, seemed uncertain about the direction of the Abe government. In her address commemorating the 94th anniversary of the March 1st Independence Movement, she stressed that "the historic dynamic of one party being a perpetrator and the other party a victim will remain unchanged even after a thousand years have passed," and argued that "in order for our two nations to heal the wounds of the past as soon as possible and march together toward a future of shared progress, it is necessary for the Japanese Government to change unreservedly and behave in a responsible manner."[41] The South Korean government reacted strongly when Deputy Prime Minister Asō Tarō and two other cabinet members visited the Yasukuni Shrine in late April during its spring festival. Foreign Minister Yun Byung-se postponed his visit to Japan.

On her first visit to Washington, DC, as ROK president, President Park Geun-hye told President Obama that "Japan needs to have a correct perception of history . . . to realize peace in Northeast Asia,"[42] and said in an interview with *The Washington Post* that "the Japanese have been opening past wounds and have been letting them fester, and this applies not only to Korea but also to other neighboring countries. . . . This arrests our ability to really build momentum, so I hope that Japan reflects upon itself."[43] President Park made an official visit to China in late June, the first time a South Korean president had visited China before going to Japan.

From Abe's perspective, President Park's attitude must have been disappointing; he himself did not visit Yasukuni and had made several gestures signaling his desire to improve relations with Seoul. However, the South Korean leader had become suspicious of the intentions of Abe and other important members of his government. According to a report in *JoongAng Ilbo*, Deputy Prime Minister Asō's remarks during his meeting with Park at her inauguration drove the president to be even more harshly critical of Japan. Asō reportedly said to Park: "In the United States they had a Civil War between the South and the North. People living in the North and South still have different historical memories and different historical perspectives. How can two countries like Korea and Japan share similar historical perceptions when even people living in the same country hold different perspectives?"[44] *JoongAng Ilbo* attributes these comments as the motivation behind Park's statements in her March 1st Movement address as well as the reason for South Korea's strong reaction to Asō's visit to the Yasukuni Shrine that April. Prime Minister Abe's legalistic interpretation of "aggression" in a Diet debate did not help either. In response to a question about ambiguity in the Murayama Statement, Abe said, "The definition of what constitutes aggression has yet to be established in academia or in the international community. Things that happened between nations will look differently depending on which side you view them from."[45] Abe was not silent on Yasukuni, either. "When did South Korea start criticizing Yasukuni? Though there was some criticism during the Kim Dae-jung administration, it was during the Rho Moo-hyun period when the criticism became louder. Before that, there had rarely been such criticism. We need to investigate why its attitude changed. . . . The same is true of China. There was no protest when the prime minister visited after Class A war criminals were included among those memorialized there. It suddenly started doing so one day. . . . It is only natural to express feelings of respect to the war dead who gave up their precious lives for the sake of their nation. We will never bend to any form of threat. We have secured the freedom [to make such visits]."[46] South Korean media reported that Abe had denied Japanese aggression, and the National Assembly passed a resolution criticizing the visits of cabinet members to Yasukuni and Abe's statement regarding history.

The foreign ministers of both countries held a meeting at the time of the ASEAN Foreign Ministers Meeting in July but were unable to improve bilateral relations. During the summer, Abe did not visit Yasukuni Shrine, despite his remarks to the Diet in April. Nevertheless, neither China nor South Korea agreed to hold bilateral summits with Japan, the opportunities for which were readily available at the many upcoming multilateral summits such as APEC, ASEAN+3 and the East Asia Summit.

The Chinese announcement on November 23 that it was establishing an air defense identification zone (ADIZ) in the East China Sea was a blow to any hopes of improving the Sino-Japanese relationship in the immediate future. Since many other countries including the United States and Japan maintain their own ADIZs, China's attempt to establish one was not in itself extraordinary; what was extraordinary was deciding to do so without consulting the countries affected by it. Japan's defense attaché in Beijing was notified only 30 minutes before the decision was announced. Furthermore, because the Chinese ADIZ overlaps widely with Japan's and includes airspace over the Senkaku Islands, the possibility exists for conflict with Japanese monitoring activities. The statement that "China's armed forces will take defensive emergency measures to respond to aircraft that do not cooperate in identification or refuse to follow orders"[47] caused concerns, as it implied that China intended to exercise sovereign rights over airspace beyond its territorial space.

Meanwhile, an episode of friendship between soldiers of South Korea and Japan turned into an embarrassing step toward a further deterioration of relations between the two countries. When a civil war erupted in South Sudan between the government headed by President Salva Kiir and a faction led by former Vice President Riek Machar, the commander of the South Korean PKO unit asked his Japanese counterpart to provide bullets to protect the South Korean encampment in which more than 15,000 civilians had taken shelter. Provision of ammunition was virtually banned under Japan's Three Principles of Arms Exports but, "given the urgent necessity and the highly humanitarian nature of the situation," the Abe government, after the deliberation of the NSC, decided that the Three Principles did not apply to this situation and ordered the SDF unit in South Sudan to supply 10,000 bullets to the South Korean unit. This was a politically risky decision for Abe because previous governments had made it clear that Japan would not provide any ammunition even if requested by the UN Secretary General. However, the South Korean government, fearing it would be accused of cooperating with Japan, denied that the need for ammunition had been "urgent" and reportedly conveyed its "strong regret" that Japan had used the incident for "political purposes," i.e., an alleged attempt to tie the provision of ammunition to an enlargement of Japan's military role.[48] "I can't believe it," Abe told a close associate on December 25. "We provided them with bullets!"[49] On the next day, Abe Shinzō visited the Yasukuni Shrine.

As Abe had repeatedly mentioned, "it was a matter of greatest regret" that he had not visited Yasukuni when he had first been prime minister. After winning a majority in the upper house election in July 2013, he had broader support than when he was out of power, but when he went to Yasukuni this time, he had his traditional nationalist supporters in mind. He had refrained from visiting the shrine in the hope of improving relations with China and South Korea. But given the recent episodes with both countries, better relations must have appeared nearly hopeless. Visiting the shrine would certainly worsen those relations, but not visiting had not achieved anything. Better pay back the debt to his traditional friends now and wait until China and South Korea realized that they would have to deal with him for the foreseeable future.

Immediately after his visit, he issued the following statement:

> Today, I paid a visit to Yasukuni Shrine and expressed my sincere condolences, paid my respects and prayed for the souls of all those who had fought for the country and made ultimate sacrifices. I also visited Chinreisha, a remembrance memorial to pray for the souls of all the people regardless of nationalities who lost their lives in the war, but [are] not enshrined in Yasukuni Shrine. . . .
>
> Japan must never wage a war again. This is my conviction based on the severe remorse for the past. I have renewed my determination before the souls of the war dead to firmly uphold the pledge never to wage a war again. . . .
>
> Regrettably, it is a reality that the visit to Yasukuni Shrine has become a political and diplomatic issue. Some people criticize the visit to Yasukuni as paying homage to war criminals, but the purpose of my visit today, on the anniversary of my administration's taking office, is to report before the souls of the war dead how my administration has worked for one year and to renew the pledge that Japan must never wage a war again.
>
> It is not my intention at all to hurt the feelings of the Chinese and Korean people. It is my wish to respect each other's character, protect freedom and democracy, and build friendship with China and Korea with respect, as did all the previous Prime Ministers who visited Yasukuni Shrine.[50]

Quite predictably, Chinese and South Koreans voiced their objections. Both governments released official statements of protest. But probably the most painful to Abe came from its ally, the US Embassy in Tokyo:

Japan is a valued ally and friend. Nevertheless, the United States is disappointed that Japan's leadership has taken an action that will exacerbate tensions with Japan's neighbors.

The United States hopes that both Japan and its neighbors will find constructive ways to deal with sensitive issues from the past, to improve their relations, and to promote cooperation in advancing our shared goals of regional peace and stability.

We take note of the Prime Minister's expression of remorse for the past and his reaffirmation of Japan's commitment to peace.[51]

China engaged in new tactics to criticize Japan; instead of allowing its people to take to the streets in anti-Japanese rampages, it ordered its ambassadors all around the world to engage in an anti-Japanese propaganda campaign. Within a month after Abe's visit to the shrine, Chinese ambassadors and diplomats in 73 countries and international organizations wrote op-eds and held media interviews as if in a competition to outdo one another in criticizing Abe and Japan. Cui Tiankai, the Chinese ambassador to the United States, for example, argued in his op-ed carried by *The Washington Post*:

The recent homage cannot be separated from the prime minister's denial of Japan's wartime atrocities, and it colors his initiative to revise Japan's constitution to transform its Self-Defense Forces into a military force capable of projecting power outside Japan. This aggressive posture imperils regional security and economic prosperity. By contrast, Japan's acceptance of and repentance for its war crimes would build a foundation for peace and security in the world's most economically dynamic region.

The Yasukuni war shrine is ground zero for the unrepentant view of Japan's wartime aggression. Established in the 19th century to honor Japan's war dead, the shrine imparted a spiritual dimension to Japanese militarism and colonial rule during World War II and became a revered living symbol of that militarism.[52]

Japanese ambassadors all around the world also engaged in this verbal sparring. As Sasae Ken'ichirō, Japanese ambassador to the United States, bluntly pointed out, "It is not Japan that most of Asia and the international community worry about; it is China" and went on to assert:

> [T]he Yasukuni Shrine, which was the focus of Beijing's most recent round of anti-Japan commentaries, is a place where the souls of those who sacrificed their lives for the country since the Meiji Restoration of 1868 have been enshrined. Japanese people visit the shrine to pray for the souls of the war dead—more than 2.4 million—not to glorify war or honour or justify a small number of Class A war criminals. . . .
>
> It is important to note that China began raising this issue with political motives in 1985. At that time, more than 20 visits by prime ministers to Yasukuni had gone unchallenged, even after 14 Class A war criminals had been enshrined there in 1978.[53]

The op-ed battle did not last long. No top-ranking Chinese leader or Politburo member, including Xi Jinping, said much about Japan. The number of Chinese tourists to Japan did not go down in January, and it increased in subsequent months. Since Japanese direct investment in China had declined in 2013 and declined further in 2014, the Chinese leaders must have thought that it was inadvisable to repeat the worsening of relations of 2012. Domestic politics in Japan were different from what they had been in 2012. Then, the DPJ's popularity was at its nadir, and Prime Minister Noda had been pressured to dissolve the Diet. Now, Abe had a solid majority in both houses, and the approval rate of his cabinet did not decrease much after his visit to Yasukuni. On the contrary, according to an *Asahi Shimbun* poll conducted in late January, 41 percent supported Abe's visit to the shrine while 46 percent opposed it; the approval rate of Prime Minister Abe himself was 50 percent, a 4 percent increase from its poll conducted on December 7, the day after the secrecy protection act was passed.[54] The Yasukuni visit was more popular than the secrecy protection act. Seeing these figures, and given the solid support that Abe enjoyed and the economic necessity for better relations with Japan, Beijing cautiously explored ways to improve political ties with Tokyo.

Before China unilaterally designated the ADIZ, Xi Jinping made an important speech at a conference on diplomacy with neighboring countries, which was held on October 24 and 25, 2013, presided over by Premier Li Keqiang and attended by all the members of the Polit-buro Standing Committee. In it Xi stressed the strategic importance of good relations with neighboring countries and stated that "the concepts of friendship, sincerity, benefit and inclusiveness should be highlighted." His statement that "the basic principle of diplomacy with neighbors is to treat them as friends and partners, to make them feel safe and to help them develop" did not appear, at least to the Japanese, to be consistent with the imposition of an air defense iden-tification zone, but after the subsequent turbulent experiences with the ADIZ and Abe's Yasukuni visit, China may have decided to apply this basic principle to its diplomacy with Japan as well. As Xi said, "China and neighboring countries should meet and visit each other more frequently."[55]

Now that Prime Minister Abe had fulfilled his commitment to his conservative friends, he welcomed any moves on the part of Beijing to improve ties with Japan. Fukuda Yasuo, who had many acquain-tances in China as a result of his long government career as well as a good Sino-Japanese relationship during his tenure as prime minis-ter, played an important role in improving ties between Abe and Xi. In consultation with Fukuda, Abe asked him to convey the govern-ment's current thinking about Sino-Japanese relations to the Chinese leaders. Fukuda visited China secretly in June and discussed various issues facing the two countries. He told his Chinese interlocutors that Abe would not visit the Yasukuni Shrine any more. To reassure the Chinese that Fukuda really had Abe's confidence, he asked to have NSC Director-General Yachi Shōtarō accompany him to China on another confidential visit on July 28.[56] Fukuda and Yachi met with Xi Jinping and set the trend toward improved relations in motion; the target date for a bilateral meeting was the APEC Summit to be held in Beijing in early November. Xi ordered former Foreign Minister Yang Jiechi to work with Yachi. After being briefed by Fukuda and Yachi, Abe decided to send positive signals to China. In his UN speech in September, Abe refrained from any statements that might imply criticism of China. And in his policy speech to the Diet on September 29, Abe stated, "As for Japan and China, we share an inseparable relationship, and the peaceful development of China is a great opportunity for Japan. In order for Japan and China, which bear great responsibility for the peace and prosperity of the region, to build *stable friendly relations* going forward, I intend to realize a summit meeting at an early time and further develop a 'mutually beneficial relationship based on common strategic interests' through dialogue"[57] (my italics). This was the first time that Abe used "friendly relations" in regard to China in a policy speech to the Diet.

Yachi and Akiba Takeo, director-general of MOFA's International Legal Affairs Bureau, made secret visits to China in October, and Akiba's Chinese counterpart, Kong Xuanyou, made a secret visit to Tokyo on November 2. On November 6, just a few days before the Beijing APEC Summit, Yachi and Akiba visited Beijing and engaged in intensive negotiations that night. It was after 2:00 AM on November 7 that Yachi and Yang Jiechi reached a four-point agreement. Japan announced the Japanese text as well as the following English translation.

Toward the improvement of the Japan-China relations, quiet discussions have been held between the Governments of Japan and China. Both sides have come to share views on the following points:

1. Both sides confirmed that they would observe the principles and spirit of the four basic documents between Japan and China and that they would continue to develop a mutually beneficial relationship based on common strategic interests.
2. Both sides shared some recognition that, following the spirit of squarely facing history and advancing toward the future, they would overcome political difficulties that affect their bilateral relations.
3. Both sides recognized that they had different views as to the emergence of tense situations in recent years in the waters of the East China Sea, including those around the Senkaku Islands, and shared the view that, through dialogue and consultation, they would prevent the deterioration of the situation, establish a crisis management mechanism and avert the rise of unforeseen circumstances.
4. Both sides shared the view that, by utilizing various multilateral and bilateral channels, they would gradually resume dialogue in political, diplomatic and security fields and make an effort to build a political relationship of mutual trust.[58]

The agreement did not mention "Yasukuni" or the existence of "territorial disputes" over the Senkaku/Diaoyu Islands. The second point in the agreement simply indicated "some recognition" of the need to overcome "political difficulties," which the Chinese would be able to explain to their public as including the Yasukuni issue. The third point again simply acknowledged the existence of "different views" about the causes of "tense situations in recent years" around the Senkaku/Diaoyu Islands and in the East China Sea. The Chinese would be able to say that Japan had finally come to accept that there were different views on the issue. The agreement was quite satisfactory to Japan especially with regard to the third point. Tokyo had always acknowledged that differences existed between Japan and China over current conditions in the Senkakus since 1970s; what it did not accept was the existence of "territorial disputes," which implies at least some legal basis for China's claims to the islands. Furthermore, it was important for Tokyo that China agreed that "tense situations" emerged only "in recent years." Verbal agreement does not mean resolution of conflicts, however; China has continued to send ships to the territorial waters around the Senkakus ever since.

In any case, with the four-point agreement as the basis for Sino-Japanese relations, Xi Jinping and Abe Shinzō held a summit meeting at the time of the APEC Summit. Although the picture released to the press showed the two men looking the other way while shaking hands, the symbolic value of the bilateral summit was significant. From late 2014 to 2015, bilateral activities became very active in many fields. Ministerial meetings in many functional areas increased. The number of Chinese visitors to Japan reached an unprecedented level in 2015. Abe and Xi would meet again in April 2015 on the sidelines of the 60th anniversary of the Bandung Conference in Indonesia.

The relationship between Seoul and Tokyo, however, did not improve in tandem with that between Beijing and Tokyo. President Park Geun-hye had two other issues in mind. The first was the Abe administration's attitude toward history in general and the comfort women issue in particular. The South Korean government and the media became very suspicious about Abe's attitude toward the Kōno Statement when Chief Cabinet Secretary Suga Yoshihide on February 21, 2014 mentioned the possibility of investigating the drafting process

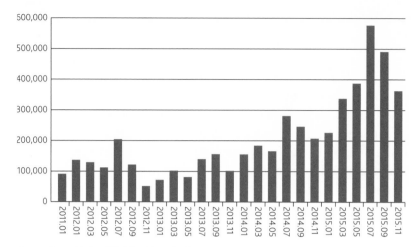

Source: Japan National Tourism Organization

Figure 11.1   Chinese Visitors to Japan

behind the statement; a South Korean foreign ministry source complained that this was "tantamount to destroying the foundation for sharing the correct view of history" and could not help but be seen as "an attempt to deny the Kōno Statement and turn back the clock of history." The South Korean media predicted that the Kōno Statement would be revised and that ROK-Japan relations would worsen.[59] When Suga announced that the government would set up a team to review the drafting process on February 28, he said that one focus of the investigation would be whether there had been consultation with the South Korean government in working out the wording of the statement.[60] The United States, seeing the continuing conflict between its two important allies in East Asia, began to stress the need for easing tensions and welcomed statements by both Suga and Abe in March that the Abe Cabinet would not revise the Kōno Statement. At the strong urging of the United States, both Abe and Park agreed to hold a trilateral meeting with President Obama in The Hague at the time of the Nuclear Security Summit. Abe's denial that the Kōno Statement would be revised was a positive factor behind Park's decision to meet him, but she continued to have suspicions about what the results of the review would be.

The report of the study group revealed no surprises; in fact, it rather supported the view that there was no need to amend the Kōno

Statement. One issue that right-wing nationalists considered critical was whether the statement had been drafted on the assumption of "forced conscription" (*kyōsei renkō*), i.e., that girls had forcibly been rounded up in a manner similar to kidnapping. Abe often said in the Diet that the Japanese government had found no evidence of forced conscription. If the drafting of the Kōno Statement had been based on an assumption different from Abe's—that is, if the underlying assumption had been that recruitment had been conducted by force—in the view of right-wing nationalists, the Statement should be revised. The report found no such assumption. The sentence in the Statement, "their recruitment, transfer, control, etc., were conducted generally against their will, through coaxing, coercion, etc.," it said, was drafted on the assumption that "coaxing, coercion, etc." did not include "forced conscription." The report also revealed that the drafting process had included frequent consultations with the South Korean government, which had accepted and expressed its appreciation for the statement as a whole.[61] The chairman of the study group, Tadaki Keiichi, a former prosecutor general, pointed out in a press conference, "We have not confirmed any fact that the Japanese side finds absolutely unacceptable. However, neither did South Korea make a concession."[62] The Korean government released its reaction to the report and criticized the Abe government for revealing diplomatic communications as contrary to the normal conduct of international diplomacy and for trying to "undermine the credibility" of the Kōno Statement.[63]

Another development that was quite important to nationalists took place in early August; the *Asahi Shimbun* officially retracted several news stories on comfort women, including items by a former Japanese soldier describing his experience of forcefully rounding up 200 young Korean girls on Jeju Island.[64] The factual credibility of his story had been doubted since the early 1990s, but the *Asahi* finally announced that it, too, had concluded that his statement was false. Since nationalists including Prime Minister Abe had long criticized the *Asahi* for publishing doubtful statements, they felt that their criticisms were vindicated. Obviously, the retraction of one soldier's lie did not negate the overall coercive nature of the comfort women system, which, as the study group's report had just revealed, was the point of the Kōno Statement. Perhaps the *Asahi* decided to retract its reports because the study group's report made it clear that the Kōno Statement had not been based on the newspaper's stories, and thus their retraction would not undermine the Statement's credibility. With the review of the Kōno Statement and the *Asahi*'s decision to retract the fabricated stories, it became much easier for Prime Minister Abe to accept the Kōno Statement, although hard-core right-wingers continued to denounce it.

A bilateral summit between Abe and Park was not easy to bring about, however. The two leaders shared tables at APEC- and ASEAN-related summits, but the South Korean government was still unwilling to hold a bilateral meeting. Both Seoul and Tokyo came to a vague understanding, however, that in 2015, they should take advantage of the establishment of diplomatic relations in 1965 to improve bilateral relations. And so on June 22, 2015, Abe participated in the ceremony marking the 50th anniversary in Tokyo hosted by the South Korean Embassy, and Park attended the ceremony in Seoul hosted by the Japanese Embassy. "In order to advance ties between the two countries, I will make efforts with President Park," Abe said. "This year is a historic opportunity for the two nations to move toward the future," said Park.[65]

Seoul, however, was still unsure about what Abe's attitude toward history would be in the statement he was planning to issue commemorating the 70th anniversary of the end of the Second World War in 2015. Along with the anti-Abe media in Japan, it suspected that Abe's remarks on that occasion would virtually deny the credibility of the Murayama and Kōno statements. Abe assembled a group of historians and experts to review the modern history of Japan and advise him in drafting his 70th anniversary statement. Most of the group's members agreed about the aggressive nature of prewar Japan and that postwar Japan had been built on a full reflection on the disastrous mistakes made in the 1930s and 1940s. The Komeito leadership also insisted on adhering to the positions made by the Murayama and Kōno statements. But the media not just in Japan but in South Korea and elsewhere reported that Abe might produce a reactionary statement. They began to assert that Abe was not interested in repeating the four key terms in the Murayama and Kōno statements: aggression, colonial rule, feelings of deep remorse and apology.

To the surprise of many of Abe's critics, the long statement he read on August 14, 2015 included all four expressions and many more:

> Incident, aggression, war—we shall never again resort to any form of the threat or use of force as a means of settling international disputes. We shall abandon colonial rule forever and respect the right of self-determination of all peoples throughout the world.
>
> With deep repentance for the war, Japan made that pledge. Upon it, we have created a free and democratic country, abided by the rule of law, and consistently upheld that pledge never to wage a war again. While taking silent pride in the path we have walked as a peace-loving nation for as long as seventy years, we remain determined never to deviate from this steadfast course.
>
> Japan has repeatedly expressed the feelings of deep remorse and heartfelt apology for its actions during the war. In order to manifest such feelings through concrete actions, we have engraved in our hearts the histories of suffering of the people in Asia as our neighbors: those in Southeast Asian countries such as Indonesia and the Philippines, and Taiwan, the Republic of Korea and China, among others; and we have consistently devoted ourselves to the peace and prosperity of the region since the end of the war.
>
> Such position articulated by the previous cabinets will remain unshakable into the future.[66]

The media waiting to attack Abe were virtually at a loss for words. Some complained that his statements were indirect and not straightforward and that the references to colonial rule were insufficient. Although some liberals may not have been happy with Abe's statement that "We must not let our children, grandchildren, and even further generations to come, who have nothing to do with that war, be predestined to apologize," few would disagree with the sentence that follows: "Still, even so, we Japanese, across generations, must squarely face the history of the past. We have the responsibility to inherit the past, in all humbleness, and pass it on to the future." Overall, the Japanese public accepted the Abe Statement: according to a Kyodo poll conducted on August 14–15, 44.2 percent viewed the statement positively while 37 percent responded in the negative; the approval rate of the cabinet increased by 5.5 percent to 43.2 from 37.7 percent the previous month.[67]

The South Korean media expressed some criticism. While stating that Abe's statement "did not quite live up to our expectations," President Park Geun-hye, in her speech on the "70th anniversary of liberation" on August 15, also said:

> we take note of the message that was clearly conveyed to the international community; namely, that the position articulated by the previous Japanese cabinets, based on its apologies and remorse for how Japan's aggression and colonial rule caused tremendous damage and suffering to the people of many countries in Asia, and caused suffering to the "comfort women" victims, will remain unshakable into the future.[68]

Foreign Minister Yun Byung-se said on August 16 in a media interview that, if the pending China-Japan-South Korea summit took place, a bilateral meeting between Abe and Park would be possible.[69] China also refrained from harsh criticism of the Abe Statement, and when Park Geun-hye met with Xi Jinping on September 2 on the occasion of China's 70th anniversary of its victory in World War II, they agreed to hold a trilateral summit in the autumn.

The US government, too, welcomed the Abe Statement. A White House National Security spokesman said, "We welcome Prime Minister Abe's expression of deep remorse for the suffering caused by Japan during the World War II era, as well as his commitment to uphold past Japanese government statements on history."[70] When President Park Geun-hye visited the United States in late October, President Obama urged her to resolve the history issues between South Korea and Japan.[71]

On November 1, the summit meeting among the leaders of China, Japan and South Korea took place in Seoul after a two and half year hiatus. Abe held a bilateral summit with Premier Li Keqiang on the same day and the first bilateral summit with President Park Geun-hye since both of them took power. The abnormal relations between Tokyo and Seoul finally ended. The thorniest issue between the two countries, the comfort women problem, had not been resolved, but the two leaders agreed to make efforts to resolve it soon, preferably within 2015, during the 50th anniversary of the establishment of diplomatic relations in 1965.

Two judicial cases in Seoul cast a shadow over the prospects for improving bilateral relations. The former Seoul bureau chief of the *Sankei Shimbun*, a Japanese newspaper, had been indicted for defaming President Park, and a case had been brought before the Constitutional Court of South Korea on the constitutionality of the 1965 Agreement on the Settlement of Problems Concerning Property and Claims and on Economic Co-operation. On December 17, the Seoul Central District Court found the *Sankei* correspondent not guilty, and the South Korean prosecution office declared that it would not appeal. On December 23, the Constitutional Court declined to rule on the constitutionality of the case on the grounds that the issue, compensation for forced labor during colonial rule, was unrelated to the Agreement. Seeing these developments, Abe sent NSC adviser Yachi to Seoul to work out a final compromise with Lee Byung-kee, presidential chief of staff and a former ambassador to Japan. Based on their negotiations, Foreign Minister Kishida Fumio and Foreign Minister Yun Byung-se declared on December 28 that the comfort women "issue is resolved finally and irreversibly." "The Government of Japan," Kishida said, "is painfully aware of [its] responsibilities. . . . Prime Minister Abe expresses anew his most sincere apologies and remorse to all the women who underwent immeasurable and painful experiences and suffered incurable physical and psychological wounds as comfort women." Japan agreed to pay from its budget 1 billion yen to a foundation to be set up by the South Korean government to support the former comfort women. Yun said that his government "will strive to solve" the issue of the statue representing a comfort woman in front of the Japanese Embassy in Seoul "in an appropriate manner through taking measures such as consulting with related organizations about possible ways of addressing this issue." Both agreed that they "will refrain from accusing or criticizing each other regarding this issue in the international community, including at the United Nations."[72] Whether this issue is really "finally and irreversibly resolved" remains to be seen, but what is significant is that both governments have made this declaration as clearly as possible.

Asia in the Second Decade of the 21st Century

Asia nearly 40 years since Prime Minister Fukuda Takeo gave his policy speech in Manila is completely different from the Asia of the 1970s. The Asia of the past had been a place of constant warfare. Since the Opium Wars, long periods of time without major civil wars or wars between countries had hardly ever existed there. During the so-called "long peace" of the Cold-War era, Asia had not been peaceful. But no major civil war has occurred in East Asia since the end of the Cambodian Civil War. Nor have there been any wars between countries, in East Asia at least, since the China-Vietnam War in 1979. Asia during the Cold War, especially East Asia, had been a divided region. Few countries had normal international relations with China. Although tensions remain, peace has continued in the East Asia of the 21st century. The maintenance of peace, at least in East Asia, uneasy though it may be, is one of the accomplishments of 21st-century Asia thus far.

Indeed, it is this peace that is the basis for Asian prosperity and for the rapid deepening of its economic interdependence. Asia was a poor region in the 1960s; South Korea's per capita GDP in 1966 (USD 129) was lower than that of Ghana (USD 269) and much lower than that of South Africa (USD 592). Now South Korea's per capita GDP is 18 times bigger than that of Ghana and 3.8 times that of South Africa. China's GDP in the 1980s was less than one-fifth of that of Japan, but now it is more than twice Japan's GDP. There are still poor countries in Asia, but as Figure 11.2 clearly shows, country by country, Asia has undergone dynamic growth. This growth has been achieved in tandem with deepening economic interdependence among Asian countries as well as between Asia and the rest of the world.

Domestic politics within each country has also greatly changed. Democracy has become entrenched in South Korea, Taiwan, the Philippines and Indonesia, all of which had once been under authoritarian regimes. The most dramatic turn of events occurred in Myanmar, where President Thein Sein took the initiative to liberalize, with the result that the general election of 2015 has seen a peaceful transfer of power from the military to the National League for Democracy. Of course, this does not mean that the trend toward democracy has

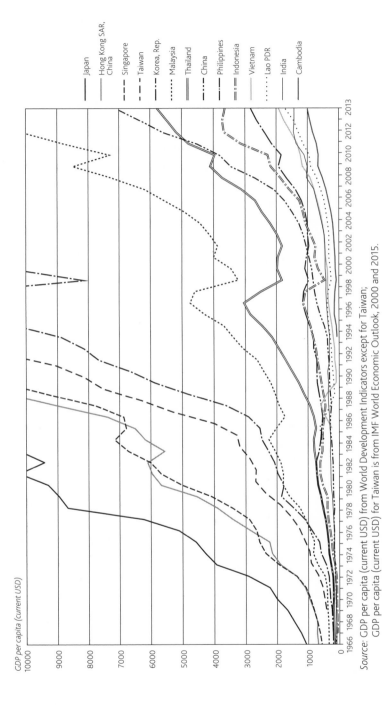

GDP per capita (current USD)

Source: GDP per capita (current USD) from World Development Indicators except for Taiwan;
GDP per capita (current USD) for Taiwan is from IMF World Economic Outlook, 2000 and 2015.

Figure 11.2 Per Capita GDP in Asian Countries

followed a straight line. In Thailand, democratization seemed to be progressing when its constitution was revised following the Asian economic crisis. Then the business tycoon Thaksin Shinawatra took advantage of democratization, entered politics and won support in the countryside by conducting pork-barrel spending in the provinces. The inner circle of his administration was always suspected of corruption. Between 2005 and 2006, the political situation was chaotic, and finally in the autumn of 2006, the army brought his administration to an end by staging a bloodless coup while Prime Minister Thaksin was out of the country. Politics in Thailand has not been stable since. Whenever the military and the anti-Thaksin elites in Bangkok decide to hold elections and return to civilian rule, the Thaksin faction supported by people in rural areas has won. Thaksin's youngest sister, Yingluck Shinawatra, became prime minister after the election in July 2011, but a military coup toppled her government in 2014.

In Malaysia and Singapore, the changeover from capable, idiosyncratic, if ironfisted, leaders to technocrats is proceeding. The Malaysia of Abdullah Badawi and Najib Razak is gradually shaking off the authoritarian aura of the Mahathir era and moving toward a moderate government. In Singapore, there are no signs that the overwhelming predominance of the People's Action Party will waver even after the death of Lee Kuan Yew in 2015. The task for both countries, which are implementing pro forma popular sovereignty and the rule of law, is probably how to transform their technocratic and often anti-liberal "hegemonies" into a more liberal system of governance. Cambodia, once the scene of genocide, still suffers from the problem of poverty, but since the chaos of 1997, peaceful elections have been held, although the three-decade-long rule of Prime Minister Hun Sen has continued to show an authoritarian streak. There are no signs of change in the political system of Brunei under the enlightened despotism of Sultan Bokiah. But even within Brunei there seems to be a strong awareness that the development of human resources is a task for the 21st century.

Trends in China, Vietnam and Laos promoting change from within socialist systems have also been dynamic. Although challenges to Communism as the ruling party are still not allowed, in both China and Vietnam transition in the supreme leadership has continued to be peaceful, and political reform is advancing, albeit slowly. On the economic side, however, the changes in those two countries over the past 40 years have been phenomenal. Although Laos continues to experience difficulties with economic development, even so, it is enthusiastic about economic exchange.

The country where stagnation and isolation persist is North Korea. The North has shown no signs of changing the despotic nature of its regime since Kim Jong Un took power after the death of Kim Jong Il in December 2012, and it continues to be in conflict with the international community over the nuclear issue. It conducted a nuclear weapons test in February 2013 and again in January 2016. Japan under Prime Minister Abe engaged with North Korea in an effort to resolve the abduction issue. The two sides reached an agreement in Stockholm in 2014, in which Pyongyang said it would open an investigation into those abducted and missing while Tokyo promised to lift sanctions. The agreement collapsed, however, when the Abe government decided to impose sanctions again because of the North's nuclear weapons and missile tests in early 2016.

In addition to these changes in the countries of East Asia themselves, relations with other Asian countries have been developing to an extent that would have been unimaginable 30 to 40 years ago. An outstanding example of this is the strengthening of relations between East Asia and India, where economic liberalization has been taking place since 1990. China has improved its relations with India; Japan, too, has strengthened its ties there, and there is a partnership between ASEAN and India as well. Even the countries of Central Asia, which were part of the Soviet Union during the Cold War, are groping toward relationships with China and Japan. Along with the interdependence of and deepening relations within East Asia, relations with the Asia that surrounds it, and with the countries of the Pacific and elsewhere, are progressing in multifaceted ways.

The complex web of regional institutions has also developed to an extent unimaginable in the 1980s. Now the ASEAN Summit, ASEAN+3 Summit and East Asia Summit have, along with the APEC Summit, become routine annual events. All these frameworks also involve ministerial meetings and senior officials meetings (SOMs). ASEAN, which since its founding in 1967 had existed without any legally binding documents, finally in 2007 agreed on the ASEAN Charter as the organization's constitution. Even before that, ASEAN member states had agreed in 2003 to establish an ASEAN Security Community, an ASEAN Economic Community and an ASEAN Social and Cultural Community by 2020. In 2007, they decided to accelerate the process of community-building and realized the formation of these communities in 2015.

Even from the perspective of cultural phenomena, the trend toward Asian integration is becoming pronounced. Whether one accepts the existence of the deep-rooted commonality of Asian-ness that underpinned Okakura Tenshin's thesis that "Asia is one," on the surface at least, the overwhelming impression that travelers to Asia have consistently been conscious of has been its diversity. Now that situation is in the process of changing. It seems possible to say that a common culture—what might be called an "East Asian way of life"—may be emerging, especially among the East Asian urban middle class.[73]

In South Korea, when President Kim Dae-jung decided to liberalize the introduction of Japanese culture, there were fears that South Korean popular culture would be swept away by Japanese pop culture. What, in fact, happened was just the opposite. Although it was only natural that Japanese *anime* and dramas would be readily watched in South Korea, what has been even more impressive is the "Korean Wave," the boom in Korean pop culture dramas that are filling the TV screens not just of Japan but of all the countries of East Asia.

In the past, tourists traveling in Asian countries used to be overwhelmingly Japanese. Now, the nationalities of tourists in Asia are very diverse. While there are still many Japanese at tourist sites throughout Asia, there are also South Koreans, Taiwanese and, now, in vast numbers, mainland Chinese. In Asia 30 years ago, the opportunities for ordinary people to meet other ordinary people were extremely limited. This is the first time in history that people-to-people contact exists in Asia on such a large scale.

But these changes cannot necessarily be said to be irreversible. To repeat, the reason that Asia, especially East Asia, now seems to be stepping up its degree of integration is mainly because the region is at peace and because economic and other forms of intercourse are unobstructed. If a phenomenon like the Cold War were to occur once again, or, above all, if a war were to break out, Asia might revert to the fragmented region it once was.

In that sense, we still have to keep a watchful eye on geopolitical conditions in North Korea, the Taiwan Strait, the East China Sea and the South China Sea. North Korea has continued to defy international pressure and refuses to terminate its nuclear and missile programs. Though tremendously dismayed by North Korean behavior, China has been extremely reluctant to apply serious sanctions against Pyongyang probably in the belief that the collapse of the regime would be worse for China than the continuing existence of a North Korea capable of launching long-range nuclear missiles. Given the determination of the North Korean regime to develop its nuclear and missile technology and China's reluctance to impose serious sanctions on the North, Japan needs to strengthen its deterrence measures against Pyongyang in close cooperation with South Korea and the United States. In view of the recent reconciliation between Tokyo and Seoul, the three allies need to work together closely to create a system of effective deterrence and defense on the Korean peninsula. The fundamental uncertainty with respect to North Korea is that, while it is likely to pursue its nuclear weapons capability, its inhumane regime may face a sudden collapse from within. Japan, South Korea and the United States need to maintain close working relations with China and Russia in preparation for such a contingency.

In comparison with the decade after the 1996 Taiwan Strait crisis, the possibility of the Taiwan Strait issue immediately giving rise to an armed conflict is extremely low because of the change in PRC policy toward Taiwan, the conciliatory attitude of the Ma Ying-jeou government and the huge increase in economic interdependence between Taiwan and the mainland. Although the election in 2016 of the Democratic Progressive Party's Tsai Ing-wen as President so far does not appear to be bringing the Taiwan Strait issue back into contention, caution on both sides of the strait is essential to maintain stability. If mishandled, the situation there has the possibility of developing into an armed confrontation between China and the United States. Although it is inconceivable that China could instantly overwhelm Taiwan militarily, year by year, the military balance is tilting in China's favor.

Situations in the East China Sea and the South China Sea also have to be watched carefully. As the last two chapters described,

Japan and China continue to experience a tense relationship over a group of small islands in the East China Sea. An agreement was reached in 2014 to bring relations back into a normal pattern. But the need for the two countries to create a crisis management system remains unchanged. Japan needs to urge China to establish a more reliable mechanism to monitor and prevent accidental interactions in sensitive areas. The resolution of territorial disputes in the South China Sea appears very difficult since the Chinese legal claim to the area based on its "nine-dash line" is so different from current mainstream views of international maritime law. Unilateral land claims over disputed areas by China and other countries are not productive for stabilizing international politics in the South China Sea.

"An Asia that is slowly becoming one" has been one of the themes of this book. What sort of relationship with Asia has Japan wrestled with in the past 40 years? That has been another theme. Data exist that indicate the fruits of Japan's Asian relationships—the results of an opinion poll called the AsiaBarometer which is carried out in all the regions of Asia.[74] One of the questions in this survey is "Do you think that Japan has a good influence or a bad influence on [your country]?" The results of the surveys conducted in almost all areas of Asia between 2003 and 2006 are shown in Figure 11.3. Judging from the numbers that combine "good influence" and "rather good influence," one can see that Japan is considered to have a positive influence in the overwhelming majority of Asian countries. In almost all the countries of Southeast Asia, South Asia and Central Asia, Japan is rated very highly. "Japan in Asia" is a country that is perceived as having a good influence by most Asian peoples. Almost 40 years ago, Prime Minister Fukuda Takeo advocated the importance of "heart-to-heart" contact as the pillar of his Fukuda Doctrine. The result of Japan's contact with Asia over those years can be said to manifest itself in Japan's high positive ratings.

A closer look at the table, however, shows that this is only part of the Asian evaluation of Japan. The ratings for Japan in East Asia, especially in China and South Korea, are strikingly low. Moreover, as one can see by tracing the years in which the surveys were taken, China's assessment of Japan in 2003, 2005 and 2006 has gotten markedly worse with every passing year. Japan has been unable to

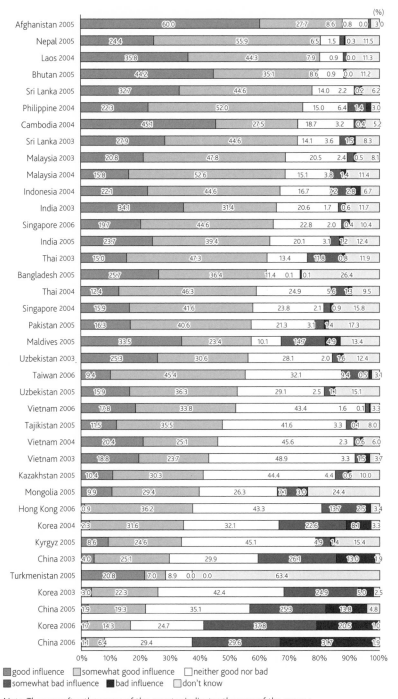

(%)

Country	good influence	somewhat good influence	neither good nor bad	somewhat bad influence	bad influence	don't know
Afghanistan 2005	60.0	27.7	8.6	0.8	0.0	3.0
Nepal 2005	24.4	55.9	6.5	1.5	0.3	11.5
Laos 2004	35.8	44.3	7.9	0.9	0.0	11.3
Bhutan 2005	44.2	35.1	8.6	0.9	0.0	11.2
Sri Lanka 2005	32.7	44.6	14.0	2.2	0.2	6.2
Philippine 2004	22.3	52.0	15.0	6.4	1.4	3.0
Cambodia 2004	45.1	27.5	18.7	3.2	0.4	5.2
Sri Lanka 2003	27.9	44.6	14.1	3.6	1.5	8.3
Malaysia 2003	20.8	47.8	20.5	2.4	0.5	8.1
Malaysia 2004	15.8	52.6	15.1	3.8	1.4	11.4
Indonesia 2004	22.1	44.6	16.7	7.2	2.8	6.7
India 2003	34.1	31.4	20.6	1.7	0.6	11.7
Singapore 2006	19.7	44.6	22.8	2.0	0.4	10.4
India 2005	23.7	39.4	20.1	3.1	1.2	12.4
Thai 2003	15.0	47.3	13.4	11.8	0.8	11.9
Bangladesh 2005	25.7	36.4	11.4	0.1	0.1	26.4
Thai 2004	12.4	46.3	24.9	5.6	1.3	9.5
Singapore 2004	15.9	41.6	23.8	2.1	0.9	15.8
Pakistan 2005	16.3	40.6	21.3	3.1	1.4	17.3
Maldives 2005	33.5	23.4	10.1	14.7	4.9	13.4
Uzbekistan 2003	25.3	30.6	28.1	2.0	1.6	12.4
Taiwan 2006	9.4	45.4	32.1	9.4	0.5	3.1
Uzbekistan 2005	15.9	36.3	29.1	2.5	1.1	15.1
Vietnam 2006	17.8	33.8	43.4	1.6	0.1	3.3
Tajikistan 2005	11.5	35.5	41.6	3.3	0.1	8.0
Vietnam 2004	20.4	25.1	45.6	2.3	0.6	6.0
Vietnam 2003	18.8	23.7	48.9	3.3	1.5	3.7
Kazakhstan 2005	10.4	30.3	44.4	4.4	0.6	10.0
Mongolia 2005	9.9	29.4	26.3	7.1	3.0	24.4
Hong Kong 2006	0.9	36.2	43.3	13.7	2.5	3.4
Korea 2004	2.3	31.6	32.1	22.6	8.1	3.3
Kyrgyz 2005	8.6	24.6	45.1	4.9	1.4	15.4
China 2003	4.0	25.1	29.9	26.1	13.0	1.9
Turkmenistan 2005	20.8	7.0	8.9	0.0	0.0	63.4
Korea 2003	3.0	22.3	42.4	24.9	5.0	2.5
China 2005	1.9	19.3	35.1	25.3	13.8	4.8
Korea 2006	1.7	14.3	24.7	37.8	20.5	1.0
China 2006	1.1	6.4	29.4	29.6	31.7	1.9

0% 10% 20% 30% 40% 50% 60% 70% 80% 90% 100%

■ good influence ☐ somewhat good influence ☐ neither good nor bad
■ somewhat bad influence ■ bad influence ☐ don't know

Note: The year after the name of the country indicates the year of the survey.

Figure 11.3   Japan's Influence (AsiaBarometer Survey)

build "heart-to-heart" relations with its nearest neighbors, China and South Korea. As our description of the last two chapters amply demonstrated, from 2011 to 2015, Japan's relations with South Korea and China were abnormally bad. In the first two decades of the 21st century, this is yet another "Japan in Asia."

As this book has shown, the two "Japans in Asia" are the result of Japanese interaction with the rest of Asia over many years. The Fukuda Doctrine, ODA in Asia, direct investment in Southeast Asia, participation in the Cambodian peace process, the founding of APEC, the Japan-North Korea normalization talks, grappling with the history problem, the response to the Asian economic crisis, dealing with the abductee issue, relations with China—all these have been serious efforts. Japan has been on the receiving end of many initiatives and responses from the rest of Asia as well as from the rest of the world, some more or less predictable and many totally unexpected. It has been able to respond to the developmental needs of Southeast Asia and South Asia over the long term as well as in situations of crisis. In this sense, relations with many Southeast Asian countries have gone through virtuous cycles. China has had its own agenda for realizing the "Chinese Dream," and South Korean domestic politics has not easily allowed the government to strike a strategic deal with Japan. Different Japanese political leaders have had their distinct conceptions of what constitutes the right relation with China and South Korea. Depending on the combination of personalities and political needs in Japan, China and South Korea, relationships have sometimes been trapped in a vicious cycle within the complicated domestic politics of the three countries.

Prime Minister Abe succeeded in normalizing relations with both China and South Korea by the end of 2015. His relations with Southeast Asian and South Asian countries have always been good, and his sense of the strong importance of the alliance with the United States remains unshaken. Japan's domestic political foundation has never been more solid. The Fukuda Doctrine in 1977 emphasized "heart-to-heart contact" with Southeast Asia in mind.

It should now be the goal of Japanese diplomacy to achieve "heart-to-heart contact" with all the peoples of Asia including those in the Northeast.

Notes

In citing works in the notes, the short title has generally been used after the first occurrence.

Preface to the Japanese Edition

1 Tanaka Akihiko, *Nit-Chū kankei, 1945–1990* [Sino-Japanese relations, 1945–1990], (Tokyo: Tōkyō Daigaku Shuppankai, 1991) and *Anzen hoshō: sengo 50nen no mosaku* [Security: the 50-year postwar search], (Tokyo: Yomiuri Shimbunsha, 1997).

2 See, for example, Tanaka Akihiko, *Sekai shisutemu* [The world system], (Tokyo: Tōkyō Daigaku Shuppankai, 1989); *Atarashii "chūsei": 21-seiki no sekai shisutemu* [The new "Middle Ages": the world system in the 21st century], (Tokyo: Nihon Keizai Shimbunsha, 1996), *The New Middle Ages: The World System in the 21st Century*, trans. Jean Connell Hoff, (Tokyo: International House of Japan, 2002); *Wādo poritikusu: gurōbarizēshon no naka no Nihon gaikō* [Word politics: Japanese diplomacy under globalization], (Tokyo: Chikuma Shobō, 2000); and *Fukuzatsusei no sekai: "tero no seiki" to Nihon* [The world of complexity: Japan and the "century of terrorism"], (Tokyo: Keisō Shobō, 2003).

Chapter 1
Asia before the End of the Cold War

1 See Tanaka, *The New Middle Ages,* Chapter 1. The standard history of the Cold War, written after it ended, is John Lewis Gaddis, *The Cold War: A New History* (New York: Penguin Press, 2005).

2 For this change in strategy and Japanese-Chinese relations in the 1970s, see Tanaka, *Nit-Chū kankei,* Chapter 3; and Mōri Kazuko, *Nit-Chū kankei: sengo kara shinjidai e* [Japanese-Chinese relations from the postwar period to the new era], (Tokyo: Iwanami Shoten, 2006), Chapter 2.

3 Even standard histories of postwar Japanese foreign relations do not contain much analysis that deals comprehensively with relations between Japan and Asia. See Watanabe Akio, ed., *Sengo Nihon no taigai seisaku: kokusai kankei no hen'yō to Nihon no yakuwari* [Postwar Japan's foreign policy: changes in international relations and Japan's role], (Tokyo: Yūhikaku, 1985); Iokibe Makoto, ed., *Sengo Nihon gaikōshi* [Postwar Japanese diplomacy], rev. ed. (Tokyo: Yūhikaku, 2006),

translated as Iokibe Makoto and Robert D. Eldridge, *The Diplomatic History of Postwar Japan* (London; New York: Routledge, 2011). Suehiro Akira and Yamakage Susumu, eds., *Ajia seiji keizairon: Ajia no naka no Nihon o mezashite* [A discussion of Asian politics and economics: moving toward a Japan in Asia], (Tokyo: NTT Shuppan, 2001), and Miyagi Taizō, ed., *Sengo Nihon no Ajia gaikō* [Japan's postwar Asia diplomacy], (Tokyo: Mineruva Shobō, 2015) make a useful correction to this tendency. Watanabe Akio, *Ajia Taiheiyō no kokusai kankei to Nihon* [Japan and Asia-Pacific international relations], (Tokyo: Tōkyō Daigaku Shuppankai, 1992) includes an insightful chapter on the region's various relations with Japan. Ōba Mie, *Ajia Taiheiyō chiiki keisei e no dōtei: Kyōkai kokka Nichi-Gō aidentiti mosaku to chiikishugi* [The process of forming the Asia-Pacific region: regionalism and border states Japan and Australia's search for identity], (Kyoto: Mineruva Shobō, 2004) deals head on with the identity of Japan and Australia vis-à-vis the Asia-Pacific region. For an attempt to explain regional systems in Asia and Japan's place in them from a long-term historical perspective with a special focus on the maritime regions, there is Shiraishi Takashi, *Umi no teikoku: Ajia o dō kangaeru ka* [Maritime empires: how should we think about Asia?], (Tokyo: Chūō Kōron Shinsha, 2000). A convenient overview of the international political history of East Asia in the sense of Northeast Asia from the 19th through the 21st centuries is Kawashima Shin and Hattori Ryūji, eds., *Higashi Ajia kokusai seijishi* [The international political history of East Asia], (Nagoya: Nagoya Daigaku Shuppankai, 2007), but it is light on Southeast Asia. Books that provide overviews of the politics and economies of each of the countries or territories in Asia have increased in recent years. See, among others, Kojima Tomoyuki, Kokubun Ryōsei, et al., eds., *Higashi Ajia*, Kokusai jōsei bēshikku shirīzu 1 [East Asia; Basics of International Affairs Series 1], (Tokyo: Jiyū Kokuminsha, 1997); Satō Hiroshi and Iwasaki Ikuo, eds., *Ajia seiji dokuhon* [Asian politics reader], (Tokyo: Tōyō Keizai Shinpōsha, 1998); Kuroyanagi Yoneji, et al., eds., *Tōnan/Minami Ajia, Oseania*, Kokusai jōsei bēshikku shirīzu 2 [Southeast/South Asia, Oceania; Basics of International Affairs Series 2], (Tokyo: Jiyū Kokuminsha, 2001); Watanabe Toshio, ed., *Ajia keizai dokuhon* [Asian economy reader], 3rd ed. (Tokyo: Tōyō Keizai Shinpōsha, 2003); Hara Yōnosuke, ed., *Ajia keizairon* [Discussion of the Asian economy], rev. ed. (Tokyo: NTT Shuppan, 2001).

4   Yamada Hiroshi, *Poru Poto (kakumei)shi: gyakusatsu to hakai no yonenkan* [The history of Pol Pot (and his revolution): four years of genocide and destruction], (Tokyo: Kōdansha, 2004), p. 154; and Imagawa Yukio, *Kanbojia to Nihon* [Cambodia and Japan], (Tokyo: Rengō Shuppan, 2000), p. 44.

5   Miyake Wasuke, *Gaikō ni shōri wa nai: dare mo shiranai Nihon gaikō*

ura no ura (There are no victories in diplomacy: behind the behind-the-scenes Japanese diplomacy that no one knows], (Tokyo: Fusōsha, 1990), p. 165.

6 Tomiyama Yasushi, *Kanbojia senki: minzoku wakai e no michi* [Cambodian war diaries: the path to ethnic reconciliation], (Tokyo: Chūō Kōronsha, 1992), p. 40.

7 On international politics vis-à-vis Vietnam after the Vietnam War, see Nakano Ari, *Gendai Betonamu no seiji to gaikō: kokusai shakai sannyū e no michi* [Politics and diplomacy in Vietnam today: the road to entry into the international community], (Tokyo: Akatsuki Inshokan, 2006).

8 For a multifaceted analysis of Japanese diplomacy in the 1970s, see Nihon Seiji Gakkai, ed., *Nenpō seijigaku: kiki no Nihon gaikō: 70 nendai* [The Annuals of the Japanese Political Science Association: Japanese diplomacy in crisis: the 70s], (Tokyo: Iwanami Shoten, 1997).

9 For a comprehensive analysis of relations between Japan and Southeast Asia up to this period with a focus on relations with China as well, see Okabe Tatsumi, *Tōnan Ajia to Nihon no shinro: "hannichi" no kōzō to Chūgoku no yakuwari* [Southeast Asia and the course for Japan to follow: "anti-Japanese" structure and China's role], (Tokyo: Nihon Keizai Shimbunsha, 1976).

10 A fairly recent study is Wakatsuki Hidekazu, *"Zenhōi gaikō" no jidai: reisen hen'yōki no Nihon to Ajia 1971–80nen* [The era of "omni-directional diplomacy": Japan and Asia in the period of Cold-War change, 1971–80], (Tokyo: Nihon Keizai Hyōronsha, 2006).

11 The English translation of Prime Minister Fukuda's speech in Manila (Fukuda Doctrine Speech) can be found online as part of the Institute for Advanced Studies on Asia's "The World and Japan" database project at http://worldjpn.grips.ac.jp/documents/texts/docs/19770818.S1E.html.

12 Ochi Takao, "Detantoki no Nihon gaikō: Fukuda seiken no gaikō wakugumi" [Japanese diplomacy in an age of détente: the diplomatic framework of the Fukuda administration], MA thesis, Graduate School of Law and Politics, Tokyo University, 2004.

13 Tomoda Seki, *Nyūmon gendai Nihon gaikō: Nit-Chū kokkō seijōka igo* [Introduction to modern Japanese diplomacy: after the normalization of Japanese-Chinese diplomatic relations], (Tokyo: Chūō Kōronsha, 1988), pp. 55–63; Sudō Sueo, "Hendōki no Nihon gaikō to Tōnan Ajia" [Japanese diplomacy and Southeast Asia in a period of transition], in Nihon Seiji Gakkai, ed., *Nenpō seijigaku*, pp. 43–58; Sudō Sueo, *The Fukuda Doctrine and ASEAN: New Dimensions in Japanese Foreign Policy* (Singapore: Institute of Southeast Asian Studies, 1992); Soeya Yoshihide, "Vietnam in Japan's Regional Policy," in Nishihara Masashi and James W. Morley, eds., *Vietnam Joins the World* (Armonk, NY: M.E. Sharpe, 1997), pp. 175–99.

14   See Soeya, "Vietnam in Japan's Regional Policy," p. 176.

15   Japan paid reparations to Burma, the Philippines, Indonesia and South Vietnam worth about USD 1.012 billion and extended grant aid as quasi-reparation to Laos, Cambodia, Thailand, Burma, Republic of Korea, Malaysia, Singapore, and Micronesia worth USD 495 million. Quasi-reparations (*jun baishō*) were virtual reparations in the form of grant aid to those countries that waived reparations claims in the San Francisco Peace Treaty, those not applicable as a war party against Japan such as the ROK, and to Burma after formal reparations ended. See Ministry of Foreign Affairs, "Japan's Official Development Assistance White Paper 2004: 'Accomplishments and Progress of 50 Years'" (Ministry of Foreign Affairs, 2004), p. 27.

16   Gaimushō Keizai Kyōryokukyoku, ed., *Wagakuni no seifu kaihatsu enjo 1* [Japan's official development assistance 1], (Tokyo: Kokusai Kyōryoku Suishin Kyōkai, 1991), pp. 22 and 82.

17   Prime Minister Suzuki Zenkō's Bangkok Speech, January 19, 1981, online (in Japanese) on "The World and Japan" database at http://worldjpn. grips.ac.jp/documents/texts/exdpm/19810119.S1J.html. Kokusai Kyōryoku Jigyōdan, *Hitozukuri, kunizukuri, kokoro no fureai: Kokusai Kyōryoku Jigyōdan 25 nenshi* [People-building, country-building, heart-to-heart exchanges: the 25-year history of the Japan International Cooperation Agency], (Tokyo: Kokusai Kyōryoku Jigyōdan, 1999), p. 77.

18   Prime Minister Nakasone Yasuhiro's Kuala Lumpur Speech, May 8, 1983, online (in Japanese) on "The World and Japan" database at http:// worldjpn.grips.ac.jp/documents/texts/exdpm/19830508.S1J.html; "Yonmannin no shinnichika o sodatete 30nen" [30 years training 40,000 Japanophiles], online (in Japanese) at http://www.jica.go.jp/topics/ news/2014/2o15o217_01.html.

19   For the role of World Bank loans to Japan, see Ōta Yasuo and Arima Yoshiyuki, *Sengo fukkō hiroku: Segin yūshi ni manabu Nippon saisei* [Hidden history of postwar reconstruction: lessons of World Bank loans for Japan's re-generation], (Tokyo: Nihon Keizai Shimbun Shuppansha, 2012).

20   For the origins and an evaluation of the project, see Shimomura Yasutami, "Tojōkoku no ōnāshippu to enjo kōka: Tai Tōbu rinkai kaihatsu keikaku no jirei" [Developing country ownership and aid effectiveness: the case of Thailand's Eastern Seaboard Development Plan], Hosei University Repository, March 31, 2000, online (in Japanese) at http://repo.lib. hosei.ac.jp/bitstream/10114/3642/1/ning_1-1_simomura.pdf.

21   Tomiyama, *Kanbojia senki*, p. 7.

22   Ibid., p. 78.

23   Imagawa, *Kanbojia to Nihon*, p. 56.

24   For systematic comparative analyses of the democratization process in Asia, see, among others, Takeda Yasuhiro, *Minshuka no hikaku seiji: Higashi Ajia shokoku no taisei hendō katei* [Comparative politics of

democratization: the process of regime change in the countries of East Asia], (Kyoto: Mineruva Shobō, 2001); Fujiwara Kiichi, "'Minshuka' no seiji keizaigaku: Higashi Ajia ni okeru taisei hendō" [The political-economy of "democratization": regime change in East Asia], in Tōkyō Daigaku Shakai Kagaku Kenkyūjo, ed., *Gendai Nihon shakai 3: kokusai hikaku 2* [Modern Japanese society 3: an international comparison 2], (Tokyo: Tōkyō Daigaku Shuppankai, 1992).

25 Fujiwara Kiichi, "Firipin ni okeru 'minshushugi' no seido to undō" [The "democracy" movement and system in the Philippines], *Shakai Kagaku Kenkyū* [Journal of Social Science] 40,1 (1988), 1–94; Asano Yukiho, *Firipin: Marukosu kara Akino e* [The Philippines: from Marcos to Aquino], (Tokyo: Ajia Keizai Kenkyūjo, 1992); Takeda, *Minshuka no hikaku seiji*, Chapter 5, section 1.

26 Shiraishi, *Umi no teikoku*, p. 172.

27 Economic data derived from World Development Indicators on the World Bank's online database, data.worldbank.org.

28 George P. Shultz, *Turmoil and Triumph: My Years as Secretary of State* (New York: Scribner's, 1993), p. 616.

29 The US, which did not want to make its support for Corazon Aquino obvious, did not respond to this request. Shultz, *Turmoil and Triumph*, pp. 619–20.

30 Ibid., p. 624.

31 Ibid., pp. 632–36.

32 Ronald Reagan, *An American Life, The Autobiography* (New York: Simon & Schuster, 1990), p. 365.

33 Shultz, *Turmoil and Triumph*, p. 636.

34 On South Korean politics, see Kimiya Tadashi, *Kankoku: minshuka to keizai hatten no dainamizumu* [South Korea: the dynamism of democratization and economic development], (Tokyo: Chikuma Shobō, 2003); Moriyama Shigenori, *Kankoku gendai seiji* [Contemporary Korean politics], (Tokyo: Tōkyō Daigaku Shuppankai, 1998). On the political culture of the Korean peninsula, the classic study is still Gregory Henderson, *Korea: The Politics of Vortex* (Cambridge, MA: Harvard University Press, 1968). For democratization, see Takeda, *Minshuka no hikaku seiji*, Chapter 6, section 1.

35 Don Oberdorfer and Robert Carlin, *The Two Koreas: A Contemporary History*, rev. and updated ed. (New York: Basic Books, 2014), p. 99.

36 Ibid., p. 107.

37 Nakasone Yasuhiro, *Tenchi ujō: gojūnen no sengo seiji o kataru* [All sentient beings: talking about 50 years of postwar politics], (Tokyo: Bungeishunjū, 1996), p. 446. For Sejima's role, see his own account, *Sejima Ryūzō kaisōroku ikusanga* [Many mountains and rivers: Sejima Ryūzō's recollections], (Tokyo: Sankei Shimbunsha, 1995), pp. 419–44.

38 See above note 27.

39 Oberdorfer and Carlin, *Two Koreas*, p. 127.

40 Ibid., p. 128.

41 Ibid., p. 3.

42 Ibid., p. 134.

43 For a concise introduction to Taiwanese politics, see Wakabayashi Masahiro, *Taiwan: hen'yō shi chūcho suru aidentiti* [Taiwan: a changing and wavering identity], (Tokyo: Chikuma Shobō, 2001). Wakabayashi analyzes contemporaneously step by step the process that led to democratization. See also Wakabayashi Masahiro, ed., *Taiwan: tenkanki no seiji to keizai* [Taiwan: politics and the economy in a time of transition], (Tokyo: Tabata Shoten, 1987); Wakabayashi Masahiro, *Taiwan: bunretsu kokka to minshuka* [Taiwan: democratization and the fragmented state], (Tokyo: Tōkyō Daigaku Shuppankai, 1992). Takeda, *Minshuka no hikaku seiji*, Chapter 4, section 1, contains an analysis of Taiwanese democratization.

44 Wakabayashi, *Taiwan: hen'yō shi chūcho suru aidentiti*, p. 31.

45 Interesting on the language situation in Taiwan is Wakabayashi Masahiro, *Taiwan no Taiwangojin, Chūgokugojin, Nihongojin: Taiwanjin no yume to genjitsu* [Taiwan's Taiwanese speakers, Chinese speakers, Japanese speakers: the dream and reality of the Taiwanese people], (Tokyo: Asahi Shimbunsha, 1997).

46 On the 228 Incident, see He Yilin, *Ni nihachi jiken: "Taiwanjin" keisei no esunoporitikusu* [The 228 Incident: the ethnopolitics of the formation of a "Taiwanese people"], (Tokyo: Tōkyō Daigaku Shuppankai, 2003).

47 Matsuda Yasuhiro, *Taiwan ni okeru ittō dokusai taisei no seiritsu* [The establishment of a one-party system in Taiwan], (Tokyo: Keiō Gijuku Daigaku Shuppankai, 2006).

48 Takeda, *Minshuka no hikaku seiji*, p. 215.

49 Nemoto Takashi, "Seiji to keizai" [Politics and the economy], in Ayabe Tsuneo and Ishii Yoneo, eds., *Motto shiritai Myanmā*, 2nd ed. [I want to learn more about Myanmar], (Tokyo: Kōbundō, 1994), pp. 233–34.

50 Heiwa Anzen Hoshō Kenkyūjo, ed., *Ajia no anzen hoshō, 1989–1990* [Asian security, 1989–1990], (Tokyo: Asagumo Shimbunsha, 1990), p. 44.

51 Takeda, *Minshuka no hikaku seiji*, p. 226.

52 Ibid., p. 218.

Chapter 2
Northeast Asia and the End of the Cold War

1 There are an enormous number of works on Chinese politics, far too many to list here. For the most recent comprehensive overviews, see,

among others, Mōri Kazuko, *Gendai Chūgoku seiji* [Modern Chinese politics], 3rd ed. (Nagoya: Nagoya Daigaku Shuppankai, 2012); Kokubun Ryōsei, *Chūka Jinmin Kyōwakoku* [The People's Republic of China], (Tokyo: Chikuma Shobō, 1999); Kojima Tomoyuki, *Chūgoku gendaishi: kenkoku 50 nen, kenshō to tenbō* [Modern Chinese history: 50 years since founding, review and prospects], (Tokyo: Chūō Kōron Shinsha, 1999). On Chinese diplomacy, see Okabe Tatsumi, *Chūgoku no taigai senryaku* [China's foreign strategy], (Tokyo: Tōkyō Daigaku Shuppankai, 2002).

2 Amako Satoshi, *Kyoryū no taidō: Mō Takutō vs Tō Shōhei*, Chūgoku no rekishi 11 [The dragon stirs: Mao Zedong vs. Deng Xiaoping; Chinese history 11], (Tokyo: Kōdansha, 2004); Liang Zhang, ed., *The Tiananmen Papers* (New York: Public Affairs, 2001).

3 Tanaka Akihiko, "Ten'anmon jiken igo no Chūgoku o meguru kokusai kankyō" [The international environment around China after the Tiananmen incident], *Kokusai Mondai* [International Affairs] 358 (1990), 31.

4 Ibid., pp. 33–34.

5 Tanaka, *Nit-Chū kankei*, pp. 172–87.

6 The Recruit scandal was a bribery case involving the Recruit Holdings company in which it sold unlisted shares in a subsidiary to high-profile politicians and bureaucrats at low prices allowing them to take advantage of huge profits once the stocks were listed.

7 Mikuriya Takashi, Watanabe Akio (interviews, compilation), *Shushō kantei no ketsudan: Naikaku Kanbō Fukuchōkan Ishihara Nobuo no 2600-nichi* [Decisions at the Prime Minister's Official Residence: Ishihara Nobuo's 2,600 days as deputy chief cabinet secretary], (Tokyo: Chūō Kōronsha, 1997), p. 51.

8 *Asahi Shimbun* (in Japanese), morning edition, June 5, 1989.

9 *Nihon Keizai Shimbun* (in Japanese), morning edition, June 5, 1989.

10 *Asahi Shimbun* (in Japanese), evening edition, June 6, 1989.

11 Ibid., morning edition, June 8, 1989.

12 Ibid., morning edition, June 9, 1989.

13 Ibid., evening edition, June 16, 1989.

14 Japan started extending ODA to China in 1980. Yen loans—concessional loans denominated in yen—constituted the major portion of Japan's ODA to China; the term of a typical loan to China was 3 percent interest, 30-year repayment with a 10-year grace period. Japan committed its "first yen loans" to seven projects largely covering infrastructure construction worth 330.9 billion yen for the period from FY1980 to FY1984. It provided the "second yen loans" to 16 projects worth 470 billion yen for the period from FY1984 to FY1989. Prime Minister Takeshita Noboru promised to extend the "third yen loans" worth 810 billion yen for the period from FY1990 to FY1995 when he visited China in August 1988.

Thus, Japanese sanctions meant freezing the implementation of this huge loan package. Kaigai Keizai Kyōryoku Kikin, eds., *Kaigai Keizai Kyōryoku Kikin 30 nenshi* [30-year history of the Overseas Economic Cooperation Fund], (Tokyo: Kaigai Keizai Kyōryoku Kikin), pp. 129–37.

15 *Asahi Shimbun* (in Japanese), evening edition, June 27, 1989.

16 "Political Declaration: Declaration on China," July 15, 1989, online on "The World and Japan" database at http://worldjpn.grips.ac.jp/documents/texts/summit/19890715.D4E.html.

17 Deng Xiaoping, *Selected Works of Deng Xiaopng*, vol. 3, 1982–1992 (Beijing: Foreign Language Press, 1994), p. 315.

18 Ibid., p. 298.

19 Okabe, *Chūgoku no taigai senryaku*, p. 218. English translation partially based on that in Zhao Quansheng, *Interpreting Chinese Foreign Policy: The Micro-Macro Linkage Approach* (New York: Oxford University Press, 1996), pp. 53–54.

20 Foreign policy address to the 118th National Diet (special session), March 2, 1990, online (in Japanese) on "The World and Japan" database at http://worldjpn.grips.ac.jp/documents/texts/fam/19900302.SXJ.html.

21 *Asahi Shimbun* (in Japanese), evening edition, April 10, 1990.

22 Ibid., evening edition, April 13, 1990.

23 Ibid., morning edition, April 17, 1990.

24 Kim Suk-hyun, *Chū-Kan kokkō seijōka to Higashi Ajia kokusai seiji no hen'yō* [Normalization of relations between China and the ROK and changes in international politics in East Asia], (Tokyo: Akashi Shoten, 2010), p. 42; Roh Tae Woo, *Korea: A Nation Transformed, Selected Speeches* (Oxford; New York: Pergamon Press, 1990), p. 57.

25 The idea of "cross-recognition" was proposed by Kamiya Fuji in 1969 and became famous when it was put forth once again by Kissinger in 1975. Kamiya Fuji, *Chōsen hantō de okita koto okiru koto* [What has happened and will happen on the Korean peninsula], (Tokyo: PHP Kenkyūjo, 1991).

26 Kim, *Chū-Kan kokkō seijōka to Higashi Ajia kokusai seiji no hen'yō*, pp. 47–48; Roh, *Korea: A Nation Transformed*, p. 9.

27 Oberdorfer and Carlin, *Two Koreas*, p. 156.

28 Ibid., p. 159.

29 Ibid., p. 61.

30 Mikhail Sergeevitch Gorbachev, *Memoirs* (New York: Doubleday, 1996), p. 544.

31 On this visit to Pyongyang, Shevardnadze requested that future Soviet-North Korean trade be on a "cash basis," *Aera* (in Japanese), (October 9, 1990).

32 Kihl Young Whan, "North Korea's Foreign Relations: Diplomacy of Promotive Adaptation," *Journal of Northeast Asian Studies* 10,3 (1991), 34.

33 Oberdorfer and Carlin, *Two Koreas*, pp. 168–69.

34 Imamura Hiroko, *Kita Chōsen: "kyokō no keizai"* [North Korea: the "fabricated economy"], (Tokyo: Shūeisha, 2005), p. 28.

35 Suzuki Masayuki, *Kita Chōsen: shakaishugi to dentō no kyōmei* [North Korea: the resonance between socialism and tradition], (Tokyo: Tōkyō Daigaku Shuppankai, 1992). For a more journalistic account of North Korean politics and society, see Bradley K. Martin, *Under the Loving Care of the Fatherly Leader: North Korea and the Kim Dynasty* (New York: Thomas Dunne Books, 2004).

36 On the early stages of Japanese-North Korean diplomatic negotiations, see Okonogi Masao, "Nit-Chō kokkō kōshō to Nihon no yakuwari" [Japanese-North Korean diplomatic negotiations and the role of Japan], in Okonogi Masao, ed., *Posuto reisen no Chōsen hantō* [The post-Cold-War Korean peninsula], (Tokyo: Nihon Kokusai Mondai Kenkyūjo, 1994), pp. 246–73.

37 Article III of the Treaty on Basic Relations reads, "It is confirmed that the Government of the Republic of Korea is the only lawful Government in Korea as specified in Resolution 195 (III) of the United Nations General Assembly." Although the scope of this provision would seem to apply to the entire Korean peninsula, in response to a question at the House of Representatives' Foreign Affairs Committee on September 5, 1974, Matsunaga Nobuo, head of the Treaties Bureau, said, "If we look at Resolution 195, the second provision reads, 'a lawful government having effective control and jurisdiction over that part of Korea where the Temporary Commission was able to observe and consult and in which the great majority of the people of all Korea reside.'" Therefore, "we do not recognize today's South Korea and the government of South Korea as the one and only government of the entire Korean peninsula; we recognize it as a country and a government that has actual and effective control of and jurisdiction over the southern part. The understanding of the government when it signed the Treaty on Basic Relations between Japan and the Republic of Korea was exactly the same; it was, in fact, for the aim and purpose of making this clear that this provision in Article III was made" (*Shūgiin Gaimu Iinkai giroku* [Records of the House of Representatives' Foreign Affairs Committee meeting], no. 3, September 5, 1974). This statement is called the "Kimura Declaration" because it was approved by then Foreign Minister Kimura Toshio. When this was reported in South Korea, the Kimura Declaration was regarded "as a sign of Japanese perfidy and [led to] massive demonstrations; some of the demonstrators broke into the Japanese Embassy in Seoul and ransacked it." Lee Chong-sik, *Japan and Korea: The Political Dimension* (Stanford: Hoover Institute Press, 1985), p. 81. Although it is hard to imagine at the present vantage point in the 21st century, for a long time, even into the 1990s, the understanding existed in Japan (sometimes quite strongly) that North Korea was the more legitimate government of the two on the Korean peninsula. Diet member Doi Takako, for example, who induced Bureau Chief Matsunaga to make the above statement,

promoted North Korea's position in the United Nations and urged that
it be made clear that Article III of the Basic Treaty refers only to south
of the 38th parallel.

38　Tanabe Makoto, "Nit-Chō kokkō kaifuku ni kaketa Nihon Shakaitō
fukuiinchō Tanabe Makoto ga akasu: kore ga 'Kanemaru hō-Chōdan'
no butaiura da" [Tanabe Makoto, vice-chairman of the Japan Socialist
Party involved in restoring Japanese-North Korean relations, tells all:
this is what happened behind the scenes of the "Kanemaru Delegation
to North Korea"], *Gekkan Asahi* [Asahi Monthly], (December 1990), 75.

39　*Asahi Shimbun* (in Japanese), morning edition, July 7, 1989. Roh,
Korea: A Nation Transformed, p. 61.

40　*Asahi Shimbun* (in Japanese), morning edition, January 21, 1989.

41　*Shūgiin Yosan Iinkai giroku* [Records of the House of Representatives'
Budget Committee meeting] 9,1 (March 30, 1989), p. 6.

42　*Asahi Shimbun* (in Japanese), morning edition, March 30, 1989.

43　Ibid., morning edition, April 4, 1989.

44　Tanabe, "Nit-Chō kokkō kaifuku ni kaketa Nihon Shakaitō fukuiinchō Tanabe Makoto ga akasu," p. 6.

45　According to *Asahi Shimbun* reporter Kobayashi Keiji, the sequence
of events and the substance of the secret contacts are as follows. The
Ministry of Foreign Affairs had it in mind to contact North Korea
in order to resolve the Fujisan Maru affair, but no progress had been
made. Therefore, it appealed to Yoshida Takeshi, the president of the
trading company Shin Nihon Sangyō [New Japan Industry], about the
possibility of secret talks with the North "several months after" Prime
Minister Takeshita declared in the Diet his intention to talk with the
DPRK. President Yoshida was "a young entrepreneur who had inherited
a company that had been trading with North Korea since his father's
generation" and frequently traveled back and forth to North Korea; "he
also had connections with the leadership of the Workers' Party of North
Korea." Yoshida conveyed the Ministry of Foreign Affair's intentions to
North Korea, and in February 1990 the reply came from North Korea to
Yoshida, who was visiting on business, that it would accept secret talks.
Paris was agreed on as the place for the talks, and the date was set as
March 28–30. Those attending from the Japanese Foreign Ministry were
Kawashima Yutaka, deputy director-general of the Asian Affairs Bureau,
and Okamoto Tsuyoshi, deputy director of the Northeast Asian Section;
on the North Korean side were Kim Dong Chul, head of the Committee
of Cultural Relations with Foreign Countries, and Mr S, an adviser to
the Workers' Party of North Korea; and President Yoshida. The North
Korean side, "assuming that (1) there would be absolutely no recognition of two Koreas; and (2) opposed to separate membership for North
and South Korea in the UN," regarded normalization of relations with
Japan as "unthinkable at present because it would likely be in a form that

recognizes two Koreas." Deputy Director-General Kawashima explained that, "as long as it is impossible to establish diplomatic relations, it will be impossible to provide large-scale economic assistance." In addition, the No. 18 Fujisan Maru incident, as well as other issues addressed during the Kanemaru visit to North Korea, were largely discussed during these initial secret talks. It is Kobayashi's view that the fact that North Korea told Fukada Hajime, head of the Socialist Party's National Movement Bureau, that it would welcome the Kanemaru visit was because North Korea placed a high value on these secret talks. In July, Mr S visited Japan and on July 22 met with Kawashima, Okamoto and Yoshida at Izuei, an eel restaurant in Ueno; they met again on July 25 at the Miyako Hotel in Kyoto (this time without Yoshida). In August, Kobayashi met twice with Kim Dong Chul, who had come to Japan. Even before the September visit of the advance party of LDP and JSP representatives, Yoshida had gone to Pyongyang and relayed the Japanese government's views on practical matters. "Kanemaru hō-Chō e no michi wa Pari de hajimatta: Nit-Chō kōshō no butaiura" [The road to the Kanemaru visit began in Paris: behind the scenes of the Japanese-North Korean negotiations], *Aera* (December 11, 1990).

46 Ibid.

47 Ibid. (October 9, 1990). According to Tanino Sakutarō, it was in fact Tanabe Makoto who called him "that blockhead" in a French restaurant where Kanemaru, Tanabe and foreign ministry officials were holding discussions over dinner, although Kanemaru later claimed that he had scolded Tanino. Tanino Sakutarō, *Gaikō shōgenroku: Ajia gaikō, kaiko to kōsatsu* [(Diplomatic testimony: Asia diplomacy, memoirs and reflections], (Tokyo: Iwanami Shoten, 2015), p. 198.

48 Nishimura Hideki, *Kita Chōsen yokuryū: dai jūhachi Fujisan Maru jiken no shinsō* [North Korean internment: the truth about the No. 18 Fujisan Maru incident], (Tokyo: Iwanami Shoten, 2004), p. 156.

49 It should be added, however, that Kubo Wataru, vice-chairman of the Socialist Party, who was present at this meeting, says, "Naturally, we did not acknowledge the existence of any responsibility on the part of the Japanese government to pay reparations for those 45 years," Kubo Wataru, "Beniko senchō Kuriura kikanchō no shakuhō o jitsugen shita futaban no tetsuya kōshō" [The two all-night talks that led to the release of Captain Beniko and Chief Engineer Kuriura], *Gekkan Asahi* [Asahi Monthly], (December 1990), 80.

50 Shigemura Toshimitsu, *Kita Chōsen no gaikō senryaku* [North Korea's foreign strategy], (Tokyo: Kōdansha, 2000), p. 111.

51 Hiraiwa Shunji, "'Reisen no shūen' to Nanboku Chōsen kankei: heiwa kyōson seidoka e no sōkoku" ["The end of the Cold War" and North-South Korean relations: the struggle for the systematic implementation of peaceful coexistence], in Okonogi, ed., *Posuto reisen no Chōsen hantō*, p. 109.

52 Izumi Hajime, "Dainihen Chōsen Minshushugi Jinmin Kyōwakoku dainisho gaikō, gunji" [Part II, chapter 2, DPRK foreign policy, military], *Chūgoku sōran 1992 nenban* [China overview 1992 edition], (Tokyo: Kazankai, 1992), from data on p. 525.
53 Oberdorfer and Carlin, *Two Koreas*, p. 95.
54 Ibid., p. 199.
55 *Asahi Shimbun* (in Japanese), morning edition, November 10, 1989.

Chapter 3
Southeast Asia and the End of the Cold War

1 On Vietnamese politics, see Tsuboi Yoshiharu, *Betonamu shinjidai: "yutakasa" e no mosaku* [New era for Vietnam: searching for "wealth"], (Tokyo: Iwanami Shoten, 2008); Tsuboi Yoshiharu, *Betonamu gendai seiji* [Modern Vietnamese politics], (Tokyo: Tōkyō Daigaku Shuppankai, 2002); Furuta Motoo, *Betonamu no genzai* [Vietnam today], (Tokyo: Kōdansha, 1996); Shiraishi Masaya, *Betonamu: kakumei to kensetsu no hazama* [Vietnam: between revolution and nation-building], (Tokyo: Tōkyō Daigaku Shuppankai, 1993), etc.
2 Tomiyama, *Kanbojia senki*, p. 72.
3 Mikhail Gorbachev, *Gorubachofu kaisōroku* [Gorbachev *Memoirs*], trans. Kudō Seiichirō and Suzuki Yasuo (Tokyo: Shinchōsha, 1996), 2: 527.
4 Ibid., p. 502.
5 Qian Qichen, *Ten Episodes in China's Diplomacy* (New York: Harpers, 2005), p. 37.
6 Tomoda Seki, "Detaching from Cambodia," in Nishihara Masashi and James W. Morley, eds., *Vietnam Joins the World* (Armonk, NY: M.E. Sharpe, 1997), pp. 140–41.
7 Tomiyama, *Kanbojia senki*, p. 100.
8 Okabe Tatsumi, "Coping with China," in Nishihara and Morley, eds., *Vietnam Joins the World*, p. 122.
9 Qian, *Ten Episodes*, pp. 42–43.
10 Tomoda, "Detaching from Cambodia," p. 141.
11 *Mainichi Shimbun* (in Japanese), morning edition, August 27, 1988.
12 Tomiyama, *Kanbojia senki*, p. 118.
13 Ibid., pp. 132–34; Imagawa, *Kanbojia to Nihon*, pp. 80–82; Kōno Masaharu, *Wahei kōsaku: tai Kanbojia gaikō no shōgen* [Peace initiatives: witness to Cambodian diplomacy], (Tokyo: Iwanami Shoten, 1999), pp. 34–36.
14 Tomiyama, *Kanbojia senki*, pp. 148–51; Kōno, *Wahei kōsaku*, pp. 34–36.
15 "Statement by Prime Minister Takeshita on the Occasion of the Luncheon Given by the Rt. Hon. the Mayor and the Corporation of

London at the Mansion House," May 4, 1988, online at http://www.
mofa.go.jp/policy/other/bluebook/1988/1988-appendix-2.htm.

16 Ikeda Tadashi, *The Road to Peace in Cambodia: Japan's Role and Involvement*, trans. James W. Griffiths (Tokyo: Japan Times, 1998), p. 19.

17 Kōno, *Wahei kōsaku*, p. 7.

18 Ibid., p. 5.

19 Ibid., pp. 55–56.

20 Tomiyama, *Kanbojia senki*, p. 156.

21 Kōno, *Wahei kōsaku*, pp. 83–87.

22 Tomiyama, *Kanbojia senki*, pp. 157–61; Kōno, *Wahei kōsaku*, pp. 112–
34; Imagawa, *Kanbojia to Nihon*, pp. 98–100; Ikeda, *Road to Peace in
Cambodia*, pp. 66–71.

23 Kōno, *Wahei kōsaku*, p. 145; Tomiyama, *Kanbojia senki*, p. 162. For the
Baker quote, see Elizabeth Becker, *When the War Was Over: Cambodia
and the Khmer Rouge Revolution* (New York: PublicAffairs, 1998), p. 504.

24 Tomiyama, *Kanbojia senki*, p. 164.

25 Qian, *Ten Episodes*, pp. 50–51; Okabe, "Coping with China,", p. 122;
Carlyle A. Thayer, "Sino-Vietnamese Relations, The Interplay of Ideology and National Interests," *Asian Survey* (June 1994), 513–28.

26 On Japan's security policies from the Gulf crisis until the mid-1990s,
see Tanaka Akihiko, *Anzen hoshō: sengo 50nen no mosaku* [Security:
50 postwar years of trial and error], (Tokyo: Yomiuri Shimbunsha,
1997), pp. 309–22; and Tanaka Akihiko, "The Domestic Context: Japanese Politics and UN Peacekeeping," in Nishihara Masashi and Selig
Harrison, eds., *UN Peacekeeping: Japanese and American Perspectives*
(Washington, DC: Carnegie Endowment for the Humanities, 1995), pp.
89–105. On Japan's security-related policy decisions from the Gulf crisis
to the 9/11 terrorist attacks and the Iraq War, see Shinoda Tomohito,
Reisengo no Nihon gaikō: anzen hoshō seisaku no kokunai seiji katei
[Postwar Japanese diplomacy: the domestic political process behind
security policies], (Tokyo: Mineruva Shobō, 2006).

27 Seki Hajime, Ochiai Taosa, Suginoo Yoshio, *PKO no shinjitsu: shirarezaru Jieitai kaigai haken no subete* [The truth about PKO: everything
you didn't know about sending the Self-Defense Forces overseas], (Tokyo:
Keizaikai, 2004), pp. 48–49.

28 Ministry of Foreign Affairs, *Gaikō seisho* [Diplomatic bluebook], 1992
ed. (Tokyo: Ōkurashō Insatsukyoku, 1993), p. 54. For the English
translation of the PKO principles, see http://www.mofa.go.jp/policy/
un/pko/pdfs/contribution.pdf.

29 Tomiyama, *Kanbojia senki*, p. 187; *The Straits Times*, May 6, 1991.

30 Owada Hisashi, *Gaikō to wa nani ka* [What is diplomacy?], (Tokyo:
NHK Shuppan, 1996), p. 221.

31 Akashi Yasushi, *Nintai to kibō: Kanbojia no 560-nichi* [Patience and
hope: 560 days in Cambodia], (Tokyo: Asahi Shimbunsha, 1995), p. 29.

32 Sasaki Yoshitaka, *Umi o wataru Jieitai: PKO rippō to seiji kenryoku* [The Self-Defense Forces overseas: PKO legislation and political power], (Tokyo: Iwanami Shoten, 1992), p. 202.

33 Akashi, *Nintai to kibō*, p. 61.

34 Ishihara Nobuo, *Kantei 2668-nichi: seisaku kettei no butaiura* [2,668 days in the Prime Minister's Official Residence: behind the scenes of policy-making], (Tokyo: NHK Shuppan, 1995), p. 74.

35 Akashi Yasushi, *Ikiru koto ni mo kokoroseki* [In a hurry to live], (Tokyo: Chūō Kōronsha, 2001), p. 80.

36 Ibid., p. 92.

37 Ishihara, *Kantei 2668-nichi*, p. 76. See also Iokibe Makoto, Itō Motoshige, Yakushiji Katsuyuki, eds., *90-nendai no shōgen: gaikō gekihen: moto Gaimushō jimu jikan Yanai Shunji* [Witness to the 90s: diplomatic upheaval, former MOFA Vice-Minister Yanai Shunji], (Tokyo: Asahi Shimbunsha, 2007), pp. 94–105.

38 Mikuriya Takashi and Nakamura Takafusa, eds., *Kikigaki: Miyazawa Kiichi kaikoroku* [Oral history: Miyazawa Kiichi's reminiscences], (Tokyo: Iwanami Shoten, 2004), p. 301. English version: *Politics and Power in 20th-Century Japan: The Reminiscences of Miyazawa Kiichi*, translation ed. Timothy S. George (London: Bloomsbury Academic, 2015), pp. 205–6.

39 *Asahi Shimbun* (in Japanese), morning edition, May 5, 1993.

40 Ishihara, *Kantei 2668-nichi*, p. 76.

41 Imagawa, *Kanbojia to Nihon*, p. 201. Ambassador to Cambodia Imagawa deflected Brigadier General Roos's protest, saying it was an "emergency evacuation out of respect for human life."

42 Akashi, *Ikiru koto ni mo kokoroseki*, pp. 102–3.

Chapter 4
"Asia-Pacific" Experiments

1 The first meeting, held at Château de Rambouillet, France, in November 1975, was a G6 Summit, the participants of which were France, West Germany, Italy, Japan, the United Kingdom and the United States. The meeting became the G7 Summit in 1976 with the participation of Canada. From 1997 to 2014, it was called the G8 Summit with the inclusion of Russia.

2 On trends toward large-scale regionalism since the latter half of the 1980s and an analysis of them, see Yamamoto Yoshinobu, "Chiiki tōgō no seiji keizaigaku: sobyō" [The political economics of regional integration: a rough sketch], *Kokusai Mondai* [International Affairs] 452 (1997), 2–23, and his *Kokusaiteki sōgo izon* [International interdependence], (Tokyo: Tōkyō Daigaku Shuppankai, 1989).

3 Nihon Keizai Shimbunsha, ed., *Shin Nihon keizai: subete ga kawari-hajimeta* [The new Japanese economy: everything has begun to change], (Tokyo: Nihon Keizai Shimbunsha, 1988).

4 George Friedman and Meredith LeBard, *The Coming War with Japan* (New York: St Martin's Press, 1991); James Fallows, "Containing Japan," *Atlantic* (May 1989), 40–54; Edward N. Luttwak, "From Geopolitics to Geo-Economics," *The National Interest*, 20 (Summer 1990), 17–23. On the Japanese side, a work that reflects Japanese self-confidence and sense of rivalry with the US at the time is Morita Akio and Ishihara Shintarō, *The Japan That Can Say No* (New York: Simon & Schuster, 1991).

5 "Asia-Pacific Co-operative Development Group: 'Towards Cooperative Development,'" June 15, 1989, online (in Japanese) on "The World and Japan" database at http://worldjpn.grips.ac.jp/documents/texts/APEC/19890615.O1J.html.

6 On Japan's regional plans in the 1950s and 1960s, see Hoshiro Hiroyuki, *Ajia chiikishugi gaikō no yukue: 1952–1966* [The rise and fall of Japan's Asian regional diplomacy, 1952–1966], (Tokyo: Bokutakusha, 2008).

7 Basic works on ASEAN include Yamakage Susumu, *ASEAN: shinboru kara shisutemu e* [ASEAN: from symbol to system], (Tokyo: Tōkyō Daigaku Shuppankai, 1991), and his *ASEAN pawā: Ajia Taiheiyō no chūkaku e* [ASEAN power: at the core of the Asia Pacific], (Tokyo: Tōkyō Daigaku Shuppankai, 1997); Satō Kōichi, *ASEAN rejīmu: ASEAN ni okeru kaigi gaikō no hatten to kadai* [The ASEAN regime: ASEAN's conference diplomacy, its development and agenda], (Tokyo: Keisō Shobō, 2003).

8 Kojima Kiyoshi, *Japan and a Pacific Free Trade Area* (Los Angeles: University of California Press, 1971).

9 Translated into English as the *Report on the Pacific Basin Cooperation Concept* (Tokyo: Pacific Basin Cooperation Study Group, 1980), online on "The World and Japan" database at http://worldjpn.grips.ac.jp/documents/texts/APEC/19800519.O1E.html.

10 The name was subsequently changed to the Pacific Economic Cooperation Council. Kikuchi Tsutomu, *APEC: Ajia Taiheiyō shinchitsujo no mosaku* [APEC: the search for a new Asia-Pacific order], (Tokyo: Nihon Kokusai Mondai Kenkyūjo, 1995), chapters 2–4.

11 On APEC, see Kikuchi's book and Ōba, *Ajia Taiheiyō chiiki keisei e no dōtei.*

12 Funabashi Yōichi, *Ajia Taiheiyō fyūjon: APEC to Nihon* [Asia Pacific fusion: Japan and APEC], (Tokyo: Chūō Kōronsha, 1995), pp. 3, 88; *Asia Pacific Fusion: Japan's Role in APEC* (Washington, DC: Institute for International Economics, 1995), pp. 61, 58. Since the English version is not as complete, both versions will be cited as necessary.

13 Bob Hawke, *The Hawke Memoirs* (Port Melbourne: William Heinemann Australia, 1994), pp. 430–34.

14 Funabashi, *Ajia Taiheiyō fyūjon*, pp. 86–87; cf. *Asia Pacific Fusion*, p. 57.

15 Ibid., pp. 317–18; cf. *Asia Pacific Fusion*, p. 212.

16 Funabashi, *Asia Pacific Fusion*, pp. 74–75.

17 The account of the EAEC is based on Tanaka Akihiko, "The Development of the ASEAN+3 Framework," in Melissa Curley and Nicholas Thomas, eds., *Advancing East Asian Regionalism* (London; New York: Routledge, 2007), pp. 55–58. See also Satō Kōichi, "Higashi Ajia Keizai Kaigi kōsō o meguru kokusai kankei: Mahatīru kōsō to Ajia Taiheiyō kyōryoku" [International relations behind plans for an East Asian Economic Caucus: the Mahathir proposal and Asia-Pacific cooperation], *Gaikō Jihō* [International Affairs, Japan] 1286 (March 1992), 4–21, and his "EAEC kōsō to ASEAN + 3 hikōshiki shunōkaigi" [The EAEC proposal and the ASEAN + 3 informal summit talks], *Tōa* [East Asia] 404 (February 2001), 58–76.

18 *Asahi Shimbun* (in Japanese), morning edition, December 12, 1990. On December 10, Mahathir had made the plan public ahead of time at a news conference, ibid., December 11, 1990.

19 *Asahi Shimbun* (in Japanese), evening edition, December 14, 1990. English-language version in *The Straits Times*, December 14, 1990.

20 *Aera* (in Japanese), (April 23, 1991), 61.

21 *Asahi Shimbun* (in Japanese), morning edition, December 28, 1990.

22 *Aera* (in Japanese), (April 23, 1991), 61.

23 "Joint Press Statement of the Twenty-Third Meeting of the ASEAN Economic Ministers, Kuala Lumpur, Malaysia, 7–8 October 1991," cited in Termsak Chalermpalanupap, "Towards an East Asia Community," online at http://asean.org/towards-an-east-asia-community-the-journey-has-begun-by-termsak-chalermpalanupap/; *Asahi Shimbun* (in Japanese), morning edition, October 10, 1991.

24 *Asahi Shimbun* (in Japanese), morning edition, January 18, 1991.

25 James Baker, *The Politics of Diplomacy: Revolution, War, and Peace, 1989–1992* (New York: Putnam, 1995), pp. 610–11.

26 Funabashi, *Asia Pacific Fusion*, p. 208.

27 "Singapore Declaration of 1992," online on "The World and Japan" database at http://worldjpn.grips.ac.jp/documents/texts/asean/19920128.D1E.html.

28 "Joint Communique 25th ASEAN Ministerial Meeting Manila, Philippines, 21–22 July, 1992," online at http://asean.org/?static_post=joint-communique-25th-asean-ministerial-meeting-manila-philippines-21-22-july-1992.

29 "Joint Communique of the Twenty-Sixth ASEAN Ministerial Meeting Singapore, 23–24 July 1993," online at http://asean.org/?static_post=joint-communique-of-the-twenty-sixth-asean-ministerial-meeting-singapore-23-24-july-1993.

30 See Chalermpalanupap, "Towards an East Asian Community."

31 "Joint Communique of the Twenty-Seventh ASEAN Ministerial Meeting Bangkok, 22–23 July 1994," online at http://asean.
org/?static_post=joint-communique-of-the-twenty-seventh-ase-
an-ministerial-meeting-bangkok-22-23-july-1994.

32 See Chalermpalanupap, "Towards an East Asian Community."

33 "Bangkok Summit Declaration of 1995 Bangkok, 14–15 December
1995," online at http://asean.org/?static_post=bangkok-summit-decla-
ration-of-1995-bangkok14-15-december-1995.

34 See Michael Leifer, *The ASEAN Regional Forum: Extending ASEAN's
Model of Regional Security*, Adelphi Papers 302 (Oxford: Oxford University Press for the International Institute of Strategic Studies, 1996),
and Yamakage, *ASEAN pawā*, Chapter 9.

35 Soeya Yoshihide, "ASEAN to Nichi Bei Chū: ASEAN Chiiki Fōramu
o chūshin ni" [ASEAN and Japan, the US and China: the ASEAN
Regional Forum], in Soeya Yoshihide and Yamamoto Nobuto, eds.,
*Seikimatsu kara no Tōnan Ajia: sakusōsuru seiji keizai chitsujo no
yukue* [Southeast Asia from the end of the century: the complicated
course of the political economic order], (Tokyo: Keiō Gijuku Daigaku
Shuppankai, 2000), p. 5.

36 "Statement by Foreign Minister Taro Nakayama to the General Session of
the ASEAN Post Ministerial Conference," July 22, 1992, online on "The
World and Japan" database at http://worldjpn.grips.ac.jp/documents/
texts/JPSEA/19910722.O1E.html.

37 Yamakage Susumu, "Nihon ASEAN kankei no shinka to hen'yō"
[Changes in and deepening of Japan-ASEAN relations], in Yamakage Susumu, ed., *Higashi Ajia chiikishugi to Nihon gaikō* [East Asian
regionalism and Japanese diplomacy], (Tokyo: Nihon Kokusai Mondai
Kenkyūjo, 2003), pp. 18–20; Soeya, "ASEAN to Nichi Bei Chū," pp. 9–10.

38 For the 1991 Diplomatic Bluebook, see the English-language version online
at http://www.mofa.go.jp/policy/other/bluebook/1991/1991-contents.htm.

39 Kobayashi Yōtarō, "'Sai-Ajiaka' no susume" [Re-Asianize Japan], *Fore-
sight* (April 1991), 44–46. See also "Re-Asianization Does Not Mean
Isolation," *Los Angeles Times* (December 3, 1991) and "Re-Asianize
Japan," *New Perspectives Quarterly* 9,1 (Winter 1992), 20–23.

40 "Panel Report: Japan and the Asia Pacific Region in the 21st Century," December 25, 1992, online (in Japanese) on "The World and
Japan" database at http://worldjpn.grips.ac.jp/documents/texts/APEC/
19921225.O1J.html.

41 For details of domestic politics from 1989 to the middle of the 1990s,
see Gotō Kenji, *Dokyumento Heisei seijishi 1: hōkai suru 55nen taisei*
[Documentary history of politics in the Heisei era: the collapse of the
1955 system], (Tokyo: Iwanami Shoten, 2014).

Chapter 5
The Rise of China and the Crisis on the Korean Peninsula

1 Mōri Kazuko, "Tai-Soren Tō-Ō kankei" [Relations with the Soviet Union and Eastern Europe], in Chūgoku Sōran Henshū Iinkai, ed., *Chūgoku sōran 1992 nenban* [Overview of China, 1992 edition], (Tokyo: Kazankai, 1992), pp. 138–39.

2 Qian, *Ten Episodes*, p. 97.

3 Ibid., pp. 98–99.

4 Iida Masafumi, "Chūgoku to Indoneshia: kokkō saikai kōshō to sono mondaiten" [China and Indonesia: talks on the resumption of diplomatic relations and their sticking points], *Ajia Kenkyū* [Asian Studies] 44,3 (1998), 1–38. Wang Taiping, ed., *Xin Zhongguo wai jiao 50 nian, 1949–1999* [New China's diplomacy over five decades, 1949–1999], Vol. 1 (Beijing: Beijing chu ban she, 1999), pp. 312–15.

5 Tanaka Kyōko, *Kokka to imin: Tōnan Ajia Kajin sekai no hen'yō* [The state and immigrants: transformation of the world of Southeast Asian Chinese], (Nagoya: Nagoya Daigaku Shuppankai, 2002), pp. 164–88. For Singapore, see Tamura Keiko, *Shingapōru no kokka kensetsu: nashonarizumu, esunishiti, jendā* [Singapore state-building: nationalism, ethnicity, gender], (Tokyo: Akashi Shoten, 2000); and Iwasaki Ikuo, *Shingapōru kokka no kenkyū: "chitsujo to seichō" no seidoka, kinō, akutā* [A study of the Singapore state: the systematization, functions and actors of "growth and order"], (Tokyo: Fūkyōsha, 2005).

6 Lee Kuan Yew, *Ri Kuan Yū: za Shingapōru sutōri / The Singapore Story, Memoirs of Lee Kuan Yew*, trans. Komaki Toshihisa (Tokyo: Nihon Keizai Shimbunsha, 2000), 2: 487.

7 Ibid., p. 529; Wang, *Xin Zhongguo wai jiao 50 nian*, pp. 315–16.

8 Wang, *Xin Zhongguo wai jiao 50 nian*, pp. 316–17.

9 On relations between China and the Korean peninsula, see Kim Sukhyun, *Chū-Kan kokkō seijōka to Higashi Ajia kokusai seiji no hen'yō*; Masuo Chisako, "Tō Shōhei ki Chūgoku no tai-Chōsen hantō seisaku" [Chinese policy toward the Korean peninsula during the Deng Xiaoping era], *Ajia Kenkyū* [Asian Studies] 48,3 (2002); Yasuda Jun, "Chūgoku no Chōsen hantō seisaku" [China's Korean peninsula policy], in Okonogi, ed., *Posuto reisen no Chōsen hantō*; Li Chengri, "Chū-Kan kokkō seijōka o meguru Chūgoku no Chōsen hantō seisaku" [China's Korean peninsula policy on the normalization of Chinese-South Korean relations], in Suzuki Masayuki, Hiraiwa Shunji, Kurata Hideya, eds., *Chōsen hantō to kokusai seiji: reisen no tenkai to hen'yō* [The Korean peninsula and international politics: Cold-War developments and transformation], (Tokyo: Keiō Gijuku Daigaku Shuppankai, 2005).

10 Qian, *Ten Episodes*, p. 118.

11 Oberdorfer and Carlin, *Two Koreas*, p. 201; International Institute of Strategic Studies, ed., *Strategic Survey, 1991–1992* (London: Brassey's, 1992), p. 139, gives the figure as around 150.

12 "Agreement on Reconciliation, Nonaggression, and Exchanges and Cooperation between South and North Korea," December 13, 1991, online at http://csis.org/files/media/csis/pubs/issuesinsights_v08n03.pdf.

13 "President Roh Tae-woo's Declaration of Non-Nuclear Korean Peninsula Peace Initiative," December 18, 1991, online (in Japanese) on "The World and Japan" database at http://worldjpn.grips.ac.jp/documents/texts/JPKR/19911218.O1J.html. Oberdorfer and Carlin, *Two Koreas*, p. 202.

14 "Joint Declaration of South and North Korea on the Denuclearization of the Korean Peninsula," January 20, 1992, online at http://www.nti.org/media/pdfs/aptkoreanuc.pdf.

15 "The President's [George Bush] News Conference With President Roh Tae Woo of South Korea in Seoul," January 6, 1992, online at http://www.presidency.ucsb.edu/ws/?pid=20418.

16 A recent comprehensive study of Chinese-South Korean diplomatic normalization is Kim Suk-hyun's *Chū-Kan kokkō seijōka to Higashi Ajia kokusai seiji no hen'yō*. The following description is mainly dependent on this work.

17 Zhong Zhicheng, *Wei le shi jie geng mei hao: Jiang Zemin chu fang ji shi* [For a better world: the state visits of Jiang Zemin], (Beijing: Shi jie zhi shi chu ban she, 2006), p. 5. According to the same source (p. 6), when Kim Il Sung visited China a half year later, he said of China's setting up a trade office in South Korea that he "fully understood."

18 South Korean Foreign Minister Lee Sang-ock writes about this point in his memoirs, *Chŏnhwan'gi ŭi Han'guk oegyo: Yi Sang-ok chŏn Oemu Changgwan oegyo hoegorok* [South Korean diplomacy in a transition period: Lee Sang-ock memoirs], (Seoul: Sam kwa Kkum, 2002), p. 140. Quoted in Kim, *Chū-Kan kokkō seijōka to Higashi Ajia kokusai seiji no hen'yō*, pp. 100ff.

19 Qian, *Ten Episodes*, p. 124.

20 Nakagawa Yoshio, *Taiwan o mitsumeru me: teiten kansoku, gekidō no 20nen* [Focusing on Taiwan: fixed point observations, 20 years of turbulence], (Tokyo: Tabata Shoten, 1992), p. 265.

21 Oberdorfer and Carlin, *Two Koreas*, p. 192.

22 Masuo, "Tō Shōhei ki Chūgoku no tai-Chōsen hantō seisaku," p. 92.

23 Kim, *Chū-Kan kokkō seijōka to Higashi Ajia kokusai seiji no hen'yō*, p. 163.

24 Ibid., pp. 221–27.

25 Ibid., pp. 129–30.

26 The description of the Emperor's visit to China is based on Tanaka Akihiko, "Tai-Nichi kankei" [Relations with Japan], in Chūgoku Sōran

Henshū Iinkai, ed., *Chūgoku sōran 1994nenban* [Overview of China, 1994 edition], (Tokyo: Kazankai, 1994), pp. 144–52.

27 *Asahi Shimbun* (in Japanese), evening edition, October 26, 1992.

28 Ibid., morning edition, January 18, 1992.

29 Ibid., morning and evening editions, February 27, 1992.

30 *Nikkan Chūgoku Tsūshin* [Daily China News (in Japanese)], March 2, 1992.

31 *Asahi Shimbun* (in Japanese), morning edition, March 18, 1992.

32 *Nit-Chū kankei kihon shiryōshū 1949–1997* [Collection of basic documents on Japan-China relations, 1949–1997], (Tokyo: Kazankai, 1998), p. 527. For the English translation, see Ministry of Foreign Affairs, "The Senkaku Islands," March 2013, online at http://www.mofa.go.jp/region/asia-paci/senkaku/pdfs/senkaku_en.pdf.

33 *Yomiuri Shimbun* (in Japanese), morning edition, February 28, 1992.

34 *Asahi Shimbun* (in Japanese), morning edition, March 24, 1992.

35 Ibid., April 7 and 8, 1992.

36 Ibid., August 26, 1992.

37 Ibid., April 7 and 8, 1992; *Reuters News*, April 8, 1992.

38 *Nikkan Chūgoku Tsūshin*, June 15, 1992; *Reuters News*, June 11, 1992.

39 *Asahi Shimbun* (in Japanese), morning edition, June 18, 1992.

40 Ibid., July 17, 1992.

41 *Nikkan Chūgoku Tsūshin,* August 27, 1992.

42 *Yomiuri Shimbun* (in Japanese), morning edition, October 7, 1992.

43 For President Yang Shangkun's welcome at the banquet for Their Majesties the Emperor and Empress, October 23, 1992, online (in Japanese) on "The World and Japan" database at http://worldjpn.grips.ac.jp/documents/texts/JPCH/19921023.O2J.html. For a partial English translation, see *South China Morning Post,* October 24, 1992.

44 "Remarks by His Majesty the Emperor of Japan at a State-Sponsored Banquet," October 23, 1992, online (in Japanese) on "The World and Japan" database at http://worldjpn.grips.ac.jp/documents/texts/JPCH/19921023.O3J.html. For a partial English translation, see *Toronto Star,* October 23, 1992.

45 *Asahi Shimbun* (in Japanese), morning edition, October 24, 1992.

46 Deng Xiaoping, *Selected Works of Deng Xiaoping,* 3:360; http://www.china.org.cn/english/features/dengxiaoping/103331.htm.

47 Ibid., p. 363 (See the same URL cited n46.).

48 World Bank, *Global Economic Prospects and the Developing Countries, 1993* (Washington, DC: World Bank, 1993), pp. 66–67; *The Economist* (November 28, 1992), 3–6 (survey).

49 For a comprehensive evaluation of the China threat in the late 1990s, see Amako Satoshi, ed., *Chūgoku wa kyōi ka* [Is China a threat?], (Tokyo: Keisō Shobō, 1997). Attention to the rise of China became much more intense and widespread in the 21st century; see Chapter 10 for details.

50 China actually bought an incomplete aircraft carrier from Ukraine and rebuild it as *Liaoning*, China's first aircraft carrier in the 21st century. See Chapter 10 for the subsequent Chinese military buildup.

51 Imamura, *Kita Chōsen: "kyokō no keizai,"* p. 34.

52 Ibid., p. 163.

53 Oberdorfer and Carlin, *Two Koreas,* p. 181.

54 Ibid., p. 211.

55 Kenneth Quinones, *Kita Chōsen: Bei kokumushō tantōkan no kōshō hiroku* [North Korea: confidential notes of the US State Department official in charge], trans. Yamaoka Kunihiko and Yamaguchi Mizuhiko (Tokyo: Chūō Kōron Shinsha, 2000), p. 37.

56 There are subtle differences in the documents about what Kanter said to the North Koreans. According to Quinones (p. 37), Kanter mentioned a "road map" aimed at normalizing relations, but according to Sunohara Tsuyoshi, who interviewed Kanter and others, the US side did not set forth a clear plan; see his *Bei-Chō tairitsu: kaku kiki no jūnen* [US-North Korean standoff: a decade of nuclear crisis], (Tokyo: Nihon Keizai Shimbunsha, 2004), pp. 35–40.

57 Nakahira Noboru, Komaki Teruo and Igarashi Takeshi, "'Koizumi Sōri hō-Chō' e no dōtei to Nihon gaikō" [Japanese diplomacy and the steps leading up to "Prime Minister Koizumi's visit to North Korea"], *Kokusai Mondai* [International Affairs] 512 (2002), 59–60.

58 *Asahi Shimbun* (in Japanese), evening edition, October 9, 1992.

59 Quinones, *Kita Chōsen,* pp. 50–51.

60 *Asahi Shimbun* (in Japanese), morning edition, November 1, 1992.

61 Ibid., January 10, 1993.

62 Ibid., November 19, 1992.

63 "Letter dated 12 March 1993 from the Minister for Foreign Affairs of the Democratic People's Republic of Korea addressed to the President of the Security Council," online at https://ahlambauer.files.wordpress.com/2013/03/s-25405.pdf.

64 On the negotiating techniques of North Korea, see Scott Snyder, *Negotiating on the Edge: North Korean Negotiating Behavior* (Washington, DC: United States Institute of Peace Press, 1999).

65 Quinones, *Kita Chōsen,* pp. 167–92. For a discussion in English, see his "The United States in North Korea's Foreign Policy," online at http://www.ckquinones.com/wp-content/uploads/2013/11/US-in-NK-Foreign-Policy.pdf.

66 Oberdorfer and Carlin, *Two Koreas,* p. 237.

67 Ibid., p. 238.

68 Ibid., p. 247.

69 Ibid., pp. 259–61.

70 "Agreed Framework between the United States of America and the Democratic People's Republic of Korea," October 21, 1994, online on

"The World and Japan" database at http://worldjpn.grips.ac.jp/documents/texts/docs/19941021.O1E.html.

71 Tanaka Hitoshi, "Kita Chōsen kaku giwaku mondai o kensho suru" [Investigating the suspicions about North Korea's nuclear weapons], *Gaikō Fōramu* [Diplomacy Forum] 7,7 (1994), 63–64.

72 Tanaka Hitoshi and Tahara Sōichirō, *Kokka to gaikō* [The state and diplomacy], (Tokyo: Kōdansha, 2005), p. 20.

Chapter 6
The "History" Flare-up and Strains in Japan-China Relations

1 Mainichi Shimbunsha Seijibu, ed., *Tenkanki no "anpo"* ["National security" in a time of transition], (Tokyo: Mainichi Shimbunsha, 1979), p. 236. On the issues surrounding the "understanding of history" in Japanese diplomacy, see Tōgō Kazuhiko and Hatano Sumio, eds., *Rekishi mondai handobukku* [Handbook on the history problem], (Tokyo: Iwanami Shoten, 2015); Hattori Ryūji, *Gaikō dokyumento rekishi ninshiki* [The understanding of history through diplomatic records], (Tokyo: Iwanami Shoten, 2015); and Iechika Ryōko, Matsuda Yasuhiro, Dan Zuisō, eds., *Kiro ni tatsu Nit-Chū kankei: kako to no taiwa, mirai e no mosaku* [Japanese-Chinese relations at the crossroads: dialogue with the past, groping toward the future], (Kyoto: Kōyō Shobō, 2007), Chapters 1–3.

2 Tanaka Akihiko, "'Kyōkasho mondai' o meguru Chūgoku no seisaku kettei" [Chinese policy-making on the "textbook controversy"], in Okabe Tatsumi, ed., *Chūgoku gaikō: seisaku kettei no kōzō* [Chinese diplomacy: the structure of policy-making], (Tokyo: Nihon Kokusai Mondai Kenkyūjo, 1983).

3 *Asahi Shimbun* (in Japanese), morning edition, June 26, 1982.

4 "Statement by Chief Cabinet Secretary Kiichi Miyazawa on History Textbooks," August 26, 1982, online at http://www.mofa.go.jp/policy/postwar/state8208.html.

5 *Sankei Shimbun* (in Japanese), morning edition, September 7, 1982; *Asahi Shimbun* (in Japanese), morning edition, September 19, 1982. But as Kunihiro Michihiko, the ambassador to China in the early 1990s, wrote, "It is a fact that for more than ten years, at the time of the screening, the Ministry of Education has stated its opinion that 'invasion' should be changed to 'advance,' etc." Kunihiro Michihiko, "Nit-Chū gaikōshi (shiron)" [History of Japan-China diplomatic relations (a tentative study)], (unpublished document, Nihon Kokusai Mondai Kenkyūjo, 1999), p. 36. Tanino Sakutarō, another China hand in the foreign ministry, agreed. Tanino, *Ajia gaikō: kaiko to kōsatsu*, p. 104. See also Hattori, *Gaikō dokyumento rekishi ninshiki*, p. 28.

6 Quoted in Etō Naoko, "Dai-ichi-ji kyōkasho mondai, 1979nen–1982nen"

[The first textbook problem, 1979–1982], in Takahara Akio and Hattori Ryūji, eds., *Nit-Chū kankeishi, 1972–2012: 1, Seijihen* [A history of Japan-China relations, 1972–2012: Vol. 1, Politics], (Tokyo: Tōkyō Daigaku Shuppan, 2012), p. 145.

7   In 1993, I wrote the analytical paper cited above in note 2 in an attempt to deduce the political reasons behind China's launching of the anti-Japanese textbook campaign, in which I cited two reasons in addition to its desire to persuade the Japanese to stop revising history. The first was to substantiate its newly launched "independent and autonomous" foreign policy, a departure from its policy of alignment with the United States and Japan during the "new" Cold War. In the summer of 1982, China had actually accepted a deal with the United States over Taiwan despite the Reagan administration's willingness to provide Taiwan with military weapons, a compromise that seemed to contradict its "independent and autonomous" foreign policy. By standing firm on Japan, Beijing wanted to demonstrate its independence. The second reason was the need for patriotic education to reinforce the party's legitimacy as explained in the text. Etō, "Dai-ichi-ji kyōkasho mondai," relying on recently available sources, overall validates my analysis.

8   Tanaka, "Nit-Chū kankei," p. 138. Also see Tanaka Akihiko, "The Yasukuni Issue and Japan's International Relations," in Tsuyoshi Hasegawa and Kazuhiko Tōgō, eds., *East Asia's Haunted Present: Historical Memories and the Resurgence of Nationalism* (Westport, CT: Praeger Security International, 2008), pp. 119–41.

9   Nakasone, *Tenchi ujō*, p. 463. He also says on p. 492, "From the outset, I had no intention of being pressured to make repeated visits."

10   Hattori, *Gaikō dokyumento rekishi ninshiki*, pp. 64–65.

11   In 2006, it became clear that the Emperor Showa himself had disapproved of the enshrinement of Class A war criminals, and for that reason had given up visiting the shrine from 1975 on. But the impact of the Emperor's decision on the Yasukuni controversy was probably greater as a domestic issue than as a diplomatic one. *Nihon Keizai Shimbun* (in Japanese), morning edition, July 20, 2006.

12   Asian Women's Fund, *The "Comfort Women" Issue and the Asian Women's Fund* (Tokyo: Asian Women's Fund, 2004), p. 1, online at http://www.awf.or.jp/pdf/0170.pdf. As the main body of text indicates, the concepts of "comfort women" and "comfort stations" have been the sources of political contention. Some argue that the former were nothing other than "sexual slaves" and the latter "rape centers." Since prostitution had been legal in Japan until 1956, other historians argue that comfort women suffered a similar fate with those who were compelled to become prostitutes because of poverty, deception and other human-trafficking activities. For an analysis of different views of comfort women, see Kazuhiko Tōgō,

"Comfort Women: Deep Polarization in Japan on Facts and on Morality," in Hasegawa and Tōgō, eds., *East Asia's Haunted Present*, pp. 142–62.

13 *Asahi Shimbun* (in Japanese), Osaka morning edition, September 2, 1982. Asahi Shimbun Dai-sansha Iinkai [The Asahi Shimbun Co. Third-Party Committee], *Hokokusho* [Report], December 22, 2014, online (in Japanese) http://www.asahi.com/shimbun/3rd/2014122201.pdf. For an abridged summary in English, see http://www.asahi.com/shimbun/3rd/report20150728e.pdf.

14 Yoshida Seiji, *Watashi no sensō hanzai: Chōsenjin kyōsei renkō* [My war crimes: the forced conscription of Koreans], (Tokyo: San'ichi Shobō, 1983).

15 *Asahi Shimbun* (in Japanese), morning edition, January 11, 1992.

16 The *Asahi* story stated that "the number of the comfort women 'forcibly conscripted' in the name of the Women's Volunteer Corps was between 80,000 and 200,000." See the online abridged summary cited in n13.

17 Hironaka Yoshimichi, *Miyazawa seiken, 644nichi* [The Miyazawa administration, 644 days], (Tokyo: Gyōken Shuppankyoku, 1998), p. 117.

18 Study Team on the Details Leading to the Drafting of the Kono Statement etc., "Details of Exchanges Between Japan and the Republic of Korea (ROK) Regarding the Comfort Women Issue: From the Drafting of the Kono Statement to the Asian Women's Fund," June 20, 2014, p. 4, online at http://japan.kantei.go.jp/96_abe/documents/2014/__icsFiles/afieldfile/2014/06/20/JPN_ROK_EXCHANGE.pdf.

19 "Details of Exchanges," pp. 8–9; *Asahi Shimbun* (in Japanese), morning edition, March 14, 1993.

20 "Details of Exchanges," p. 13. The ROK government later stated that the consultation had been "informal": "The opinion rendered by the Korean government on the language of the Kono Statement at the time came only after Japan's repeated pleas for discussion, under the premise that it was made on an informal basis to help clarify the facts with accuracy." "Korea's Position on Japan's Review of the Details Leading to the Drafting of the Kono Statement," June 25, 2014, online at http://news.mofa.go.kr/enewspaper/mainview.php?mvid=1881&master.

21 "Statement by the Chief Cabinet Secretary Yohei Kono on the result of the study on the issue of 'comfort women,'" August 4, 1993, online at http://www.mofa.go.jp/policy/women/fund/state9308.html. On the study that served as background for this statement, see the interview with Ishihara Nobuo, the then-Deputy Chief Cabinet Secretary, in *Ajia josei kikin: Ōraru hisutorī* [Asian Women's Fund: oral history], (Tokyo: Josei No Tameno Ajia Heiwa Kokumin Kikin, 2007), pp. 37–44.

22 *Asahi Shimbun* (in Japanese), morning edition, August 5, 1993.

23 The "Agreement on the Settlement of Problems Concerning Property and Claims and on Economic Co-operation between Japan and the

Republic of Korea," concluded on June 22, 1965, contains the following articles:

Article I

1. To the Republic of Korea Japan shall:
(a) Supply the products of Japan and the services of the Japanese people, the total value of which will be so much in yen as shall be equivalent to three hundred million United States dollars ($300,000,000). . . .
(b) Extend long-term and low-interest loans up to such amount in yen as shall be equivalent to two hundred million United States dollars ($200,000,000). . . .

Article II

1. The Contracting Parties confirm that [the] problem concerning property, rights and interests of the two Contracting Parties and their nationals (including juridical persons) and concerning claims between the Contracting Parties and their nationals, including those provided for in Article IV, paragraph (a) of the Treaty of Peace with Japan signed at the city of San Francisco on September 8, 1951, is settled completely and finally.

Online on "The World and Japan" database at http://worldjpn.grips.ac.jp/documents/texts/JPKR/19650622.T9E.html.

24 *Sankei Shimbun* (in Japanese), morning edition, April 30, 1992.

25 Konoe was prime minister at the beginning of the Sino-Japanese War in 1937. He committed suicide after it was reported that he would be tried at the Tokyo Military Tribunal.

26 "Policy Speech by Prime Minister Hosokawa Morihiro to the 127th Session of the National Diet," August 23, 1993, online at http://japan.kantei.go.jp/127.html#sec5. The account here is based on Tanaka Akihiko, "Tai-Nichi kankei" [Relations with Japan], in Chūgoku Sōran Henshū Iinkai, ed., *Chūgoku sōran 1998nenban* [Overview of China, 1998 edition], (Tokyo: Kazankai, 1998), pp. 138–49.

27 *Mainichi Shimbun* (in Japanese), morning edition, March 21, 1994.

28 *Mainichi Shimbun* (Osaka; in Japanese), morning edition, May 5, 1994. English translation in "The Politics of History: History in Politics," online at http://library.fes.de/pdf-files/bueros/japan/11285.pdf.

29 "Policy Speech by Prime Minister Hata Tsutomu to the 129th Session of the National Diet," May 10, 1994, online on "The World and Japan" database (in Japanese) at http://worldjpn.grips.ac.jp/documents/texts/pm/19940510.SWJ.html.

30 "Policy Speech by Prime Minister Murayama Tomiichi to the 130th Session of the National Diet," July 18, 1994, online on "The World and Japan" database (in Japanese) at http://worldjpn.grips.ac.jp/documents/texts/pm/19940718.SWJ.html.

31 Yakushiji Katsuyuki, ed., *Murayama Tomiichi kaikoroku* [Memoirs of

Murayama Tomiichi], (Tokyo: Iwanami Shoten, 2012), pp. 189–90.

32 *Mainichi Shimbun* (in Japanese), morning edition, August 13, 1994.

33 *Nikkan Chūgoku Tsūshin* (in Japanese), August 19, 1994; for an English-language account, see *Reuters News*, August 13, 1994.

34 "Resolution to Renew the Determination for Peace on the Basis of Lessons Learned From History," June 9, 1995, online at http://www.mofa.go.jp/announce/press/pm/murayama/address9506.html.

35 Yakushiji, *Murayama Tomiichi kaikoroku*, p. 214.

36 Ibid., p. 215.

37 Tanino mentioned Hosoya Chihiro, Kitaoka Shin'ichi and Ōnuma Yasuaki as scholars he consulted. Tanino, *Ajia gaikō: kaiko to kōsatsu*, p. 255.

38 *Yomiuri Shimbun* (in Japanese), morning edition, August 9, 1995.

39 "Statement by Prime Minister Tomiichi Murayama 'On the occasion of the 50th anniversary of the war's end,'" August 15, 1995, online at http://www.mofa.go.jp/announce/press/pm/murayama/9508.html. Murayama Tomiichi, *Sō janō: Murayama Tomiichi "shushō taiken" no subete o kataru* [Well, let's see: Murayama Tomiichi tells all about his "experience as prime minister"], (Tokyo: Daisan Shokan, 1998), pp. 105–8.

40 *Nikkan Chūgoku Tsūshin* (in Japanese), August 17, 1995. *Xinhua News Agency* critique, "Tōtoi ippo, kibishii zento" [Valuable first step, challenging future], *Nikkan Chūgoku Tsūshin*, August 25, 1995. English-language translation in Tōgō Kazuhiko, *Japan and Reconciliation in Post-war Asia: The Murayama Statement and Its Implications* (Basingstoke: Palgrave Pivot, 2010), pp. 28–29.

41 Heiwa Anzen Hoshō Kenkyūjo, ed., *Ajia no anzen hoshō, 1996–1997* [Asian security, 1996–1997], (Tokyo: Asagumo Shimbunsha, 1996), pp. 181–82.

42 On the Asian Women's Fund, see *"Ianfu" mondai to Ajia Josei Kikin* [The "comfort women" controversy and the Asian Women's Fund], (Tokyo: Josei no Tame no Ajia Heiwa Kokumin Kikin, 2007); Ōnuma Yasuaki, *"Ianfu" mondai to wa nandatta no ka: media, NGO, seifu no kōzai* [What was the "comfort women" controversy? the strengths and weaknesses of the media, NGOs and the government], (Tokyo: Chūō Kōron Shinsha, 2007).

43 *Yomiuri Shimbun* (in Japanese), morning edition, June 28, 1995.

44 Asian Women's Fund, "The 'Comfort Women' Issue," pp. 17–19.

45 "Measures Taken by the Government of Japan on the Issue known as 'Comfort Women,'" October 14, 2014, online at http://www.mofa.go.jp/policy/women/fund/policy.html.

46 Ōnuma, *"Ianfu mondai" to wa nandatta no ka*, pp. 58–59.

47 Shiba Ryōtarō, *Taiwan kikō: kaidō o yuku, 40* [Taiwan travel diary: on the highways, 40], (Tokyo: Asahi Shimbunsha, 1997), p. 75.

48 On the process by which Lee Teng-hui cemented his power, see Wakabayashi, *Taiwan: hen'yō shi chūcho suru aidentiti*, pp. 152–71.

49 The most succinct account of China-Taiwan relations is Nakagawa Yoshio, *Chūgoku to Taiwan* [China and Taiwan], (Tokyo: Chūō Kōron-sha, 1998).

50 Testifying to Congress on February 15, 1995, Secretary of State Warren Christopher described a visit to the US by President Lee Teng-hui as "inconsistent with the unofficial character of our relationship" with Taiwan. On April 17, when Christopher met with Chinese Foreign Minister Qian Qichen at the UN, he said that the US would probably not issue Lee a visa. But in May, a nonbinding congressional resolution asking that Lee be issued a visa to visit the US in an unofficial capacity was passed by an overwhelming majority, a 396 to 0 vote in the House of Representatives and 97 to 1 in the Senate. James Mann, *About Face: A History of America's Curious Relationship with China from Nixon to Clinton* (New York: Alfred A. Knopf, 1999), pp. 321–32.

51 *Asahi Shimbun* (in Japanese), evening edition, March 2, 1996. The following account is based on Tanaka Akihiko, "Tai-Nichi kankei," in *Chūgoku sōran 1998nenban*, pp. 130–41.

52 *Sankei Shimbun* (in Japanese), morning edition, March 6, 1996.

53 *Asahi Shimbun* (in Japanese), morning edition, March 7, 1996.

54 *Sankei Shimbun* (in Japanese), morning edition, March 8, 1996.

55 Ibid., March 9, 1996.

56 *Asahi Shimbun* (in Japanese), morning edition, March 9, 1996.

57 *Sankei Shimbun* (in Japanese), morning edition, March 13, 1996.

58 Ibid., March 14, 1996.

59 Ibid., March 15, 1996.

60 Ibid., March 16, 1996.

61 *Asahi Shimbun* (in Japanese), morning edition, March 20, 1996.

62 Ibid., April 1, 1996.

63 Ibid., February 6, 1996.

64 Ibid., April 1, 1996.

65 *Pekin shūho* [Beijing Review] 24 (1996), 22–23.

66 *Asahi Shimbun* (in Japanese), morning edition, June 9, 1996.

67 Ibid., July 30, 1996.

68 *Nikkan Chūgoku Tsūshin* (in Japanese), July 31, 1996.

69 Ibid., August 15, 1996.

70 *Sankei Shimbun* (in Japanese), morning edition, July 17, 1996.

71 Ibid., July 26, 1996.

72 Ibid., September 11, 1996.

73 *Pekin shūho* [Beijing Review] 31 (1996), 6.

74 *Sankei Shimbun* (in Japanese), morning edition, July 18, 1996.

75 *Asahi Shimbun* (in Japanese), morning edition, August 4, 1996.

76 *Yomiuri Shimbun* (in Japanese), morning edition, September 13, 1996.

77 *Nikkan Chūgoku Tsūshin* (in Japanese), August 13, 1996.

78 Ibid., August 20, 1996.

79   Ibid., September 9, 1996.

80   Ibid., September 13, 1996.

81   *Asahi Shimbun* (in Japanese), morning edition, September 19, 1996.

82   Ibid., September 26, 1996.

83   Ibid., October 4, 1996. For an English-language account, see *The Straits Times*, October 5, 1996.

84   *Yomiuri Shimbun* (in Japanese), morning edition, October 1, 1996.

85   *Asahi Shimbun* (in Japanese), morning edition, September 27, 1996.

86   Ibid., October 5, 1996. For an English-language account, see *Reuters News*, October 5, 1996.

87   Ibid., November 24, 1996.

88   *Pekin shūho* [Beijing Review] 49 (1996), 4.

89   *Nikkan Chūgoku Tsūshin* (in Japanese), December 26, 1996.

90   Ibid., April 22, 1996.

91   *Asahi Shimbun* (in Japanese), morning edition, July 17, 1997.

92   Ibid., July 26, 1997.

93   Ibid., July 30, 1997.

94   Ibid., August 20, 1997.

95   *Nikkan Chūgoku Tsūshin* (in Japanese), August 22, 1997.

96   Ibid., August 25, 1997.

97   Ibid., August 26, 1997.

98   *Yomiuri Shimbun* (in Japanese), morning edition, September 6, 1997. For the official English translation of the Prime Minister's Beijing speech on September 5, 1997, see http://www.mofa.go.jp/region/asia-paci/china/dialogue.html.

99   *Yomiuri Shimbun* (in Japanese), morning edition, November 12, 1997.

Chapter 7

The Asian Financial Crisis

1   Itō Takatoshi, "1997nen Ajia tsūka kiki: gen'in to shinkokuka no riyū" [The 1997 Asian currency crisis: its origins and the reasons it became more serious], *Kokusai Mondai* [International Affairs], 563 (2007), 4–13. See also his "Asian Currency Crisis and the International Monetary Fund, 10 Years Later: Overview," *Asian Economic Policy Review* 2,1 (June 2007), 16–49. The characterization of "the crisis as having spread through the region like a brush fire" (p. 17) is wrong, he argues; there was both time enough and the appropriate policy measures to stop it. That is probably true, but in the final analysis, those measures could not be taken, and the crisis spread from one country to the next.

2 This is the view of leading Thai political scientist Chai-Anan Samu-davanija. Suehiro Akira, *Tai: kaihatsu to minshushugi* [Thailand: development and democracy], (Tokyo: Iwanami Shoten, 1993), p. 11. For the history of Thailand up to the 21st century, see Kakizaki Ichirō, *Monogatari Tai no rekishi: hohoemi no kuni no shinjitsu* [The history of the story of Thailand: the truth about the "land of smiles"], (Tokyo: Chūō Kōron Shinsha, 2007).

3 This, too, is Chai-Anan's theory. Suehiro, *Tai: kaihatsu to minshushugi*, p. 94.

4 World Bank, *The East Asian Miracle: Economic Growth and Public Policy* (New York: Oxford University Press, 1993).

5 Paul Krugman, "The Myth of Asia's Miracle," *Foreign Affairs* 73 (November/December 1994), 62–78.

6 Yoshitomi Masaru, *Ajia keizai no shinjitsu: kiseki, kiki, seido no shinka* [Reality of the Asian economy: miracle, crisis and institutional evolution], (Tokyo: Tōyō Keizai Shinpōsha, 2003).

7 Ibid., pp. 51–52.

8 Sakakibara Eisuke, *Nihon to sekai ga furueta hi: saibā shihonshugi no seiritsu* [The day Japan and the world shook: the birth of cyber capitalism], (Tokyo: Chūō Kōron Shinsha, 2000), p. 164.

9 According to Itō, "Asian Currency Crisis" (p. 25), this announcement by the Thai Central Bank prompted a loss of confidence in the IMF aid package and further accelerated the depreciation of the currency. With foreign reserves drying up, the IMF's USD 17.2 billion in aid was utterly insufficient to cover the USD 23.4 billion in forward contracts, and the markets lost confidence.

10 Shimomura Yasutami, "Higashi Ajia kin'yū kiki no seiji shakaiteki eikyō" [The political and social impact of the East Asian financial crisis], in Shimomura Yasutami and Inada Jūichi, eds., *Ajia kin'yū kiki no seiji keizaigaku* [The political economy of the Asian financial crisis], (Tokyo: Nihon Kokusai Mondai Kenkyūjo, 2001), p. 80. Minowa Tokuji, "Tai no tsūka kiki to sono go no keizai jōkyō" [The Thai currency crisis and subsequent economic conditions], in Itō Osamu, Okuyama Tadanobu and Minowa Tokuji, eds., *Tsūka kin'yū kiki to Higashi Ajia keizai* [The currency and financial crises and the East Asian economy], (Tokyo: Shakai Hyōronsha, 2005), p. 179.

11 *Kyōdō Tsūshin* (in Japanese), October 11, 1997.

12 On the Indonesian government, the basic work is Shiraishi Takashi, *Indoneshia*, shinpan [Indonesia, new ed.], (Tokyo: NTT Shuppan, 1996). For the collapse of the Suharto regime, see Shiraishi, *Hōkai Indoneshia wa doku e yuku* [Collapse: whither Indonesia?], (Tokyo: NTT Shuppan, 1999); Kanō Hiroyoshi, *Indoneshia ryōran* [Indonesia in confusion], (Tokyo: Bungei Shunjū, 2001); Takeda, *Minshuka no*

hikaku seiji, Chapter 5, section 2. An analysis by an important participant in Indonesian politics and economic policy-making is offered by Ginandjar Kartasasmita and Joseph J. Stern, *Reinventing Indonesia* (Singapore: World Scientific, 2016).

13 Shiraishi, *Hōkai Indoneshia wa doku e yuku*.

14 *Ajia no anzen hoshō, 1998–1999*, p. 37. For the Albright quote, see *The New York Times*, May 21, 1998.

15 Sakakibara, *Nihon to sekai ga furueta hi*, pp. 202–3.

16 *Ajia no anzen hoshō, 1998–1999*, p. 187.

17 Ibid., p. 190.

18 Hayashida Hiroaki, *Mahatīru no jirenma: hatten to konmei no Marēshia gendaishi* [Mahathir's dilemma: Malaysia's modern history of development and turmoil], (Tokyo: Chūō Kōron Shinsha, 2001), pp. 76, 82.

19 Kaneko Yoshiki, *Marēshia no seiji to esunishiti: Kajin seiji to kokumin tōgō* [Politics and ethnicity in Malaysia: Chinese politics and national integration], (Kyoto: Kōyō Shobō, 2001); Torii Takashi, ed., *Mahatīru seikenka no Marēshia: "Isurāmu senshinkoku" o mezashita 22-nen* [Malaysia under the Mahathir administration: 22 years of striving to create an "advanced country with Islamic values"], (Chiba: Ajia Keizai Kenkyūjo, 2006).

20 Hayashida, *Mahatīru no jirenma*, pp. 81–82.

21 Ibid., pp. 108–31.

22 *Ajia no anzen hoshō, 1997–1998*, p. 149.

23 Sakakibara, *Nihon to sekai ga furueta hi*, pp. 182–83.

24 Itō, "Asian Currency Crisis," p. 44.

25 Sakakibara, *Nihon to sekai ga furueta hi*, pp. 183–84.

26 Ibid., pp. 185–86.

27 Kuroda Haruhiko, *Tsūka no kōbō: en, doru, yūro, jinmingen no yukue* [The rise and fall of currencies: the fate of the yen, dollar, euro and renminbi], (Tokyo: Chūō Kōron Shinsha, 2005), p. 182.

28 Ibid., p. 172.

29 Ibid., pp. 172–73.

30 Ibid., p. 174.

31 *Asahi Shimbun* (in Japapese), morning edition, April 5, 1998.

32 *The New York Times*, July 13, 1998.

33 Suehiro and Yamakage, eds., *Ajia seiji keizairon: Ajia no naka no Nihon o mezashite*, p. 457. On the New Miyazawa Initiative, see Kishimoto Shūhei, "Ajia kin'yū senryaku no tenkai: Shin Miyazawa Kōsō o koeta hōkatsuteki shien wa jitsugen suru no ka" [The development of an Asian monetary strategy: will comprehensive aid that goes beyond the New Miyazawa Initiative ever materialize?], in Suehiro and Yamakage, eds., *Ajia seiji keizairon*, pp. 289–319. For an online English version of the Initiative, see http://www.mof.go.jp/english/international_policy/financial_cooperation_in_asia/new_miyazawa_initiative/e1e042.htm.

34 "Statement by Foreign Minister Keizo Obuchi on Japan and East Asia: Outlook for the New Millennium," May 4, 1998, English translation online at http://www.mofa.go.jp/announce/announce/1998/5/980504. html.

35 "Policy Speech by Prime Minister Keizo Obuchi at the Lecture Program hosted by the Institute for International Relations, Hanoi, Vietnam, December 16, 1998: Toward the Creation of A Bright Future for Asia," English translation online at http://www.mofa.go.jp/region/asia-paci/asean/pmv9812/policyspeech.html.

36 Michael Vatikiotis, "Help Yourself," *Far Eastern Economic Review* 162,1 (December 31, 1998/January 7, 1999), 12–13.

Chapter 8
East-Asian Regionalism and Japan

1 The account of ASEM and ASEAN+3 in this chapter is based on Tanaka, "Development of the ASEAN+3 Framework," pp. 57–65. On the ASEM formation process, see Miyamoto Mitsuo, "Ajia-Ōshū kaigi purosesu to ryōchiiki kankei no shōrai" [The ASEM process and the future of relations between the two regions], *Seikei Hōgaku* [Seikei University Law] 51 (March 2000), 15–51; Tanaka Toshirō, "Ajia-Ōshū kankei no shintenkai: ASEM no tanjō to hatten" [New developments in Asian-European relations: the birth and growth of ASEM], in Akagi Kanji and Soeya Yoshihide, eds., *Reisengo no kokusai seiji: jisshō seisaku riron* [Post-Cold-War international politics: proof, policy, theory], (Tokyo: Keiō Gijiku Daigaku Shuppankai, 1998).

2 *The Straits Times*, October 22, 1994.

3 Ibid., February 17, 1995.

4 *Asahi Shimbun* (in Japanese), morning edition, January 31, 1995.

5 Ibid.

6 Ibid., March 20, 1995.

7 *Kyōdō Tsūshin* (in Japanese), March 19, 1995.

8 *Yomiuri Shimbun* (in Japanese), morning edition, April 7, 1995; ibid. (morning edition), April 9, 1995; *Kyōdō Tsūshin* (in Japanese), April 10, 1995.

9 *Kyōdō Tsūshin* (in Japanese), April 10, 1995; *Asahi Shimbun* (in Japanese), morning edition, April 12, 1995.

10 *The Straits Times*, May 3, 1995.

11 Ibid., July 25, 1995.

12 *Asahi Shimbun* (in Japanese), morning edition, August 1, 1995.

13 *Yomiuri Shimbun* (in Japanese), evening edition, November 18, 1995; *Asahi Shimbun* (in Japanese), morning edition, November 19, 1995; *Yomiuri Shimbun* (in Japanese), morning edition, November 20, 1995.

14 *Asahi Shimbun* (in Japanese), morning edition, March 1, 1996.

15 Ibid., morning edition, December 15, 1995.

16 Ibid., morning edition, December 1, 1996; on Goh Chok Tong's and Malaysia's ideas, see Terada Takashi, "Constructing an 'East Asian' Concept and Growing Regional Identity: From EAEC to ASEAN+3," *The Pacific Review* 16 (2003), 262–64.

17 Ministry of Foreign Affairs, *Gaikō seisho 1998*, Daiichibu [Diplomatic bluebook, 1998, Part 1], (Tokyo: Ōkurashō Insatsukyoku, 1998), p. 112. English translation of the Singapore speech online at http://www.mofa.go.jp/region/asia-paci/asean/pmv9701/policy.html.

18 *Kyōdō Tsūshin* (in Japanese), January 14, 1997. That the heads of the ASEAN countries did not immediately say yes to Japan is, of course, regarded as the "ASEAN way." A report right after Prime Minister Hashimoto's ASEAN visit quoted a high-ranking official from an ASEAN country as saying, "The Asean way is the consensus way. Each Asean country will never give a categorical 'yes' until they had met as a group to discuss the matter. The proposal for the summit, [to] which several leaders have given agreement in principle, will be discussed at forthcoming Asean meetings. An Asean position will definitely emerge. The Japan-Asean Summit will become a reality." *The Straits Times*, January 22, 1997.

19 Professor Lee Poh Ping of the National University of Malaysia commented that "Japan is not the only big power operating in Southeast Asia. The other powers like China and the US may wonder why Japan should be the only country to have the regular summit with ASEAN and not China or [the] US." *The Nikkei Weekly*, January 20, 1997.

20 *Business Times*, January 15, 1997.

21 *Kyōdō Tsūshin* (in Japanese), February 20, 1997.

22 Ibid., March 27, 1997.

23 Ibid., April 29, 1997.

24 *Asahi Shimbun* (in Japanese), morning edition, June 1, 1997.

25 Satō, "EAEC kōsō to ASEAN+3 hikōshiki shunō kaigi," 64; *Tōnan Ajia Geppō* [Southeast Asian Monthly], (May 1997), 171.

26 For a discussion of ASEAN+3 in relation to the financial crisis, see Kikuchi Tsutomu, "'Higashi Ajia' chiikishugi no kanōsei: ASEAN+3 (Nit-Chū-Kan) no keii to tenbō" [The possibilities for 'East Asian' regionalism: circumstances of and prospects for ASEAN+3 (Japan, China and South Korea)], *Kokusai Mondai* [International Affairs] 494 (May 2001), 16–33.

27 *Asahi Shimbun* (in Japanese), morning edition, December 5, 1997.

28 Ibid., morning edition, December 17, 1997. According to a summary published by the Ministry of Foreign Affairs, the contents under discussion at this meeting were as follows. There was no mention in the summary of the possibility that the meetings would continue.

[a] Views were expressed that there were no prospects of recovery for ASEAN economies and its economic difficulties would continue for the coming several years. Under these circumstances, ASEAN participants expressed their expectation about the role Japan would play.

[b] On financial issues, it was confirmed that the implementation of the Manila Framework should be the priority. Some expressed concerns about the negative impact of IMF conditionality on economic activities.

[c] On ASEM, the importance of the dialogues between Europe, which was accelerating its integration with the introduction of the Euro, and East Asia was confirmed. The view was also expressed that the discussions must be deepened particularly on economic issues.

Online (in Japanese) at http://www.mofa.go.jp/mofaj/kaidan/kiroku/s_hashi/arc_97/asean97/kaigi.html; English translation in Tanaka, "Development of the ASEAN+3 Framework," p. 61.

29 *Kyōdō Tsūshin* (in Japanese), August 3, 1998.

30 *Asahi Shimbun* (in Japanese), morning edition, October 4, 1998.

31 Ibid., morning edition, December 17, 1998.

32 East Asia Vision Group Report (hereafter EAVG Report), *Towards an East Asian Community: Region of Peace, Prosperity and Progress*, p. 44. According to the summary of this meeting issued in Japanese by the Japanese Ministry of Foreign Affairs, "the proposal was made by South Korea to set up a primarily non-governmental forum [i.e., the East Asia Vision Group] for the purpose of exchanging views on ways of overcoming the economic crisis." (http://www.mofa.go.jp/mofaj/kaidan/kiroku/s_obuchi/arc_98/viet98/gaiyo.html.) As of December 1998, the scope of the EAVG had probably not yet been narrowed down. The Terms of Reference are believed to have actually been drawn up between December 1998 and July 1999, but that is not exactly clear.

33 Ministry of Foreign Affairs, Asian Bureau, *Obuchi Sōri no ASEAN to no shunōkaigi tō shusseki* [Prime Minister Obuchi's attendance at the summit meeting with ASEAN and elsewhere], (Tokyo: Gaimushō Ajiakyoku, 1999), p. 30. According to "ASEAN+Nit-Chū-Kan shunōkaigi" [ASEAN+Japan, China and South Korea summit meeting] in the same document, "it was agreed that the ASEAN+3 summit was extremely beneficial and that it would be held regularly on an ongoing basis. However, no clear proposal was made as to frequency," p. 28.

34 EAVG Report, p. 45.

35 *Asahi Shimbun* (in Japanese), morning edition, March 19, 1999.

36 *Nihon Keizai Shimbun* (in Japanese), morning edition, May 1, 1999.

37 *Kyōdō Tsūshin* (in Japanese), July 12, 1999. The East Asia Vision Group held its first meeting in Seoul on October 21–22, 1999, with

two knowledgeable private citizens as members from each country. Former Korean Foreign Minister Han Sung-joo was elected chairman from among the members. The representatives from Japan were Yoshitomi Masaru, dean of the Asian Development Bank Institute, and the author (Tanaka Akihiko).

38   Ibid., October 8, 1999.

39   *Nihon Keizai Shimbun* (in Japanese), morning edition, October 20, 1999.

40   *Asahi Shimbun* (in Japanese), morning edition, November 13, 1999; *Nihon Keizai Shimbun* (in Japanese), morning edition, November 14, 1999.

41   *Nihon Keizai Shimbun* (in Japanese), morning edition, November 26, 1999.

42   "Joint Statement on East Asia Cooperation 28 November 1999" online at http://www.asean.org/?static_post=joint-statement-on-east-asia-cooperation-28-november-1999. Specifically mentioned were cooperation in developing the Mekong River Basin, the setting up of an East Asian Business Council and the ASEAN Human Resource Development Initiative.

43   At the meeting the leaders of ASEAN, Japan, China and South Korea are said to have spent a considerable amount of time discussing the situation in Indonesia and North Korea but made no reference to the South China Sea or Taiwan Strait issue. At first, it had been intended that security issues would head the list of items in the Joint Statement, but security dropped down to seventh place. *Nihon Keizai Shimbun* (in Japanese), morning edition, November 29, 1999.

44   The participants at the ASEAN Post Ministerial Conference (PMC) are the foreign ministers of ASEAN and ASEAN's Dialogue Partners. Japan became the first ASEAN Dialogue Partner in 1978, followed by the US, Australia, New Zealand and the EU in 1979, Canada in 1980, South Korea in 1991 and India, Russia and China in 1996.

45   *Asahi Shimbun* (in Japanese), evening edition, June 28, 1995; ibid. (evening edition), October 3, 1998.

46   For a detailed account of the information-gathering satellite and Taepodong, see Sunohara Tsuyoshi, *Tanjō kokusan supai eisei: dokuji jōhōmō to Nichi-Bei dōmei* [The birth of an indigenous spy satellite: an independent intelligence network and the Japan-US alliance], (Tokyo: Nihon Keizai Shimbunsha, 2005).

47   "South-North Joint Declaration," June 15, 2000, English translation online at http://www.usip.org/sites/default/files/file/resources/collections/peace_agreements/n_skorea06152000.pdf.

48   Takeshima (Dokdo), composed of two main islands and dozens of very small islands totaling 0.20 square kilometers located 158 kilometers northwest of the Oki Islands, has been occupied by South Korea since 1954. Japan incorporated the islands into Shimane Prefecture in January 1905. In September 1954, Japan proposed that this dispute be referred

to the International Court of Justice; South Korea rejected the proposal in October of the same year (http://www.mofa.go.jp/a_o/na/takeshima/pagelwe_000065.html). For academic analysis of the dispute, see Hyŏn Tae-song, *Ryōdo nashonarizumu no tanjō: "Dokudo/Takeshima mondai" no seijigaku* [The birth of territorial nationalism: the politics of the "Dokdo/Takeshima issue"], (Kyoto: Mineruva Shobō, 2006).

49 *Yomiuri Shimbun* (in Japanese), evening edition, February 9, 1996.

50 South Korea ratified the United Nations Convention on the Law of the Sea (UNCLOS) in January 1996, and Japan did so in June. With the establishment of the new international maritime legal system, both Japan and ROK regarded it necessary to draw up a new fisheries agreement though it was almost impossible for both countries to reach a full agreement on the delimitation of the EEZ. Hashimoto and Kim Young-sam agreed to separate the negotiations on a fishery agreement from the territorial issue. The new agreement was signed in November 1977 and went into effect the following January. Cho Youn-soo, "Kaiyō o meguru Nik-Kan kankei 50nen" [50 years of Japan-South Korea maritime relations], in Kimiya Tadashi and Yi Wŏn-dŏk, eds., *Nik-Kan kankeishi, 1965–2015: 1 Seiji* [History of Japan-South Korea relations, 1965–2015: 1 Politics], (Tokyo: Tōkyō Daigaku Shuppankai, 2015), pp. 273–96.

51 *Ajia no anzen hoshō, 1998–1999*, p. 192.

52 *Asahi Shimbun* (in Japanese), morning edition, April 30, 1998.

53 Hattori, *Gaikō dokyumento rekishi ninshiki*, pp. 175–76. See also Iokibe, Itō, Yakushiji, eds., *90-nendai no shōgen: Gaikō gekihen, moto gaimushō jimujikan Yanai Shunji*, pp. 237–38.

54 "Japan-Republic of Korea Joint Declaration: A New Japan-Republic of Korea Partnership towards the Twenty-first Century," October 8, 1998, English translation online at "The World and Japan" database at http://worldjpn.grips.ac.jp/documents/texts/JPKR/19981008.D1E.html.

55 *Pekin shūho* [Beijing Review] 19 (1998), 8. *Asahi Shimbun* (in Japanese), morning edition, April 25, 1998. The account of Jiang Zemin's visit to Japan is based on Tanaka Akihiko, "Tai-Nichi kankei" [Relations with Japan], in Chūgoku Sōran Henshū Iinkai, ed., *Chūgoku sōran: 2000nenban* [China overview: the year 2000 edition], (Tokyo: Kazankai, 2000), pp. 134–44.

56 *Asahi Shimbun* (in Japanese), morning edition, July 11, 1998.

57 Ibid., August 9, 1998.

58 Ibid., November 24, 1998.

59 Ibid., November 12, 1998.

60 Funabashi Yōichi, *Za Peninshura kuesuchon: Chōsen hantō dainiji kaku kiki* [The peninsula question: the second nuclear crisis on the Korean peninsula], (Tokyo: Asahi Shimbunsha, 2006), p. 47. See also Ōshita Eiji, *Kōmura Masahiko "Shin no kokueiki o"* [Kōmura Masahiko: in pursuit of the "true national interest"], (Tokyo: Tokuma Shoten, 2010), pp. 146–58.

61 *Asahi Shimbun* (in Japanese), morning edition, November 25, 1998.

62 Ibid. (morning edition), November 27, 1998.

63 Ibid.

64 "Japan-China Joint Declaration: On Building a Partnership of Friendship and Cooperation for Peace and Development," November 26, 1998, English translation online at http://www.mofa.go.jp/region/ asia-paci/china/visit98/joint.html.

65 *Asahi Shimbun* (in Japanese), evening edition, November 28, 1998.

66 *The Economist*, December 5, 1998.

67 *The Washington Post*, December 6, 1998.

68 *Asahi Shimbun* (in Japanese), morning edition, May 22, 1999.

69 Ibid., morning edition, July 9, 1999.

70 Obuchi visited Okinawa at least four or five times when he was a student at Waseda University. Okinawa was still under American administrative control at the time, and Obuchi was active in the movement to return Okinawa to Japan. He often call Gunma, his birthplace and constituency, his first hometown, Okinawa, his second. Sano Shin'ichi, *Bonsaiden* [Biography of a mediocre prime minister], (Tokyo: Bungei Shunjū, 2003), pp. 170–73.

71 "21-seiki Nihon no Kōsō" Kondankai, ed., *Nihon no furontia wa Nihon no naka ni aru: jiritsu to kyōchi de kizuku shinseiki* [The Frontier Within: individual empowerment and better governance in the new millennium], (Tokyo: "21-seiki Nihon no Kōsō" Kondankai, 2000). An English translation of "Japan's Goals in the 21st Century" is available online at http://www.kantei.go.jp/jp/21century/report/htmls/.

72 *Nihon Keizai Shimbun* (in Japanese), morning edition, November 29, 1999.

Chapter 9
Enter Koizumi

1 Interview with Mori Yoshirō, "Kīpāson ga kataru shōgen 90nendai dai16kai Mori Yoshirō" [A key person speaks, testimony from the 90s, number 16: Mori Yoshirō], *Ronza* (January 2007), 253.

2 Just after Prime Minister Mori took office, a test revealed he had prostate cancer. Because of the timing, he did not have surgery and continued to receive "thorough radiation therapy and chemotherapy." For that reason, "from the beginning it was my intention to remain in office for only one year." He underwent surgery in July 2002 after he had resigned. Ibid., p. 253.

3 Ibid., p. 254.

4   "Shasetsu" (Editorial), *Asahi Shimbun* (in Japanese), morning edition, April 10, 2001.

5   Iijima Isao, *Koizumi kantei hiroku* [Confidential notes from Prime Minister Koizumi's Official Residence], (Tokyo: Nihon Keizai Shimbunsha, 2006), pp. 7–8.

6   Ibid., p. 107.

7   The support of Diet member Tanaka Makiko is said to have been extremely important in Koizumi's election. When he was putting together his cabinet, she reportedly said she was not interested in any position except that of foreign minister. Uesugi Takashi, *Tanaka Makiko no shōtai* [Tanaka Makiko's true face], (Tokyo: Sōshisha, 2002), p. 27.

8   Tanaka Akihiko, "Tanaka Makiko gaisō wa hayaku ji'nin subeki da" [Foreign Minister Tanaka Makiko should resign soon], *Chūō Kōron* [Central Review], (July 2001), 32–35.

9   Uesugi, *Tanaka Makiko no shōtai*, p. 27.

10   Iijima, *Koizumi kantei hiroku*, p. 107.

11   *Asahi Shimbun* (in Japanese), evening edition, April 17, 2001.

12   Interview with Nonaka Hiromu, "Kīpāson ga kataru shōgen 90nendai dai20kai Nonaka Hiromu" [A key person speaks, testimony from the 90s, number 20: Nonaka Hiromu], *Ronza* (May 2007), 251.

13   Before the LDP presidential election, Koizumi was not thought to have been particularly diligent in paying visits to the Yasukuni Shrine. He had run for president twice before but had not pledged to visit Yasukuni at those times. Yomiuri Shimbun Seijibu, *Gaikō o kenka ni shita otoko: Koizumi gaikō 2000-nichi no shinjitsu* [The man who made a fight out of diplomacy: the reality behind the 2000 days of Koizumi's diplomacy], (Tokyo: Shinchōsha, 2006), p. 223. In his recollections published in late 2015, Koizumi emphasized that it was the obligation of a prime minister to visit the shrine. He had not visited the shrine since he left office, he said. Tokoi Ken'ichi, "Koizumi Jun'ichirō dokuhakuroku" [Koizumi Jun'ichirō speaks out], *Bungei Shunjū* (January, 2016), 111.

14   *Asahi Shimbun* (in Japanese), evening edition, October 4, 2001.

15   Ibid., morning edition, October 9, 2001.

16   Yomiuri Shimbun Seijibu, *Gaikō o kenka ni shita otoko*, p. 30.

17   Ibid., p. 21.

18   Ibid., p. 24.

19   Iijima, *Koizumi kantei hiroku*, p. 150.

20   Yomiuri Shimbun Seijibu, *Gaikō o kenka ni shita otoko*, p. 35. English translation in Funabashi, *The Peninsula Question*, p. 5.

21   "Japan-DPRK Pyongyang Declaration," September 17, 2002, English translation online on "The World and Japan" database at http://world-jpn.grips.ac.jp/documents/texts/JPKR/20020917.D1E.html.

22 Funabashi, *The Peninsula Question*, p. 40, says that Fukuda and Abe clashed over this question. According to Yomiuri Shimbun Sei-jibu, *Gaikō o kenka ni shita otoko*, Tanaka Hitoshi insisted that they should be sent back to North Korea, while Nakayama Kyōko and Yachi Shōtarō insisted they should not be. According to Tanaka and Tahara, *Kokka to gaikō*, p. 64, Tanaka Hitoshi said he was not against the five remaining in Japan. Although Iijima stresses the importance of Abe's role, when asked about Fukuda and Tanaka's views, "I know nothing about that," was his response. Tahara Sōichirō (chief editor), *Ofu reko! Bessatsu, Saikō kenryoku no kenkyū: Koizumi kantei no shin-jitsu, Iijima Isao zen hishokan ga kataru!* [Off the record special issue: A study of supreme power; the facts inside Prime Minister Koizumi's Official Residence, former executive secretary Iijima Isao tells all], (Tokyo: Asukomu, 2007), p. 186.

23 The United States and Japan were not able to strike a deal in the "Early Voluntary Sectoral Liberalization" (EVSL) negotiations, which origi-nated out of the APEC leaders' agreement in 1996 on the desirability of accelerating liberalization in the sectors that would have a positive effect on economic growth. Eight sectors—toys, marine products, environmental goods and services, chemical products, forest products, jewelry and precious metals, medical instruments and equipment— were chosen as priority sectors. The US proposed a package deal to lib-eralize all the sectors simultaneously while Japan strongly opposed it as a violation of the spirit of "voluntary liberalization." Both sides were unable to work out a compromise by the time of the APEC Summit at Kuala Lumpur in 1998, and the EVSL got nowhere. Okamoto Jirō, ed., *APEC sōki jiyūka kyōgi no seiji katei: kyōyūsarenakatta konsensasu* [The political process of the APEC EVSL negotiations: the consensus that was not shared], (Tokyo: Ajia Keizai Kenkyūjo, 2001).

24 *Asahi Shimbun* (in Japanese), morning edition, March 25, 2000; *Nihon Keizai Shimbun* (in Japanese), morning edition, March 25, 2000; the account of ASEAN+3 in this chapter is based on Tanaka Akihiko, "The Development of the ASEAN+3 Framework," pp. 65–68.

25 *Nihon Keizai Shimbun* (in Japanese), morning edition, May 7, 2000; *Nikkei Kin'yū Shimbun* (in Japanese), May 8, 2000; it is fairly clear that Japan's Ministry of Finance was the force behind the Chiang Mai Ini-tiative, but the ministry was cautious about letting that impression spread, perhaps because of the past failure of the AMF plan; *Nikkei Kin'yū Shimbun*, May 12, 2000. On the reasons for China's support, finance ministry officials suggested that "it probably thought that, having seen the Asian economic crisis with its own eyes, there was nothing more important than strengthening the cooperative frame-work." *Asahi Shimbun* (in Japanese), morning edition, May 7, 2000.

26 *Nihon Keizai Shimbun* (in Japanese), morning edition, May 9, 2000.

27 Ibid., May 3, 2000.

28 "East Asia grouping to be formalised within ASEAN," *Agence France-Presse*, July 25, 2000.

29 *Nihon Keizai Shimbun* (in Japanese), morning edition, August 22, 2000.

30 Ibid., evening edition, October 7, 2000; ibid., morning edition, October 8, 2000. Three priority areas were agreed on (IT; small- and medium-sized enterprises, components- and parts-supply industries; and trade and investment) as well as rules to determine items of cooperation. These latter were (1) items that would benefit all the member countries; (2) those in which at least two countries from both ASEAN and Japan, China and South Korea would participate; and (3) those for which the participating countries would bear the costs.

31 "Press Statement by Prime Minister Yoshiro Mori," November 25, 2000, online at http://www.mofa.go.jp/region/asia-paci/asean/conference/asean3/press0011.html.

32 *Asahi Shimbun* (in Japanese), morning edition, November 26, 2000. Perhaps because this free-trade zone plan attracted extremely strong interest in the Japanese media, the mere possibility of a "working subcommittee" to consider setting up such an area was reported, while there was virtually no mention of the East Asia Study Group, the establishment of which had actually been agreed upon. That group, in fact, was supposed to review the report of the Vision Group and also explore the prospects for free trade and an East Asia Summit. That said, since the Vision Group itself was discussing the possibility of free trade and an East Asia Summit, reviewing its report would amount to the same thing. As a matter of fact, however, although the decision to set up the East Asia Study Group took place in November 2000, it was not clear what specifically the group was supposed to do. Even when it came to reviewing the Vision Group's proposals, the latter was then in the midst of drawing those proposals up and would not submit them until the autumn of 2001.

33 *Nihon Keizai Shimbun* (in Japanese), evening edition, October 16, 2000.

34 *Asahi Shimbun* (in Japanese), evening edition, November 24, 2000.

35 Ibid., morning edition, May 11, 2001; *Nihon Keizai Shimbun* (in Japanese), morning edition, May 11, 2001. The agreement with South Korea was signed on July 4; with Thailand on July 30; with the Philippines on August 27; and with Malaysia on October 5.

36 *Nihon Keizai Shimbun* (in Japanese), morning edition, November 1, 2001.

37 Ibid., November 6, 2001.

38 *Asahi Shimbun* (evening edition) November 6, 2001. The China-ASEAN FTA came into effect on January 1, 2010.

39 "Opening Statement by Prime Minister Junichiro Koizumi at the Press Conference Following the ASEAN+3 Summit Meeting," November 6, 2001, online at http://japan.kantei.go.jp/koizumispeech/2001/1106asean_e.html.

40 East Asia Vision Group Report 2001, "Towards an East Asian Community: Region of Peace, Prosperity and Progress," online at http://www.mofa.go.jp/region/asia-paci/report2001.pdf.

41 "Press Statement by the Chairman of the 7th ASEAN Summit and the 5th ASEAN+3 Summit Brunei Darussalam, 5 November 2001," online at http://asean.org/?static_post=press-statement-by-the-chairman-of-the-7th-asean-summit-and-the-5th-asean-3-summit-brunei-darussalam-5-november-2001.

42 According to the *Asahi Shimbun* (in Japanese) morning edition, November 7, 2001, the headline in a local English-language newspaper on the 5th read "The Stage is Set for China," welcoming the visit of Premier Zhu Rongji, and a headline referring to "His Courage and Vision" introduced President Kim Dae-jung.

43 A noteworthy aspect of this address, found online at http://www.mofa.go.jp/region/asia-paci/pmv0201/speech.html, is that while speaking about making maximum use of the ASEAN+3 framework, he says, "I expect that the countries of ASEAN, Japan, China, the Republic of Korea, Australia and New Zealand will be core members of such a community." While Japan had been actively pushing for the ASEAN+3 framework from 1997 on, for a while it lost sight of the plan to include Australia and New Zealand. Although the closeness of what might be called Japan's special relation with Australia and New Zealand did not change, it is not known why the plan to add those two countries, which dated back to 1995, was raised again at this stage.

44 Japan concluded bilateral EPAs with Singapore (2002), Malaysia (2006), Thailand (2007), Indonesia (2008), Brunei (2008), the Philippines (2008), and Vietnam (2009). The ASEAN-Japan Comprehensive Economic Partnership Agreement (AJCEP) was signed in 2008 and went into effect as each signatory completed its domestic ratification process. As of 2016, AJCEP has gone into effect with all the ASEAN countries except Indonesia. "Framework for Comprehensive Economic Partnership between Japan and the Association of South East Asian Nations," online at http://www.mofa.go.jp/region/asia-paci/asean/pmv0310/framework.html.

45 To be precise, in the case of Japan, the level assigned to attend was the deputy minister for Foreign Affairs. But a working group was set up under the EASG, and substantive deliberations seem to have proceeded at this level. Although it was regarded as a bureau-chief-level position, in fact, the person in charge for Japan was the head of the Regional Policy Division in the Asian and Oceanian Affairs Bureau.

46 "Final Report of the East Asia Study Group," pp. 50, 59; online at http://www.mofa.go.jp/region/asia-paci/asean/pmv0211/report.pdf.

47 Although both the EAVG and EASG reports refer to an "East Asian Summit," the meeting came to be called the East Asia Summit.

48 Ōba Mie, *Jūsōteki chiiki to shite no Ajia: tairitsu to kyōzon no kōzu* [Asia as multiple overlapping regions: structure of conflict and cooperation], (Tokyo: Yūhikaku, 2014), pp. 161–63.

49 On US-Chinese relations in regard to the Six-Party Talks, see Kurata Hideya, "Rokusha kaidan no seiritsu katei to Bei-Chū kankei" [US-Chinese relations and the process behind the establishment of the Six-Party Talks], in Takagi Seiichirō, ed., *Bei-Chū kankei: reisengo no kōzō to tenkai* [US-Chinese relations, their post-Cold-War structure and development], (Tokyo: Nihon Kokusai Mondai Kenkyūjo, 2007), pp. 67–92. For post-Cold-War US-Chinese relations as a whole, this book provides the most up-to-date analysis.

50 Funabashi, *The Peninsula Question*, p. 267.

51 *Asahi Shimbun* (in Japanese), morning edition, December 3, 2002.

52 Ibid., evening edition, March 12, 2003; Imamura, *Kita Chōsen: "kyokō no keizai,"* p. 45; Funabashi, *The Peninsula Question*, p. 324.

53 Funabashi, *The Peninsula Question*, p. 333.

54 On the Shanghai Cooperation Organization, see Iwashita Akihiro, technical editor, *Seisaku teigen wagakuni no yūrashia gaikō: Shanhai Kyōryoku Kikō o tegakari ni* [Japan's Eurasian diplomacy: using the Shanghai Cooperation Organization as a key], (Tokyo: Nihon Kokusai Mondai Kenkyūjo, 2007), online in Japanese at http://www2.jiia.or.jp/pdf/report/h18_eurasia.pdf.

55 "Joint Statement of the Fourth Round of the Six-Party Talks," September 19, 2005, online on "The World and Japan" database, at http://worldjpn.grips.ac.jp/documents/texts/JPKR/20050919.D1E.html.

56 Oberdorfer and Carlin, *Two Koreas*, p. 418.

57 For Japanese-Chinese relations between 2001 and 2003, see Tanaka Akihiko, "Tai-Nichi kankei" [Relations with Japan], in Chūgoku Sōran Henshū Iinkai, eds., *Chūgoku sōran 2004nenban* [Overview of China, 2004 edition], (Tokyo: Gyōsei, 2004), pp. 135–46.

58 *Asahi Shimbun* (in Japanese), morning edition, October 9, 2001.

59 Ibid., evening edition, March 15, 2002; ibid., morning edition, May 24, 2002; ibid., morning edition, July 18, 2002.

60 Ibid., morning and evening editions, October 28, 2002.

61 For Japanese-Chinese relations after this period, see Tanaka Akihiko, "Tai-Nichi kankei" [Relations with Japan], in Chūgoku Sōran Henshū Iinkai, eds., *Chūgoku sōran 2005–2006nenban* [Overview of China, 2005–2006 edition], (Tokyo: Gyōsei, 2006), pp. 147–58.

62 *Asahi Shimbun* (in Japanese), morning edition, October 9, 2003.

63 Shimizu Yoshikazu, *Chūgoku ga "han-Nichi" o suteru hi* [The day China stops being anti-Japanese], (Tokyo: Kōdansha, 2006), p. 115.

64 *Asahi Shimbun* (in Japanese), morning edition, November 2, 2003.

65 Shimizu, *Chūgoku ga "han-Nichi" o suteru hi*, pp. 50–62.

66 It must be added, however, that Prime Minister Koizumi himself had expressed negative views on the issue of permanent membership on the UN Security Council before he became prime minister. But by the summer of 2004, the arguments of the foreign ministry bureaucrats had prevailed. Prime Minister Koizumi himself had become strongly aware that the climactic moment would be the UN General Assembly in the fall of 2005 and accordingly formulated plans to actively promote UN diplomacy himself.

67 On Japan's UN diplomacy in this period, see Kitaoka Shin'ichi, *Kokuren no seiji rikigaku: Nihon wa doko ni iru no ka* [Political dynamics of the United Nations: where does Japan stand?], (Tokyo: Chūō Kōron Shinsha, 2007).

68 In the September 19, 2005 edition of the *Nihon Keizai Shimbun*, the author wrote, "Leaders who have won elections by a landslide, as Prime Minister Koizumi has now, can generally be said to be in an extremely favorable position when it comes to promoting diplomacy. As for the diplomacy they promote, they no longer need to fear domestic criticism, and it makes it difficult for the foreign countries that are their diplomatic counterparts to engage in negotiations that take advantage of weaknesses at home." Based on this assumption, "if Prime Minister Koizumi were to state that he would not pay a visit to the Yasukuni Shrine during his time in office, I think the situation would improve considerably. There are those who say that Japanese-Chinese relations won't improve because China will continue to criticize even if Koizumi gives up the Yasukuni visits, but I don't think so. Even with public opinion on the Internet in China, it is possible to see a kind of admiration for Koizumi's strong performance. Now, when Japanese-Chinese relations are fixated on the Yasukuni issue, by letting go of it, I think it would be all the more possible to produce a "Koizumi effect" on Japanese-Chinese relations as a whole. Even if anti-Japanese sentiments don't change, at least the Chinese leadership will no longer have any reason to refuse visits by Japanese and Chinese heads of state to each other's country, and it will be easier from now on to ask that China's anti-Japanese education policy be corrected."

69 "Basic Strategies for Japan's Foreign Policy in the 21st Century: New Era, New Vision, New Diplomacy," November 28, 2002, Executive Summary online at http://japan.kantei.go.jp/policy/2002/1128tf_e.html.

70 During the Koizumi administration, at the Ministry of Foreign Affairs in 2004, the Consular and Emigration Affairs Department was promoted to the Consular Affairs Bureau, and the Treaties Bureau was renamed the International Legal Affairs Bureau; the Intelligence and

Analysis Bureau was abolished, and in its place a Director-General of the Intelligence and Analysis Service was established. In 2006, in tandem with the reform of ODA, ODA-related departments of the Economic Cooperation Bureau and the Multilateral Cooperation Department were consolidated to form the new International Cooperation Bureau. A Director-General for Global Issues was also established to take charge of ODA as well as measures to deal with poverty and infectious diseases.

Chapter 10
Six Prime Ministers in Six Years

1 Forty-six percent in 2008 and 47 percent in 2013. NHK Hōsō Bunka Kenkyūjo, *Gendai Nihonjin no ishiki kōzō* [Structure of the consciousness of contemporary Japanese], 8th ed. (Tokyo: NHK Hōsō Shuppan Kyōkai, 2015), pp. 102–3. The importance of "non-party" voters has long been discussed in the standard texts on Japanese politics. See, for example, Itō Mitsutoshi, Tanaka Aiji, and Mabuchi Masaru, *Seiji katei-ron* [Theories of the political process], (Tokyo: Yūhikaku, 2000), pp. 118–21.

2 China agreed to resume policy dialogues by early 2006; comprehensive policy dialogues at the vice-ministerial level took place February 10–11 and May 7–9, and a foreign ministers' meeting was held in Qatar on May 23. Ministry of Foreign Affairs, *Gaikō seisho 2007* [Diplomatic bluebook 2007], (Tokyo: Gaimushō, 2007), p. 28.

3 Kokubun Ryōsei, Soeya Yoshihide, Takahara Akio and Kawashima Shin, *Nit-Chū kankeishi* [History of Sino-Japanese relations], (Tokyo: Yūhikaku, 2013), pp. 221–22. Trans. Keith Krulak, *Japan-China Relations in the Modern Era* (London; New York: Routledge, 2017), pp. 168–69.

4 NHK News, August 3, 2006.

5 Ibid., August 4, 2006.

6 Uesugi Takashi, *Kantei hōkai: Abe seiken meisō no ichinen* [Collapse in the Prime Minister's Official Residence: one year of floundering in the Abe administration], (Tokyo: Shinchōsha, 2007), p. 58.

7 Yachi Shōtarō and Takahashi Masayuki, *Gaikō no senryaku to kokorozashi* [Strategy and aspirations of diplomacy], (Tokyo: Sankei Shimbun Shuppan, 2009), pp. 40–41.

8 *Shūgiin Honkaigi gijiroku* [Plenary session proceedings of the House of Representatives], October 2, 2006.

9 Ibid., October 3, 2006.

10 "Japan-China Joint Press Statement," October 8, 2006, English translation online at http://www.mofa.go.jp/region/asia-paci/china/joint0610.html.

11 The Japan-China Joint History Research project held its first meeting on December 26, 2006. The joint research committee consisted of ten

Japanese and ten Chinese historians; they held four meetings, the last of which was in December 2009, and submitted their report in January 2010. The report is a "parallel history" consisting of separate Japanese and Chinese analyses of pre-modern and modern Sino-Japanese history, drafts of which were commented on and discussed among the commissioned authors (19 Japanese and 29 Chinese). The parallel analyses naturally resulted in different interpretations (for example, the number of victims in the Nanjing Massacre), but the general thrust appeared to be largely shared by the participants. Though the drafts on the history of the two countries after the Second World War were written, they have not been published, apparently because of sensitivity in China. See the summary (in Japanese) on the Foreign Ministry website, September 2010 at http://www.mofa.go.jp/mofaj/area/china/rekishi_kk.html and Kitaoka Shin'ichi and Bu Ping, eds., *"Nit-Chū rekishi kyōdō kenkyū" hōkokusho* [Report of the "Japan-China Joint History Research"], 2 vols. (Tokyo: Bensei Shuppan, 2014).

12　*Kyōdō Tsūshin* (in Japanese), April 12, 2007; "Speech by Premier Wen Jiabao . . . at the Japanese Diet," April 13, 2007, English translation online at http://www.fmprc.gov.cn/mfa_eng/wjb_663304/zzjg_663340/yzs_663350/gjlb_663354/2721_663446/2725_663454/t311544.shtml.

13　Ibid. The text that was passed out beforehand contained a section that read, "After the war, Japan embarked on the path of peaceful development, and became a leading economic power and influential member in the international community. As a friendly neighbor of Japan, the Chinese people support the Japanese people in their continued pursuit of peaceful development," but Wen Jiabao skipped over this part. It is unclear whether or not he did so intentionally.

14　Ministry of Foreign Affairs, *Gaikō seisho 2002* [Diplomatic bluebook 2002], (Tokyo: Gaimushō, 2002), p. 119.

15　"Confluence of the Two Seas," August 22, 2007, English translation on the "World and Japan" database at http://worldjpn.grips.ac.jp/documents/texts/exdpm/20070822.S1E.html.

16　The name of this plan was not established at the time, but it later came to be called the JENESYS Programme: Japan East Asia Network of Exchange for Students and Youths.

17　"Arc of Freedom and Prosperity: Japan's Expanding Diplomatic Horizons," November 30, 2006, English translation online at http://www.mofa.go.jp/announce/fm/aso/speech0611.html.

18　"Policy Speech by Prime Minister Shinzo Abe to the 166th Session of the Diet," January 26, 2007, English translation online at http://japan.kantei.go.jp/abespeech/2007/01/26speech_e.html.

19　"Policy Speech by Minister for Foreign Affairs Taro Aso to the 166th Session of the Diet," January 26, 2007, English translation online at http://www.mofa.go.jp/announce/fm/aso/speech0701.html.

20 Abe Shinzō and Hibi Toshifumi, "Kaiyōsei daichōen o kokufuku suru" [Overcoming ulcerative colitis], *Shōkaki no hiroba* [Forum on the digestive system] 1 (2012), 3–6, online (in Japanese) at http://www.jsge.or.jp/citizen/hiroba/pdf/now01.pdf.

21 Details of these negotiations have not been made fully public. Watanabe Tsuneo, editor-in-chief of the *Yomiuri Shimbun*, and former Prime Minister Mori played intermediary roles. But what Fukuda and Ozawa actually discussed is not clear. See Gotō, *Heisei seijishi*, 3:97–102, and Mori Yoshirō, *Watashi no rirekisho, Mori Yoshirō kaikoroku* [My CV: the memoirs of Mori Yoshirō], (Tokyo: Nihon Keizai Shimbun Shuppansha, 2013), pp. 250–53.

22 Takenaka Harukata, *Sangiin to wa nanika, 1947–2010* (What is the House of Councillors? 1947–2010), (Tokyo: Chūō Kōron Shinsha, 2010), pp. 259, 277–81.

23 Adapted from the *Analects*; the Confucian original is "Reanimate the Old and Know the New" (*wengu zhixin*).

24 "Joint Statement between the Government of Japan and the Government of the People's Republic of China on Comprehensive Promotion of a 'Mutually Beneficial Relationship Based on Common Strategic Interests,'" English translation at http://www.mofa.go.jp/region/asia-paci/china/joint0805.html.

25 "Speech by Chinese President Hu Jintao at Waseda University," June 9, 2008, English translation at http://www.fmprc.gov.cn/mfa_eng/wjdt_665385/zyjh_665391/t464200.shtml.

26 Anami Yūsuke, "Senryakuteki gokei kankei no mosaku to Higashi Shinakai mondai 2006nen–2008nen" [The search for a strategic, mutually beneficial partnership and the East China Sea problem, 2006–2008], in Takahara Akio and Hattori Ryūji, eds., *Nit-Chū kankeishi 1972–2012*, 1: *Seiji* [History of Sino-Japanese relations, 1972–2012, 1: Politics], (Tokyo: Tōkyō Daigaku Shuppankai, 2012), pp. 443–85.

27 *Asahi Shimbun* (in Japanese), evening edition, April 11, 2008. See Kim Chan Hung, "Nippon no tai Kita-Chōsen kōshō patān ni kansuru kenkyū" [A study of patterns of Japan's normalization negotiations with North Korea], PhD dissertation, University of Tokyo (2014), pp. 364–436.

28 *Mainichi Shimbun* (in Japanese), April 13, 2008.

29 Ibid., August 12, 2008.

30 Gotō, *Heisei seijishi*, 3:115–37.

31 "When the Pacific Ocean Becomes an 'Inland Sea': Five Pledges to a Future Asia that 'Acts Together,'" May 22, 2008, English translation at http://japan.kantei.go.jp/hukudaspeech/2008/05/22speech_e.html.

32 Gotō, *Heisei seijishi*, 3:171–72.

33 Shimizu Yoshikazu, *"Chūgoku mondai" no kakushin* [Core of the "China problem"], (Tokyo: Chikuma Shobō, 2009), pp. 22–25.

34 According to Shimizu Yoshikazu, an unidentified Chinese source told him that the commander went ahead without permission but was not

particularly punished for it. Shimizu Yoshikazu, "Taigai kyōkō shisei no kokunai seiji" [Domestic politics behind the assertive foreign posture], in Kokubun Ryōsei, ed., *Chūgoku wa ima* [China, now], (Tokyo: Iwanami Shoten, 2011), p. 12.

35 "Manifesto: Detailed Policies, The Democratic Party of Japan's Platform for Government," p. 28, English translation online at https://www.dpj.or.jp/english/manifesto/manifesto2009.pdf.

36 Yakushiji Katsuyuki, *Shōgen Minshutō seiken* [Testimony: inner politics of the DPJ], (Tokyo: Kōdansha, 2012), p. 35.

37 Ibid., pp. 37, 87.

38 Gotō, *Heisei seijishi*, 3:279.

39 *The New York Times*, August 26, 2009.

40 According to Foreign Minister Maehara Seiji, in Yakushiji, *Shōgen Minshutō seiken*, p. 66.

41 Yamaguchi Jirō and Nakakita Kōji, eds., *Minshutō seiken to wa nan datta no ka? Kī pāsontachi no shōgen* [What was the DPJ government? testimonies of key figures], (Tokyo: Iwanami Shoten, 2014), p. 98.

42 "'CAMPUS Asia' Monitoring on Quality Assurance," online at http://www.niad.ac.jp/n_kokusai/campusasia/monitoring_english_report_english.pdf. The number of students participating in the project is given in "Kyanpasu Ajia no jōkyō ni tsuite" [On the situation of CAMPUS Asia], a document dated November 20, 2015 provided to the author by the Ministry of Education, Culture, Sports, Science and Technology.

43 "Statement by Prime Minister Naoto Kan," August 10, 2010, English translation online at http://japan.kantei.go.jp/kan/statement/201008/10danwa_e.html.

44 Nihon Saiken Inishiatibu, *Minshutō seiken shippai no kenshō* [Examination of the failures of the DPJ government], (Tokyo: Chūō Kōron Shinsha, 2013), pp. 140–44; Anami, "Senryakuteki gokei kankei no mosaku," p. 470.

45 Itō Gō and Takahara Akio, "Minshutō seiken tanjō ikō no Nit-Chū kankei 2009–2012nen" [Sino-Japanese relations since the birth of the DPJ government, 2009–2012], in Takahara and Hattori, *Nit-Chū kankeishi 1972–2012*, 1: 487–501.

46 In the same essay, Itō and Takahara point out that Hu Jintao's directive in July 2009 was *jianchi taoguang yanghui jiji yousuo zuowei* (maintain concealing our capacity and positively do what we can). By adding "positively" (*jiji*) to another phase of Deng's, "do what we can," Hu suggested that China should become more assertive. For Deng's original dictum, see Chapter 2, p. 41.

47 *Gaikō seisho 2011*, p. 68.

48 "National Defense Program Guidelines for FY2011 and beyond," December 17, 2010, English translation at http://www.mod.go.jp/e/d_act/d_policy/pdf/guidelinesFY2011.pdf.

49 "Policy Speech by Prime Minister Naoto Kan at the 176th Extraordinary Session of the Diet," October 1, 2010, English translation at http://japan.kantei.go.jp/kan/statement/201010/01syosin_e.html.

50 For a comparison between prewar Japan and the Fukushima crisis, see Funabashi Yōichi, *Genpatsu haisen: kiki no rīdāshippu to wa* [Defeat at the nuclear power plant: what constitutes leadership in a crisis?], (Tokyo: Bungei Shunjū, 2014).

51 "Assistance by U.S. Forces in the Aftermath of the Great East Japan Earthquake (Operation Tomodachi)," English translation at http://www.mofa.go.jp/j_info/visit/incidents/pdfs/tomodachi.pdf.

52 Japanese Red Cross Society, "Japan Earthquake & Tsunami," English-language website at http://www.jrc.or.jp/eq-japan2011/index.html.

53 "Taiwan kara no shien" [Support from Taiwan], on the Interchange Association, Japan website (in Japanese) at http://www.koryu.or.jp/ez3_contents.nsf/Top/6BE18444C925CE364925785C00299F24?OpenDocument.

54 "Higashi Nihon daishinsai, kaigai shien matome" [The Great East Japan Earthquake: summary of foreign support], (in Japanese) at http://wikiwiki.jp/h4j/#e7321lb8.

55 Based on Fukunaga Kei, *Mindanao wahei* [Mindanao peace], (Tokyo: Iwanami Bukkusentā, 2014); Uesugi Yūji, "Wahei shien de no gaikō to kaihatsu no renkei" [Alignment between diplomacy and development in peace assistance], *Kaigai Jijō* [Journal of International Affairs] 63 (October 2015), 1–16; and my conversations with leaders of both the government of the Philippines and the MILF when I visited an MILF camp and Manila several times from 2012 to 2015.

56 Gotō, *Heisei seijishi*, 3:440–46.

57 For the broader social basis of opposition to the TPP, see Megumi Naoi and Shujiro Urata, "Free Trade Agreements and Domestic Politics: The Case of the Trans-Pacific Partnership Agreement," *Asian Economic Policy Review* 8,2 (December 2013), 326–49; and on pp. 352–53 of the same issue, Akihiko Tanaka, "Comment on 'Free Trade Agreements and Domestic Politics: The Case of the Trans-Pacific Partnership Agreement.'"

58 "ANNEX for ASEAN Security Community Plan of Action," at http://www.asean.org/?static_post=annex-for-asean-security-community-plan-of-action.

59 "Addressing Myanmar's Debt Issues," April 21, 2011, English translation at http://www.mofa.go.jp/region/asia-paci/myanmar/thein_sein_1204/myanmar_debt_issues_en.html.

60 A slightly revised version of the English translation of the Court's findings found at http://nadesiko-action.org/wp-content/uploads/2013/06/Challenge-against-Act-of-omission-involving-Article-3.pdf.

61 *Nihon Keizai Shimbun* (in Japanese), morning edition, December 19, 2011.

62 Noda's statement in Yamaguchi and Nakakita, *Minshutō seiken to wa nan datta no ka?* p. 244.

63 *Mainichi Shimbun* (in Japanese), September 2, 2013; *Nihon Keizai Shimbun* (in Japanese), morning edition, January 11, 2015.

64 *The Asahi Shimbun*, August 15, 2012.

65 *Nihon Keizai Shimbun* (in Japanese), August 14, 2012.

66 Sunohara Tsuyoshi, *Antō Senkaku kokuyūka* [Secret strife behind the nationalization of the Senkakus], (Tokyo: Shinchōsha, 2013), p. 53. English account of the Heritage Foundation speech in *The Guardian*, April 19, 2012.

67 Sunohara, *Antō Senkaku kokuyūka*, pp. 114–15.

68 Hamamoto Ryōichi, *Shirīzu Chaina Wotchi 2: Shū Kinpei no kyōken seiji de Chūgoku wa doko e mukau no ka?: 2012–2013nen* [Series China Watch 2: Where is China heading under Xi Jinping's high-handed politics: 2012–2013], (Kyoto: Mineruva Shobō, 2014), p. 129.

69 Itō and Takahara, "Minshutō seiken tanjō ikō no Nit-Chū kankei," p. 497.

70 Noda Yoshihiko, "Heisei 24nen: Senkaku kokuyūka, Ishihara chiji to mikkai no yoru, ketsudan shita" [2012: I decided to nationalize the Senkakus the evening I had a secret meeting with Governor Ishihara], *Bungei Shunjū* (January 2016), 355–56.

71 Sunohara, *Antō Senkaku kokuyūka*, p. 148.

72 Noda's testimony in Yamaguchi and Nakakita, *Minshutō seiken to wa nan datta no ka?* pp. 234–35.

73 Sunohara, *Antō Senkaku kokuyūka*, p. 198.

74 "Statement by Yang Jiechi at [the] 67th UN General Assembly," September 27, 2012, English translation online at http://www.voltairenet.org/article176041.html.

75 "Statement made by H.E. Mr. Kazuo Kodama . . . following the statement made by H.E. Mr Yang Jiechi," English translation online at http://www.mofa.go.jp/announce/speech/un2012/un_0928.html.

76 "Remarks of Rebuke against Japan's Statement. . . ," October 16, 2012, English translation online at http://www.china-un.org/eng/gdxw/t976699.htm.

77 Sunohara, *Antō Senkaku kokuyūka*, pp. 142–43.

78 "Chūka jinmin kyōwakoku no kaijō hoan kikan" (Maritime law enforcement agencies in the PRC), online (in Japanese) at https://ja.wikipedia.org/wiki/chukajinmin kyowakoku no kaijo hoan kikan/ (The Japanese Wikipedia entry is more complete than the English version).

79 Hamamoto, *Shū Kinpei no kyōken seiji de Chūgoku wa doko e mukau no ka?*, pp. 140–41.

80 Ibid., pp. 152–53.

81 *The New York Times*, October 25, 2012.

82 Gotō, *Heisei seijishi*, 3:530.

Chapter 11
Abe's Come-back

1 "Japan is Back," February 22, 2013 at the Center for Strategic and International Studies, online at http://www.mofa.go.jp/announce/pm/abe/us_20130222en.html.

2 Richard L. Armitage and Joseph S. Nye, "The U.S.-Japan Alliance: Anchoring Stability in Asia" (Washington, DC: Center for Strategic and International Studies, 2012), p. 1, online at http://csis.org/files/publication/120810_Armitage_USJapanAlliance_Web.pdf.

3 Many of the prominent right-wing nationalists who supported Abe's run for the LDP presidential election are listed in Ogawa Eitarō, *Kokka no meiun: Abe seiken kiseki no dokyumento* [The fate of the nation: records of the Abe administration's miracle], (Tokyo: Gentōsha, 2013), pp. 68–74.

4 For Suga's view of Abe, see Gotō, *Heisei seijishi*, 3:520–22 and Ogawa, *Kokka no meiun*, pp. 32–33.

5 "Policy Speech by Prime Minister Shinzō Abe to the 183rd Session of the Diet," January 28, 2013, English translation online at http://japan.kantei.go.jp/96_abe/statement/201301/28syosin_e.html. "Three arrows" is the author's translation; the official English translation translates *sanbon no ya* as "three prongs."

6 Bank of Japan, "Introduction of the 'Quantitative and Qualitative Monetary Easing,'" April 4, 2013, online at https://www.boj.or.jp/en/announcements/release_2013/k130404a.pdf.

7 *Nihon Keizai Shimbun* (in Japanese), April 4 and 27, 2013.

8 Ibid., April 22, 2013, December 28, 2012.

9 "Factsheet on Japan-ASEAN Relations," February 2013, online at http://www.mofa.go.jp/region/asia-paci/asean/factsheet.html.

10 "Myanmā no entai saimu no kaishō ni tsuite" [On the cancellation of Myanmar's overdue debts], January 30, 2013, online (in Japanese) at http://www.mofa.go.jp/mofaj/press/release/25/1/pdfs/20130130_02_1.pdf.

11 "Debt-Relief Measure for Myanmar," May 26, 2013, online at http://www.mofa.go.jp/press/release/press6e_000096.html.

12 "Signing of Exchange of Notes concerning Yen Loan to Myanmar," May 26, 2013, online at http://www.mofa.go.jp/press/release/press6e_000094.html.

13 "Vision Statement on ASEAN-Japan Friendship and Cooperation: Shared Vision, Shared Identity, Shared Future," online at http://www.asean.org/wp-content/uploads/images/2013/resources/40thASEAN-Japan/finalvision%20statement.pdf, and "Joint Statement of the ASEAN-Japan Commemorative Summit: 'Hand in hand, facing

regional and global challenges,'" online at http://www.mofa.go.jp/ files/000022451.pdf.

14 "Japan-ASEAN Commemorative Summit (Japan's ODA to ASEAN)," online at http://www.mofa.go.jp/files/000070232.pdf.

15 "Nihon o torimodosu" [Taking back Japan], LDP campaign platform 2012, online (in Japanese) at http://jimin.ncss.nifty.com/pdf/j_file2012.pdf.

16 "Joint Statement by the United States and Japan," online at http://www. mofa.go.jp/mofaj/kaidan/s_abe2/vti_1302/pdfs/1302_us_02.pdf.

17 *Nihon Keizai Shimbun* (in Japanese), December 10, 2013.

18 "Cabinet Decision on Development of Seamless Security Legislation to Ensure Japan's Survival and Protect its People," July 1, 2014, online at http://japan.kantei.go.jp/96_abe/decisions/2014/__icsFiles/afield-file/2014/07/03/anpohosei_eng.pdf.

19 *Asahi Shimbun* (in Japanese), September 20, 2015; *Nihon Keizai Shimbun* (in Japanese), September 20, 2015.

20 *Asahi Shimbun* (in Japanese), September 19, 2015; *The Asahi Shimbun*, September 19, 2015.

21 Ibid.

22 *Korean News*, September 19, 2015.

23 Hamamoto Ryōichi, "Chūgoku no dōkō" [Trends in China], *Tōa* [East Asia], 548 (February 2013), 39.

24 Tsukamoto Sōichi, "Chōsen hantō no dōkō" [Trends on the Korean peninsula], *Tōa*, 548 (February 2013), 70.

25 *Nihon Keizai Shimbun* (in Japanese), September 15, 2012.

26 Ibid., October 18, 2012.

27 Hamamoto, *Shū Kinpei no kyōken seiji de Chūgoku wa doko e mukau no ka: 2012–2013nen*, pp. 185–86.

28 *Asahi Shimbun* (in Japanese), February 6, 2013; *The New York Times*, February 5, 2013; Hamamoto, *Shū Kinpei no kyōken seiji de Chūgoku wa doko e mukau no ka: 2012–2013nen*, pp. 205–9.

29 *The New York Times*, February 8, 2013.

30 *Nihon Keizai Shimbun* (in Japanese), morning and evening edition, February 9, 2013.

31 Ibid., February 23, 2013.

32 *Asahi Shimbun* (in Japanese), morning edition, April 24, 2013.

33 *Nihon Keizai Shimbun* (in Japanese), June 21, 2013.

34 Ibid., July 29, 2013.

35 *China Daily*, July 30, 2013.

36 *Nihon Keizai Shimbun* (in Japanese), August 13, 2013.

37 Ibid., September 30, 2013.

38 Yomiuri Shimbun Seijibu, *Nit-Chū-Kan gaikō sensō* [Japan-China-South Korea diplomatic wars], (Tokyo: Shinchōsha, 2014), p. 134.

39 *Asahi Shimbun* (in Japanese), morning edition, January 5, 2013; *Daily Yomiuri*, January 6, 2013.

40 *Asahi Shimbun* (in Japanese), morning edition, January 9, 2013.

41 "Address by President Park Geun-hye on the 94th March 1st Independence Movement Day," March 4, 2013, online at http://www.korea.net/NewsFocus/policies/view?articleId=106019.

42 *Asahi Shimbun* (in Japanese), May 8, 2013; *The Asahi Shimbun*, May 8, 2013.

43 *The Washington Post*, May 7, 2013.

44 Quoted in *Asia's Alliance Triangle: US-Japan-South Korea Relations at a Tumultuous Time*, ed. Gilbert Rozman (New York: Palgrave Macmillan, 2015), p. 96; cf. *Korea JoongAng Daily*, April 24, 2013.

45 *Kokkai kaigiroku kensaku sisutemu* [Database system for the minutes of the Diet], Sangiin Yosan Iinkai [House of Councillors, Budget Committee], no. 10, April 23, 2013; English translation in *The Washington Post*, April 26, 2013. On May 15, Abe stated that he never said that Japan had not engaged in aggression, *Kokkai kaigiroku kensaku sisutemu*, Sangiin Yosan Iinkai, no. 18, May 15, 2013.

46 *Kokkai kaigiroku kensaku sisutemu*, Sangiin Yosan Iinkai, no. 11, April 24, 2013; cf. *The Asahi Shimbun*, April 25, 2013.

47 *The New York Times*, November 23, 2013.

48 *Nihon Keizai Shimbun* (in Japanese), December 25, 2013; "Contribution in Kind to the United Nations Mission in the Republic of South Sudan," December 24, 2013, online at http://japan.kantei.go.jp/96_abe/decisions/2013/1224unmiss_ccs_e.html.

49 *Nihon Keizai Shimbun* (in Japanese), December 27, 2013.

50 "Pledge for everlasting peace," December 26, 2013, online at http://japan.kantei.go.jp/96_abe/statement/201312/1202986_7801.html.

51 "Statement on Prime Minister Abe's December 26 Visit to Yasukuni Shrine," December 26, 2013, online at http://jp.usembassy.gov/statement-prime-minister-abes-december-26-visit-yasukuni-shrine/.

52 *The Washington Post*, January 9, 2014.

53 *The Nation*, January 22, 2014.

54 *Asahi Shimbun* (in Japanese), morning edition, December 8, 2013, and January 28, 2014.

55 "Let the Sense of Community of Common Destiny Take Deep Root in Neighboring Countries," October 25, 2013, online at http://www.fmprc.gov.cn/mfa_eng/wjb_663304/wjbz_663308/activities_663312/t1093870.shtml.

56 *Nihon Keizai Shimbun* (in Japanese), morning edition, January 18, 2015. Fukuda told the Nikkei correspondent that the June visit was "not secret at all. You simply didn't notice it."

57 "Policy Speech . . . to the 187th Session of the Diet," September 29, 2014, online at http://japan.kantei.go.jp/96_abe/statement/201409/policyspch.html.

58 "Regarding Discussions toward Improving Japan-China Relations," November 7, 2014, online at http://www.mofa.go.jp/a_o/c_m1/cn/page4e_000150.

html. The following is the English translation issued by the Chinese government:

> The two sides reached a four-point principled agreement on handling and improving the bilateral relations:
>
> First, the two sides have affirmed that they will follow the principles and spirit of the four political documents between China and Japan and continue to develop the China-Japan strategic relationship of mutual benefit.
>
> Second, in the spirit of "facing history squarely and looking forward to the future", the two sides have reached some agreement on overcoming political obstacles in the bilateral relations.
>
> Third, the two sides have acknowledged that different positions exist between them regarding the tensions which have emerged in recent years over the Diaoyu Islands and some waters in the East China Sea, and agreed to prevent the situation from aggravating through dialogue and consultation and establish crisis management mechanisms to avoid contingencies.
>
> Fourth, the two sides have agreed to gradually resume political, diplomatic and security dialogue through various multilateral and bilateral channels and to make efforts to build political mutual trust.

"China and Japan Reach Four-Point Principled Agreement on Handling and Improving Bilateral Relations," November 7, 2014, online at http://www.fmprc.gov.cn/mfa_eng/zxxx_662805/t1208360.shtml.

59 *Asahi Shimbun* (in Japanese), morning edition, February 22, 2014; *The Asahi Shimbun*, February 22, 2014.

60 *Asahi Shimbun* (in Japanese), evening edition, February 28, 2014; "Press Conference by the Chief Cabinet Secretary," February 28, 2014, online at http://japan.kantei.go.jp/tyoukanpress/201402/28_p.html.

61 "Details of Exchanges Between Japan and the Republic of Korea (ROK) Regarding the Comfort Women Issue," June 20, 2014, online at http://www.mofa.go.jp/files/000042171.pdf.

62 *Asahi Shimbun* (in Japanese), morning edition, June 21, 2014; *The Mainichi*, June 21, 2014.

63 "Korea's Position on Japan's Review of the Details Leading to the Drafting of the Kōno Statement," June 25, 2014, online at http://news.mofa.go.kr/enewspaper/mainview.php?mvid=1881&master.

64 *Asahi Shimbun* (in Japanese), morning edition, August 5, 2014.

65 *The Korea Times*, June 22, 2015, online at http://www.koreatimes.co.kr/www/news/nation/2015/06/116_181382.html.

66 "Statement by Prime Minister Shinzo Abe," August 14, 2015, online at http://japan.kantei.go.jp/97_abe/statement/201508/0814statement.html.

67 *Nihon Keizai Shimbun* (in Japanese), morning edition, August 16, 2015.

68 "Commemorative Address by President Park Geun-hye on the 70th Anniversary of Liberation," August 15, 2015, online at http://www.koreasociety.org/policy/commemorative_address_by_president_park_geun-hye_on_the_70th_anniversary_of_liberation.html.

69 *Asahi Shimbun* (in Japanese), evening edition, August 18, 2015.

70 *The Japan Times*, August 16, 2015, online at http://www.japantimes.co.jp/news/2015/08/16/national/politics-diplomacy/u-s-lauds-abe-wwii-anniversary-statement/#.VrmNsMfxa-Q; "Statement by NSC Spokesperson Ned Price on Japanese Prime Minister Abe's Statement on the 70th Anniversary of the End of World War II," August 14, 2015, online at https://obamawhitehouse.archives.gov/the-press-office/2015/08/14/statement-nsc-spokesperson-ned-price-japanese-prime-minister-abe%E2%80%99s.

71 *Asahi Shimbun* (in Japanese), morning edition, October 18, 2015.

72 "Announcement by Foreign Ministers of Japan and the Republic of Korea at the Joint Press Occasion," December 28, 2015, online at http://www.mofa.go.jp/a_o/na/kr/page4e_000364.html.

73 "East Asian way of life" is the author's coinage. On the present state of, and possibilities for, a shared culture of this kind in modern Asia, see Shiraishi Takashi, "Higashi Ajia chiiki keisei to 'kyōtsū bunkaken'" [The formation of the East Asian region and a "common cultural sphere"], in Soeya Yoshihide and Tadokoro Masayuki, eds., *Nihon no Higashi Ajia kōsō* [Japan's conception of East Asia], (Tokyo: Keiō Gijuku Daigaku Shuppankai, 2004), pp. 11–30, and Aoki Tamotsu, "'Konsei bunka' no tenkai to hirogaru 'toshi chūkansō'" [The development of a "hybrid culture" and the expanding "urban middle class"], in Itō and Tanaka, eds., *Higashi Ajia Kyōdōtai to Nihon no shinro*, pp. 67–115.

74 The AsiaBarometer began at the initiative of Professor Inoguchi Takashi and is a project in which the author also participates. For an overview of the project see Inoguchi Takashi, ed., *Ajia Baromētā: toshibu no kachikan to seikatsu sutairu* [The AsiaBarometer: urban value systems and lifestyles], (Tokyo: Akashi Shoten, 2005) and the AsiaBarometer website (https://www.asiabarometer.org). The Pew Research Center conducted a similar survey examining mutual perceptions among Asia-Pacific countries in 2015, showing a very similar pattern to the AsiaBarometer survey, i.e., Japan enjoys very favorable views from most Asian countries except China and South Korea. Bruce Stokes, "How Asia-Pacific Publics See Each Other and Their National Leaders," September 2, 2015, online at http://www.pewglobal.org/files/2015/09/Pew-Research-Center-Asian-Views-of-Each-Other-Report-FINAL-September-2-2015.pdf.

Bibliography

All the websites cited in this Bibliography were valid as of May 12, 2017.

Abe Shinzō. "Confluence of the Two Seas." August 22, 2007. Parliament of the Republic of India. http://worldjpn.grips.ac.jp/documents/texts/exdpm/20070822.S1E.html.

———. "Japan is Back." February 22, 2013. Center for Strategic and International Studies, Washington, DC. http://www.mofa.go.jp/announce/pm/abe/us_20130222en.html.

———. "Pledge for everlasting peace." December 26, 2013. http://japan.kantei.go.jp/96_abe/statement/201312/1202986_7801.html.

———. "Policy Speech by Prime Minister Shinzo Abe to the 166th Session of the Diet." January 26, 2007. http://japan.kantei.go.jp/abe-speech/2007/01/26speech_e.html.

———. "Policy Speech by Prime Minister Shinzo Abe to the 183rd Session of the Diet." January 28, 2013. http://japan.kantei.go.jp/96_abe/statement/201301/28syosin_e.html.

———. "Policy Speech by Prime Minister Shinzo Abe to the 187th Session of the Diet." September 29, 2014. http://japan.kantei.go.jp/96_abe/statement/201409/policyspch.html.

———. "Statement by Prime Minister Shinzo Abe." August 14, 2015. http://japan.kantei.go.jp/97_abe/statement/201508/0814statement.html.

———, and Hibi Toshifumi. "Kaiyōsei daichōen o kokufuku suru" [Overcoming ulcerative colitis]. Shōkaki no hiroba [Forum on the digestive system] 1 (2012), 3–6. http://www.jsge.or.jp/citizen/hiroba/pdf/now01.pdf.

Abe Administration. "Cabinet Decision on Development of Seamless Security Legislation to Ensure Japan's Survival and Protect its People." July 1, 2014. http://japan.kantei.go.jp/96_abe/decisions/2014/__icsFiles/afieldfile/2014/07/03/anpohosei_eng.pdf.

———. "Contribution in Kind to the United Nations Mission in the Republic of South Sudan." December 24, 2013. http://japan.kantei.go.jp/96_abe/decisions/2013/1224unmiss_ccs_e.html.

"Agreement on Reconciliation, Nonaggression, and Exchanges and Cooperation between South and North Korea." December 13, 1991. http://csis.org/files/media/csis/pubs/issuesinsights_v08n03.pdf.

Akashi Yasushi. Ikiru koto ni mo kokoroseki [In a hurry to live]. Tokyo: Chūō Kōronsha, 2001.

———. Nintai to kibō: Kanbojia no 560-nichi [Patience and hope: 560 days in Cambodia]. Tokyo: Asahi Shimbunsha, 1995.

Amako Satoshi. *Kyoryū no taidō: Mō Takutō vs Tō Shōhei: Chūgoku no rekishi 11* [The dragon stirs: Mao Zedong vs. Deng Xiaoping; Chinese history 11]. Tokyo: Kōdansha, 2004.

——, ed. *Chūgoku wa kyōi ka* [Is China a threat?]. Tokyo: Keisō Shobō, 1997.

Anami Yūsuke. "Senryakuteki gokei kankei no mosaku to Higashi Shinakai mondai 2006nen–2008nen" [The search for a strategic, mutually beneficial partnership and the East China Sea problem, 2006–2008]. In Takahara Akio and Hattori Ryūji, eds. *Nit-Chū kankeishi 1972–2012, 1: Seiji* [History of Sino-Japanese relations, 1972–2012, 1: Politics], pp. 443–85. Tokyo: Tōkyō Daigaku Shuppankai, 2012.

Aoki Tamotsu. "'Konsei bunka' no tenkai to hirogaru 'toshi chūkansō'" [The development of a "hybrid culture" and the expanding "urban middle class"]. In Itō Ken'ichi and Tanaka Akihiko, eds. *Higashi Ajia Kyōdōtai to Nihon no shinro* [East Asian Community and Japan's course], pp. 67–115. Tōkyō : Nihon Hōsō Shuppan Kyōkai, 2005.

Armitage, Richard L., and Joseph S. Nye. "The U.S.-Japan Alliance: Anchoring Stability in Asia." Washington, DC: Center for Strategic and International Studies, 2012. http://csis.org/files/publication/120810_Armitage_USJapanAlliance_Web.pdf.

Asahi Shimbun Dai-sansha Iinkai [The Asahi Shimbun Co. Third-Party Committee]. *Hokokusho* [Report]. December 22, 2014. In Japanese. http://www.asahi.com/shimbun/3rd/2014122201.pdf. English summary: http://www.asahi.com/shimbun/3rd/report20150728e.pdf.

Asano Yukiho. *Firipin: Marukosu kara Akino e* [The Philippines: from Marcos to Aquino]. Tokyo: Ajia Keizai Kenkyūjo, 1992.

ASEAN (Association of Southeast Asian Nations). "ANNEX for ASEAN Security Community Plan of Action." June 14, 2012. http://www.asean.org/?static_post=annex-for-asean-security-community-plan-of-action.

——. "Bangkok Summit Declaration of 1995 Bangkok, 14–15 December 1995." http://asean.org/?static_post=bangkok-summit-declaration-of-1995-bangkok14-15-december-1995.

——. East Asia Vision Group Report. *Towards an East Asian Community: Region of Peace, Prosperity and Progress.* http://www.asean.org/wp-content/uploads/images/archive/pdf/east_asia_vision.pdf.

——. "Final Report of the East Asia Study Group." http://www.mofa.go.jp/region/asia-paci/asean/pmv0211/report.pdf.

——. "Joint Communique 25th ASEAN Ministerial Meeting Manila, Philippines, 21–22 July, 1992." http://asean.org/?static_post=-joint-communique-25th-asean-ministerial-meeting-manila-philippines-21-22-july-1992.

——. "Joint Communique of the Twenty-Sixth ASEAN Ministerial Meeting Singapore, 23–24 July 1993." http://asean.org/?static_post=-

joint-communique-of-the-twenty-sixth-asean-ministerial-meeting-singapore-23-24-july-1993.

———. "Joint Communique of the Twenty-Seventh ASEAN Ministerial Meeting Bangkok, 22–23 July 1994." http://asean.org/?static_post=-joint-communique-of-the-twenty-seventh-asean-ministerial-meeting-bangkok-22-23-july-1994.

———. "Joint Statement on East Asia Cooperation 28 November 1999." http://www.asean.org/?static_post=joint-statement-on-east-asia-cooperation-28-november-1999.

———. "Press Statement by the Chairman of the 7th ASEAN Summit and the 5th ASEAN+3 Summit Brunei Darussalam, 5 November 2001." http://asean.org/?static_post=press-statement-by-the-chairman-of-the-7th-asean-summit-and-the-5th-asean-3-summit-brunei-darussalam-5-november-2001.

———. "Vision Statement on ASEAN-Japan Friendship and Cooperation: Shared Vision, Shared Identity, Shared Future." http://www.asean.org/wp-content/uploads/images/2013/resources/40thASEAN-Japan/final-vision%20statement.pdf.

AsiaBarometer. *See* Inoguchi Takashi.

Asian Women's Fund. *Ajia Josei Kikin: Ōraru hisutorī* [Asian Women's Fund: oral history]. Tokyo: Josei No Tame no Ajia Heiwa Kokumin Kikin, 2007.

———. "The 'Comfort Women' Issue and the Asian Women's Fund." Tokyo: Asian Women's Fund, 2004. http://www.awf.or.jp/pdf/0170.pdf.

———. *"Ianfu" mondai to Ajia Josei Kikin* [The "comfort women" controversy and the Asian Women's Fund]. Tokyo: Josei no Tame no Ajia Heiwa Kokumin Kikin, 2007.

Asō Tarō. "Arc of Freedom and Prosperity: Japan's Expanding Diplomatic Horizons." November 30, 2006. http://www.mofa.go.jp/announce/fm/aso/speech0611.html.

———. "Policy Speech by Minister for Foreign Affairs Taro Aso to the 166th Session of the Diet." January 26, 2007. http://www.mofa.go.jp/announce/fm/aso/speech0701.html.

Baker, James. *The Politics of Diplomacy: Revolution, War, and Peace, 1989–1992*. New York: Putman, 1995.

Bank of Japan. "Introduction of the 'Quantitative and Qualitative Monetary Easing.'" April 4, 2013. https://www.boj.or.jp/en/announcements/release_2013/k130404a.pdf.

Becker, Elizabeth. *When the War Was Over: Cambodia and the Khmer Rouge Revolution*. New York: PublicAffairs, 1998.

CAMPUS Asia. "'CAMPUS Asia' Monitoring on Quality Assurance." March 2014. http://www.niad.ac.jp/n_kokusai/campusasia/monitoring_english_report_english.pdf.

Chalermpalanupap, Termsak. "Towards an East Asia Community." October 19,2002.http://asean.org/towards-an-east-asia-community-the-journey-has-begun-by-termsak-chalermpalanupap/.

Cho Youn-soo. "Kaiyō o meguru Nik-Kan kankei 50nen" [50 years of Japan-South Korea maritime relations]. In Kimiya Tadashi and Yi Wŏn-dŏk, eds., *Nik-Kan kankeishi, 1965–2015: 1, Seiji* [History of Japan-South Korea relations, 1965–2015: 1, Politics], pp. 273–96. Tokyo: Tōkyō Daigaku Shuppankai, 2015.

Democratic Party of Japan. "Manifesto: Detailed Policies, The Democratic Party of Japan's Platform for Government." 2009. https://www.dpj.or.jp/english/manifesto/manifesto2009.pdf.

Deng Xiaoping. *Selected Works of Deng Xiaoping, 3: 1982–1992.* Beijing: Foreign Languages Press, 1994. https://dengxiaopingworks.wordpress.com.

Etō Naoko. "Dai-ichi-ji kyōkasho mondai, 1979nen–1982nen" [The first textbook problem, 1979–1982]. In Takahara Akio and Hattori Ryūji, eds., *Nit-Chū kankeishi, 1972–2012, 1: Seijihen* [A history of Japan-China relations, 1972–2012: 1, Politics]. Tokyo: Tōkyō Daigaku Shuppankai, 2012.

Fallows, James. "Containing Japan." *Atlantic* (May 1989), 40–54.

Friedman, George, and Meredith LeBard. *The Coming War with Japan.* New York: St Martin's Press, 1991.

Friedrich-Ebert-Stiftung Tokyo Office. "The Politics of History: History in Politics." December 2014. http://library.fes.de/pdf-files/bueros/japan/11285.pdf.

Fujiwara Kiichi. "Firipin ni okeru 'minshushugi' no seido to undō" [The "democracy" movement and system in the Philippines]. *Shakai Kagaku Kenkyū* [Journal of Social Science] 40,1 (1988), 1–94.

———. "'Minshuka' no seiji keizaigaku: Higashi Ajia ni okeru taisei hendō" [The political-economy of "democratization": regime change in East Asia]. In Tōkyō Daigaku Shakai Kagaku Kenkyūjo, ed., *Gendai Nihon shakai 3: kokusai hikaku 2* [Modern Japanese society 3: an international comparison 2]. Tokyo: Tōkyō Daigaku Shuppankai, 1992.

Fukuda Takeo. "Fukuda Doctrine Speech." August 18, 1977. Manila. http://worldjpn.grips.ac.jp/documents/texts/docs/19770818.S1E.html.

Fukuda Yasuo. "When the Pacific Ocean Becomes an 'Inland Sea': Five Pledges to a Future Asia that 'Acts Together.'" May 22, 2008. http://japan.kantei.go.jp/hukudaspeech/2008/05/22speech_e.html.

Fukunaga Kei. *Mindanao wahei* [Mindanao peace]. Tokyo: Iwanami Bukkusentā, 2014.

Funabashi Yōichi. *Ajia Taiheiyō fyūjon: APEC to Nihon* [Asia Pacific fusion: Japan and APEC]. Tokyo: Chūō Kōronsha, 1995. English version: *Asia Pacific Fusion: Japan's Role in APEC.* Washington, DC: Institute for International Economics, 1995.

———. *Genpatsu haisen: kiki no rīdāshippu to wa* [Defeat at the nuclear power plant: what constitutes leadership in a crisis?]. Tokyo: Bungei Shunjū, 2014.

———. *Za Peninshura kuesuchon: Chōsen hantō dainiji kaku kiki* [The peninsula question: the second nuclear crisis on the Korean peninsula]. Tokyo: Asahi Shimbunsha, 2006. English version: *The Peninsula Question: A Chronicle of the Second Korean Nuclear Crisis.* Washington, DC: The Brookings Institution Press, 2007.

Furuta Motoo. *Betonamu no genzai* [Vietnam today]. Tokyo: Kōdansha, 1996.

Gaddis, John Lewis. *The Cold War: A New History.* New York: Penguin Press, 2005.

Gaimushō Keizai Kyōryokukyoku, ed. *Wagakuni no seifu kaihatsu enjo 1* [Japan's official development assistance 1]. Tokyo: Kokusai Kyōryoku Suishin Kyōkai, 1991.

Gorbachev, Mikhail Sergeevitch. *Gorubachofu kaisōroku* [Gorbachev Memoirs]. Trans. Kudō Seiichirō and Suzuki Yasuo. 2 vols. Tokyo: Shinchōsha, 1996.

———. *Memoirs.* New York: Doubleday, 1996.

Gotō Kenji. *Dokyumento Heisei seijishi 1: hōkai suru 55nen taisei* [Documentary history of politics in the Heisei era 1: the collapse of the 1955 system]. Tokyo: Iwanami Shoten, 2014.

Hamamoto Ryōichi. "Chūgoku no dōkō: Nichi-Bei Dōmei kyōka ni ugoku Abe seiken o keikai suru Chūgoku" [Trends in China: China cautious about the Abe administration's moves to strength the Japan-US Alliance]. *Tōa* [East Asia] 548 (February 2013), 38–52.

———. *Shirīzu Chaina Wotchi 2: Shū Kinpei no kyōken seiji de Chūgoku wa doko e mukau no ka?: 2012–2013nen* [Series China Watch 2: Where is China heading under Xi Jinping's high-handed politics: 2012–2013]. Kyoto: Mineruva Shobō, 2014.

Hara Yōnosuke, ed. *Ajia keizairon* [Discussion of the Asian economy]. Rev. ed. Tokyo: NTT Shuppan, 2001.

Hashimoto Ryūtarō. "Hashimoto Sōri no ASEAN to no shunōkaigi" [Prime Minister Hashimoto's summit meeting with ASEAN]. December 17, 1997. http://www.mofa.go.jp/mofaj/kaidan/kiroku/s_hashi/arc_97/asean97/kaigi.html.

———. "Japan-China Relations in the New Age." September 5, 1997, Beijing. http://www.mofa.go.jp/region/asia-paci/china/dialogue.html.

———. "Reforms for the New Era of Japan and ASEAN." January 14, 1997, Singapore. http://www.mofa.go.jp/region/asia-paci/asean/pmv9701/policy.html.

Hata Tsutomu. "Policy Speech by Prime Minister Hata Tsutomu to the 129th Session of the National Diet." May 10, 1994 (in Japanese). http://world-jpn.grips.ac.jp/documents/texts/pm/19940510.SWJ.html.

Hattori Ryūji. *Gaikō dokyumento rekishi ninshiki* [The understanding of history through diplomatic records]. Tokyo: Iwanami Shoten, 2015.

Hawke, Bob. *The Hawke Memoirs*. Port Melbourne: William Heinemann Australia, 1994.

Hayashida Hiroaki. *Mahatīru no jirenma: hatten to konmei no Marēshia gendaishi* [Mahathir's dilemma: Malaysia's modern history of development and turmoil]. Tokyo: Chūō Kōron Shinsha, 2001.

He Yilin. *Ni nihachi jiken: "Taiwanjin" keisei no esunoporitikusu* [The 228 Incident: the ethnopolitics of the formation of a "Taiwanese people"]. Tokyo: Tōkyō Daigaku Shuppankai, 2003.

Heiwa Anzen Hoshō Kenkyūjo, ed. *Ajia no anzen hoshō, 1989–1990* [Asian security, 1989–1990]. Tokyo: Asagumo Shimbunsha, 1990.

―――. *Ajia no anzen hoshō, 1996–1997* [Asian security, 1996–1997]. Tokyo: Asagumo Shimbunsha, 1996.

Henderson, Gregory. *Korea: The Politics of Vortex*. Cambridge, MA: Harvard University Press, 1968.

Hiraiwa Shunji. "'Reisen no shūen' to Nanboku Chōsen kankei: heiwa kyōson seidoka e no sōkoku" ["The end of the Cold War" and North-South Korean relations: the struggle for the systematic implementation of peaceful coexistence]. In Okonogi Masao, ed., *Posuto reisen no Chōsen hantō* [The post-Cold-War Korean peninsula]. Tokyo: Nihon Kokusai Mondai Kenkyūjo, 1994.

Hironaka Yoshimichi. *Miyazawa seiken, 644nichi* [The Miyazawa administration, 644 days]. Tokyo: Gyōken Shuppankyoku, 1998.

Hoshiro Hiroyuki. *Ajia chiikishugi gaikō no yukue: 1952–1966* [The rise and fall of Japan's Asian regional diplomacy, 1952–1966]. Tokyo: Bokutakusha, 2008.

Hosokawa Morihiro. "Policy Speech by Prime Minister Hosokawa Morihiro to the 127th Session of the National Diet." August 23, 1993. http://japan.kantei.go.jp/127.html#sec5.

Hu Jintao. "Speech by Chinese President Hu Jintao at Waseda University." June 9, 2008. http://www.fmprc.gov.cn/mfa_eng/wjdt_665385/zyjh_665391/t464200.shtml.

Hyŏn Tae-song. *Ryōdo nashonarizumu no tanjō: "Dokkudo/Takeshima mondai" no seijigaku* [The birth of territorial nationalism: the politics of the "Dokdo/Takeshima issue"]. Kyoto: Mineruva Shobō, 2006.

Iechika Ryōko, Matsuda Yasuhiro, and Dan Zuisō, eds. *Kiro ni tatsu Nit-Chū kankei: kako to no taiwa, mirai e no mosaku* [Japanese-Chinese relations at the crossroads: dialogue with the past, groping toward the future]. Kyoto: Kōyō Shobō, 2007.

Iida Masafumi. "Chūgoku to Indoneshia: kokkō saikai kōshō to sono mondaiten" [China and Indonesia: talks on the resumption of diplomatic relations and their sticking points]. *Ajia Kenkyū* [Asian Studies] 44,3 (1998), 1–38.

Iijima Isao. *Koizumi kantei hiroku* [Confidential notes from Prime Minister Koizumi's Official Residence]. Tokyo: Nihon Keizai Shimbunsha, 2006.

Ikeda Tadashi. *The Road to Peace in Cambodia: Japan's Role and Involvement*. Trans. James W. Griffiths. Tokyo: Japan Times, 1998.

Imagawa Yukio. *Kanbojia to Nihon* [Cambodia and Japan]. Tokyo: Rengō Shuppan, 2000.

Imamura Hiroko. *Kita Chōsen: "kyokō no keizai"* [North Korea: the "fabricated economy"]. Tokyo: Shūeisha, 2005.

Inoguchi Takashi, ed. *Ajia Barometā: toshibu no kachikan to seikatsu sutairu* [The AsiaBarometer: urban value systems and lifestyles]. Tokyo: Akashi Shoten, 2005. https://www.asiabarometer.org.

International Institute of Strategic Studies, ed. *Strategic Survey, 1991–1992*. London: Brassey's, 1992.

Iokibe Makoto, ed. *Sengo Nihon gaikōshi* [Postwar Japanese diplomacy]. Rev. ed. Tokyo: Yūhikaku, 2006. English version: Iokibe Makoto and Robert D. Eldridge. *The Diplomatic History of Postwar Japan*. London; New York: Routledge, 2011.

―――, Itō Motoshige and Yakushiji Katsuyuki, eds. *90nendai no shōgen: gaikō gekihen, moto gaimushō jimujikan Yanai Shunji* [Testimony of the 1990s series: turmoil in diplomacy, former Vice-Minister of Foreign Affairs, Yanai Shunji]. Tokyo: Asahi Shimbunsha, 2007.

Ishihara Nobuo. *Kantei 2668-nichi: seisaku kettei no butaiura* [2,668 days in the Prime Minister's Official Residence: behind the scenes of policy-making]. Tokyo: NHKShuppan, 1995.

Itō Gō, and Takahara Akio. "Minshutō seiken tanjō ikō no Nit-Chū kankei 2009–2012nen" [Sino-Japanese relations since the birth of the DPJ government, 2009–2012]. In Takahara Akio and Hattori Ryūji, eds., *Nit-Chū kankeishi 1972–2012: 1, Seiji* [History of Sino-Japanese relations, 1972–2012: 1, Politics], pp. 487–501. Tokyo: Tōkyō Daigaku Shuppankai, 2012.

Itō Mitsutoshi, Tanaka Aiji, and Mabuchi Masaru. *Seiji katei-ron* [Theories of the political process]. Tokyo: Yūhikaku, 2000.

Itō Takatoshi. "1997nen Ajia tsūka kiki: gen'in to shinkokuka no riyū" [The 1997 Asian currency crisis: its origins and the reasons it became more serious]. *Kokusai Mondai* [International Affairs] 563 (2007), 4–13.

―――. "Asian Currency Crisis and the International Monetary Fund, 10 Years Later: Overview." *Asian Economic Policy Review* 2,1 (June 2007), 16–49.

Iwasaki Ikuo. *Shingapōru kokka no kenkyū: "chitsujo to seichō" no seidoka, kinō, akutā* [A study of the Singapore state: the systematization, functions and actors of "growth and order"]. Tokyo: Fūkyōsha, 2005.

Iwashita Akihiro, technical editor, *Seisaku teigen wagakuni no yūrashia gaikō: Shanhai Kyōryoku Kikō o tegakari ni* [Japan's Eurasian diplomacy: using the Shanghai Cooperation Organization as a key]. Tokyo:

Nihon Kokusai Mondai Kenkyūjo, 2007. http://www2.jiia.or.jp/pdf/report/h18_eurasia.pdf.

Izumi Hajime. "Dainihen Chōsen Minshushugi Jinmin Kyōwakoku dainishō gaikō, gunji" [Part II, chapter 2, DPRK foreign policy, military]. *Chūgoku sōran 1992nenban* [China overview 1992 edition]. Tokyo: Kazankai, 1992.

Japan-China Joint History Research project. September 2010 (in Japanese). http://www.mofa.go.jp/mofaj/area/china/rekishi_kk.html.

JICA (Japan International Cooperation Agency). *Hitozukuri, kunizukuri, kokoro no fureai: Kokusai Kyōryoku Jigyōdan 25 nenshi* [People-building, country-building, heart-to-heart exchanges: the 25-year history of the Japan International Cooperation Agency]. Tokyo: Kokusai Kyōryoku Jigyōdan, 1999.

———. "Yonmannin no shinnichika o sodatete 30nen" [30 years training 40,000 Japanophiles]. February 17, 2015 (in Japanese). http://www.jica.go.jp/topics/news/2014/20150217_01.html.

"Joint Declaration of South and North Korea on the Denuclearization of the Korean Peninsula." January 20, 1992. http://www.nti.org/media/pdfs/aptkoreanuc.pdf.

"Joint Declaration" of September 28, 1990 on Japan-DPRK normalization. Cited in C. Kenneth Quinones, "Japan's Engagement of the DPRK, 1990–2000," online at http://www.ckquinones.com/wp-content/uploads/2013/11/JAPANS-ENGAGEMENT-OF-THE-DPRK.pdf.

Kaigai Keizai Kyōryoku Kikin, eds. *Kaigai Keizai Kyōryoku Kikin 30nenshi* [30-year history of the Overseas Economic Cooperation Fund]. Tokyo: Kaigai Keizai Kyōryoku Kikin, 1992.

Kakizaki Ichirō. *Monogatari Tai no rekishi: hohoemi no kuni no shinjitsu* [The history of the story of Thailand: the truth about the "land of smiles"]. Tokyo: Chūō Kōron Shinsha, 2007.

Kamiya Fuji. *Chōsen hantō de okita koto okiru koto* [What has happened and will happen on the Korean peninsula]. Tokyo: PHP Kenkyūjo, 1991.

Kan Naoto. "Policy Speech by Prime Minister Naoto Kan at the 176th Extraordinary Session of the Diet." October 1, 2010. http://japan.kantei.go.jp/kan/statement/201010/01syosin_e.html.

———. "Statement by Prime Minister Naoto Kan." August 10, 2010. http://japan.kantei.go.jp/kan/statement/201008/10danwa_e.html.

Kaneko Yoshiki. *Marēshia no seiji to esunishitī: Kajin seiji to kokumin tōgō* [Politics and ethnicity in Malaysia: Chinese politics and national integration]. Kyoto: Kōyō Shobō, 2001.

Kanō Hiroyoshi. *Indoneshia ryōran* [Indonesia in confusion]. Tokyo: Bungei Shunjū, 2001.

Kartasasmita, Ginandjar, and Joseph J. Stern. *Reinventing Indonesia.* Singapore: World Scientific, 2016.

Kawashima Shin, and Hattori Ryūji, eds. *Higashi Ajia kokusai seijishi* [The international political history of East Asia]. Nagoya: Nagoya Daigaku Shuppankai, 2007.

Kihl Young Whan. "North Korea's Foreign Relations: Diplomacy of Promotive Adaptation." *Journal of Northeast Asian Studies* 10,3 (1991), 30–45.

Kikuchi Tsutomu. *APEC: Ajia Taiheiyō shinchitsujo no mosaku* [APEC: the search for a new Asia-Pacific order]. Tokyo: Nihon Kokusai Mondai Kenkyūjo, 1995.

———. "'Higashi Ajia' chiikishugi no kanōsei: ASEAN+3 (Nit-Chū-Kan) no keii to tenbō" [The possibilities for 'East Asian' regionalism: circumstances of and prospects for ASEAN+3 (Japan, China and South Korea)]. *Kokusai Mondai* [International Affairs] 494 (May 2001), 16–33.

Kim Chan Hung. "Nippon no tai Kita-Chōsen kōshō patān ni kansuru kenkyū" [A study of patterns of Japan's normalization negotiations with North Korea]. PhD dissertation. University of Tokyo, 2014.

Kim Suk-hyun. *Chū-Kan kokkō seijōka to Higashi Ajia kokusai seiji no hen'yō* [Normalization of relations between China and the ROK and changes in international politics in East Asia]. Tokyo: Akashi Shoten, 2010.

Kimiya Tadashi. *Kankoku: minshuka to keizai hatten no dainamizumu* [South Korea: the dynamism of democratization and economic development]. Tokyo: Chikuma Shobō, 2003.

Kishimoto Shūhei. "Ajia kin'yū senryaku no tenkai: Shin Miyazawa Kōsō o koeta hōkatsuteki shien wa jitsugen suru no ka" [The development of an Asian monetary strategy: will comprehensive aid that goes beyond the New Miyazawa Initiative ever materialize?]. In Suehiro Akira and Yamakage Susumu, eds., *Ajia seiji keizairon* [Asian political economy: toward Japan in Asia], pp. 289–319. Tokyo: NTT Shuppan, 2001.

Kitaoka Shin'ichi. *Kokuren no seiji rikigaku: Nihon wa doko ni iru no ka* [Political dynamics of the United Nations: where does Japan stand?]. Tokyo: Chūō Kōron Shinsha, 2007.

———, and Bu Ping, eds. *"Nit-Chū rekishi kyōdō kenkyū" hōkokusho* [Report of the "Japan-China Joint History Research"]. 2 vols. Tokyo: Bensei Shuppan, 2014.

Kobayashi Keiji. "Kanemaru hō-Chō e no michi wa Pari de hajimatta: Nit-Chō kōshō no butaiura" [The road to the Kanemaru visit began in Paris: behind the scenes of the Japanese-North Korean negotiations]. *Aera* (December 11, 1990).

Kobayashi Yōtarō. "Re-Asianization Does Not Mean Isolation." *Los Angeles Times* (December 3, 1991).

———. "Re-Asianize Japan." *New Perspectives Quarterly* 9,1 (Winter 1992), 20–23.

———. "'Sai-Ajiaka' no susume" [Re-Asianize Japan]. *Foresight* (April 1991), 44–46.

Kodama Kazuo. "Statement by H.E. Mr. Kazuo Kodama . . . following the statement made by H.E. Mr Yang Jiechi." September 27, 2012. http://www.mofa.go.jp/announce/speech/un2012/un_0928.html.

Koizumi Jun'ichirō. "Opening Statement by Prime Minister Junichiro Koizumi at the Press Conference Following the ASEAN+3 Summit Meeting." November 6, 2001. http://japan.kantei.go.jp/koizumi-speech/2001/1106asean_e.html.

———. "Speech by Prime Minister Junichiro Koizumi: Japan and ASEAN in East Asia." January 14, 2002. http://www.mofa.go.jp/region/asia-paci/pmv0201/speech.html.

Kojima Kiyoshi. *Japan and a Pacific Free Trade Area.* Los Angeles: University of California Press, 1971.

Kojima Tomoyuki. *Chūgoku gendaishi: kenkoku 50nen, kenshō to tenbō* [Modern Chinese history: 50 years since founding, review and prospects]. Tokyo: Chūō Kōron Shinsha, 1999.

———, Kokubun Ryōsei, et al., eds. *Higashi Ajia: Kokusai jōsei bēshikku shirīzu 1* [East Asia; Basics of International Affairs Series 1]. Tokyo: Jiyū Kokuminsha, 1997.

Kokkai kaigiroku kensaku sisutemu [Database system for the minutes of the Diet]. Sangiin Yosan Iinkai [House of Councillors, Budget Committee]. No. 10, April 23, 2013; no. 11, April 24, 2013; no. 18, May 15, 2013.

Kokubun Ryōsei. *Chūka Jinmin Kyōwakoku* [The People's Republic of China]. Tokyo: Chikuma Shobō, 1999.

———, Soeya Yoshihide, Takahara Akio, and Kawashima Shin. *Nit-Chū kankeishi* [History of Sino-Japanese relations]. Tokyo: Yūhikaku, 2013. English version: *Japan-China Relations in the Modern Era.* Trans. Keith Krulak. London; New York: Routledge, 2017.

Kōno Masaharu. *Wahei kōsaku: tai Kanbojia gaikō no shōgen* [Peace initiatives: witness to Cambodian diplomacy]. Tokyo: Iwanami Shoten, 1999.

Kōno Yōhei. "Statement by the Chief Cabinet Secretary Yohei Kono on the result of the study on the issue of 'comfort women.'" August 4, 1993. http://www.mofa.go.jp/policy/women/fund/state9308.html.

Krugman, Paul. "The Myth of Asia's Miracle." *Foreign Affairs* 73 (1994), 62–78.

Kubo Wataru. "Beniko senchō Kuriura kikanchō no shakuhō o jitsugen shita futaban no tetsuya kōshō" [The two all-night talks that led to the release of Captain Beniko and Chief Engineer Kuriura]. *Gekkan Asahi* [Asahi Monthly], (December 1990).

Kunihiro Michihiko. "Nit-Chū gaikōshi (shiron)" [History of Japan-China diplomatic relations (a tentative study)]. Unpublished document. Nihon Kokusai Mondai Kenkyūjo, 1999.

Kurata Hideya. "Rokusha kaidan no seiritsu katei to Bei-Chū kankei" [US-Chinese relations and the process behind the establishment of the Six-Party Talks]. In Takagi Seiichirō, ed., *Bei-Chū kankei: reisengo no kōzō to tenkai* [US-Chinese relations, their post-Cold-War structure and development], pp. 67–92. Tokyo: Nihon Kokusai Mondai Kenkyūjo, 2007.

Kuroda Haruhiko. *Tsūka no kōbō: en, doru, yūro, jinmingen no yukue* [The rise and fall of currencies: the fate of the yen, dollar, euro and renminbi]. Tokyo: Chūō Kōron Shinsha, 2005.

Kuroyanagi Yoneji, et al., eds. *Tōnan/Minami Ajia, Oseania: Kokusai jōsei bēshikku shirīzu* 2 [Southeast/South Asia, Oceania; Basics of International Affairs Series 2]. Tokyo: Jiyū Kokuminsha, 2001.

Lee Chong-sik. *Japan and Korea: The Political Dimension*. Stanford: Hoover Institute Press, 1985.

Lee Kuan Yew. *Ri Kuan Yū: za Shingapōru sutōri / The Singapore Story, Memoirs of Lee Kuan Yew*. Trans. Komaki Toshihisa. 2 vols. Tokyo: Nihon Keizai Shimbunsha, 2000.

Lee Sang-ock. *Chŏnhwan'gi ŭi Han'guk oegyo: Yi Sang-ok chŏn Oemu Changgwan oegyo hoegorok* [South Korean diplomacy in a transition period: Lee Sang-ock memoirs]. Seoul: Sam kwa Kkum, 2002.

Leifer, Michael. *The ASEAN Regional Forum: Extending ASEAN's Model of Regional Security*. Adelphi Papers 302. Oxford: Oxford University Press for the International Institute of Strategic Studies, 1996.

Li Baodong "Remarks of Rebuke against Japan's Statement on Diaoyu Dao . . . ." October 16, 2012. http://www.china-un.org/eng/gdxw/t976699.htm.

Li Chengri. "Chū-Kan kokkō seijōka o meguru Chūgoku no Chōsen hantō seisaku" [China's Korean peninsula policy on the normalization of Chinese-South Korean relations]. In Suzuki Masayuki, Hiraiwa Shunji, and Kurata Hideya, eds., *Chōsen hantō to kokusai seiji: reisen no tenkai to hen'yō* [The Korean peninsula and international politics: Cold-War developments and transformation]. Tokyo: Keiō Gijuku Daigaku Shuppankai, 2005.

Liang Zhang, ed. *The Tiananmen Papers*. New York: Public Affairs, 2001.

Liberal Democratic Party. "Nihon o torimodosu" [Taking back Japan]. LDP campaign platform 2012 (in Japanese). http://jimin.ncss.nifty.com/pdf/j_file2012.pdf.

Luttwak, Edward N. "From Geopolitics to Geo-Economics." *The National Interest* 20 (Summer 1990), 17–23.

Mainichi Shimbunsha Seijibu, ed. *Tenkanki no "anpo"* ["National security" in a time of transition]. Tokyo: Mainichi Shimbunsha, 1979.

Mann, James. *About Face: A History of America's Curious Relationship with China from Nixon to Clinton*. New York: Alfred A. Knopf, 1999.

Martin, Bradley K. *Under the Loving Care of the Fatherly Leader: North Korea and the Kim Dynasty*. New York: Thomas Dunne Books, 2004.

Masuo Chisako. "Tō Shōhei ki Chūgoku no tai-Chōsen hantō seisaku" [Chinese policy toward the Korean peninsula during the Deng Xiaoping era]. *Ajia Kenkyū* [Asian Studies] 48,3 (2002), 77–101.

Matsuda Yasuhiro. *Taiwan ni okeru ittō dokusai taisei no seiritsu* [The establishment of a one-party system in Taiwan]. Tokyo: Keiō Gijuku Daigaku Shuppankai, 2006.

Mikuriya Takashi, and Nakamura Takafusa, eds. *Kikigaki: Miyazawa Kiichi kaikoroku* [Oral history: Miyazawa Kiichi's reminiscences]. Tokyo: Iwanami Shoten, 2004. English version. *Politics and Power in 20th-Century Japan: The Reminiscences of Miyazawa Kiichi*. Translation ed. Timothy S. George. London: Bloomsbury Academic, 2015.

———, and Watanabe Akio (interviews, compilation), *Shushō kantei no ketsudan: Naikaku Kanbō Fukuchōkan Ishihara Nobuo no 2600-nichi* [Decisions at the Prime Minister's Official Residence: Ishihara Nobuo's 2,600 days as deputy chief cabinet secretary]. Tokyo: Chūō Kōronsha, 1997.

Ministry of Defense (Japan). "National Defense Program Guidelines for FY 2011 and beyond." December 17, 2010. http://www.mod.go.jp/e/d_act/d_policy/pdf/guidelinesFY2011.pdf.

Ministry of Foreign Affairs (DPRK). "Letter dated 12 March 1993 from the Minister for Foreign Affairs of the Democratic People's Republic of Korea addressed to the President of the Security Council." https://ahlambauer.files.wordpress.com/2013/03/s-25405.pdf.

Ministry of Foreign Affairs (Japan). "Addressing Myanmar's Debt Issues." April 21, 2011. http://www.mofa.go.jp/region/asia-paci/myanmar/thein_sein_1204/myanmar_debt_issues_en.html.

———. "Announcement by Foreign Ministers of Japan and the Republic of Korea at the Joint Press Occasion." December 28, 2015. http://www.mofa.go.jp/a_o/na/kr/page4e_000364.html.

———. "Debt-Relief Measure for Myanmar." May 26, 2013. http://www.mofa.go.jp/press/release/press6e_000096.html.

———. "Details of Exchanges Between Japan and the Republic of Korea (ROK) Regarding the Comfort Women Issue." June 20, 2014. http://www.mofa.go.jp/files/000042171.pdf.

———. "Factsheet on Japan-ASEAN Relations." February 2013. http://www.mofa.go.jp/region/asia-paci/asean/factsheet.html.

———. "Framework for Comprehensive Economic Partnership between Japan and the Association of South East Asian Nations." October 8, 2003. http://www.mofa.go.jp/region/asia-paci/asean/pmv0310/framework.html.

———. *Gaikō seisho 1991* [Diplomatic Bluebook]. Tokyo: Ōkurashō Insatsukyoku, 1991. English translation: http://www.mofa.go.jp/policy/other/bluebook/1991/1991-contents.htm.

———. *Gaikō seisho 1992* [Diplomatic bluebook]. Tokyo: Ōkurashō Insatsukyoku, 1993. English translation of PKO principles: http://www.mofa.go.jp/policy/un/pko/pdfs/contribution.pdf.

———. *Gaikō seisho 1998, Daiichibu* [Diplomatic bluebook, 1998, Part 1]. Tokyo: Ōkurashō Insatsukyoku, 1998. English translation: http://www.mofa.go.jp/policy/other/bluebook/1998/index.html.

————. *Gaikō seisho 2002* [Diplomatic bluebook 2002]. Tokyo: Gaimushō, 2002. English translation: http://www.mofa.go.jp/policy/other/bluebook/2002/index.html.

————. *Gaikō seisho 2007* [Diplomatic bluebook 2007]. Tokyo: Gaimushō, 2007. English translation: http://www.mofa.go.jp/policy/other/bluebook/2007/index.html.

————. "Japan's Official Development Assistance White Paper 2004: 'Accomplishments and Progress of 50 Years.'" Economic Cooperation Bureau, Ministry of Foreign Affairs, 2004. http://www.mofa.go.jp/policy/oda/white/2004/part1-2.pdf.

————. "Japan-ASEAN Commemorative Summit: Japan's ODA to ASEAN." http://www.mofa.go.jp/files/000070232.pdf.

————. "Japan-China Joint Declaration: On Building a Partnership of Friendship and Cooperation for Peace and Development." November 26, 1998. http://www.mofa.go.jp/region/asia-paci/china/visit98/joint.html.

————. "Japan-China Joint Press Statement." October 8, 2006. http://www.mofa.go.jp/region/asia-paci/china/joint0610.html.

————. "Japanese Territory: Takeshima." July 30, 2015. http://www.mofa.go.jp/a_o/na/takeshima/page1we_000065.html.

————. "Joint Statement between the Government of Japan and the Government of the People's Republic of China on Comprehensive Promotion of a 'Mutually Beneficial Relationship Based on Common Strategic Interests.'" May 10, 2008. http://www.mofa.go.jp/region/asia-paci/china/joint0805.html.

————. "Joint Statement by the United States and Japan." November 12, 2011. http://www.mofa.go.jp/mofaj/kaidan/s_abe2/vti_1302/pdfs/1302_us_02.pdf.

————. "Joint Statement of the ASEAN-Japan Commemorative Summit: 'Hand in hand, facing regional and global challenges.'" http://www.mofa.go.jp/files/000022451.pdf.

————. "Measures Taken by the Government of Japan on the Issue known as 'Comfort Women.'" October 14, 2014. http://www.mofa.go.jp/policy/women/fund/policy.html.

————. "Myanmā no entai saimu no kaishō ni tsuite" [On the cancellation of Myanmar's overdue debts]. January 30, 2013 (in Japanese). http://www.mofa.go.jp/mofaj/press/release/25/1/pdfs/20130130_02_1.pdf .

————. "A New Initiative to Overcome the Asian Currency Crisis (New Miyazawa Initiative). http://www.mof.go.jp/english/international_policy/financial_cooperation_in_asia/new_miyazawa_initiative/ele042.htm.

————. *Nit-Chū kankei kihon shiryōshū 1949–1997* [Collection of basic documents on Japan-China relations, 1949–1997]. Tokyo: Kazankai, 1998. English translation: "The Senkaku Islands." March 2013. http://www.mofa.go.jp/region/asia-paci/senkaku/pdfs/senkaku_en.pdf.

————. "Regarding Discussions toward Improving Japan-China Relations." November 7, 2014. http://www.mofa.go.jp/a_o/c_m1/cn/page4e_000150.html.

————. "Signing of Exchange of Notes concerning Yen Loan to Myanmar." May 26, 2013. http://www.mofa.go.jp/press/release/press6e_000094.html.

Ministry of Foreign Affairs (PRC). "China and Japan Reach Four-Point Principled Agreement on Handling and Improving Bilateral Relations." November 7, 2014. http://www.fmprc.gov.cn/mfa_eng/zxxx_662805/st1208360.shtml.

————. "Let the Sense of Community of Common Destiny Take Deep Root in Neighboring Countries." October 25, 2013. http://www.fmprc.gov.cn/mfa_eng/wjb_663304/wjbz_663308/activities_663312/t1093870.shtml.

Ministry of Foreign Affairs (ROK). "Korea's Position on Japan's Review of the Details Leading to the Drafting of the Kono Statement." June 25, 2014. http://news.mofa.go.kr/enewspaper/mainview.php?m-vid=1881&master.

Minowa Tokuji. "Tai no tsūka kiki to sono go no keizai jōkyō" [The Thai currency crisis and subsequent economic conditions]. In Itō Osamu, Okuyama Tadanobu and Minowa Tokuji, eds., Tsūka kin'yū kiki to Higashi Ajia keizai [The currency and financial crises and the East Asian economy]. Tokyo: Shakai Hyōronsha, 2005.

Miyagi Taizō, ed. Sengo Nihon no Ajia gaikō [Japan's postwar Asia diplomacy]. Tokyo: Mineruva Shobō, 2015.

Miyake Wasuke. Gaikō ni shōri wa nai: dare mo shiranai Nihon gaikō ura no ura [There are no victories in diplomacy: behind the behind-the-scenes Japanese diplomacy that no one knows]. Tokyo: Fusōsha, 1990.

Miyamoto Mitsuo. "Ajia-Ōshū kaigi purosesu to ryōchiiki kankei no shōrai" [The ASEM process and the future of relations between the two regions]. Seikei Hōgaku [Seikei University Law] 51 (March 2000), 15–51.

Miyazawa Kiichi. "Statement by Chief Cabinet Secretary Kiichi Miyazawa on History Textbooks." August 26, 1982. http://www.mofa.go.jp/policy/postwar/state8208.html.

Mōri Kazuko. Gendai Chūgoku seiji [Modern Chinese politics]. 3rd ed. Nagoya: Nagoya Daigaku Shuppankai, 2012.

————. Nit-Chū kankei: sengo kara shinjidai e [Japanese-Chinese relations from the postwar period to the new era]. Tokyo: Iwanami Shoten, 2006.

————. "Tai-Soren Tō-Ō kankei" [Relations with the Soviet Union and Eastern Europe]. In Chūgoku Sōran Henshū Iinkai, ed., Chūgoku sōran 1992nenban [Overview of China, 1992 edition]. Tokyo: Kazankai, 1992.

Mori Yoshirō. "Kīpāson ga kataru shōgen 90nendai dai16kai Mori Yoshirō" [A key person speaks, testimony from the 90s, number 16: Mori Yoshirō]. Ronza 140 (January 2007), 243–56.

———. "Press Statement by Prime Minister Yoshiro Mori." 25 November 2000. http://www.mofa.go.jp/region/asia-paci/asean/conference/asean3/press0011.html.

———. *Watashi no rirekisho, Mori Yoshirō kaikoroku* [My CV: the memoirs of Mori Yoshirō]. Tokyo: Nihon Keizai Shimbun Shuppansha, 2013.

Morita Akio, and Ishihara Shintarō. *The Japan That Can Say No.* New York: Simon & Schuster, 1991.

Moriyama Shigenori. *Kankoku gendai seiji* [Contemporary Korean politics]. Tokyo: Tōkyō Daigaku Shuppankai, 1998.

Murayama Tomiichi. "Policy Speech by Prime Minister Murayama Tomiichi to the 130th Session of the National Diet." July 18, 1994 (in Japanese). http://worldjpn.grips.ac.jp/documents/texts/pm/19940718.SWJ.html.

———. "Resolution to Renew the Determination for Peace on the Basis of Lessons Learned From History." June 9, 1995. http://www.mofa.go.jp/announce/press/pm/murayama/address9506.html.

———. *Sō janō: Murayama Tomiichi "shushō taiken" no subete o kataru* [Well, let's see: Murayama Tomiichi tells all about his "experience as prime minister"]. Tokyo: Daisan Shokan, 1998.

———. "Statement by Prime Minister Tomiichi Murayama 'On the occasion of the 50th anniversary of the war's end.'" August 15, 1995. http://www.mofa.go.jp/announce/press/pm/murayama/9508.html.

Nakagawa Yoshio. *Chūgoku to Taiwan* [China and Taiwan]. Tokyo: Chūō Kōronsha, 1998.

———. *Taiwan o mitsumeru me: teiten kansoku, gekidō no 20nen* [Focusing on Taiwan: fixed point observations, 20 years of turbulence]. Tokyo: Tabata Shoten, 1992.

Nakahira Noboru, Komaki Teruo, and Igarashi Takeshi. "'Koizumi Sōri hō-Chō' e no dōtei to Nihon gaikō" [Japanese diplomacy and the steps leading up to "Prime Minister Koizumi's visit to North Korea"]. *Kokusai Mondai* [International Affairs] 512 (2002), 58–75.

Nakano Ari. *Gendai Betonamu no seiji to gaikō: kokusai shakai sannyū e no michi* [Politics and diplomacy in Vietnam today: the road to entry into the international community]. Tokyo: Akatsuki Inshokan, 2006.

Nakasone Yasuhiro. Kuala Lumpur Speech. May 8, 1983 (in Japanese). http://worldjpn.grips.ac.jp/documents/texts/exdpm/19830508.S1J.html.

——— *Tenchi ujō: gojūnen no sengo seiji o kataru* [All sentient beings: talking about 50 years of postwar politics]. Tokyo: Bungei Shunjū, 1996.

Nakayama Tarō. "Foreign policy address to the 118th National Diet (special session)." March 2, 1990 (in Japanese). http://worldjpn.grips.ac.jp/documents/texts/fam/19900302.SXJ.html.

———. "Statement by Foreign Minister Taro Nakayama to the General Session of the ASEAN Post Ministerial Conference." July 22, 1992. http://worldjpn.grips.ac.jp/documents/texts/JPSEA/19910722.O1E.html.

Naoi Megumi, and Shujiro Urata. "Free Trade Agreements and Domestic Politics: The Case of the Trans-Pacific Partnership Agreement." *Asian Economic Policy Review* 8,2. (December 2013), 326–49.

Nemoto Takashi. "Seiji to keizai" [Politics and the economy]. In Ayabe Tsuneo and Ishii Yoneo, eds., *Motto shiritai Myanmā* [I want to learn more about Myanmar]. 2nd ed. Tokyo: Kōbundō, 1994.

NHK Hōsō Bunka Kenkyūjo. *Gendai Nihonjin no ishiki kōzō* [Structure of the consciousness of contemporary Japanese]. 8th ed. Tokyo: NHK Hōsō Shuppan Kyōkai, 2015.

Nihon Keizai Shimbunsha, ed. *Shin Nihon keizai: subete ga kawarihajimeta* [The new Japanese economy: everything has begun to change]. Tokyo: Nihon Keizai Shimbunsha, 1988.

Nihon Saiken Inishiatibu. *Minshutō seiken shippai no kenshō* [Examination of the failures of the DPJ government]. Tokyo: Chūō Kōron Shinsha, 2013.

Nihon Seiji Gakkai, ed. *Nenpō seijigaku: kiki no Nihon gaikō: 70nendai* [The Annals of the Japanese Political Science Association: Japanese diplomacy in crisis: the 70s]. Tokyo: Iwanami Shoten, 1997.

Nishigaki Akira, Shimomura Yasutami, and Tsuji Kazuto. *Kaihatsu enjo no keizaigaku* [The economics of development assistance]. 4th ed. Tokyo: Yūhikaku, 2009.

Nishimura Hideki. *Kita Chōsen yokuryū: dai jūhachi Fujisan Maru jiken no shinsō* [North Korean internment: the truth about the No. 18 Fujisan Maru incident]. Tokyo: Iwanami Shoten, 2004.

Noda Yoshihiko. "Heisei 24nen: Senkaku kokuyūka, Ishihara chiji to mikkai no yoru, ketsudan shita" [2012: I decided to nationalize the Senkakus the evening I had a secret meeting with Governor Ishihara]. *Bungei Shunjū* (January 2016), 355–57.

Nonaka Hiromu. "Kīpāson ga kataru shōgen 90nendai dai20kai Nonaka Hiromu" [A key person speaks, testimony from the 90s, number 20: Nonaka Hiromu]. *Ronza* 144 (May 2007), 245–56.

Ōba Mie. *Ajia Taiheiyō chiiki keisei e no dōtei: kyōkai kokka Nichi-Gō aidentiti mosaku to chiikishugi* [The process of forming the Asia-Pacific region: regionalism and border states Japan and Australia's search for identity]. Kyoto: Mineruva Shobō, 2004.

———. *Jūsōteki chiiki to shite no Ajia: tairitsu to kyōzon no kōzu* [Asia as multiple overlapping regions: structure of conflict and cooperation]. Tokyo: Yūhikaku, 2014.

Oberdorfer, Don, and Robert Carlin, *The Two Koreas: A Contemporary History*. Rev. and updated ed. New York: Basic Books, 2014.

Obuchi Keizō. "Obuchi Sōri no ASEAN to no shunōkaigi tō shusseki" [Prime Minister Obuchi's attendance at the summit meeting with ASEAN and elsewhere]. Tokyo: Gaimushō Ajiakyoku, 1999.

————. "Policy speech by Prime Minister Keizo Obuchi at the Lecture Program hosted by the Institute for International Relations, Hanoi, Vietnam, December 16, 1998: Toward the Creation of A Bright Future for Asia." http://www.mofa.go.jp/region/asia-paci/asean/pmv9812/policy-speech.html.

————. "Statement by Foreign Minister Keizo Obuchi on Japan and East Asia: Outlook for the New Millennium." May 4, 1998. http://www.mofa.go.jp/announce/announce/1998/5/980504.html.

Ochi Takao. "Detantoki no Nihon gaikō: Fukuda seiken no gaikō wakugumi" [Japanese diplomacy in an age of détente: the diplomatic framework of the Fukuda administration]. MA thesis. Graduate School of Law and Politics, Tokyo University, 2004.

Ogawa Eitarō. *Kokka no meiun: Abe seiken kiseki no dokyumento* [The fate of the nation: records of the Abe administration's miracle]. Tokyo: Gentō-sha, 2013.

Okabe Tatsumi. *Chūgoku no taigai senryaku* [China's foreign strategy]. Tokyo: Tōkyō Daigaku Shuppankai, 2002.

————. "Coping with China." In Nishihara Masahi and James Morley, eds., *Vietnam Joins the World*, pp. 117–33. Armonk, NY: M.E. Sharpe, 1997.

————. *Tōnan Ajia to Nihon no shinrō: "hannichi" no kōzō to Chūgoku no yakuwari* [Southeast Asia and the course for Japan to follow: "anti-Japanese" structure and China's role]. Tokyo: Nihon Keizai Shimbunsha, 1976.

Okamoto Jirō, ed. *APEC sōki jiyūka kyōgi no seiji katei: kyōyūsarenakatta konsensasu* [The political process of the APEC EVSL negotiations: the consensus that was not shared]. Tokyo: Ajia Keizai Kenkyūjo, 2001.

Okonogi Masao. "Nit-Chō kokkō kōshō to Nihon no yakuwari" [Japanese-North Korean diplomatic negotiations and the role of Japan]. In Okonogi Masao, ed., *Posuto reisen no Chōsen hantō* [The post-Cold-War Korean peninsula], pp. 246–73. Tokyo: Nihon Kokusai Mondai Kenkyūjo, 1994.

Ōnuma Yasuaki. *"Ianfu" mondai to wa nandatta no ka: media, NGO, seifu no kōzai* [What was the "comfort women" controversy? the strengths and weaknesses of the media, NGOs and the government]. Tokyo: Chūō Kōron Shinsha, 2007.

Ōshita Eiji. *Kōmura Masahiko "Shin no kokueiki o"* [Kōmura Masahiko: in pursuit of the "true national interest"]. Tokyo: Tokuma Shoten, 2010.

Ōta Yasuo, and Arima Yoshiyuki. *Sengo fukkō hiroku: Segin yūshi ni manabu Nippon saisei* [Hidden history of postwar reconstruction: lessons of World Bank loans for Japan's re-generation]. Tokyo: Nihon Keizai Shimbun Shuppansha, 2012.

Owada Hisashi. *Gaikō to wa nani ka* [What is diplomacy?]. Tokyo: NHK Shuppan, 1996.

Pacific Basin Cooperation Study Group. *Report on the Pacific Basin Cooperation Concept.* Tokyo: Pacific Basin Cooperation Study Group, 1980. http://worldjpn.grips.ac.jp/documents/texts/APEC/19800519.O1E.html.

Park, Geun-hye. "Address by President Park Geun-hye on the 94th March 1st Independence Movement Day." March 4, 2013. http://www.korea.net/NewsFocus/policies/view?articleId=106019.

———— "Commemorative Address by President Park Geun-hye on the 70th Anniversary of Liberation." August 15, 2015. http://www.koreasociety.org/ policy/commemorative_address_by_president_park_geun-hye_on_the_70th_ anniversary_of_liberation.html.

Prime Minister's Commission on Japan's Goals in the 21st Century. "21-seiki Nihon no Kōsō" Kondankai, ed. *Nihon no furontia wa Nihon no naka ni aru: jiritsu to kyōchi de kizuku shinseiki* [The Frontier Within: individual empowerment and better governance in the new millennium]. Tokyo: "21-seiki Nihon no Kōsō" Kondankai, 2000. English translation: "Japan's Goals in the 21st Century." http://www.kantei.go.jp/jp/21century/report/htmls/.

Prime Minister's Task Force on Foreign Relations. "Basic Strategies for Japan's Foreign Policy in the 21st Century: New Era, New Vision, New Diplomacy." November 28, 2002. http://japan.kantei.go.jp/policy/2002/1128tf_e.html.

Qian Qichen. *Ten Episodes in China's Diplomacy.* New York: Harpers, 2005.

Quinones, Kenneth. *Kita Chōsen: Bei kokumushō tantōkan no kōshō hiroku* [North Korea: confidential notes of the US State Department official in charge]. Trans. Yamaoka Kunihiko and Yamaguchi Mizuhiko. Tokyo: Chūō Kōron Shinsha, 2000.

————. "The United States in North Korea's Foreign Policy." http://www.ckquinones.com/wp-content/uploads/2013/11/US-in-NK-Foreign-Policy.pdf.

Reagan, Ronald. *An American Life, The Autobiography.* New York: Simon & Schuster, 1990.

Roh Tae-woo. *Korea: A Nation Transformed, Selected Speeches.* Oxford; New York: Pergamon Press, 1990.

————. "President Roh Tae-woo's Declaration of Non-Nuclear Korean Peninsula Peace Initiative." December 18, 1991 (in Japanese). http://worldjpn.grips.ac.jp/documents/texts/JPKR/19911218.O1J.html.

Rozman, Gilbert, ed. *Asia's Alliance Triangle: US-Japan-South Korea Relations at a Tumultuous Time.* New York: Palgrave Macmillan, 2015.

Sakakibara Eisuke. *Nihon to sekai ga furueta hi: saibā shihonshugi no seiritsu* [The day Japan and the world shook: the birth of cyber capitalism]. Tokyo: Chūō Kōron Shinsha, 2000.

Sano Shin'ichi. *Bonsaiden* [Biography of a mediocre prime minister]. Tokyo: Bungei Shunjū, 2003.

Sasaki Yoshitaka. *Umi o wataru Jieitai: PKO rippō to seiji kenryoku* [The Self-Defense Forces overseas: PKO legislation and political power]. Tokyo: Iwanami Shoten, 1992.

Satō Hiroshi, and Iwasaki Ikuo, eds. *Ajia seiji dokuhon* [Asian politics reader]. Tokyo: Tōyō Keizai Shinpōsha, 1998.

Satō Kōichi. *ASEAN rejīmu: ASEAN ni okeru kaigi gaikō no hatten to kadai* [The ASEAN regime: ASEAN's conference diplomacy, its development and agenda]. Tokyo: Keisō Shobō, 2003.

———. "EAEC kōsō to ASEAN + 3 hikōshiki shunōkaigi" [The EAEC proposal and the ASEAN + 3 informal summit talks]. *Tōa* [East Asia] 404 (February 2001), 58–76.

———. "Higashi Ajia Keizai Kaigi kōsō o meguru kokusai kankei: Mahatīru kōsō to Ajia Taiheiyō kyōryoku" [International relations behind plans for an East Asian Economic Caucus: the Mahathir proposal and Asia-Pacific cooperation]. *Gaikō Jihō* [International Affairs, Japan] 1286 (March 1992), 4–21.

Sejima Ryūzō. *Sejima Ryūzō kaisōroku ikusanga* [Many mountains and rivers: Sejima Ryūzō's recollections]. Tokyo: Sankei Shimbunsha, 1995.

Seki Hajime, Ochiai Taosa and Suginoo Yoshio. *PKO no shinjitsu: shirarezaru Jieitai kaigai haken no subete* [The truth about PKO: everything you didn't know about sending the Self-Defense Forces overseas]. Tokyo: Keizaikai, 2004.

Shiba Ryōtarō. *Taiwan kikō: kaidō o yuku*, 40 [Taiwan travel diary: on the highways, 40]. Tokyo: Asahi Shimbunsha, 1997.

Shigemura Toshimitsu. *Kita Chōsen no gaikō senryaku* [North Korea's foreign strategy]. Tokyo: Kōdansha, 2000.

Shimizu Yoshikazu. *Chūgoku ga "han-Nichi" o suteru hi* [The day China stops being anti-Japanese]. Tokyo: Kōdansha, 2006.

———. *"Chūgoku mondai" no kakushin* [Core of the "China problem"]. Tokyo: Chikuma Shobō, 2009.

———. "Taigai kyōkō shisei no kokunai seiji" [Domestic politics behind the assertive foreign posture]. In Kokubun Ryōsei, ed., *Chūgoku wa ima* [China, now]. Tokyo: Iwanami Shoten, 2011.

Shimomura Yasutami. "Higashi Ajia kin'yū kiki no seiji shakaiteki eikyō" [The political and social impact of the East Asian financial crisis]. In Shimomura Yasutami and Inada Jūichi, eds., *Ajia kin'yū kiki no seiji keizaigaku* [The political economy of the Asian financial crisis]. Tokyo: Nihon Kokusai Mondai Kenkyūjo, 2001.

———. "Tojōkoku no ōnāshippu to enjo kōka: Tai Tōbu rinkai kaihatsu keikaku no jirei" [Developing country ownership and aid effectiveness: the case of Thailand's Eastern Seaboard Development Plan]. Hosei University Repository, March 31, 2000 (in Japanese). http://repo.lib. hosei.ac.jp/bitstream/10114/3642/1/ning_1-1_simomura.pdf.

Shinoda Tomohito. *Reisengo no Nihon gaikō: anzen hoshō seisaku no kokunai seiji katei* [Postwar Japanese diplomacy: the domestic political process behind security policies]. Tokyo: Mineruva Shobō, 2006.

Shiraishi Masaya. *Betonamu: kakumei to kensetsu no hazama* [Vietnam: between revolution and nation-building]. Tokyo: Tōkyō Daigaku Shuppankai, 1993.

Shiraishi Takashi. "Higashi Ajia chiiki keisei to 'kyōtsū bunkaken'" [The formation of the East Asian region and a "common cultural sphere"]. In Soeya Yoshihide and Tadokoro Masayuki, eds., *Nihon no Higashi Ajia kōsō* [Japan's conception of East Asia]. Tokyo: Keiō Gijuku Daigaku Shuppankai, 2004.

———. *Hōkai Indoneshia wa doko e yuku* [Collapse: whither Indonesia?]. Tokyo: NTT Shuppan, 1999.

———. *Indoneshia, shinpan* [Indonesia, new ed.]. Tokyo: NTT Shuppan, 1996.

———. *Umi no teikoku: Ajia o dō kangaeru ka* [Maritime empires: how should we think about Asia?]. Tokyo: Chūō Kōron Shinsha, 2000.

Shūgiin Gaimu Iinkai giroku [Records of the House of Representatives' Foreign Affairs Committee meeting]. No. 3, September 5, 1974.

Shūgiin Honkaigi gijiroku [Plenary session proceedings of the House of Representatives]. October 2–3, 2006.

Shūgiin Yosan Iinkai giroku [Records of the House of Representatives' Budget Committee meeting]. March 30, 1989.

Shultz, George P. *Turmoil and Triumph: My Years as Secretary of State*. New York: Scribner's, 1993.

Snyder, Scott. *Negotiating on the Edge: North Korean Negotiating Behavior*. Washington, DC: United States Institute of Peace Press, 1999.

Soeya Yoshihide. "ASEAN to Nichi-Bei-Chū: ASEAN Chiiki Fōramu o chūshin ni" [ASEAN and Japan, the US and China: the ASEAN Regional Forum]. In Soeya Yoshihide and Yamamoto Nobuto, eds., *Seikimatsu kara no Tōnan Ajia: sakusōsuru seiji keizai chitsujo no yukue* [Southeast Asia from the end of the century: the complicated course of the political economic order]. Tokyo: Keiō Gijuku Daigaku Shuppankai, 2000.

———. "Vietnam in Japan's Regional Policy." In Nishihara Masashi and James W. Morley, eds., *Vietnam Joins the World*, pp. 175–99. Armonk, NY: M.E. Sharpe, 1997.

"South-North Joint Declaration." June 15, 2000. http://www.usip.org/sites/default/files/file/resources/collections/peace_agreements/n_skorea06152000.pdf.

Stokes, Bruce. "How Asia-Pacific Publics See Each Other and Their National Leaders." September 2, 2015. http://www.pewglobal.org/files/2015/09/Pew-Research-Center-Asian-Views-of-Each-Other-Report-FINAL-September-2-2015.pdf.

Study Team on the Details Leading to the Drafting of the Kono Statement etc. "Details of Exchanges Between Japan and the Republic of Korea

(ROK) Regarding the Comfort Women Issue: From the Drafting of the Kono Statement to the Asian Women's Fund." June 20, 2014. http://japan.kantei.go.jp/96_abe/documents/2014/__icsFiles/afieldfile/2014/06/20/JPN_ROK_EXCHANGE.pdf.

Sudō Sueo. *The Fukuda Doctrine and ASEAN: New Dimensions in Japanese Foreign Policy*. Singapore: Institute of Southeast Asian Studies, 1992.

———. "Hendōki no Nihon gaikō to Tōnan Ajia" [Japanese diplomacy and Southeast Asia in a period of transition]. In Nihon Seiji Gakkai, ed., *Nenpō seijigaku: kiki no Nihon gaikō: 70nendai* [The Annals of the Japanese Political Science Association: Japanese diplomacy in crisis: the 70s], pp. 43–58. Tokyo: Iwanami Shoten, 1997.

Suehiro Akira. *Tai: kaihatsu to minshushugi* [Thailand: development and democracy]. Tokyo: Iwanami Shoten, 1993.

———, and Yamakage Susumu, eds. *Ajia seiji keizairon: Ajia no naka no Nihon o mezashite* [A discussion of Asian politics and economics: moving toward a Japan in Asia]. Tokyo: NTT Shuppan, 2001.

Suga Yoshihide. "Press Conference by the Chief Cabinet Secretary." February 28, 2014. http://japan.kantei.go.jp/tyoukanpress/201402/28_p.html.

Sunohara Tsuyoshi. *Antō Senkaku kokuyūka* [Secret strife behind the nationalization of the Senkakus]. Tokyo: Shinchōsha, 2013.

———. *Bei-Chō tairitsu: kaku kiki no jūnen* [US-North Korean standoff: a decade of nuclear crisis]. Tokyo: Nihon Keizai Shimbunsha, 2004.

———. *Tanjō kokusan supai eisei: dokuji jōhōmō to Nichi-Bei dōmei* [The birth of an indigenous spy satellite: an independent intelligence network and the Japan-US alliance]. Tokyo: Nihon Keizai Shimbunsha, 2005.

Suzuki Masayuki. *Kitachōsen: shakaishugi to dentō no kyōmei* [North Korea: the resonance between socialism and tradition]. Tokyo: Tōkyō Daigaku Shuppankai, 1992.

Suzuki Zenkō. Bangkok Speech. January 19, 1981 (in Japanese). http://world-jpn.grips.ac.jp/documents/texts/exdpm/19810119.S1J.html.

Tahara Sōichirō, chief editor. *Ofu reko! Bessatsu, Saikō kenryoku no kenkyū: Koizumi kantei no shinjitsu, Iijima Isao zen hishokan ga kataru!* [Off the record special issue: A study of supreme power; the facts inside Prime Minister Koizumi's Official Residence, former executive secretary Iijima Isao tells all]. Tokyo: Asukomu, 2007.

Takeda Yasuhiro. *Minshuka no hikaku seiji: Higashi Ajia shokoku no taisei hendō katei* [Comparative politics of democratization: the process of regime change in the countries of East Asia]. Kyoto: Mineruva Shobō, 2001.

Takenaka Harukata. *Sangiin to wa nanika, 1947–2010* [What is the House of Councillors? 1947–2010]. Tokyo: Chūō Kōron Shinsha, 2010.

Takeshita Noboru. "Statement by Prime Minister Takeshita on the Occasion of the Luncheon Given by the Rt. Hon. the Mayor and the Corporation of London at the Mansion House." May 4, 1988. http://www.mofa.go.jp/policy/other/bluebook/1988/1988-appendix-2.htm.

Tamura Keiko. *Shingapōru no kokka kensetsu: nashonarizumu, esunishiti, jendā* [Singapore state-building: nationalism, ethnicity, gender]. Tokyo: Akashi Shoten, 2000.

Tanabe Makoto. "Nit-Chō kokkō kaifuku ni kaketa Nihon Shakaitō fuku-iinchō Tanabe Makoto ga akasu: kore ga 'Kanemaru hō-Chōdan' no butaiura da" [Tanabe Makoto, vice-chairman of the Japan Socialist Party involved in restoring Japanese-North Korean relations, tells all: this is what happened behind the scenes of the "Kanemaru Delegation to North Korea"]. *Gekkan Asahi* [Asahi Monthly], (December 1990).

Tanaka Akihiko. *Anzen hoshō: sengo 50nen no mosaku* [Security: 50 postwar years of trial and error]. Tokyo: Yomiuri Shimbunsha, 1997.

———. *Atarashii "chūsei": 21-seiki no sekai shisutemu.* Tokyo: Nihon Keizai Shimbunsha, 1996. English version: *The New Middle Ages: The World System in the 21st Century.* Trans. Jean Connell Hoff. Tokyo: International House of Japan, 2002.

———. "Comment on 'Free Trade Agreements and Domestic Politics: The Case of the Trans-Pacific Partnership Agreement.'" *Asian Economic Policy Review* 8,2 (December 2013), 352–53.

———. "The Development of the ASEAN+3 Framework." In Melissa Curley and Nicholas Thomas, eds., *Advancing East Asian Regionalism*, pp. 52–73. London; New York: Routledge, 2007.

———. "The Domestic Context: Japanese Politics and UN Peacekeeping." In Nishihara Masashi and Selig Harrison, eds., *UN Peacekeeping: Japanese and American Perspectives*, pp. 89–105. Washington, DC: Carnegie Endowment for the Humanities, 1995.

———. "'Kyōkasho mondai' o meguru Chūgoku no seisaku kettei" [Chinese policy-making on the "textbook controversy"]. In Okabe Tatsumi, ed., *Chūgoku gaikō: seisaku kettei no kōzō* [Chinese diplomacy: the structure of policy-making]. Tokyo: Nihon Kokusai Mondai Kenkyūjo, 1983.

———. *Nit-Chū kankei, 1945–1990* [Japanese-Chinese relations, 1945–1990]. Tokyo: Tōkyō Daigaku Shuppankai, 1991.

———. "Tai-Nichi kankei" [Relations with Japan]. In Chūgoku Sōran Henshū Iinkai, ed., *Chūgoku sōran 1994nenban* [Overview of China, 1994 edition], pp. 144–52. Tokyo: Kazankai, 1994.

———. "Tai-Nichi kankei" [Relations with Japan]. In Chūgoku Sōran Henshū Iinkai, ed., *Chūgoku sōran 1998nenban* [Overview of China, 1998 edition], pp. 138–49. Tokyo: Kazankai, 1998.

———. "Tai-Nichi kankei" [Relations with Japan]. In Chūgoku Sōran Henshū Iinkai, ed., *Chūgoku sōran: 2000nenban* [Overview of China, 2000 edition], pp. 134–44. Tokyo: Kazankai, 2000.

———. "Tai-Nichi kankei" [Relations with Japan]. In Chūgoku Sōran Henshū Iinkai, ed., *Chūgoku sōran 2004nenban* [Overview of China, 2004 edition], pp. 135–46. Tokyo: Gyōsei, 2004.

——. "Tai-Nichi kankei" [Relations with Japan]. In Chūgoku Sōran Hen-shū Iinkai, ed., *Chūgoku sōran 2005–2006nenban* [Overview of China, 2005–2006 edition], pp. 147–58. Tokyo: Gyōsei, 2006.

——. "Tanaka Makiko gaisō wa hayaku ji'nin subeki da" [Foreign Minister Tanaka Makiko should resign soon]. *Chūō Kōron* [Central Review] 116 (July 2001), 32–35.

—— "Ten'anmon jiken igo no Chūgoku o meguru kokusai kankyō" [The international environment around China after the Tiananmen incident]. *Kokusai Mondai* [International Affairs] 358 (1990), 30–45.

——. "The Yasukuni Issue and Japan's International Relations." In Hasegawa Tsuyoshi and Tōgō Kazuhiko, eds., *East Asia's Haunted Present: Historical Memories and the Resurgence of Nationalism*, pp. 119–41. Westport, CT: Praeger Security International, 2008.

Tanaka Hitoshi. "Kita Chōsen kaku giwaku mondai o kensho suru" [Investigating the suspicions about North Korea's nuclear weapons]. *Gaikō Fōramu* [Journal of Japanese perspectives on diplomacy] 7,7 (1994), 59–64.

——, and Tahara Sōichirō. *Kokka to gaikō* [The state and diplomacy]. Tokyo: Kōdansha, 2005.

Tanaka Kyōko. *Kokka to imin: Tōnan Ajia Kajin sekai no hen'yō* [The state and immigrants: transformation of the world of Southeast Asian Chinese]. Nagoya: Nagoya Daigaku Shuppankai, 2002.

Tanaka Toshirō. "Ajia-Ōshū kankei no shintenkai: ASEM no tanjō to hatten" [New developments in Asian-European relations: the birth and growth of ASEM]. In Akagi Kanji and Soeya Yoshihide, eds., *Reisengo no kokusai seiji: jisshō seisaku riron* [Post-Cold-War international politics: proof, policy, theory]. Tokyo: Keiō Gijiku Daigaku Shuppankai, 1998.

Tanino Sakutarō. *Gaikō shōgenroku: Ajia gaikō, kaiko to kōsatsu* [Diplomatic testimony: Asia diplomacy, memoirs and reflections]. Tokyo: Iwanami Shoten, 2015.

Terada Takashi. "Constructing an 'East Asian' Concept and Growing Regional Identity: From EAEC to ASEAN+3." *The Pacific Review* 16 (2003), 251–77.

Thayer, Carlyle A. "Sino-Vietnamese Relations, The Interplay of Ideology and National Interests." *Asian Survey* (June 1994), 513–28.

Tōgō Kazuhiko. "Comfort Women: Deep Polarization in Japan on Facts and on Morality." In Hasegawa Tsuyoshi and Tōgō Kazuhiko, eds., *East Asia's Haunted Present: Historical Memories and the Resurgence of Nationalism*, pp. 142–62. Westport, CT: Praeger Security International, 2008.

——. *Japan and Reconciliation in Post-war Asia: The Murayama Statement and Its Implications.* [Basingstoke]: Palgrave Pivot, 2010.

——, and Hatano Sumio, eds. *Rekishi mondai handobukku* [Handbook on the history problem]. Tokyo: Iwanami Shoten, 2015.

Tokoi Ken'ichi. "Koizumi Jun'ichirō dokuhaku" [Koizumi Jun'ichirō speaks out]. *Bungei Shunjū* (January 2016).

Tomiyama Yasushi. *Kanbojia senki: minzoku wakai e no michi* [Cambodian war diaries: the path to ethnic reconciliation]. Tokyo: Chūō Kōronsha, 1992.

Tomoda Seki. "Detaching from Cambodia." In Nishihara Masashi and James W. Morley, eds., *Vietnam Joins the World*, pp. 134–53. Armonk, NY: M.E. Sharpe, 1997.

———. *Nyūmon gendai Nihon gaikō: Nit-Chū kokkō seijōka igo* [Introduction to modern Japanese diplomacy: after the normalization of Japanese-Chinese diplomatic relations]. Tokyo: Chūō Kōronsha, 1988.

Torii Takashi, ed. *Mahatīru seikenka no Marēshia: "Isurāmu senshinkoku" o mezashita 22-nen* [Malaysia under the Mahathir administration: 22 years of striving to create an "advanced country with Islamic values"]. Chiba: Ajia Keizai Kenkyūjo, 2006.

Tsuboi Yoshiharu. *Betonamu gendai seiji* [Modern Vietnamese politics]. Tokyo: Tōkyō Daigaku Shuppankai, 2002.

———. *Betonamu shinjidai: "yutakasa" e no mosaku* [New era for Vietnam: searching for "wealth"]. Tokyo: Iwanami Shoten, 2008.

Tsukamoto Sōichi. "Chōsen hantō no dōkō: Pak Kuneshi no 'yoku-chi-sa-ji' to Kita Chōsen no 'Shinnen no ji' fukkatsu" [Trends on the Korean peninsula: Park Geun-hye's "do unto others" and North Korea's revival of its "New Year's message"]. *Tōa* [East Asia] 548 (February 2013), 66–74.

Uesugi Takashi. *Kantei hōkai: Abe seiken meisō no ichinen* [Collapse in the Prime Minister's Official Residence: one year of floundering in the Abe administration]. Tokyo: Shinchōsha, 2007.

———. *Tanaka Makiko no shōtai* [Tanaka Makiko's true face]. Tokyo: Sōshi-sha, 2002.

Uesugi Yūji. "Wahei shien de no gaikō to kaihatsu no renkei" [Alignment between diplomacy and development in peace assistance]. *Kaigai Jijō* [Journal of International Affairs] 63 (October 2015), 51–66.

Vatikiotis, Michael. "Help Yourself." *Far Eastern Economic Review* 162,1 (December 31, 1998/January 7, 1999), 12–13.

Wakabayashi Masahiro. *Taiwan: bunretsu kokka to minshuka* [Taiwan: democratization and the fragmented state]. Tokyo: Tōkyō Daigaku Shuppankai, 1992.

———. *Taiwan: hen'yō shi chūcho suru aidentiti* [Taiwan: a changing and wavering identity]. Tokyo: Chikuma Shobō, 2001.

———. *Taiwan no Taiwangojin, Chūgokugojin, Nihongojin: Taiwanjin no yume to genjitsu* [Taiwan's Taiwanese speakers, Chinese speakers, Japanese speakers: the dream and reality of the Taiwanese people]. Tokyo: Asahi Shimbunsha, 1997.

———, ed. *Taiwan: tenkanki no seiji to keizai* [Taiwan: politics and the economy in a time of transition]. Tokyo: Tabata Shoten, 1987.

Wakatsuki Hidekazu. *"Zenhōi gaikō" no jidai: reisen hen'yōki no Nihon to Ajia 1971–80nen* [The era of "omni-directional diplomacy": Japan and Asia in the period of Cold-War change, 1971–80]. Tokyo: Nihon Keizai Hyōronsha, 2006.

Wang Taiping, ed. *Xin Zhongguo wai jiao 50 nian, 1949–1999* [New China's diplomacy over five decades, 1949–1999]. 3 vols. Beijing: Beijing chu ban she, 1999.

Watanabe Akio. *Ajia Taiheiyō no kokusai kankei to Nihon* [Japan and Asia-Pacific international relations]. Tokyo: Tōkyō Daigaku Shuppankai, 1992.

———, ed. *Sengo Nihon no taigai seisaku: kokusai kankei no hen'yō to Nihon no yakuwari* [Postwar Japan's foreign policy: changes in international relations and Japan's role]. Tokyo: Yūhikaku, 1985.

Watanabe Toshio, ed. *Ajia keizai dokuhon* [Asian economy reader]. 3rd ed. Tokyo: Tōyō Keizai Shinpōsha, 2003.

Wen Jiabao. "Speech by Premier Wen Jiabao . . . at the Japanese Diet." April 13, 2007. http://www.fmprc.gov.cn/mfa_eng/wjb_663304/zzjg_663340/yzs_663350/gjlb_663354/2721_663446/2725_663454/t311544.shtml.

World and Japan database. "Agreed Framework between the United States of America and the Democratic People's Republic of Korea." October 21, 1994. http://worldjpn.grips.ac.jp/documents/texts/docs/19941021.O1E.html.

———. "Agreement on the Settlement of Problems Concerning Property and Claims and on Economic Co-operation between Japan and the Republic of Korea." June 22, 1965. http://worldjpn.grips.ac.jp/documents/texts/JPKR/19650622.T9E.html.

———. "Asia-Pacific Co-operative Development Group: 'Towards Cooperative Development.'" June 15, 1989 (in Japanese). http://worldjpn.grips.ac.jp/documents/texts/APEC/19890615.O1J.html.

———. "Japan-DPRK Pyongyang Declaration." September 17, 2002. http://worldjpn.grips.ac.jp/documents/texts/JPKR/20020917.D1E.html.

———. "Japan-Republic of Korea Joint Declaration: A New Japan-Republic of Korea Partnership towards the Twenty-first Century." October 8, 1998. http://worldjpn.grips.ac.jp/documents/texts/JPKR/19981008.D1E.html.

———. "Joint Statement of the Fourth Round of the Six-Party Talks." September 19, 2005. http://worldjpn.grips.ac.jp/documents/texts/JPKR/20050919.D1E.html.

———. "Panel Report: Japan and the Asia Pacific Region in the 21st Century." December 25, 1992 (in Japanese). http://worldjpn.grips.ac.jp/documents/texts/APEC/19921225.O1J.html.

———. "Political Declaration: Declaration on China." July 15, 1989. http://worldjpn.grips.ac.jp/documents/texts/summit/19890715.D4E.html.

———. "Remarks by His Majesty the Emperor of Japan at a State-Sponsored Banquet." October 23, 1992 (in Japanese). http://worldjpn.grips.ac.jp/documents/texts/JPCH/19921023.O3Jhtml.

———. "Singapore Declaration of 1992." http://worldjpn.grips.ac.jp/documents/texts/asean/19920128.D1E.html.

World Bank. *The East Asian Miracle: Economic Growth and Public Policy.* New York: Oxford University Press, 1993.

———. *Global Economic Prospects and the Developing Countries,* 1993. Washington, DC: World Bank, 1993.

———. *World Development Indicators.* data.worldbank.org.

Yachi Shōtarō, and Takahashi Masayuki. *Gaikō no senryaku to kokorozashi* [Strategy and aspirations of diplomacy]. Tokyo: Sankei Shimbun Shuppan, 2009.

Yakushiji Katsuyuki. *Shōgen Minshutō seiken* [Testimony: inner politics of the DPJ]. Tokyo: Kōdansha, 2012.

———, ed. *Murayama Tomiichi kaikoroku* [Memoirs of Murayama Tomiichi]. Tokyo: Iwanami Shoten, 2012.

Yamada Hiroshi. *Poru Poto (kakumei)shi: gyakusatsu to hakai no yonenkan* [The history of Pol Pot (and his revolution): four years of genocide and destruction]. Tokyo: Kōdansha, 2004.

Yamaguchi Jirō, and Nakakita Kōji, eds. *Minshutō seiken to wa nan datta no ka? Kī pāsontachi no shōgen* [What was the DPJ government?: testimonies of key figures]. Tokyo: Iwanami Shoten, 2014.

Yamakage Susumu. *ASEAN pawā: Ajia Taiheiyō no chūkaku e* [ASEAN power: at the core of the Asia Pacific]. Tokyo: Tōkyō Daigaku Shuppankai, 1997.

———. *ASEAN: shinboru kara shisutemu e* [ASEAN from symbol to system]. Tokyo: Tōkyō Daigaku Shuppankai, 1991.

———. "Nihon ASEAN kankei no shinka to hen'yō" [Changes in and deepening of Japan-ASEAN relations]. In Yamakage Susumu, ed., *Higashi Ajia chiikishugi to Nihon gaikō* [East Asian regionalism and Japanese diplomacy]. Tokyo: Nihon Kokusai Mondai Kenkyūjo, 2003.

Yamamoto Yoshinobu. "Chiiki tōgō no seiji keizaigaku: sobyō" [The political economics of regional integration: a rough sketch]. *Kokusai Mondai* [International Affairs] 452 (1997), 2–23.

———. *Kokusaiteki sōgo izon* [International interdependence]. Tokyo: Tōkyō Daigaku Shuppankai, 1989.

Yang Jiechi. "Statement by Yang Jiechi at [the] 67th UN General Assembly." September 27, 2012. http://www.voltairenet.org/article176041.html .

Yang Shangkun. Welcome Speech at the banquet for the Emperor. October 23, 1992 (in Japanese). http://worldjpn.grips.ac.jp/documents/texts/JPCH/19921023.O2J.html.

Yasuda Jun. "Chūgoku no Chōsen hantō seisaku" [China's Korean peninsula policy]. In Okonogi Masao, ed., *Posuto reisen no Chōsen hantō* [The Korean peninsula after the Cold War]. Tokyo: Nihon Kokusai Mondai Kenkyūjo, 1994.

Yomiuri Shimbunsha Seijibu. *Gaikō o kenka ni shita otoko: Koizumi gaikō 2000-nichi no shinjitsu* [The man who made a fight out of diplomacy: the reality behind the 2000 days of Koizumi's diplomacy]. Tokyo: Shinchōsha, 2006.

———. *Nit-Chū-Kan gaikō sensō* [Japan-China-South Korea diplomatic wars]. Tokyo: Shinchōsha, 2014.

Yoshida Seiji. *Watashi no sensō hanzai: Chōsenjin kyōsei renkō* [My war crimes: the forced conscription of Koreans]. Tokyo: San'ichi Shobō, 1983.

Yoshitomi Masaru. *Ajia keizai no shinjitsu: kiseki, kiki, seido no shinka* [Reality of the Asian economy: miracle, crisis and institutional evolution]. Tokyo: Tōyō Keizai Shinpōsha, 2003.

Zhao Quansheng. *Interpreting Chinese Foreign Policy: The Micro-Macro Linkage Approach.* New York: Oxford University Press, 1996.

Zhong Zhicheng. *Wei le shi jie geng mei hao: Jiang Zemin chu fang ji shi* [For a better world: the state visits of Jiang Zemin]. Beijing: Shi jie zhi shi chu ban she, 2006.

Index

About the Author

Tanaka Akihiko is president of the National Graduate Institute for Policy Studies (GRIPS) in Tokyo. His academic specialties include theories of international politics, contemporary international relations in East Asia, and Japan's foreign policy. He obtained his BA in International Relations at the University of Tokyo in 1977 and his PhD in Political Science at Massachusetts Institute of Technology in 1981. After returning to Japan, he was a researcher at the Research Institute for Peace and Security. In 1983, he became a research associate at the College of Arts and Sciences, the University of Tokyo, and was named associate professor in 1984. In 1990 he moved to the Institute of Oriental Culture (now the Institute for Advanced Studies on Asia, or IASA, of the University of Tokyo) and was associate professor there until 1998 when he became professor. He was director of the Institute of Oriental Culture 2002–2006, executive vice president of the University of Tokyo 2009–2011, vice president there 2011–2012, and president of the Japan International Cooperation Agency (JICA) 2012–2015. After leaving JICA, he was reappointed as a professor at IASA 2015–2017. He was also a visiting professor at Ruhr University, Bochum, Germany, in 1986, and a senior associate member at St Antony's College, Oxford, from 1994 to 1995. In 2012 Professor Tanaka received the Medal of Honor with Purple Ribbon (*shiju hōshō*) for his academic achievements. His numerous books and articles in Japanese and English include *The New Middle Ages: The World System in the 21st Century* (Tokyo: The International House of Japan, 2002), *Posuto kuraishisu no sekai* [The post-crisis world], (Tokyo: Nihon Keizai Shimbun Shuppansha, 2009), and *Kokusai funsō: riron to rekishi* [International conflict: theory and history], (Tokyo: Yūhikaku, 2011), a translation with Murata Kōji of *Understanding International Conflicts: An Introduction to Theory and History* by Joseph S. Nye, Jr., and David A. Welch.

About the Translator

Jean Connell Hoff has been a translator for almost 40 years. Among the many books she has translated is *The New Middle Ages: The World System in the 21st Century* by Tanaka Akihiko. She is pleased to add another work by the same author to her résumé.

(英文版)アジアのなかの日本
Japan in Asia: Post-Cold-War Diplomacy

2017年5月31日 第1刷発行

著　者　田中明彦
訳　者　ジーン・コーネル・ホフ
発行所　一般財団法人出版文化産業振興財団
〒101-0051　東京都千代田区神田神保町3-12-3
電　話　03-5211-7282(代)
ホームページ　http://www.jpic.or.jp/

印刷・製本所　大日本印刷株式会社